The Dispersion of Power

The Dispersion of Power

A Critical Realist Theory of Democracy

Samuel Ely Bagg

OXFORD
UNIVERSITY PRESS

Great Clarendon Street, Oxford, OX2 6DP,
United Kingdom

Oxford University Press is a department of the University of Oxford.
It furthers the University's objective of excellence in research, scholarship,
and education by publishing worldwide. Oxford is a registered trade mark of
Oxford University Press in the UK and in certain other countries

© Samuel Ely Bagg 2024

The moral rights of the author have been asserted

All rights reserved. No part of this publication may be reproduced, stored in
a retrieval system, or transmitted, in any form or by any means, without the
prior permission in writing of Oxford University Press, or as expressly permitted
by law, by licence or under terms agreed with the appropriate reprographics
rights organization. Enquiries concerning reproduction outside the scope of the
above should be sent to the Rights Department, Oxford University Press, at the
address above

You must not circulate this work in any other form
and you must impose this same condition on any acquirer

Published in the United States of America by Oxford University Press
198 Madison Avenue, New York, NY 10016, United States of America

British Library Cataloguing in Publication Data

Data available

Library of Congress Control Number: 2023939194

ISBN 9780192848826

DOI: 10.1093/oso/9780192848826.001.0001

Printed and bound in the UK by
Clays Ltd, Elcograf S.p.A.

Links to third party websites are provided by Oxford in good faith and
for information only. Oxford disclaims any responsibility for the materials
contained in any third party website referenced in this work.

Sabeel Rahman, David Ragazzoni, Enzo Rossi, Élise Rouméas, Jay Ruckelshaus, Paul Sagar, Alex Sayegh, Andreas Schedler, Eric Schliesser, David Schmidtz, Jonathan Schwartz, Mohamed Sesay, Abe Singer, Yves Sintomer, Matt Sleat, Sarah Song, Jeff Spinner-Halev, Brian Spisiak, Tom Spragens (RIP), Gopal Sreeenivasan, Zofia Stemplowska, Annie Stilz, Peter Stone, Collis Tahzib, Pierre Vandamme, Muhammad Velji, Camila Vergara, Vertika, Merlin Wehrs, Stuart White, Laurence Whitehead, Matt Whitt, Will Wittels, David Wong, and Deva Woodly—among many others who have doubtless been unintentionally omitted.

I am also very grateful for the material support and intellectual community provided by the University Scholars Program, Kenan Institute for Ethics, and Council on European Studies at Duke; the Research Group on Constitutional Studies and GRIPP at McGill; and Nuffield College at Oxford. I presented parts of the project multiple times at all of these places, as well as panels at APSA, APT, ASPP, MANCEPT, MPSA, SPSA, and WPSA, and workshops at Arizona, Berkeley, Copenhagen, IDEA, Illinois, KCL, Loyola Chicago, UNC, Princeton, Reading, Uppsala, Utrecht, Villa Vigoni, and Yale Law School. I thank the audiences at all of these talks for their feedback and engagement.

Parts of Chapter 8 are drawn from "The Power of the Multitude: Answering Epistemic Challenges to Democracy," published by the *American Political Science Review*, and parts of Chapter 9 from "Fighting Power with Power: The Administrative State as a Weapon against Private Power," published by *Social Philosophy and Policy*. I am grateful to Cambridge University Press, in both cases, for permission to reprint revised versions of that material here.

My greatest debts, finally, are to my partner EB, who has witnessed and supported this project from the very beginning—and is the only person more relieved than I am to see it finally completed. She has shown me other worlds, and for that I feel much more than gratitude.

Columbia, South Carolina, March 2023

always kept me on my toes, pushing me to sharpen my ideas as they began to take their final form. Special thanks go to Shai Agmon, Jacob Barrett, Teresa Bejan, Udit Bhatia, Sarah Bufkin, Ying Chan, Jamie Draper, Des King, Cécile Laborde, Maxime Lepoutre, David Miller, Temi Ogunye, Zeynep Pamuk, Charlie Richards, Ẹniọlá Ṣóyẹmí, Tony Taylor, and Jo Wolff, whose feedback was especially generous and insightful. At South Carolina, I am exceptionally grateful for the support of Doug Thompson, as well as my fellow junior faculty, who made me feel at home right away. Outside of my home institutions, I am especially indebted to feedback and encouragement from Alyssa Battistoni, Mark Brown, Simone Chambers, Kevin Duong, Kevin Elliott, Sean Ingham, Rob Jubb, Amy Kapczynski, Steven Klein, Jeffrey Lenowitz, Jason Maloy, John Medearis, Vijay Phulwani, Andy Sabl, Melissa Schwartzberg, Rogers Smith, and David Wiens. And finally, I am deeply grateful for the astute editorial eye of Michael Schulson, who did his best to make the final manuscript fit for public consumption, as well as Dominic Byatt, my extremely patient editor at Oxford University Press.

Many others helped shape the book as well. I have benefited greatly from exchanges with Rufaida Al Hashmi, Aaron Ancell, Ben Ansell, Gordon Arlen, Frédérick Armstrong, Albena Azmanova, Alice Baderin, Rochana Bajpai, Chitralekha Basu, Edana Beauvais, Pablo Beramendi, Gerald Berk, Aberdeen Berry, Mark Bevir, Susan Bickford, Paul Billingham, Sarah Birch, Mariana Borges, Geoffrey Brennan (RIP), Luke Bretherton, Lucy Britt, Dan Butt, Monica Byrne, Federica Carugati, Martin Caver, Emilee Chapman, Eric Cheng, Matt Cole, Pepper Culpepper, Michael Da Silva, Sam DeCanio, Peter Dietsch, Lisa Disch, Oliver Dowlen, Andy Eggers, Gideon Elford, Alice El-Wakil, Cécile Fabre, Evan Fox-Decent, Liz Frazer, Fede Fuchs, Mike Gadomski, John Gastil, Mollie Gerver, Vafa Ghazavi, Pablo Gilabert, Jeff Green, Aaron Greenberg, Malachi Hacohen, Nora Hanagan, Michael Hannon, Katy Hansen, Lisa Herzog, Mie Inouye, Turku Isiksel, Kate Jackson, Kieran Jimenez, McKenzie Johnson, Amy Kapczynski, Emily Katzenstein, John Keane, Tae-Yeoun Keum, Ewan Kingston, Nik Kirby, Sharon Krause, Melis Laebens, Hélène Landemore, Claudia Landwehr, Antong Liu, Dan Luban, Eric MacGilvray, Emma MacKinnon, Iain MacLean, Ian MacMullen, Ruairí Maguire, Elliott Mamet, Jorge Mangonnet, Jane Mansbridge, Lois McNay, Alison McQueen, Alfred Moore, Jeannie Morefield, Sam Moyn, James Muldoon, Russell Muirhead, Jan-Werner Müller, Mike Munger, Sofia Nässtrom, Mike Neblo, Kalypso Nicolaidis, Bill Novak, Josh Ober, David Owen, Vicky Paniagua, Philip Pettit, Ryan Pevnick, Anne Phillips, Natasha Piano, Barbara Piotrowska, Alex Prescott-Couch, Janosch Prinz, Jed Purdy,

Acknowledgements

I have been writing this book, in one form or another, for most of my adult life. It has consumed me in all of the best ways that a decade-long project can consume a person—and in others as well. The first draft was a PhD dissertation, written partly for my advisers at Duke, and partly for myself: to paraphrase Joan Didion, sometimes we write to know what we think. Yet as I finished this version amid the upheavals of 2016–17, its abstraction and introspection seemed inappropriate to the growing urgency of questions about understanding and improving democracy. Except for the title, scarcely a word remains from that draft, and in the six years since, I have rewritten it three times. The first time was at McGill, in Canada, where I held my first postdoctoral fellowship, and hosted my first workshop on the manuscript. The second time was at Nuffield College, Oxford, in the UK, where I held another fellowship, and another workshop—and once again saw the world transformed by the social and political earthquakes of 2020–1. By the time I finished my third and final revision, I found myself back in the US South; this time in my first year on the tenure track at the University of South Carolina.

Certain convictions have motivated me throughout this process: some recurring frustrations with the ways democracy is talked about, and some basic intuitions about why it really matters. With each rewrite, though, my arguments changed significantly, in dialogue with the changing world around me, as well as the ocean of generous feedback I received along the way. Even more than most books, I suspect, this one owes its shape to the rich intellectual communities that supported its long gestation, and so there are a great many people to thank.

At Duke, I owe special thanks to my mentors Michael Gillespie, Ruth Grant, Alex Kirshner, Wayne Norman, and especially Jack Knight—who cultivated my love of political theory and gave me space to pursue such an ambitious project—as well as my colleagues Nolan Bennett, Mike Hawley, Chris Kennedy, Alex Oprea, Aaron Roberts, and Isak Tranvik. My two years at McGill were crucial in shaping the project into its current form—thanks especially to incisive commentary from Arash Abizadeh and Jacob Levy, as well as particularly enlightening conversations with Kelsey Brady, Rob Goodman, Catherine Lu, Victor Muñiz-Fraticelli, Will Roberts, Daniel Weinstock, and Yves Winter. The unmatched political theory community at Oxford

~ for EB, who sees ~

Contents

Introduction   1

PART ONE   DEMOCRATIC FOUNDATIONS

1. A Critical Realist Theory of Democracy   13
2. Beyond Responsive Representation   36
3. Beyond Participatory Inclusion   55

PART TWO   DEMOCRATIC PRINCIPLES

4. What Is State Capture?   79
5. Structuring Public Power: The Liberal Demands of Democracy   108
6. Dispersing Private Power: The Radical Demands of Democracy   124
7. Resisting State Capture as a Democratic Ideal   146

PART THREE   DEMOCRATIC PRACTICES

8. The Power of the Multitude: A Realistic Defense of Elections   177
9. Fighting Power with Power: An Agenda for Democratic Policy   195
10. Organizing for Power: A Paradigm for Democratic Action   212
    Conclusion   239

Bibliography   244
Index   271

Introduction

Beginning in late 2018, a massive protest movement shook French society and politics to the core. Named for the characteristic "yellow vests" (or *gilets jaunes*) worn by demonstrators, the movement was initially sparked by opposition to a fuel tax thought to unfairly burden middle- and working-class people. However, the protestors' demands soon expanded to include broader measures of economic justice—such as a wealth tax and a higher minimum wage—as well as reforms to enable more direct popular input into political decisions.

Within weeks, French President Emmanuel Macron had rescinded the fuel tax, but by then it was too late to dissipate the substantial political energy that had coalesced around the *gilets jaunes*, and eventually, Macron decided to counter with an ambitious democracy initiative of his own. After encouraging a "Great Debate" involving more than 10,000 local meetings and 2 million online comments, he convened a Citizens' Convention for Climate (CCC) composed of 150 randomly selected citizens, who were tasked with proposing solutions to the climate crisis that would then be put directly to the people in a referendum.

Each side in this political drama claimed the mantle of democracy. For one, defenders of the offending fuel tax pointed out that it was not imposed by a foreign power or lawless dictator, but rather by elected representatives who had recently been chosen by the people of France themselves. In this context, the *gilets jaunes* were accused of using disruptive and sometimes illegal tactics to circumvent the legitimate processes of representative democracy.

In response, of course, protestors drew on their own theories of democracy. Since the dawn of modern representative government, critics have noted its tendency to favor wealthy elites, insisting (like the *gilets jaunes*) that genuine rule of the people requires more direct popular input via initiatives, referendums, and other tools. And if disruptive protest is what it takes to achieve such reforms against the resistance of entrenched elites, it is easy to see why advocates of democracy might embrace such movements, rather than deriding them as a populist scourge.

2 The Dispersion of Power

Rather than confining popular input to intermittent elections or ceding all control to volatile plebiscites, finally, Macron's innovations aimed to encourage deliberation. The Great Debate urged citizens to redirect their political energy from adversarial confrontation to respectful discussions that could shift public opinion informally, while the deliberative CCC was formally empowered to set the agenda. Implicit throughout Macron's approach is a view of democracy as a process of reason-giving, such that the collective will is not simply aggregated via majority vote, but is rather constructed through collaborative discussion and mutual learning.

As many democratic societies face growing challenges along similar lines, parallel debates about how best to protect and enrich democracy are playing out around the globe—and each contending vision in these debates has clear virtues. In this book, however, I argue that none offers a fully persuasive account of why democracy matters and how to make it better. Despite the many differences between them, all three focus on how certain collective decisions are made, rather than how power is distributed more broadly—and in doing so, they lead us astray.

To be sure: representative elections, direct participation, and reasonable deliberation all play key roles in broader processes of democratic decision-making. The root cause of the very real pathologies that all three visions of democracy aim to address, however, lies not in any specific method of decision-making, but rather in the background asymmetries of social and economic power that shape the outcomes of *whatever* decision procedures are used—allowing wealthy and powerful groups to capture state institutions for their own partial interests.

Consider what actually happened with the CCC, which was widely celebrated by advocates of deliberative and participatory innovation. According to many observers, the 150 randomly selected participants made a good faith effort, with expert help, to craft responsible solutions to the challenges of climate change. Buoyed by a massive social rebellion against self-serving technocratic elites, meanwhile, they bitterly resisted anything they saw as an attempt by elites to bias the results, and ultimately produced a highly ambitious program of climate mitigation policies. This ambition, however, proved to be their undoing. Rather than letting the people vote on their proposals right away, as promised, Macron simply vetoed the most radical—like a 4 percent tax on wealth—and watered down many others, before holding the promised popular referendum (see Ehs and Mokre 2021; Courant 2021).

For its defenders, this was a vindication of the representative system: the policies crafted by ordinary citizens would never have worked, they argued, so it was right for elected leaders to step in. For advocates of deliberative and participatory innovations, however, it was a tragic missed opportunity to rethink the way we make decisions together. For many of the *gilets jaunes*, meanwhile, Macron's betrayal was further evidence of the corruption endemic to representative politics, and of the need for a direct popular voice in government.

In focusing their attention on finding the correct processes of collective decision-making, however, all three groups are missing the point. No matter what procedures we use to construct and aggregate preferences, the range of possible outcomes will always be constrained by the underlying balance of social forces—and given the distribution of power in contemporary France, policies that posed such a fundamental challenge to the core interests of wealthy and powerful elites simply never had a chance. This is not to say that such policies could *never* be implemented, but if and when they are, it will not be a matter of instituting a certain electoral reform or participatory innovation. Instead, it will reflect far deeper shifts in the distribution of power. And unless we account for this fundamental fact of political life, we cannot fully appreciate why democracy matters or how to make it better—in France or anywhere else.

This book proposes a way of thinking about democracy that does better on this score, highlighting the underlying power relations that inevitably shape the outcomes of whatever procedures we use to make collective decisions. In doing so, however, it goes against the grain of much contemporary democratic thinking—which, like all the visions we have just examined, often revolves around an ideal of democracy as *collective self-rule*. I now offer a brief outline of that ideal, and contrast it to the alternative I propose: democracy as *resisting state capture*.

Two ideals of democracy: Collective self-rule and resisting state capture

When asked why democracy is valuable, many people are likely to draw upon the thought that everyone deserves a fair say in the decisions that affect their lives. Humans are constantly governed by forces beyond our control, but the ideal of *collective self-rule* embodies the hope that we can regain some control by subjecting those forces to processes of collective decision-making in which everyone has a fair say. Reflecting this ideal, many existing practices aim to bring about some form of *equal control over collective decisions*, while many approaches to democratic reform aim to make that control *more* equal or extend it to *more* decisions.

4   The Dispersion of Power

The ideal of collective self-rule makes perfect sense if we are asking how individuals who cooperate on shared projects should ideally make decisions about those projects. Moreover, it tracks with everyday experiences of collective decision-making that many of us have in our communities and workplaces, where we successfully resolve our differences by talking to each other, making compromises, and—if necessary—voting. The collective control experienced by many participants in such localized processes, however, is not a good model of how democratic politics works on the scale of modern states. At this level, the analytical clarity provided by a focus on individual contributions to certain processes of decision-making becomes a liability, clouding our judgments about why democracy matters and how to make it better.

In aiming to provide a more reliable guide to such judgments, I begin not from any stylized situation, but from the observation that politics is ultimately oriented around competition for access to state power. Given the uniquely concentrated power of modern states, the results are especially dire when a single group achieves uncontested control. Meanwhile, even groups whose control is incomplete can often divert state institutions from their public purposes, coopting parts of the state for private ends. At the same time, modern states can also be powerful tools for advancing human interests—just so long as no can corrupt them in this way. The key question, then, is how we can keep any of the groups contending for access to state power from attaining such unilateral or outsized control. And that question, in turn, gives rise to the ideal I articulate and defend in this book: democracy as *resisting state capture*.

At a basic level, this ideal is oriented to the same goal as collective self-rule: keeping state power tethered to a general public interest. As I explain in the next chapter, this is why both can plausibly be understood as ideals of democracy—and why, on certain readings, we can even interpret them as complements rather than rivals. On such readings, they are simply pitched at different levels, such that the ideal of resisting state capture spells out what is required in practice by some highly abstract version of collective self-rule. For reasons I discuss below, however, the ideal of collective self-rule is far more often spelled out in ways that generate a misleading emphasis on decision-making at the expense of background power relations—just like all three visions at work in the episode of Macron vs. the *gilets jaunes*.

Regardless of what we call them, what I am interested in here is the contrast between two ways of understanding what democracy is, why it matters, and how to make it better. Rather than pinning the value of existing democratic practices on their ability to realize equal control over collective decisions, for one, my account highlights their role in keeping inter-group competition from degenerating into violence, as well as the limited incentives they create for leaders to pursue the public interest. Rather than aiming to further equalize individual control over a wider range of decisions, meanwhile, it implies that democratic action and reform should strive to maintain a roughly *egalitarian balance of social forces*, thereby ensuring that whatever decision-making procedures are used, the results will not favor any group too heavily.

In practice, the democratization agenda implied by this ideal includes procedural reforms that allow ordinary citizens to scrutinize and punish elite malfeasance, substantive policies that redistribute power from hegemonic to counter-hegemonic groups, and—most crucially—the organization of collective power among the latter. As I illustrate in Chapter 4, the biggest source of capture in most electoral democracies is the organized collective power of wealthy elites (among other powerful groups whose character varies from place to place), and the first priority of democratic action and reform must therefore be to build countervailing forms of organized collective power that can prevent these groups from getting their way every time.

The stakes of this choice between two ways of thinking are high. If I am right, prevailing theories do not provide the best way of defending democracy against the serious challenges it faces. For one, a growing chorus of theoretical criticism calls out for a more robust, realistic, and broadly compelling response than is currently available. We need a better account, relying on realistic and widely shared premises, of why existing electoral democracies deserve fierce loyalty despite their many flaws. Even more crucially, the widening gyre of democratic decline in seemingly every part of the globe calls out for a more promising practical agenda for protecting and enriching democracy on the ground. This book aims to provide both—and more.

A critical realist approach: Joining realist skepticism and radical critique

According to the ideal of collective self-rule, democracy matters because it allows us to make collective decisions on equal terms. Some argue that electoral practices are sufficient for this purpose (Waldron 1999), while others hold that it requires expanding the range of decisions open to popular input (Hagglund 2019), including more people in those decisions (Landemore 2020), or making their input more deliberative (Lafont 2019). Despite its popularity, of course, this ideal has not escaped critical scrutiny altogether, and this book draws in particular on two broad traditions that I call "realist skepticism" and "radical critique." Though divergent in many respects and rarely brought together, they converge on certain key worries about the ideal of collective self-rule, grounded in a shared concern with background power relations.

First, analysts belonging to the tradition of realist skepticism have long pointed out that elections do not institutionalize an attractive form of collective self-rule, and probably never could (Achen and Bartels 2016). Because they offer such coarse-grained accountability, even the fairest electoral procedures leave ample room for various elites to achieve their interests behind the scenes. As social choice theorists have argued, meanwhile, this is true not just of elections but any collective choice procedures (Weale 2018). Even if these obstacles could be surmounted, finally, a trove of evidence from public opinion and political psychology indicates that most political behavior is powerfully motivated by social identity (Lodge and Taber 2013), creating further opportunities for elite manipulation. The persistence of commonsense views of collective self-rule in the face of such evidence has been called "the scandal of modern democratic thought" (J. Green 2009: 68), and it leaves us ill-prepared to explain the real value of electoral practices in the face of growing challenges from anti-democratic forces.

Second, thinkers in a more radical tradition of critique have emphasized that everything we do is structured by broader systems of advantage such as class, race, and gender, which do not simply disappear when all are granted formal equality in certain collective decision-making procedures. In seeking to legitimize political power by subjecting it to collective decisions, indeed, aspirations for collective self-rule can serve to conceal these asymmetries, along with the histories of domination that have created them (Dhillon 2017). From national elections down to local participatory institutions, background inequalities inevitably shape the agenda of collective decision-making procedures, as well as the types of participatory practices and political values that are legible within them (Sanders 1997). Intentionally or not, many popular strategies of democratic reform thus end up serving the interests of wealthy and powerful elites, enabling them to defuse contestation and co-opt or demobilize potential opponents (Lee 2014). Collaborative participation in collective decision-making procedures can be useful in some contexts, but the pervasive focus on them among democratic reformers serves to obscure or even undermine the oppositional strategies necessary to overcome the profound asymmetries that characterize all contemporary democracies to one degree or another.

This book is distinguished in part by its willingness to draw extensively on both traditions, as reflected in the "critical realist" label. A key insight of both, for instance, is that no decision-making procedure can be perfectly collective, allowing us to make choices together on truly equal terms. Against the widespread hope that law and social power can be made legitimate if citizens share equally in authoring it, therefore, realist skeptics and radical critics both suggest that the rules governing our lives will always remain in some sense foreign to us. Indeed, any decision-making process that claims to fully legitimize power threatens to conceal—and thus perpetuate—whatever power relations inevitably remain in the background (Honig 1993).

As such, I argue, we should replace the precise, *positive* goal of collective authorization with the deliberately imprecise, *negative* goal of resisting capture—a loose category designed to encompass an ever-shifting variety of concrete threats. My account thus reframes democracy as an ongoing process of partisan opposition to whichever groups pose the greatest threats at a given time, not a fixed set of neutral procedures for resolving disagreements among equals. Recognizing the vast uncertainty of social life, more generally, I aim to draw rough heuristics for judgment, rather than exceptionless principles or authoritative practical conclusions.

Accounting for the dispiriting evidence presented by realist skeptics, on the one hand, the ideal of resisting state capture offers a defense of the broadly liberal, constitutional, electoral form of democracy that already exists in many countries—despite its many deficits—which remains robust, realistic, and broadly compelling. While elections cannot achieve genuine collective self-rule, in short, they can and often do obstruct politicians' efforts to entrench their position and capture state power entirely for themselves. This makes them indispensable for any modern political project aimed at keeping public power tethered to the public interest.

At the same time, electoral democracy is also consistent with vast asymmetries in private power—asymmetries which, if allowed to stand, will reliably feed back into politics. In line with the demands of radical critics, therefore, my approach also refocuses reform on the goal of *dispersing power*. In evaluating an outcome's democratic credentials, I argue, we must care not only about the formal decision procedures used to reach it, but also the distribution of organizational capacity among groups: i.e., their informal ability to shape outcomes. As such, the key priority of democratic reform must be to mitigate disparities among groups in terms of private power resources, coordination rights, and other components of organizational capacity.

The core claim of this book can thus be stated as follows: as compared to conventional interpretations of collective self-rule, the ideal of resisting state capture offers a better account of why democracy matters and how to make it better, because it focuses on underlying power relations rather than specific processes of collective decision-making.

Chapter 1 explores the normative and methodological foundations for this claim, while Chapters 2 and 3 illustrate how my critique of collective self-rule applies to the two most influential versions of that ideal: "responsive representation" and "participatory inclusion." Due to the structure of social choices and the motivated character of reasoning, Chapter 2 shows, various elites will always be able to shape "collective" decisions in their favor. As such, the justification and legitimacy of democratic institutions cannot rest on the claim that they are responsive to the popular will, and reform should not focus primarily on making electoral processes more responsive. Meanwhile, Chapter 3 shows that deliberative forums and other participatory decision-making procedures are no less susceptible to manipulation and capture by elites, and that an exclusive focus on them is therefore just as inadequate.

The rest of the book explores the alternative way of thinking that I propose, beginning with an examination of state capture in Chapter 4. Defined as the use of public power to pursue private interests at the expense of the public, this concept incorporates disparate problems—ranging from regulatory capture, corruption, and clientelism to authoritarianism, oligarchy, and racial caste systems—and my exploration of it integrates insights from the history of political thought with the latest research in contemporary social science. Building on this conceptual foundation, the next three chapters then outline the basic political orientation suggested by the ideal of resisting state capture. Chapter 5 outlines its three broadly liberal components: principles of *constitutionalism*, *competition*, and *universalism*. Chapter 6 then shows how the radical priorities of *anti-monopoly*, *countervailing power*, and *systemic redistribution* follow from the same organizing principles. Finally, Chapter 7 explores the utopian horizon and broader political orientation implied by this ideal, before using it to work through tough cases.

Chapter 8 applies this general framework to the evaluation of existing practices of electoral democracy. Compared to the most salient alternatives, I show, these practices reliably disable certain tactics that incumbents can use to entrench their power, thus obstructing the worst forms of state capture. This explains their value in measured and realistic terms, while nevertheless providing a robust reply to critics of democracy. Chapter 9 then offers a novel vision of democratization, casting it as a matter not just of how certain decisions are made, but also of which general approach to state involvement the state takes in each policy area, how those policy tools are structured internally, and what forms of popular oversight are enabled. Of course, we can hardly expect states that are captured by wealthy elites to implement such radically democratizing policies: instead, we must force their hand by building countervailing power, on a massive scale, outside of the state—and Chapter 10 identifies one promising approach to this task. Drawing together the practices of radical labor unions as well as certain community organizations and movement groups, I develop a model of "organizing for power" that enables counter-hegemonic groups to build collective countervailing power.

This provides a sharp contrast to popular models of democratic reform—including all of those at work in the episode of Macron vs. the *gilets jaunes*. In short, I conclude, enriching democracy does require expanding popular participation, but not in the ways most often envisioned by democratic reformers. Modern democracy is not a collaborative process for making decisions, but a way of organizing competition for public power, which at present is pervasively biased in favor of wealthy elites and other groups with concentrated private power and organizational capacity. What deeper democratization requires, then, is not more channels for direct individualized input into collective decision-making procedures, but more effective ways of organizing mass collective action by ordinary people, in direct opposition to organized elite interests. And amid the escalating challenges faced by democracies around the globe, this account of democratic priorities is the most important practical contribution of the book.

PART ONE
DEMOCRATIC FOUNDATIONS

Trust those who seek the truth; doubt those who find it.
—**André Gide**

1
A Critical Realist Theory of Democracy

At the heart of this book is a contrast between two ways of thinking about what democracy is, why it is valuable, and how to make it better. Its core claim is quite simple: conceiving democracy as collective self-rule leads us astray in a number of important ways, and we would do better to understand it in terms of resisting state capture instead. This preliminary sketch, however, leaves many questions unanswered. What exactly is a "way of thinking," for instance, and what are the stakes of "conceiving" or "understanding" democracy in one way rather than another? How should we interpret evaluative phrases such as "lead us astray" and "do better"? Apart from their intrinsic interest, the way I answer these questions is part of what makes my approach distinctive, and this chapter is devoted to explaining it.[1]

1.1 Collective self-rule and resisting state capture as mid-level ideals

Our political judgments are inevitably informed, shaped, and motivated—in both conscious and unconscious ways—by a wide variety of beliefs, norms, principles, intuitions, assumptions, and habits of thought. I refer to these diverse influences on our judgment, collectively, as *heuristics*. At times, their role may be quite direct. For instance, a politician might explicitly endorse a certain principle of distributive justice, and actively consult it when deciding which healthcare policy to promote. Most of the time, though, the process by which various heuristics come to influence our political action is far less direct—indeed, we will often be entirely unaware of their influence. The practice of political theory arises from those relatively rare moments of reflection when we do step back and assess which heuristics are shaping our judgment and whether they are serving us as well as they could.

---

[1] Like many others who see political theory as continuous with other forms of political thought and action, I have often felt unsatisfied with the abstract and idealized character of much contemporary political theory, and my previous work has explicitly addressed the question of how to do political theory in a more 'grounded' or 'realistic' way (Bagg 2016, 2022b). In this book, these methodological concerns are largely confined to the background, but my approach does reflect the commitments laid out more comprehensively in prior work.

What it means for a heuristic to "serve us well," of course, is a controversial question, about which political theorists disagree strongly. Rather than taking a stand in these debates, I simply say that a heuristic serves a political agent well whenever they find, on reflection, that it seems to point them in the right direction, by whatever ultimate standard seems right to them.[2] All it means for a heuristic to be useful or reliable, in other words, is that *we find it* useful or reliable, all things considered—a formulation that is compatible with diverse views about both the meta-ethical grounding and the substantive content of our foundational normative commitments.[3]

As a practice, then, normative political theory aims to refine the heuristics we use, gradually bringing them into closer alignment with our overall sense of the right thing to do, across a range of political circumstances. And in many cases, more specifically, the goal is to arrive at a set of heuristics that are interrelated and mutually supportive, and which (taken together) give rise to a relatively consistent way of engaging the political world. A key aim of *political theorizing* as a practice, in other words, is to produce coherent *political theories*—i.e., the kind of thing I am concerned with in this book. Like most of the ideals, conceptions, values, and other normative frameworks discussed by political theorists, in other words, the terms "collective self-rule" and "resisting state capture" refer to reasonably coherent collections of interrelated and mutually supportive heuristics, which come together to shape the judgments of the agents who accept or otherwise internalize them in certain relatively consistent ways.

Again, crucially, agents need not *explicitly* endorse a theory or ideal in order for it to shape their judgments. If a particular conception of freedom or justice is embedded in the fabric of social meaning, for instance, it can implicitly shape the judgments of agents who have never actively endorsed it, and cannot articulate it explicitly. An Indigenous farmer in Chiapas and a financial analyst in Madrid will likely understand such terms in very different ways—even if neither can articulate their understanding precisely. And whether or not they are consciously recognized, such intuitive differences in understanding can still have a profound influence on how political agents perceive political problems, make judgments in response, and design the legal and political institutions that structure their common interactions.

---

[2] As a pragmatist, I find it useful to think in terms of Elizabeth Anderson's (2014) gloss of John Dewey's pragmatist moral theory, whereby a normative heuristic is a proposal of the form, 'try it, you'll like it' (see Bagg 2016). However, it is not necessary to be a pragmatist in this sense to follow the rest of my argument.

[3] In evaluating whether a heuristic points us in the right direction, for instance, we might be evaluating its validity as a 'hypothetical' imperative—judging whether it accords with whatever 'internal' reasons we happen to accept—or as a 'categorical' imperative—judging whether it reflects 'external' reasons that are equally valid for everyone, no matter what we think. My formulation is purposefully neutral between these two readings.

These initial observations allow me to restate the core argument of the book in more precise terms. To begin with, I observe, an ideal of collective self-rule explicitly informs the way that many people think about what democracy is, why it is valuable, and how to make it better—including many political theorists, social scientists, and policymakers. Meanwhile, the same ideal implicitly shapes the behavior of a much larger group—plausibly including most citizens of existing democracies—along with many of the institutions they have built. Unfortunately, I argue, this influence has not been entirely benign. To be sure, the ideal of collective self-rule has inspired many people to valuable forms of political action, and is likely worth preserving in some form. Yet it also consistently leads to certain consequential errors in judgment, whose basic outlines I explore shortly. For that reason, its spell ought to be broken, and its influence reduced (Dunn 2014). In many contexts where people currently employ an ideal of collective self-rule, in short, I argue that an ideal of resisting state capture would serve them better.

To be clear: this does not imply that with enough reflection, *everyone* would eventually come to agree that the ideal of resisting state capture provides more reliable guidance. For one, it aims to be compatible with a wide range of plausible commitments, not with all possible views. Similarly, its claim is not to provide perfect guidance in all circumstances, but simply to guide our judgments in three specific areas more reliably than prominent ideals of collective self-rule. In particular, these areas are: (1) evaluating existing practices of electoral democracy; (2) developing an agenda for the reform of law and policy; and (3) setting priorities for civic action and participation outside the state. Given a wide range of normative assumptions, that is, the ideal of resisting state capture offers a more persuasive defense of electoral democracy, as well as a more promising agenda for action and reform. I outline the domain-specific heuristics offered by each ideal below, and summarize them in Table 1.1 at the end of the chapter.

In a very broad sense, this discussion can be said to take place at the level of "nonideal theory." For two reasons, however, I generally avoid this language. Because ideals of resisting state capture and collective self-rule can both be justified with reference to a range of different normative foundations, for one, neither must be oriented to any *specific* normative foundation. While they may be normatively subordinate to more basic values, similarly, they need not be *practically* subordinate—meaning that we need not settle on a precise account of normative foundations before we can responsibly say anything about what they demand in practice. And in both of these ways, they challenge the traditional framework of ideal and nonideal theory.

Instead, I understand the theories of collective self-rule and resisting state capture as *mid-level* ideals. In other words, each constitutes a collection of interrelated and mutually supportive heuristics, whose role is not to determine which ideals we should adopt at the highest level of abstraction, or which values we should treat as most basic, but rather to help us translate these foundational normative commitments into consistent and reliable practical judgments. People who turn to collective self-rule when addressing tasks of democratic judgment may have many different ultimate justifications for pursuing that goal, and may also interpret its practical demands in a variety of different ways. Each unique version of the ideal thus translates abstract normative premises into concrete heuristics and substantive conclusions in a distinctive way. Of course, this is precisely what the ideal of resisting state capture does as well. My claim is that it does so more reliably—or in other words, that it yields a more reliable *mid-level ideal*.

My choice to focus on domain-specific heuristics and mid-level ideals, without saying much about their ultimate foundations, is part of what makes my approach distinctive. Some who are accustomed to traditional ways of doing political philosophy may object that we can make practical judgments responsibly only once we have settled more foundational questions. In light of the severe practical and epistemic limitations we face, however, it strikes me that it is the priority often given to articulating precise accounts of normative foundations that should be regarded as irresponsible. As I have argued elsewhere, in short, we have good reasons to be skeptical of any precise account of human interests (Bagg 2021). We can be relatively more secure, however, in identifying concrete threats to those interests (Bagg 2022b). By building our theories around those commitments we can articulate with relatively greater confidence and precision, then—rather than those with logical priority—we can economize on certainty.

Indeed, this explains how collective self-rule and resisting state capture manage to achieve the distinctive balance between concreteness and broad applicability that makes both especially useful as mid-level ideals. Though neither yields guidance about *all* cases, both address many of the most important recurring judgments facing citizens of modern societies. And the reason for this is that both are *democratic* ideals, addressed to the *predicament of modern politics*.

1.2 Collective self-rule and resisting state capture as thick democratic ideals

The fundamental fact of modern politics is the singularly concentrated power of the modern state—which, under the international state system, sets the terms on which all other entities and groups interact. The predicament of modern politics thus arises from the enormous possibilities for both good and evil such states present. On the one hand, they can promote human interests on unprecedented scales—advancing broadly shared goals such as physical security, economic growth, social and scientific progress, cultural production, and environmental protection with extraordinary efficiency. For precisely the same reasons, on the other hand, they also pose extremely serious threats to human interests. Indeed, all of the greatest promises and greatest dangers currently faced by the human species are either directly caused or profoundly mediated by modern states. Because of the self-reinforcing character of the international state system, meanwhile, this fundamental predicament is unlikely to change any time soon. The central question of modern politics, then, is the following: how can we maximize the good states do while minimizing the dangers they pose? How, in other words, can we keep the concentrated public power of states reliably tethered to the public interest?

The central answer, in short, is democracy. Historically, most practices now understood as liberal or democratic—along with the theories devised to justify them—arose in a context characterized by the growing dangers of state power in the modern world (El Amine 2016). And to the extent that they provide an effective response to the predicament of modern politics, it is because they enact specific constellations of constraining and empowering forces, granting state actors certain capabilities while constraining them to follow certain rules and respond to certain incentives. Under the social and political conditions created by these practices, state actors are more likely to pursue public projects that serve human interests, as compared to their counterparts in other regimes, who face different constellations of forces.

The (liberal) imperative of constraint is often understood as opposed to the (democratic) imperative of empowerment. And there are, of course, real tensions: too much constraint makes it difficult for state actors to pursue public projects, while too little enables them to pursue their private ends instead. It is a mistake, however, to understand these imperatives as fundamentally opposed. Both ultimately serve the same goal of *enabling* state actors to advance broad public interests, in part by *preventing* them from using their power for private ends. The real value of many liberal *and* democratic practices, in other words, is to increase the likelihood that *when* state actors use public power, they do so in ways that serve broadly shared human interests. And what this requires is not a generic balance between constraint and empowerment, but a *specific* constellation of constraining and empowering practices that together push state actors in that direction. Rather than treating democracy as a *thin* ideal comprising only paradigmatic empowering practices, like elections and participation, I understand it as a *thick* ideal that also includes constraining practices commonly seen as liberal, like rights and the rule of law.

Understood in this thicker sense, democracy refers to the entire set of practices that help us keep the concentrated public power of the state tethered to the public interest, in response to the predicament of modern politics. This definition allows us to incorporate many elements of the familiar package of practices adopted by contemporary liberal democracies like Norway and Japan, and thus tracks standard usage. At the same time, it is also revisionist in several key respects. As noted, thick democratic ideals may include practices like minority rights, which are often seen as liberal *rather than* democratic. In addition, they may also incorporate radical demands that are often seen as substantive rather than procedural—or, relatedly, as demands of justice rather than democracy—such as the redistribution of wealth and social privilege.

That said, my aim is not to declare a monopoly on the term "democracy," and I readily admit that there are contexts in which thinner accounts of democracy may be useful. For the purpose of empirical measurement, for instance, we may want to define "democracy" simply as competitive elections. In other contexts, it may be more useful to define it in terms of participation by ordinary people—as when comparing political parties and firms that are hierarchically structured with those that are organized "democratically." Finally, we may find it useful to discuss institutions with certain outwardly egalitarian features, like referendums or citizens' assemblies, as "democratic" in some sense, relative to those that rely more obviously on meritocratic hierarchies, like the judicial system or bureaucratic administration.

Even in such cases, though, this language has drawbacks. Referendums often serve to *entrench* elite rule (Weale 2018). Intra-party democracy can hinder leaders' ability to maneuver against rival parties, thus undermining competitiveness at the systemic level (Rosenbluth and Shapiro 2018). Despite their superficial "democraticity," such practices do not effectively keep public power tethered to the public interest, and thus do not merit wholehearted endorsement as genuinely democratic according to the thicker standard I propose. As Jan-Werner Müller (2016) observes, more broadly, framing liberalism and democracy as opposing forces plays into the hands of authoritarians like Viktor Orbán, who claim that attacking liberal institutions unleashes popular sovereignty from anti-democratic limits. While it is possible to retort within the terms of this oppositional framing—arguing that liberalism provides necessary restraints on democracy's excesses—Müller shows that this reply is both strategically and conceptually confused: suppressing opponents and the rule of law really does undermine *democracy* in any sense that is worth wanting. Although thinner accounts of democracy may be useful for certain analytical purposes, then, a thicker standard is called for whenever the "democraticity" of a practice is taken to stand in for its overall value—as it so often is today.

Still, we must also be wary of stretching the concept of democracy too far. If it is to remain an ideal of democracy—rather than justice or something else—even a thick ideal must refrain from committing to any particular picture of what the public interest actually is. Rather than relying on a specific conception of the *first-order* goals we must pursue, in other words, it should refer only to *second-order* concerns about how power can be organized to maximize the likelihood that state actors pursue valuable first-order goals (see Knight and Johnson 2011).

To be sure: certain basic assumptions must be made in order to get any normative argument off the ground. In what follows, for instance, I do assume that we should weight the interests of all people equally, and that their interests include certain forms of objective welfare as well as some subjective experience of freedom. However, my argument in this book hinges on the contention that we can say quite a bit about which *practices* are best able to keep public power tethered to the public interest, without going into too much additional detail about the definition of the public interest or related concepts such as welfare, freedom, and equality. Whether we aim to universalize freedom as nondomination, achieve social equality, or maximize average utility—among many other conceptions of the ultimate ends we might pursue in politics—I argue that we have robust reasons to endorse a wide range of democratic practices.

To begin with, it is widely accepted that certain *procedural* rules, like competitive elections and the rule of law, help constrain state actors to the pursuit of broadly shared public interests—even among those who disagree about which public interests should be pursued. Meanwhile, certain *substantive* policies, ranging from hate speech regulations to social insurance schemes, are sometimes defended on similar grounds: i.e., not because they are required by first-order goals such as justice or welfare, but because they enable fairer decision-making or otherwise serve second-order democratic goals. In this book, I defend an especially wide range of policies on these grounds—from antitrust and the right to strike to unconditional wealth transfers. Like elections and the rule of law, I will argue, all of these practices help keep public power tethered to the public interest, and this gives us a strong reason to pursue them.

That, however, is an argument for future chapters. For now, the key point of this discussion is that it enables us to understand how mid-level ideals of collective self-rule and resisting state capture are able to generate reasonably concrete guidance across such a broad range of contexts. Because they are addressed to a specific task—i.e., keeping public power tethered to the public interest—they offer more concrete guidance than can be directly inferred from fundamental principles. Because this task arises necessarily from the pervasive predicament of modern politics, meanwhile, their guidance will be relevant to many of the most important judgments that consistently confront political agents in the modern world. And because we can say quite a bit about how to achieve this task without relying on any particular account of the public interest, they are compatible with a range of different normative foundations.

This completes my account of the common role played by ideals of collective self-rule and resisting state capture. As thick, mid-level ideals of democracy relying exclusively on second-order concerns, in short, they tell us how to keep public power tethered to the public interest, without presuming any particular account of what the public interest is or why we should pursue it. Crucially, however, they play that role in different ways—suggesting different domain-specific heuristics in response to the three tasks I set out above: i.e., evaluating existing practices of electoral democracy, developing an agenda for policy reform, and setting priorities for civic action and participation outside the state. The next two sections outline the heuristics offered by each ideal in greater detail, as summarized in Table 1.1 at the end of the chapter.

1.3 The ideal of collective self-rule: Equal control over collective decisions

A great many theories of democracy are structured in one way or another by the aspiration for collective self-rule. All draw upon the same basic intuition—i.e., that we can keep public power tethered to the public interest by giving every member of society an equal say over its use—and can thus be understood as oriented towards the shared goal of achieving *equal control over collective decisions*. Yet this goal can be specified in many different ways, and in this respect, two key dimensions of variation emerge as especially important.

The first concerns which decisions must be subjected to collective control. Liberals, for instance, often limit their scope of concern to coercive political power, while radicals argue for collective control over various forms of economic, social, and cultural power. The second concerns which capacities must be guaranteed to all, in order to ensure they share equally in that control. Some argue that giving everyone a vote in majoritarian elections is sufficient (Waldron 1999), for instance, while others maintain that more extensive rights (Brettschneider 2010), more significant deliberative contributions (Lafont 2019), or more background equality (Kolodny 2014b), are required for a sufficiently egalitarian process of will formation.

Both questions are ultimately about which forms of power deserve our normative concern, and ideals of collective self-rule can thus be usefully arrayed along a spectrum—ranging from those employing narrow definitions of power (Dahl 1957) in service of minimalist accounts of democracy (Dahl 1961), to those demanding collective control over a wider range of decisions, by equalizing a wider range of power resources (Hayward 2000). On the first dimension, more expansive accounts aim to make *more decisions* collectively, at the limit implying a utopian horizon of *full socialization* with nearly all realms of social life at least potentially subject to collective control. On the second dimension, expansive accounts strive to make decisions *more collectively*, with a corresponding horizon of *ideal deliberation* in which decisions result from sincere and egalitarian exchanges of reasons. Meanwhile, particular versions of self-rule offer particular domain-specific heuristics for evaluating and improving existing democracies.

Some view electoral democracy as sufficient on its own to realize an important form of self-rule—enabling decision-making on terms equal enough to endow outcomes with authority. When elected officials claim that their decisions are democratically legitimate because they reflect "the will of the people," for instance, they implicitly employ this sort of view (Weale 2018). And although few democratic theorists accept this commonsense view as such, some license similar inferences through sophisticated means—arguing, for instance, that majority rule possesses a brute fairness unmatched by other decision procedures (Waldron 1999).

That said, theorists of collective self-rule more often reach the opposite conclusion, arguing that decision-making conditions in existing democracies are *not* equal enough for the resulting decisions to count as genuinely collective. In some cases, the alleged democratic deficits may be as shallow as the organization of the electoral system, implying that with certain reforms—proportional representation, for instance, or referendums, or limits on campaign spending—elected officials could rightly claim the sort of democratic authority to which current leaders are not yet entitled. Where some claim a first-past-the-post system featuring majoritarian procedures at the district level realizes collective decision-making, for instance, others insist that proportional representation within higher-level political units is required.

For more radical critics, meanwhile, the profound deficits of existing democracies cannot be entirely resolved through any such institutional reforms. In order to represent the true will of the people and lay rightful claim to democratic authority, they argue, decisions about public power would need to reflect a far more egalitarian process of will formation. Accordingly, it is the dream of equal control over the *formation of a collective will* that drives their agenda for institutional reform, as well as their priorities for civic action and participation outside the state. Though the process they imagine would still typically culminate in elections, radical critics of electoral democracy enumerate various combinations of extra-electoral procedures, substantive policies, social practices, and background conditions, which must accompany elections in order for the decision-making process be considered genuinely collective overall. Most commonly, this means deliberative forums governed by norms of mutual reason-giving; oriented towards collaboration and compromise; and characterized by greater social and material equality.

At times, the logic of collective self-rule has even been used to justify *eliminating* elections entirely. Indeed, nearly every modern ideology that eschews competitive elections does so in the name of a "purer" or "more direct" form of collective self-rule—from Mussolini's fascism to Stalin's "dictatorship of the proletariat." Meanwhile, analogous demands for "direct representation" animate the plebiscitary appeal of contemporary populists like Recep Tayyip Erdoğan, Viktor Orbán, Jair Bolsonaro, and Narendra Modi (Müller 2016). Of course, such (proto-)authoritarians play fast and loose with the logic of collective control, and we rightly recognize their claims to realize the "will of the people" as cynical and dangerous obfuscations. Yet if realist skeptics and radical critics are right to suggest that even the "healthiest" electoral democracies *also* fail to achieve genuinely collective decision-making—as I will argue in Chapter 2—elected leaders may have no better claim to this form of democratic legitimacy. And while most alternatives to elections are no longer taken seriously by political theorists, one has received growing attention: lottocracy. Given that elections cannot realize collective self-rule, in other words, some argue that the true aims of democracy would be better served by replacing elected leaders with randomly chosen citizens (Guerrero 2014; Landemore 2020).

Collective self-rule can thus be interpreted in a dizzying variety of ways, motivating an almost limitless variety of political projects. As I have acknowledged, many of these projects are valuable—and indeed, the aspiration for collective self-rule will not always serve us poorly as an ideal. In certain contexts, for one, it can motivate critical forms of solidarity and collective action. At a high level of abstraction, meanwhile, it can even be construed as compatible with my arguments in the rest of the book—in a sense to be explained momentarily.

The trouble comes, in my view, when vague aspirations for self-rule are concretely specified along the two dimensions discussed above: i.e., when precise answers are given about which decisions must be subjected to collective control, and which capacities equalized in order to achieve it. Once this happens, ideals of collective self-rule typically focus our attention on certain moments and procedures of political decision-making, and certain contributions that individuals can make within them. And while those procedures are often quite important, the emphasis they are granted by many ideals of collective self-rule often ends up obscuring various group-based power asymmetries that may be less visible, salient, or easily measurable.

This is precisely what goes wrong, for instance, with the two most influential concrete interpretations of the aspiration for collective self-rule in contemporary political life, which I identify as the common-sense ideal of "responsive representation," and the widespread demand for "participatory inclusion." As I demonstrate in Chapters 2 and 3, respectively, both conceptions of the goals of democracy identify it closely with certain processes of collective decision-making. The domain-specific heuristics they generate for evaluating institutions and prioritizing among possible reforms thus place too much emphasis on the existence of such processes—and formal equality among individuals within them—while ignoring the pervasive influence of group-based power asymmetries on the outcomes of whatever procedures are used. As such, the efforts of political agents who have internalized those ideals to defend and improve democratic institutions will not reliably help keep public power tethered to the public interest.

Of course, not *all* ideals of collective self-rule specify the goal of equal control in ways that obscure power relations. Some may eschew concrete specification altogether, preferring to remain at a high level of abstraction—indeed, this is one way to understand the thrust of certain recent developments in democratic theory. For one, philosophers have increasingly recognized that no decision procedure could give everyone the ability to control the conditions of their lives simultaneously (Christiano 1996). Noting that the right procedures might still grant everyone equal social *standing*, however, they have abandoned freedom-based accounts of democracy in favor of equality-based accounts (Christiano 2008; Kolodny 2014b; Viehoff 2014; J. Wilson 2019). Similarly, deliberative theorists have increasingly recognized that, from a broader social perspective, certain forms of nondeliberative action can have a deliberative function (Lepoutre 2018; I. M. Young 2001). As such, they have rejected the singular emphasis on reasonable speech that had been implied by earlier theories, instead evaluating political action on the basis of its role in the broader "deliberative system" of society (Fung 2005; Mansbridge et al. 2012).

Both trends correct the mistakes of prior theories by retreating from the latter's emphasis on certain decision procedures—i.e., majoritarian elections and reasonable deliberation—and arguing that background asymmetries must be seriously mitigated before genuinely collective decisions can be made. Though both ultimately strive for a form of equal control over collective decisions, therefore, they interpret terms like "control" and "decisions" so expansively that their scope of concern becomes indistinguishable from the background power structure itself.

To the extent that these and other versions of collective self-rule genuinely remain at such a high level of abstraction, therefore, they avoid leading us astray. Without more details about how such highly abstract aims can best be pursued in particular circumstances, however, such ideals will be unable to generate the sort of concrete, domain-specific heuristics that help us address key tasks of democratic judgment. And if we attempt to fill in these details in the way that is perhaps most naturally suggested by the goal of equal control over collective decisions—i.e., by specifying which decisions must be subjected to collective control, and which capacities must be equalized in order to achieve that control—we will be likely once again to emphasize processes of collective decision-making at the expense of background power relations.

Instead, I argue, those who seek to realize one of these highly abstract versions of collective self-rule should fill in this gap between ideal and reality with the mid-level heuristics associated with the ideal of resisting state capture, which I outline and defend in what follows. Though I have thus far presented these two ideals as rivals, in other words, they can also be plausibly understood as complements. On this reading, the two ideals simply operate at different levels of abstraction, such that resisting state capture spells out what it takes in practice to realize some highly abstract version of collective self-rule. The former thus appears as a revisionary *interpretation* of what the latter demands, rather than as a wholesale *alternative* to it—providing the domain-specific heuristics needed to address key tasks of democratic judgment.

In what follows, however, I continue to frame these two ideals of democracy primarily as rivals rather than complements. Although the domain-specific heuristics I defend under the rubric of resisting state capture *can* be understood to follow from a highly abstract conception of collective self-rule, for one, they can *also* be justified as effective ways of pursuing other ultimate values as well—including many conceptions of freedom, equality, welfare, or justice. More importantly, the heuristics themselves differ substantially and systematically from those most *commonly* derived from ideals of collective self-rule. Let us now examine how.

1.4 The ideal of resisting state capture: An egalitarian balance of social forces

As with collective self-rule, the most basic aim of resisting state capture is to keep public power tethered to the public interest, in response to the predicament of modern politics. Like ideals of collective self-rule, moreover, the ideal of resisting state capture pursues this aim by attempting to equalize influence over public power, in a very general sense. It diverges from the most prominent versions of collective self-rule, however, in the way it translates this highly abstract aim into a set of concrete, domain-specific heuristics. In evaluating existing practices and setting priorities for action and reform, most centrally, the ideal of resisting state capture focuses on sustaining an *egalitarian balance of social forces*—through constant mitigation of asymmetries in private power and organizational capacity—rather than attaining *equal control over collective decisions* through specific processes of will formation and decision-making.

The central motivation for this shift in focus—from equal control over collective decisions to an egalitarian balance of social forces—lies in the overlapping insights of certain realist and radical traditions of thinking about democracy, which jointly give rise to my *critical realist* approach. Despite the differences between them, I observe, realist skeptics and radical critics converge in their insistence that asymmetries in private power will always structure public institutions—no matter what we do to equalize control—and that this undermines the singular faith in collective decision-making implied by conventional democratic ideals. Put differently, the crucial insight of many thinkers in both realist and radical traditions is that many influences on public power operate outside formal processes of decision-making—and that in seeking to equalize influence over public power, we cannot confine our concern to such processes.

I explore these critical claims in great detail over the next several chapters. First, however, I must clarify the distinctive assumptions behind my own approach, as well as the domain-specific heuristics it suggests. And in the first respect, three features are worth highlighting: its *pluralistic* conception of state power, its focus on *groups* as the central units of political life, and its embrace of *competition* rather than collaboration as the fundamental activity of politics.

Unlike many ideals of collective self-rule, for one, the ideal of resisting state capture conceives the state as a pluralistic and internally differentiated entity. The Hobbesian notion that the state is (or should be) a singular sovereign authority is at least partly responsible—via Rousseau—for the pervasive focus on collective decision-making in democratic theory. In reality, however, state power is often highly disaggregated and subdivided into many distinct organs and institutions, which may be at cross purposes. Even when authority appears highly centralized, meanwhile, hierarchical state structures are effective only to the extent that they are at least implicitly supported by a sufficiently powerful coalition of actors with access to coercive capacity, wealth, social prestige, and other sources of private power. In practice, then, any decision-making procedure we use to determine state action will only function effectively if it is supported by this same sort of coalition. And as a result, the shape and outcomes of this procedure will predictably reflect the relative power of the members of that coalition.

This leads us to the second point. Where ideals of collective self-rule almost universally focus on equalizing control among individuals, the ideal of resisting state capture conceives politics primarily as a *group* activity. To be clear: individuals are still the ultimate units of *normative* concern, and I recognize of course that individuals can be important political actors. However, focusing on the relative power of the groups they belong to turns out to be a useful normative and theoretical shortcut—enabling the mid-level ideal of resisting state capture to generate concrete practical implications without improperly restricting our scope of political concern. And in this context, it is worth exploring why this shortcut works so well.

Perhaps most obviously, all politics requires collective action and coalition-building, meaning that much of our political activity will be undertaken explicitly in groups. Even when we do not *intentionally* act as part of a group, meanwhile, extensive psychological research concludes that our political behavior is still pervasively *motivated* by our group affiliations and other social identities. The nature of these groups varies widely, ranging from tight-knit kinship networks and elite cabals to broad-based political parties and loosely defined ethnic or cultural identities. Still, the point remains that we *participate* in politics primarily as members of groups, of one kind or another.[4] At the same time, state action also *affects* us primarily as members of such groups. States might distribute benefits or burdens, for instance, to people of certain families, lineages, tribes, ethnicities, and linguistic groups; to members of certain races, religions, social classes, and political factions; or to participants in certain industries, professions, businesses, organizations, clubs, or elite networks. Even more broadly, laws typically apply to us not as individuals, but rather in virtue of belonging to certain legal categories—and we thus share interests with others who belong to those categories.

Though the ultimate unit of normative concern remains the individual, then, the mid-level ideal of resisting state capture gains real-world traction in part by focusing on the relative power of the groups they belong to. More specifically, it is set in motion by the observation that many of the most significant threats to human interests in the modern world can be traced either directly or indirectly to the use of state power by certain groups to promote their interests at the expense of others. Its foremost aim, then, is to prevent any group from gaining the sort of unilateral control over state institutions that would enable them to perpetrate these threats. Put differently, the ideal of resisting state capture aims to keep public power tethered to something like a broadly shared public interest by preventing certain kinds of *deviations* from it—namely, those that result from the capture of public power by particular groups—and endorses as democratic all practices that help prevent these deviations. More than any specific process of decision-making, then, modern politics is about ensuring that no group achieves complete and permanent victory in the competition among groups for access to state power.

Indeed, this embrace of competition is the final distinctive feature of my approach that I will discuss. Ideals of collective self-rule typically see democracy as a process of co-creation—implying either that oppositional and adversarial practices necessarily threaten democratic legitimacy, or that they are appropriate only as a second best, when collaboration is precluded, and when they can be justified with reference to a horizon of mutual understanding or sincere compromise. By contrast, the ideal of resisting state capture assumes that groups will always compete for access to state power, and aims primarily to ensure that no group can dominate this competition.

---

[4] To be clear, I do not claim that no one ever seeks the *common* good or *public* interest. Many people clearly do. At least some people, some of the time, however, *will* be seeking their own partial or private interests. Thanks to motivated reasoning, meanwhile, even those who perceive themselves to be working for the public interest will have views of it that are biased in ways that reliably favor their interests and the interests of their group.

More specifically, its foremost aim is to maintain a roughly egalitarian balance in the "organizational capacity" of different groups—i.e., their ability to coordinate widespread collective action by mobilizing power resources such as coercive force, material wealth, and social prestige. Rather than seeing oppositional contestation as theoretically marginal, and as a last resort in practice, the ideal of resisting state capture thus conceives it as paradigmatically democratic in theory, and central in practice to all democratic societies.

In this context, the main purpose of electoral democracy is to steer this competition toward channels that are relatively less dangerous and destructive than contests of brute coercive force. When inter-group competition for state power spills over into political violence, in short, the results are often extremely harmful to human interests—both in the immediate sense that war causes massive destruction, and also because the winners of military conflicts often attain an especially comprehensive level of control over state institutions, enabling especially dangerous forms of capture and abuse. On any plausible account of human interests, therefore, preventing inter-group competition from spilling over into violence will be central to protecting them. And the practices of electoral democracy—namely, competitively elections with universal suffrage, as supported by certain constitutional limits and universal guarantees—offer the most reliable method of doing so. The record of electoral democracies is hardly perfect on this score, but no alternative is *more* effective. As I argue at length in subsequent chapters, electoral democracy is thus an indispensable part of any plausible response to the predicament of modern politics.

At the same time, the formal procedures of electoral decision-making are hardly sufficient, on their own, to resist these additional forms of capture. Before such procedures even begin, wealthy elites and other privileged groups exert outsized influence over the terms upon which they will be conducted—shaping which issues make it to the political agenda, how those issues are constructed in order to activate certain interests and identities, and how those interests and identities are organized into political coalitions and party platforms. They may then influence electoral results in various ways—perhaps most prominently by funding certain parties and candidates. After formal electoral procedures are over, finally, those with outsized power have further opportunities to influence which policies are made, as well as how they are actually implemented, using everything from blatant bribery of elected and appointed officials, to a range of subtler career-driven incentives and cultural influences. At every stage, in sum, wealthy elites and others with concentrated private power are far more successful than other groups at ensuring that public power in electoral democracies serves their interests.

On the one hand, then, existing practices of electoral democracy prevent any group from having the kind of pervasive control over the state that would allow them to do whatever they want—and for that, they are *indispensable*. On the other hand, wealthy elites and others with outsized private power and organizational capacity still enjoy systematic advantages in every electoral democracy, meaning that these practices are also profoundly *insufficient*. And where ideals of collective self-rule often emphasize one of these crucial insights at the expense of the other, the ideal of resisting state capture is designed to keep both squarely in view. That is what makes its approach to the first concrete task of political judgment distinctively promising. Eschewing the undue enthusiasm of minimalist ideals of collective self-rule as well as the undue pessimism of many expansive versions, it suggests an attitude of *measured appreciation* towards electoral democracy. Under reasonably favorable conditions, it reminds us, electoral democracy can keep public power very loosely tethered to the public interest—but without additional practices, this tether will always remain quite loose, and may get looser over time.

Our next question thus follows quite naturally: which additional practices might deepen, enrich, and safeguard democracy by further tightening the connection between public power and the public interest? As I examine in Chapter 2, democratic reformers who seek to expand responsive representation typically focus on reforming electoral procedures, for instance by restricting campaign finance or moving to a proportional system. As I show in Chapter 3, meanwhile, those influenced by an ideal of participatory inclusion promote a variety of collaborative decision-making procedures outside of elections—ranging from participatory budgeting to citizens' assemblies—whose aim is to include ordinary people more directly in a wider range of decisions. In addition, finally, more expansive versions of collective self-rule will sometimes advocate social welfare programs and other substantive policies, on the avowedly democratic grounds that they make the conditions of collective will formation more egalitarian.

Many of these familiar institutional reforms can protect public power to some extent, and thus merit some degree of support. Their democratic impact is often overestimated, however—and more important priorities are often neglected—due to the pervasive focus of democratic theorists and reformers on how decisions are made, rather than the underlying power relations that shape the outcomes of whatever procedures are used. At least within electoral democracies, most of the greatest threats to the public interest can be traced to capture by wealthy elites and other groups with outsized private power and organizational capacity. And no matter how collective decision-making is structured, such groups will find ways to influence the results. So long as massive group-based asymmetries remain, therefore, reforms to elections and other decision-making procedures will only ever achieve marginal progress on democratic goals. As powerful groups learn how to manipulate whatever new rules have been implemented, indeed, any gains made through such institutional reforms will likely dissipate further with time.

In developing its agenda for action and reform, therefore, the ideal of resisting state capture aims directly at mitigating these underlying asymmetries in private power and organizational capacity. To the extent that they serve this goal, it offers conditional support for certain popular institutional reforms, such as campaign finance restrictions and participatory budgeting initiatives. Yet it eschews the uncritical embrace, overzealous expectations, and special urgency often granted to such procedural fixes by democratic reformers influenced by ideals of responsive representation and/or participatory inclusion. The substantive demands for background equality implied by expansive versions of collective self-rule are closer to the mark, meanwhile, but even here, the aim of most democratic theorists and reformers is to ensure that each individual has sufficient resources to participate, and not to address the group-based asymmetries that are the ultimate cause of most capture in electoral democracies.

Though the ideal of resisting state capture offers some degree of support to certain common reform proposals, then, it grants far greater priority to a less familiar set of strategies for deeper democratization, focused directly on mitigating these underlying asymmetries. As I explore in Chapter 9, this includes procedural mechanisms that use *impartial oversight* to prevent powerful groups from turning outsized organizational capacity into policy influence—like the "citizen juries" I have defended at greater length elsewhere. It also includes explicit efforts to limit the resources and coordination rights of groups whose systematic advantages make them *hegemonic* (e.g., wealth taxes and antitrust law), support organization among groups whose structural position makes them *counter-hegemonic* (e.g., protections for unions), and flatten the overall distribution of private power across groups (e.g., wealth transfers). Rather than guaranteeing certain capacities to each person—as implied by the generic goal of ensuring background equality—these policies adopt the more specific goal of *corrective partiality*.

In setting an agenda for popular participation, finally, the ideal of resisting state capture highlights practices that are narrowly targeted at building *organized collective power* among particular counter-hegemonic groups—i.e., those who possess the least concentrated private power, and those who are most likely to contest and undermine the outsized power of wealthy elites and other hegemonic groups—rather than encouraging generic forms of civic virtue. In particular, the only thing that can reliably force concessions from entrenched hegemonic interests is costly collective action by large and diverse groups of ordinary people, sustained over long periods of time. And it is this sort of sustained, well-organized popular participation that is most urgently needed to defend and enrich democracy.

In this respect, my approach diverges from certain prominent strands of radical democratic theory. It implies, for one, that *spontaneous* action is not uniquely democratic. Rather, its long-term democratic value depends entirely on whether the energy it generates in the short term is effectively translated into lasting organizational capacity among counter-hegemonic groups. Similarly, it is a mistake to regard *internally democratic* organization as intrinsically valuable across all contexts. To be sure: some degree of internal democracy is necessary within unions, parties, and other organizations that claim to represent counter-hegemonic groups—both in order to keep leaders accountable, and in order to build solidarity and commitment among the rank and file. Yet given that some degree of hierarchy is *also* necessary to enable those organizations to wield power effectively, *more* internal democracy is not always better.

What sorts of popular participation should we turn to instead, in order to build sustainable and effective organizations of countervailing power? Chapter 10 begins to address this highly complex question, noting a remarkable convergence on certain practices of "organizing for power" among successful organizers in unions, community groups, and social movements, and analyzing key features of this promising model. My reflections here are avowedly provisional, however, and I stop short of exploring how the solidarity and organizational capacity developed in face-to-face contexts can be scaled up to generate countervailing power at national or international scales. Though this question remains beyond my scope in this book, I conclude by arguing that it is one of the most important for democratic theorists to address.

1.5 The scope and limits of a critical realist approach

This is hardly the only dilemma the book leaves unresolved. In such cases, however, my approach still leaves us with a kind of guidance: namely, that further inquiry and disagreement should be oriented around broadly empirical claims about which groups pose the greatest threats of capture, and which practices will enable us to resist those threats most effectively. This reflects my efforts to economize on certainty: i.e., to build from those claims that merit the greatest confidence, rather than those which are logically or normatively fundamental. And while I am confident in my basic commitment to respecting the interests of all human beings equally, it seems to me that many empirical regularities merit a relatively higher degree of confidence than any *precise* normative account of exactly what human interests are or why they are worth respecting. Rather than seeking an unwarranted degree of precision in defining foundational normative concepts, then, I aim to make theoretical progress through broadly empirical forms of inquiry.

Some might worry that the empirical knowledge we get from history and social science will never be nearly certain enough to warrant definitive conclusions. For me, though, that is precisely the point: where disputes at the theoretical level tend to generate a clash of competing certainties, disputes at the level of flawed empirical inquiry and context-sensitive normative judgment foreground the real uncertainty we face in deeply complex political situations. The merits of judicial review, for instance, are often seen to turn on which conception of collective self-rule is correct: i.e., whether majoritarian elections are sufficient (e.g., Waldron 1999), or whether equal control can only be achieved if certain basic rights are protected from hostile majorities by counter-majoritarian forces (e.g., Dworkin 1996). By contrast, my approach promotes contextual inquiry about the relative dangers of capture involved in each option. This may not yield a definitive answer, but in my view, it leads to more responsible practices of judgment and discussion—and ultimately, a more cumulative theoretical project (Bagg 2016).

The empirical claims I rely upon are certainly contestable. Not everyone will share my conviction, for instance, that public power in all democracies disproportionately benefits those with great wealth, and perpetuates other systems of categorical advantage. Still, even those who doubt such claims may still find it useful to employ the general framework I present. Such readers may eschew some of the conclusions I draw from the ideal of resisting state capture, in other words, yet find that it nevertheless structures their judgments about existing practices, future priorities, and concrete dilemmas in ways they find normatively satisfying on the whole, once they substitute their preferred assumptions. If so, the book can clarify our disagreements, by highlighting the predictions and judgments responsible for our divergent conclusions.

It bears repeating, finally, that my aim here is not to describe an ideally just society, nor the best overall response to particular circumstances. Instead, my aim is to explain why democracy matters and how to make it better. Like other democratic theories, then, it does not directly address forms of inequality and capture located either below or above the level of states—not to mention the broader first-order aims we may have. In many cases, political actors will need to weigh the demands of democracy at the state level against these other concerns. That said, the ideal of resisting state capture does address some of these concerns indirectly—and even where it does not, it can sometimes speak directly to practice regardless.

As I document in Chapter 4, for instance, most ostensibly private forms of domination and oppression are supported by legal structures, and thus reflect state capture. Similarly, extreme inequality between the Global North and South persists, in part, because the most powerful states and international institutions are captured by the citizens—and especially the elites—of the North. Meanwhile, the severity of the climate crisis is partly attributable to the influence of "fossil capital" (Malm 2015) on those same governments and institutions. In all these cases, any plausible solution will focus on undermining the power of global elites, while fostering the countervailing power of their most salient opponents: i.e., national organizations and parties pressing the interests of ordinary people (Aronoff et al. 2019; Purdy 2019). Though concerns of private domination and global justice remain beyond my scope in this book, then, my wager is that incorporating them would not drastically change my overall conclusions.

In particular, the urgency of goals such as fighting climate change does not justify the use of authoritarian methods (e.g., Mittiga 2022). As I argue in Chapter 8, in short, doing so would create structures that could all too easily be usurped by opponents of climate action, generating outcomes even worse than those achieved under democracy. No matter how strong they are, then, our first-order reasons to fight climate change cannot "outweigh" our second-order reasons to maintain democratic institutions: rather, the urgency of the former only reinforces the latter. Of course, this applies only when second-order democratic reasons are strong and unambiguous. When they are weak or uncertain, first-order reasons will prevail by default. And in between these poles, there are cases of genuine conflict between first- and second-order reasons. Still, there are fewer than we might initially expect—and as such, we can often assume that the most democratic practices are also the best overall.

With these caveats in mind, then, let us begin to examine what those practices are. Table 1.1 below summarizes the arguments I have just outlined, and indicates where further discussion of each issue can be found—thus serving as a reading guide for the rest of the book.

Table 1.1 Summary: collective self-rule and resisting state capture as democratic ideals

	Collective Self-Rule (democracy as collective co-authorship of law)	**Resisting State Capture** (democracy as group competition for power)
Political Orientation What general goals does each ideal set for the foreseeable future?	*Equal Control over Collective Decisions*: keep public power tethered to the public interest by subjecting it to collective control → expand participation by individuals in processes of will formation / decision-making (see §1.3)	*Egalitarian Balance of Social Forces*: keep public power tethered to the public interest by ensuring no groups can manipulate it for private ends → mitigate asymmetries between groups (see §1.4, §7.2, §9.1–2)
Concrete Heuristics (addressing the three key tasks of democratic judgment) How does each ideal evaluate existing practices of electoral democracy?	*Minimalist Views*: control enabled by elections is equal enough for legitimacy (danger: grants unwarranted legitimacy) (see §2.1–2) *Expansive Views*: elections are unequal and thus insufficient for legitimacy (danger: fails to explain real value) (see §3.4)	*Measured Appreciation*: elections are indispensable (because they limit extreme capture), but also profoundly insufficient (because they enable many other forms of capture, especially by wealthy elites and advantaged groups) (see §4, §5, §8)
What agenda is suggested for the reform of institutions and policy?	*Responsive Representation*: reform redesigning electoral process to ensure policy tracks public opinion (see §2.3) *Participatory Inclusion*: include more people more directly (and deliberatively) in more decisions (see §3.1–3) *Background Equality*: make processes of will formation more egalitarian by expanding welfare state programs (see §3.4)	*Impartial Oversight*: limit the ability of any group to capture the state via contestatory oversight procedures (with ordinary citizens as impartial defenders of the public interest) (see §9.4) *Corrective Partiality*: balance organizational capacity by constraining hegemonic groups, aiding counter-hegemonic groups, and flattening the overall distribution of power (see §6, §9.3)

	Which priorities are implied for civic action and participation outside the state?	*Generic Civic Virtue*: emphasize collaborative, deliberative, individualized forms of participation; turn to oppositional, group-based contestation only as a last resort; treat internal "democracy" as presumptively and intrinsically valuable (see §3.1–3)	*Countervailing Power*: prioritize oppositional organization among counter-hegemonic groups; value internal "democracy" only if and when it enhances collective power (see §6, §10)
Democratic Dilemmas	How does each ideal navigate tensions among democratic demands?	*Theoretical Resolution*: debate and inquiry on theoretical terrain: i.e., which definition is correct? (see §1.5) (e.g., if democracy = majority rule, judicial review is bad; but if democracy = minority rights, judicial review is good)	*Empirical Resolution*: debate and inquiry on empirical terrain: i.e., which choice minimizes capture? (see §7.3, §9.1) (e.g., judicial review is valuable only if and when its tendency to limit abuse outweighs its tendency to entrench elite power)
Utopian Horizon	What vague direction is set by each ideal for the very distant future?	*Full Socialization*: make *more* decisions collectively → expand scope to economy / society / culture (see §7.1) *Ideal Deliberation*: make decisions *more* collectively → expand reach of reasonable / egalitarian discourse (see §7.1)	*Dispersion of Private Power*: equalize private power among groups → limit the need for collective decision-making by decentralizing choices where possible, while also minimizing inequalities of influence over choices that must be made collectively (see §7.1)

2
Beyond Responsive Representation

This chapter addresses the commonsense view that democracy is valuable because—and to the extent that—elected leaders obey the will of the people. This is perhaps the most widespread and influential version of the ideal of collective self-rule, and it is ubiquitous in contemporary democratic life. Every time a political leader claims that their electoral victory authorizes them to act in the name of the people, for instance, they trade on this view. Yet so do their opponents, when they point to polling data or street protest as more reliable indicators of what the people want. After all, the idea that democracy means the will of the people is constantly reinforced by everything from civics textbooks and news articles to TV spots and bumper sticker slogans.

I call this the ideal of *responsive representation*.[1] It holds, centrally, that democracy should enact a *principal–agent* relationship between voters and representatives, whereby the latter (the "agents") faithfully execute the stable, coherent, and independent policy priorities of the former (the "principal"). And something like it shapes how many people think about why democracy matters and how to make it better. While acknowledging that elections fall short of allowing citizens to author the laws directly, for instance, many political scientists argue that they enable citizens to prospectively choose among elites and/or retrospectively punish those who fail to serve their interests (Fearon 1999). In assessing different systems, meanwhile, many refer to the alignment of state policy with majority preferences, as expressed in opinion polls (Erikson 2015; Jacobs and Shapiro 2000). In light of this, finally, many popular proposals for democratic reform focus on removing salient barriers to responsiveness in the electoral system—which, depending on the system, may take the form of nonpartisan redistricting, proportional representation, restrictions on campaign finance and lobbying, or more direct popular participation in legislation, among many other institutional fixes.

Like many versions of collective self-rule, the ideal of responsive representation gets a lot right. In an important sense, elections do authorize winners to act—and when large majorities oppose their actions, it is indeed a bad sign.

---

[1] Similar views have been described as the 'vocal model' (J. Green 2009), 'folk theory' (Achen and Bartels 2016), or 'bedrock norm' (Disch 2011).

The Dispersion of Power. Samuel Ely Bagg, Oxford University Press. © Samuel Ely Bagg (2024).
DOI: 10.1093/oso/9780192848826.003.0003

Meanwhile, electoral democracies do typically enjoy greater responsiveness than other regimes, and reforms like nonpartisan redistricting and limits on campaign finance are typically good ideas. Like most versions of collective self-rule, however, the ideal of responsive representation tells only part of the story—placing too much emphasis on the processes through which individual preferences are aggregated to generate collective decisions, and not enough on background power relations among groups.

Given the structure of collective decisions and the social determinants of political behavior, I argue, even the fairest possible electoral procedures will always be susceptible to capture by wealthy elites and other powerful interests—reflecting the underlying balance of power among different groups in society. And while this often generates a mismatch between public opinion and policy, responsiveness is not a reliable indicator of democratic health. For reasons I explore below, on the one hand, extensive capture by powerful groups is consistent with high levels of responsiveness. Though low responsiveness is usually a bad sign, on the other hand, it does not *necessarily* indicate capture. The ideal of responsive representation thus fails to offer a fully compelling account of why democracy matters and how to make it better.

2.1 Capture via collective indeterminacy: Social choice and agenda control

As noted in the Introduction, ideals of collective self-rule may draw some of their intuitive plausibility from an analogy with decision-making in small groups—and this is especially true of responsive representation. In a small group with relatively equal power and broadly shared interests, considering a limited number of issues at a time, it seems sufficient to ensure that everyone has an equal opportunity to inform themselves, present their views, and vote. Under such conditions, indeed, it makes sense that participants may feel that they have reached a genuinely collective decision, even if they do not get the outcome they originally preferred.

To state what should be obvious, however, the nature and scale of modern democratic politics makes this analogy irrelevant several times over. In a group of five people, each person may make a unique contribution, and perhaps the same could even be said for an assembly of 500 or 5000. The conceit is simply untenable, however, in a society of 5 million, where a limited number of perspectives will inevitably dominate discussion, and any individual's vote is vanishingly unlikely to matter. Even more importantly, the number of distinct choices made each year by modern states—including bills that come before legislative bodies, the rulings of state bureaucracies, and so on—is on the scale of millions. Under such conditions, even the most well-informed citizens will never be aware of the vast majority of what is done "in their name," much less able to develop a coherent opinion about it. The result is a fundamental mismatch between the vast number of policy choices states must make, and the extremely coarse accountability mechanism of elections, which gives rise to pervasive indeterminacy about the majority will and ultimately enables elite manipulation.

The basic problem is that voters cannot make their support of a given candidate or party conditional on more than a few highly salient issues at once. If limiting immigration is what matters most to a particular voter, for instance, and there is only one viable party that promises to do so, she may vote for that party despite strongly disagreeing with the rest of its platform. And while other voters may find different issues most salient, only a limited number of issues typically occupy public attention at a given time. What this means is that on nearly all other issues—i.e., issues that no large group of voters finds salient—representatives will be free to ignore constituent preferences without facing major electoral consequences (Culpepper 2010). And on these non-salient issues, they are likely to cater instead to well-resourced elites who can exert influence and demand concessions from politicians behind the scenes.[2]

This intuitive account of how the indeterminacy inherent to collective choice procedures facilitates elite capture can be generalized and formalized using the tools of social choice theory (SCT). In particular, a key result of SCT is that whenever voter preferences are structured in certain reasonably common ways, there can be no true majority will, because whatever decision is reached, at least one majority will prefer some alternative (Arrow 1951; Riker 1982; Weale 2018). For instance, imagine that in a country at war, about a third of the population wants to withdraw all troops, while another third favors staying the course but would rather not commit more troops, and a final third favors a troop surge in order to guarantee victory but prefers to withdraw entirely rather than staying in a quagmire. In this case, any decision will be opposed by a majority: withdrawal by those who favor staying the course or a surge; staying the course by advocates of withdrawal or a surge; and a surge by those who favor withdrawal or staying the course. Social choice

---

[2] Some aim to mitigate this problem by insisting that citizens vote on each issue separately, rather than being forced to choose between fixed platforms. Even if it were possible for everyone to vote on each of the millions of decisions modern states make, however, the evidence on referendums and other forms of mass direct democracy suggests that they are no less susceptible to elite manipulation (Weale 2018).

theorists say that preferences structured in this way lack a single peak, leaving no true majority opinion about the preferred policy, only several *potential* majorities.

On many discrete political issues, of course, voter preferences will not exhibit this peculiar structure. However, a similar phenomenon occurs whenever there are multiple issues at stake in a single vote—so long as preferences about those issues vary independently of one another. Consider a situation, for instance, where a third of the population supports both abortion and redistribution, and a third opposes both, while a sixth each supports one but not the other. In this situation, any platform or policy settlement that includes a stance on both issues will be opposed by a majority, generating the same situation as above: i.e., there is no *true* majority will about which platform should be adopted, only several *potential* majorities. When multiple issues must be bundled together, then—as party platforms do for thousands of issues—we might expect many possible majorities, yielding great indeterminacy.

In theory, preferences structured in this way could yield active cycling between outcomes supported by different majority coalitions. Every time a policy settlement were reached, that is, it would quickly be overturned by a majority that opposes it, whose proposed replacement would in turn be overturned by a new majority. Given the difficulty of building coalitions in practice, however, not all potential majorities are actualized. Instead of constant instability, we more often observe *latent* cycles—i.e., preference structures that could in theory support such cycling but do not in practice. And the most significant effect of such latent preference cycles, it turns out, is to generate opportunities for elite manipulation behind the scenes. When there is no determinate answer about which option is preferred by a majority, in short, the choice between potential majority platforms must be made on unrelated, "arbitrary" grounds. Yet crucially, this does not imply that outcomes will be chosen at *random*. Instead, they will likely reflect the interests of those best able to use extra-procedural mechanisms—ranging from direct control of politicians to subtle forms of influence over media and culture—to shape the political agenda, and thereby resolve any indeterminacies in their favor.

Any group with outsized access to these extra-procedural means can be called an *elite*, in contrast to *ordinary people* whose primary source of political power lies in the electoral process itself. And while the most prominent elites will vary across circumstances, a critical factor in determining whose interests will be favored in any context is *organizational capacity*: i.e., the ability of groups to coordinate and act collectively in defense of shared interests.

Given the incentives facing elected politicians, credible threats from organized groups to withdraw key forms of support will be felt far more directly than the vague possibility that disorganized ordinary voters will defect *en masse* from their coalition (Jacobs and Shapiro 2000). As such, groups with high organizational capacity will be best able to influence outcomes in their favor.

There are many determinants of organizational capacity, and different elites will draw upon different sources of strength. As Mancur Olson (1965) famously pointed out, for instance, it is generally easier for smaller groups to overcome collective action problems, and this is at least part of what explains the success of certain special interest groups in lobbying for policies that serve their interests while harming everyone else. In the grand scheme of things, however, a more important determinant of a group's organizational capacity is the access of members to private power resources including social clout, cultural capital, and especially material wealth. As I elaborate at length in Chapter 4, indeed, wealthy elites in all contemporary democracies employ myriad tools to influence officials behind the scenes—ranging from campaign funding (Lessig 2011), lobbying (Lindsey and Teles 2017), legislative subsidies (Hall and Deardorff 2006), and descriptive representation (Carnes 2013) to cultural capture (Kwak 2013) and the threat of capital flight (Lindblom 1982)—and thereby ensure their interests are protected.

According to recent studies of unequal responsiveness across income groups, these efforts bear quite a bit of fruit.[3] In a famous study of the US, for instance, Gilens and Page (2014) found that the preferences of lower- and middle-income Americans had virtually *no* independent impact on state policy. Policy does sometimes align with the preferences of lower- and middle-income Americans, but only when those preferences happen to align with the preferences of wealthy Americans—or, in certain rare cases, when they are exceptionally well organized around specific issues. Where income groups diverge, by contrast, policy nearly always reflects the preferences of the wealthy. And though the US is sometimes treated as an outlier in this respect, researchers have uncovered similar patterns in many other democracies (Giger, Rosset, and Bernauer 2012; Hopkin and Lynch 2016; Lupu and Warner 2021; Peters and Ensink 2015; Schakel 2021).

What should we take from all of this? The headline conclusion people often draw from SCT is that—given certain plausible assumptions about the

---

[3] Scholars of public opinion distinguish between *congruence*, the degree to which policy outcomes match voter preferences at a given time, and *responsiveness*, the degree to which outcomes change over time in response to changes in voter preferences (Beyer and Hänni 2018). For my purposes, however, this distinction is not important, and both are included in my concept of responsive representation.

structure of voter preferences—there is no such thing as a genuinely collective will. And the importance of this conclusion, where it holds, should not be understated: in short, it means that any discourse about the popular will, or the will of the people, or even the will of the majority, is basically nonsensical. At times it can be harmless or even useful nonsense, but in many cases it is put to sinister use, conferring the sheen of democratic legitimacy upon outcomes that do not deserve it.

Nevertheless, proponents of SCT have sometimes exaggerated its importance. For one, voter preferences may not vary along multiple dimensions as often as we might expect (Mackie 2003). Meanwhile, studies of unequal responsiveness have been criticized on both substantive and methodological grounds (Elkjær and Klitgaard 2021)—and whatever inequalities do exist between income groups, policy outcomes in electoral democracies still exhibit higher *overall* congruence with public opinion than the dismal picture drawn here would suggest (Brooks and Manza 2006; Burstein 2003). Even if it does not constitute a collective will in any theoretically precise sense, the congruence measured by such studies might still be valuable.

In an important recent book, finally, Sean Ingham (2019) affirms the core SCT finding that there is often no genuine will of *the* people (or even *the* majority), while showing that the more general idea of "popular control" *can* be given a coherent interpretation. In short, he argues, a majority who share a preference can be said to have control not only when that preference is actually realized, but also when that preference *would* be realized, *if* they cared about it enough. While it is not usually meaningful to speak of a single collective will on any particular issue, then, a degree of popular control exists whenever *all potential* majorities within a population possess this counterfactual ability to change any outcomes they care about strongly enough.[4]

---

[4] This is not a particularly demanding criterion: all it requires is that any majority, if it devoted all of its energies to realizing a single shared preference, would eventually be able to realize it. And if a potential majority must sacrifice everything else in order to achieve its shared preference, its control is quite weak compared to that of other potential majorities, which can achieve their preferences without sacrificing much at all. In addition to this minimal threshold, then, Ingham also articulates a maximalist ideal of popular control, whereby each majority has the highest degree of control compatible with every majority having the same amount. It is hard to overstate the significance of Ingham's contribution, which in my view offers the only interpretation of popular rule whose coherence does not depend on restrictive assumptions about preference structures, and thus resolves decades of controversies surrounding SCT. Nevertheless, Ingham's account of 'rule by multiple majorities' still relies on unstable and manipulable individual preferences, and thus faces the worries I raise in the following section. As an ideal, meanwhile, it has few clear practical implications, for its minimal threshold is already met by nearly all existing democracies—and possibly even some non-democracies—while the maximalist ideal it promotes is too utopian to provide concrete guidance. Even if we accept maximal popular control as our ultimate goal, then, we will still need a mid-level ideal, like resisting state capture, to determine how best to pursue it.

These considerations should make us wary of over- or misinterpreting SCT. In my view, however, it still has crucial lessons for democratic theory. On the one hand, voter preferences do sometimes exhibit latent cycles—and when they do, we have reason to be skeptical of the widespread focus among democratic reformers on the structure of electoral institutions. Some form of responsive representation may remain coherent as a goal, but if preferences are structured such that any collective choice procedure will inevitably generate indeterminacies that are subject to elite manipulation, we will not get far by pursuing the kind of institutional reforms often associated with that goal. If we aim to pursue a coherent version of responsive representation, rather, my interpretation of SCT implies that we should focus on remedying asymmetries in the organizational capacity of different groups, since this is what will really determine whose preferences are reflected in policy. Even if we retain the ideal of responsive representation in an abstract sense, in other words, the best way to advance it will be to adopt the practices of resisting state capture, rather than those it is normally taken to imply.

Where empirical results cast doubt on the assumptions of SCT, on the other hand, they do so in a way that only lends further *support* to my core practical inference: i.e., that the proper focus of democratic reform is balancing organizational capacity among groups, via substantively redistributive policy and countervailing organizing outside of the state, rather than enhancing responsive representation through reform of collective decision procedures. And in fact, the tools of SCT can help to clarify why this is. Given what we know about how voters form political preferences, in short, the absence of latent cycles is very unlikely to indicate a genuine principal–agent relationship between voters and their representatives, free of elite manipulation. Instead, the process of *individual* will formation involves significant indeterminacies of its own, which are no less susceptible to asymmetrical influence by wealthy elites and others with outsized organizational capacity. I turn now to explore that process, and the ways in which it favors powerful groups.

2.2 Capture via individual indeterminacy: The construction of social identities

The key assumption of the dispiriting picture drawn in the previous section is that voter preferences will vary along multiple dimensions, giving rise to many potential majorities and creating indeterminacies that can be exploited by elites with outsized organizational capacity. And if citizens formed their views about political issues independently, this assumption might be justified. In reality, however, citizen preferences are highly correlated with one another—so much so, indeed, that in many cases the views of citizens on thousands of seemingly unrelated issues can be accurately captured by a *single* left–right dimension.

In the US, for instance, it just so happens that pro-life voters tend to be hawks who oppose redistribution, while pro-choice voters tend to be doves who support redistribution. Meanwhile, those with more extreme views in one area tend to have more extreme views in other areas as well. Even more remarkably, their views on less salient issues like central bank policy, sentencing guidelines, bankruptcy law, trade deals, tort reform, and intellectual property can *also* be reliably predicted by their general placement on the very same left–right spectrum. Such alignments are not perfect, of course, and secondary dimensions do play an important role in electoral politics—perhaps increasingly so in many European democracies.[5] Given the vast dimensionality of the *available* issue space, however, the degree to which preferences do line up along a single dimension, at least in certain political contexts, is nothing short of astonishing.

Where it exists, this alignment rescues the possibility of attaining responsive representation via elections (Mackie 2003). If most citizens have only one major preference that reliably predicts everything else—i.e., their position on a left–right spectrum—then an election with only two viable parties or coalitions *can* deliver responsiveness to majority opinion. All it needs to do is track the position of the median voter along this left–right spectrum, which is precisely what elections are often thought to do (Downs 1957). Whether this represents a desirable normative outcome, however, depends crucially on what explains this miraculous alignment.

One possibility here is that the alignment of preferences along a left–right spectrum is the result of reasonable deliberation on equal terms (Knight and Johnson 1994). If so, this can be celebrated as part of the process of collective self-rule, whereby citizens come together and make collective decisions not only about what to do, but also about the terms on which to make those decisions—i.e., the proper questions to ask, the relevant policy platforms to choose from, and other features of the political agenda. While it will rarely yield *consensus*, in other words, deliberation can serve to *structure* our disagreements along a single dimension, thereby facilitating more robust

---

[5] For instance, the left–right spectrum is most closely associated with preferences over economic redistribution, and a common cross-cutting dimension has sometimes been called the 'GAL–TAN' spectrum, pitting green, alternative, libertarian (GAL) against traditionalist, authoritarian, nationalist (TAN) values. Albert Weale (2018) develops an extended example of social choice problems using these dimensions.

correlations between preferences and policy. And if citizens really do remain equal and autonomous while structuring their disagreements in this way, we can plausibly interpret this as a key phase in a genuinely collective process of will formation.

Unfortunately, empirical research casts serious doubt on this optimistic supposition. In practice, voters' knowledge of politically relevant facts is subpar (Somin 2016), while their preferences about specific issues are often constructed on the spot, reflecting measurement strategies rather than an authentic, underlying will (Zaller 1992). Even if they are stable over time, moreover, this does not guarantee that a voter's beliefs, opinions, and values are internally consistent: they may express preferences for lower taxes *and* better services, for instance, without considering how the tension between these two demands might be resolved. This is not to disparage ordinary voters: given the infinitesimal chance their vote will make a difference, it is rational for people not to inform themselves—and even if they tried, no single person could become an expert about *all* of the thousands of policies at stake in most elections. Still, what this means is that on most issues, most of the time, the preferences of most voters are simply indeterminate—making a principal–agent relationship between voters and leaders impossible.

Even when a voter's opinions appear stable, coherent, and well informed, meanwhile, they do not necessarily reflect a genuine process of autonomous reflection and choice. What the evidence suggests, rather, is that the explanations we give for our political views are often post-hoc rationalizations of affective attachments driven largely by social identity (D. Green, Palmquist, and Schickler 2002; Lodge and Taber 2013; L. Mason 2018).[6] This reflects a broad consensus in cognitive science that human reasoning is not a neutral process of truth-seeking, but rather a motivated activity (Kunda 1990), often aimed at protecting the social groups we belong to (Kahan et al. 2007). Preferences formed via deliberation and introspection thus reflect an authentic or autonomous will no more reliably than those created arbitrarily on the spot.

More specifically, reasoning about our views may help us explain to ourselves *why* we hold them, but it will only rarely yield substantial *changes* to those views. Indeed, the evidence suggests that becoming well informed simply leads people to become more confident in the opinions which they would likely have held anyway—and *less* likely to change their minds (Bartels 2002;

---

[6] More technically, this means that social identity is highly predictive of party affiliation and other forms of political behavior, and there is good evidence that social identity is the more foundational element, bearing much of the causal responsibility in this relationship (Achen and Bartels 2016: 232–67).

Kahan 2012; McKee and Stuckler 2010; Nyhan and Reifler 2010). Where low-information voters are usually nonideological—expressing an idiosyncratic assortment of weakly held views that may be out of step with their voting patterns—high-information voters hold stronger and more ideologically consistent views because they are better able to pick up on elite cues and adopt the policy preferences associated with their political identity.

Collectively, these findings constitute a paradigm for understanding political behavior that we may call *social identity theory* (SIT). Like any scholarly approach, the details of SIT are subject to continual debate, but given the vast quantity of evidence amassed by its proponents, few would question its basic claim that social identity exerts a distinctively powerful influence on political preferences and behavior. Partisan identity is a classic example, since partisanship is a salient identity category in the US, where much of the initial research in this area was conducted. It is important to emphasize, however, that this is not essential to SIT as such.[7] On the contrary, one of its core assumptions is that everyone always has multiple overlapping social identities, which may change, vary in salience, or shift meaning over time. Its key claim, rather, is that changes in political preferences and behaviors are largely attributable to shifts of this kind: i.e., changes in the interpretation and salience of social identities.

As I interpret it, then, the most important implication of SIT is that the ability to influence the meaning and salience of widely shared social identities is a key form of political power. Indeed, a key strategy of political campaigns and social movements aiming to build majority coalitions is to mobilize certain identities, demobilize others, and shape how people understand the identities they find salient. No less impactful in this regard, however, are schools, churches, union halls, museums, memorials, and other spaces of political education; as well as the broader set of cultural and media institutions that shape how people interpret social reality and place themselves within it—including print journalism, talk radio, cable news, and social media, as well as advertising and narrative storytelling. Finally, scholarship on "policy feedback" shows that the structure of social insurance programs and other substantive policies can often exert a powerful influence on the social identities of those affected by them as well (Pierson 1993).

---

[7] Early versions of social identity theory framed partisanship as the 'unmoved mover' underlying all political behavior (Campbell et al. 1960), but this narrow view has long since been abandoned. Partisanship can be a very strong identity, and is often correlated with other salient identities like race or class, but its salience varies—as demonstrated by its steadily declining salience in Western Europe over the past half century (Mair 2013).

On the one hand, political actors might use these tools to shape how voters *interpret* their identities—for instance by inducing major parties to endorse certain policies, in the hope that their partisans will follow suit. Again, however, partisanship is not the only social identity that can serve this purpose: political actors may also use the various means of identity construction to associate their favored beliefs and preferences with identities grounded in class, race, gender, religion, profession, or region, among many others. On the other hand, political actors can also influence voter behavior by shifting the relative *salience* of existing identities, or even by inventing and promoting new social identities. For instance, wealthy elites can often reduce effective support for redistributive policies among the poor not by severing the robust association between those policies and class identity, but rather by increasing the salience of cross-cutting identities associated with indifference or opposition to redistribution.

Among the most blatant and successful of these efforts is the mobilization of racial identity by wealthy white people in many societies to prevent alliances between poor people of different races. In many societies around the globe since the beginning of European colonization and settlement in the fifteenth century, the ruling class has consisted of wealthy white elites. An obvious danger to their power, then, has been that poorer whites would join forces with nonwhites to demand greater power and threaten the material interests of the ruling class. And in a wide variety of contexts, in a wide variety of different ways, wealthy white elites have successfully prevented this outcome through a strategy of "divide-and-conquer" along racial lines, making racial identity salient relative to other identities grounded in class, region, lifestyle, and so on.

The impact of this strategy on the course of world history is hard to understate. Many scholars trace racialized slavery, and even racial categories themselves, to this precise set of calculations by wealthy white elites (Allen 1994, 1997; Williams 1944). Since Atlantic slavery was abolished, meanwhile, the ability of wealthy whites to mobilize racial identity in defending their material interests has been credited with everything from the failure of Reconstruction in the US (Du Bois 1935) to the weakness of its labor movement and welfare state (Katznelson 2013; R. M. Smith 1993). And as I explore in Chapter 4, wealthy elites in other contexts have successfully mobilized identities grounded in ethnicity, nationality, religion, gender, and many others for the same purpose: i.e., to undermine threatening forms of economic solidarity.

To be clear: strategies that target the social identity of voters are not inherently nefarious. As constructivist theorists of representation insist, rather, *all* mass politics revolves around the efforts of competing political actors to shift the meaning and salience of various identities, in ways that will generate a majority coalition behind their platform (Disch 2021). Despite the constant attempts of wealthy elites to undermine it, for instance, working-class identity has often been an especially powerful source of solidarity, and is widely credited with enabling the achievements of twentieth-century social democratic parties. Meanwhile, cross-cutting identities grounded in categories such as race, gender, ethnicity, religion, and caste can be interpreted in ways that facilitate broader solidarity rather than undermining it. As I explore in my discussion of organizing in Chapter 10, such tactics are in fact essential for emancipatory projects.

The conclusion we should draw from SIT, then, is that even where preference structures do not generate the sort of collective indeterminacies highlighted by SCT—meaning that elections *can* bring about substantial responsiveness to public opinion—this does not vindicate the ideal of responsive representation. To the extent that people have stable and coherent preferences about political issues, these are often endogenous to cues from various elites. When a victorious party implements the platform it sold to voters, a rough correlation between public opinion and state policy will emerge, and it may appear the majority has gotten what it wanted. Yet the causal arrow runs mostly in the opposite direction. Rather than reflecting a principal-agent relationship, that is—whereby leaders enact the stable, pre-existing, independently formulated wishes of voters—the relatively high responsiveness observed in many electoral democracies more likely reflects successful efforts by political elites to shape the views of their constituents.

As Lisa Disch summarizes, then, the ideal of responsive representation "describes neither how democratic representation should work, how it does work, nor how it lets us down" (2021: 2). And accordingly, the program of reform it implies—aiming to make public officials and policy responsive to a public opinion that is largely constructed by political elites in the first place—will not reliably point us in the right direction. Disch takes this as a hopeful message, and in certain ways it is: after all, once we abandon the principal-agent model of how representation should work, we need not mourn its inevitable failures, and can develop other metrics for evaluating acts of representation. As noted above, moreover, I agree that not all attempts to shape social identity (or "make constituencies," in her terms) are manipulative or bad. Nevertheless, even Disch understates the extent to which this process is biased towards certain groups, especially those with great wealth. Like Mouffe, Laclau, and others she draws from, then, she places too much faith in strategic rhetorical shifts by well-placed elites.

As I argued above, those with outsized private power and organizational capacity will be better positioned to take advantage of the opportunities for extra-procedural influence afforded by indeterminacies about the collective will—and the same is true of the individual-level indeterminacies highlighted in this section. Those with greater access to the means of agenda control, in short, will also enjoy greater access to the means of constituency-making and identity construction. And while this does not mean that democracy is doomed, it does mean that a program of deeper democratization must be about much more than the top-level strategic and rhetorical choices of representatives and other political elites. Once again, in other words, my conclusion is that what really matters for democracy is the underlying balance of social forces—and that the primary goal of those who seek to protect and enrich democracy must therefore be to create a more egalitarian distribution of organizational capacity.

2.3 Responsive representation as a guide to core tasks of democratic judgment

In Chapter 1, I suggested that conventional ideals of collective self-rule tend to lead us astray on three key tasks of democratic judgment: (1) evaluating existing practices of electoral democracy; (2) developing an agenda for legal and policy reform; and (3) setting priorities for civic action and participation outside the state. The aim of the present chapter is to show how this applies to the most common and influential version of collective self-rule in contemporary life: the ideal of responsive representation. And in pursuing this aim, I have examined two major paradigms in the study of politics: social choice theory and social identity theory.

On the one hand, I have argued, SCT shows that on many issues, in many contexts, there is simply no determinate collective will to be found. As such, elections or any other collective choice procedure will generate opportunities for various elites—i.e., those with outsized private power and organizational capacity—to shape outcomes in their favor behind the scenes. Even in contexts where voter preferences do give rise to a determinate majority view about some issue, on the other hand, SIT shows that this "collective will" should not typically be regarded as a trustworthy reflection of preferences formed autonomously by the individuals involved, much less a genuine public interest. Instead, we should expect that these preferences strongly reflect social identities whose meaning and salience are themselves subject to disproportionate influence by elites. In both cases, of course, there are caveats to be made and exceptions to be noted. Nevertheless, the overall lesson of each paradigm on its own—and especially of both, taken together—is clear. The results of collective decision procedures such as elections will often appear as if they are genuinely collective decisions, when in fact they reliably reflect the interests of groups with greater organizational capacity. And in short, that is why the ideal of responsive representation is inadequate as a guide to the three tasks of judgment listed above.

To begin with, one of the key practical roles of democratic theory is to help us explain to ourselves, and to others, why certain existing democratic practices and institutions are valuable. For instance, judges and bureaucrats within democracies are frequently called upon to make decisions about how to interpret and implement those institutions, and in doing so, they take cues—implicitly and often explicitly—from prevailing accounts of their ultimate purpose and value. No less importantly, such accounts also shape how ordinary citizens view and enact their role, as well as their sense of whether democracy is living up to its promises. Finally, these accounts also shape the arguments and strategies of those who seek to defend democratic practices from attack, or promote them where they do not yet exist. For all of these reasons, it matters a great deal whether our explanation of the value of democracy is robust to empirical scrutiny and the lived experience of ordinary citizens, and compelling to people with a wide range of perspectives. And on each dimension, my arguments in this chapter have cast serious doubt on the suitability of responsive representation as a democratic ideal.

Consider what Bernardo Zacka (2022: 23) and Kate Jackson (2022: 781) have called the "transmission belt" model of administrative legitimacy, which holds that acts of bureaucratic agencies are democratically legitimate only when (and because) they are authorized by the will of the people, as revealed through elections and enacted by elected representatives. Since bureaucrats are not directly elected, this model suggests, they should have minimal independent discretion, and agency action should instead be controlled as directly as possible by elected officials with the proper sort of democratic authority. In the US, for instance, libertarians use the transmission belt model to argue that, as the bearer of popular sovereignty, Congress cannot legitimately delegate its lawmaking authority to unelected agency officials—and that much of the administrative state is therefore illegitimate (Hamburger 2014). Emphasizing presidential rather than congressional elections as the proper source of authorization, others use similar logic to justify empowering top *executive* officials (E. A. Posner and Vermeule 2011).

The very existence of such widely diverging conclusions, however—reflecting contrary interpretations of *which* elected officials are the true bearers of popular sovereignty—points to the fundamental instability of this logic. At least within highly complex, large-scale modern democracies of the kind we are discussing, Kate Jackson (2022: 781) observes, "the diverse multiplicity of citizens could never find a common will"—especially not one that is "expressed through the law-making of elected representatives." As such, those aiming to limit bureaucratic discretion on the grounds that it represents an illegitimate delegation of authority from the genuine bearer(s) of popular sovereignty are effectively "grant[ing] statutory law-making more democratic credentials than it deserves," and aiming to "prevent the delegation of something that simply may not exist" in the first place: i.e., a singular and well-defined popular will.

In this sense, the transmission belt model of administrative legitimacy clearly reflects the ideal of responsive representation. And as Jackson shows, fealty to it can have a devastating impact on democracy. When judges aim to preserve a pristine principal–agent relationship between public officials and "the people" that has never existed (and could never be achieved), their error is not simply that of pursuing a noble but unreachable ideal. In shifting power from independent bureaucrats to centralized executives or politicized legislatures, rather, they are effectively undermining the ability of public officials to act in the public interest, and thus actively *harming* democracy, in any plausibly comprehensive sense of that ideal.

There are very real democratic worries about granting agency officials excessive discretion. Indeed, the question of how to ensure that bureaucrats and other unelected officials reliably act in the public interest is among the most important for democratic theorists to address—and in subsequent chapters, I begin to pursue it. The point of this chapter, however, is that elections are not uniquely democratic, and thus cannot be expected to accomplish this feat on their own. On my account, no procedure can be regarded as a singularly reliable route to democratic legitimacy. It is because they endow a specific procedure with such singular democratic authority that the various juridical doctrines derived from a transmission-belt model tend to lead us astray. And the same can be said of many other prominent legal and normative theories that rely implicitly on unrealistic theories of democratic authorization. Most scholars and practitioners assume that popular referendums are required to endow major constitutional changes with the proper sort of democratic legitimacy, for instance, but this logic falls apart once we adopt a more realistic perspective on how such decisions actually get made, along the lines articulated here (see Lenowitz 2021). I return to these concerns in Chapter 9, where I develop a different way of thinking about democratization and legitimation beyond the electoral system.

The ideal of responsive representation also distorts the way ordinary people engage with democratic politics. Most obviously, citizens who see representative institutions as a vehicle for responsiveness will naturally grow frustrated with their inability to deliver on this promise, and may become cynical, disengaged, and perhaps susceptible to the appeals of authoritarian populists peddling "more direct" methods of realizing popular sovereignty. Some such disappointment may be inherent to the structure of representative democracy—and if so, populism may be its permanent shadow (Müller 2016). Perhaps its potency could be limited, however, if our democratic ideals set more realistic expectations to begin with.

In light of the arguments in this chapter, finally, the ideal of responsive representation is poorly suited to the task of rebutting democracy's critics and explaining its value to those who may be more skeptical. If responsiveness is such an elusive goal, in other words—and if popular preferences are so pervasively shaped by social identities to begin with—political leaders deciding whether to transition from autocracy to democracy might reasonably wonder whether such a transition is worth the sacrifice of efficiency it may seem to entail.[8]

The good news for advocates of democracy is that better accounts of its value are available. As I argue in subsequent chapters, the ideal of resisting state capture offers more robust reasons to favor democratic over nondemocratic practices, a more realistic account of the role ordinary citizens can play, and a more reliable standard for determining which procedures are *most* democratic. So far, however, this only covers the first of the three tasks of democratic judgment discussed above. What about our agenda for reform? Even if responsive representation does not offer the best account of existing institutions, it might still be a worthy goal.

There is certainly a grain of truth here. All else equal, greater responsiveness is usually a good thing, and many of the strategies that aim to improve it are probably worth pursuing. For several reasons, however, this should not be seen as the central aim of democratic action or reform. To begin with, responsiveness deficits are not *always* bad: democrats should celebrate, for instance, when counter-majoritarian institutions block racist laws preferred by a majority. Even when they are problematic, meanwhile, responsiveness deficits may not be the *most fundamental* problems. Jim Crow laws did exacerbate Black disadvantage in the US South by eliminating responsiveness to

---

[8] In subsequent chapters, I suggest that democracy does *not* entail such sacrifices, at least in the long run. Here, my point is simply that democrats are more likely to convince those skeptical of democracy's instrumental merits by engaging these concerns directly, rather than insisting they are superseded by intrinsic concerns whose salience varies across contexts.

Black voters, for instance, but this was a *symptom* of the broader disease of white supremacy, not its underlying cause. And indeed, Black disadvantage hardly ended after the Voting Rights Act of 1965 removed many crucial barriers to responsiveness.

Even if we assume responsiveness *is* the core issue, finally, strategies aimed directly at making representatives more responsive are often counterproductive. For instance, early modern advocates of republican self-government tended to see smaller political units as more hospitable to genuine popular control—and where larger political units were necessary, they typically embraced single-member districts as a natural way to preserve direct accountability and responsiveness. As we now understand, however, local government can be highly corrupt, while single-member districts reliably enable gerrymandering, machine politics, pork-barrel politics, and various other modes of capture by powerful interests—not to mention a tendency towards two-party duopoly that is widely reviled by ordinary voters almost everywhere it exists.

Partly in response to these disappointed hopes, meanwhile, many reformers in the late nineteenth and early twentieth centuries reformulated their ambitions, de-emphasizing accountability to *local* public opinion in favor of responsiveness to *mass* public opinion (see Rosanvallon 2018: 6–9). For instance, US Progressives demanded mechanisms like recall elections and direct primaries as crucial tools for undermining the outsized influence of "Gilded Age" oligarchs. Around the world, democratizing reformers sought an "imperative mandate" to keep politicians more closely tied to the popular will, and increasingly eschewed single-member districts altogether, in favor of large multi-member districts with proportional representation.

Once again, however, the results of such electoral reforms were underwhelming. Even where they did improve responsiveness on the margins, they put only a small dent (at best) in problems of corruption, inequality, monopoly power, and money in politics (Caughey and Warshaw 2018). In some cases, meanwhile, they backfired completely: direct primaries on the US model appear no less susceptible to manipulation by wealthy elites than general elections, for instance, while evidence from Europe suggests that more "inclusive" procedures actually make parties *less* representative of voters (Hazan and Rahat 2010; Spies and Kaiser 2014).

Nevertheless, enthusiasm for such engineering solutions continues apace—especially in the United States—as democratic activists tout their favored voting systems (Drutman 2020) or campaign finance rules (Lessig 2011) as silver bullets for democratic decline. And indeed, many of these reforms would probably improve outcomes on the margins. Yet the bottom line is that pervasive capture by wealthy elites remains even in those European democracies—often idealized by US progressives—which have successfully minimized threats such as voter suppression, gerrymandering, and the fundraising imperative that are still rampant in the US (J. Green 2016). As it turns out, for instance, strict campaign finance regulations can actually reduce responsiveness by entrenching existing parties as a "cartel" (Katz and Mair 2018).

This should not be surprising. As I have emphasized throughout, elites with concentrated private power will always have strong incentives and outsized ability to use extra-electoral means to influence outcomes, and we should expect them to do so whenever indeterminacy in majority opinion allows—even if reforms require them to innovate new means (Issacharoff and Karlan 1999; Weschle 2022). As a result, electoral reforms that close particular influence channels may bring about marginal and temporary gains in responsiveness, but even these will tend to erode over time, as wealthy elites adapt to the new rules of the game. As Ian Shapiro observes, such tools "might be dreamed up by the disempowered, but once established they become available for the powerful and well-resourced as well. This has been the story of primaries, ballot initiatives, and much social movement politics" (2016b: 176).

At least partly for the reasons adduced in this chapter, the real troubles lie much deeper than the design of electoral procedures, and by the mid- to late-twentieth century, many democratic idealists had begun looking elsewhere. Some located the problem in uneducated or uninformed masses, and saw the solution in better education and more active political engagement (Addams 1902; Dewey 1927). Others placed the blame on a more sinister form of *miseducation* or ideology, which distorted people's view of their interests, and theorized a form of undistorted deliberative communication as the only plausible remedy (Habermas 1984, 1987; Mansbridge 1980). Still others traced the trouble to the scale of mass politics, and turned their attention to direct participation in decision-making at the level of the workplace, the school, and the local community—all of which would be valuable for their own sake while serving as a training ground for the broader political arena (Barber 1984; Pateman 1970).

Despite their diverse motivations and theoretical commitments, many of these twentieth-century democratic reformers converged on a broadly similar account of what was practically necessary for collective self-rule. This common platform for remedying the defects of mass electoral politics can be encapsulated in the phrase "participatory inclusion." To the extent that public opinion is distorted by ideology or insufficient information, for one, reasonable deliberation among citizens is upheld as the best hope of clearing away these distortions. To the extent that some citizens are excluded or disengaged from such discussions, meanwhile, those citizens must be invited or induced to participate on equal terms. In other words, the processes through which the demos formulates and enacts a collective will must be rationalized and equalized through collaborative participation in all sorts of collective decisions outside of elections.

This is a tempting view. Among those theorists and reformers who share my concerns about common-sense ideals of responsive representation, indeed, the ideal of participatory inclusion is almost certainly the most popular alternative vision of what collective self-rule requires. In the next chapter, however, I argue that it is no more promising as a guide to democratic action.

3
Beyond Participatory Inclusion

The ideal of participatory inclusion is arguably the most practically significant contribution of twentieth century political theory. No single figure can claim anything like the influence of Locke and Montesquieu on the American founders, or of Rousseau on the French Revolutionaries, or of Marx on their twentieth-century heirs. Yet over the past hundred years, a diverse range of thinkers have observed the shortcomings of responsive representation through elections, and concluded that genuine collective self-rule would require more active participation, by a wider range of people, in an array of collaborative decision-making procedures outside of elections. And in an age otherwise indifferent to theoretical scribblings, this convergent embrace of participatory inclusion has had a remarkable impact. In the episode explored in the Introduction, for instance, *both* Macron and the *gilets jaunes* protestors appealed to different versions of this ideal.

Yet despite its genuine insights and widespread appeal, the ideal of participatory inclusion is ultimately misguided. In the previous chapter, I showed why a "critical realist" approach informed by diverse traditions of realist skepticism and radical critique presses us to look beyond the ideal of collective self-rule as responsive representation. And while the ideal of participatory inclusion advances in many ways over this commonsense model, it retains a conception of democracy as a fair process of decision-making—i.e., as a set of procedures through which individual citizens resolve their disagreements and reach genuinely collective decisions on equal terms. As I show in this chapter, therefore, it fails to reckon adequately with the dynamics of political power and social inequality highlighted by a critical realist approach.

As with responsive representation, of course, the ideal of participatory inclusion is popular in part because it gets a great deal right. Just as electoral reforms to increase responsiveness can sometimes help keep public power tethered to the public interest, collaborative procedures oriented to particular decisions can promote that democratic goal under the right conditions. Those conditions are quite limited, however, and in profoundly unequal societies like ours, a singular focus on such collaborative procedures obscures more urgent priorities. As such, widespread participation in collaborative processes of decision-making should not be seen as inherently democratic;

much less as the overriding goal and central priority of democratic action and reform. Instead, we must identify those specific forms of popular participation that most reliably obstruct capture by wealthy elites and other powerful groups—a task I take up in the rest of the book. In seeking to enhance democracy via institutional reform and civic action, in sum, we must look beyond generic forms of participatory inclusion.

3.1 Participatory inclusion as a response to failures of responsive representation

The intellectual and political roots of the ideal of participatory inclusion are quite diverse. Within European political thought, for instance, one can trace the lineage of related ideas and practices all the way back to Athens and Rome, via the (civic) republicans of the late medieval and early modern eras. Forerunners can also be found in the revolutionary forms of popular participation glorified by eighteenth and nineteenth century radicals, as well as in the institutionalized forms of civic participation praised by liberals like Tocqueville and Mill. In its contemporary form, however, the ideal of participatory inclusion is a direct response to the disappointments and failures of modern mass democracy and the associated logic of responsive representation. As such, it did not fully take shape until the consolidation of electoral regimes with widespread suffrage and broad-based political parties in the late nineteenth and early twentieth centuries.

In short, many on both sides of nineteenth century struggles over suffrage imagined that when the working class finally got the vote, they would dismantle key structures of inequality and elite privilege, including private property. By the early twentieth century, however, it became clear that this was not going to happen. As "democratic realists" (or "elite theorists") like Robert Michels (1915) began to observe, on the one hand, working-class parties that sought change through parliamentary means tended to generate internal elites who became invested in maintaining existing institutions, and thus ended up serving to soften and conceal the rule of wealthy elites rather than obstructing it.[1] On the other hand, generations of radicals watched in horror as working-class parties that rejected such sterile electoralism in favor of revolutionary violence were routinely captured, in even more sinister ways,

---

[1] Other prominent thinkers in this tradition include Gaetano Mosca, Vilfredo Pareto, Max Weber, Joseph Schumpeter, and Walter Lippmann. For insightful analysis, see the work of Natasha Piano (e.g., 2019).

by top-level leaders who deployed the rhetoric of "democratic centralism" to justify brutally repressive forms of personal rule.

The various ideals and practices that I collect under the umbrella concept of participatory inclusion emerged in the wake of these twin failures, and can be understood as reactions to them. If electoral democracy on its own was incapable of realizing genuine collective self-rule, yet dispensing with elections altogether seemed to invite too much danger, it was only common sense to suggest that the path to a truer democracy lay in the proliferation of additional forums for collective will formation and decision-making within a broadly electoral system.

Depending on the specific political and intellectual context facing particular actors, of course, this basic intuition appeared in many different guises. Perhaps its earliest proponents emerged in the United States—shaped by its longer experience with mass parties and grassroots activism, as well as its racial divisions and relatively weak labor movement. Drawing on groundwork laid by "labour republicans" and populists in the late nineteenth century (Gourevitch 2015), a diverse array of American activists and intellectuals in the early twentieth century came to embrace widespread political participation, outside of traditional representative institutions, as the best way for ordinary people to take back control from political machines and Gilded Age plutocrats (Emerson 2019; Rahman 2016; Stears 2010).

Some of their proposed solutions, like recall elections, were straightforward applications of the ideal of responsive representation discussed in the last chapter—aiming to make public officials more responsive through electoral reforms. Others, meanwhile, began to stress the importance of direct popular participation in lawmaking. Perhaps the most prominent of these were initiatives and referendums, which combined the goal of responsive representation—i.e., bringing legislation into line with mass public opinion through periodic mass voting—with the mechanism of direct popular participation. In addition, however, some early-twentieth-century Progressives began to articulate a more distinctive participatory model—focusing on smaller-scale deliberative processes and more fine-grained tasks of rule-making and implementation (Emerson 2019: 61–147; Rahman 2016: 78–96)—which more fully and faithfully reflects the ideal of participatory inclusion as I understand it. Much more than any kind of mass voting, whether in representative elections or policy referendums, reforms based on this distinctive model would entail a transformation in the quality and intensity of participation expected of ordinary people, who would be charged not merely with choosing between competing elites (á la Schumpeter 1942), but with actively constructing the rules that govern their lives.

These proposals were fiercely criticized by "realists" and "elitists," of course—including rival Progressives—who doubted that ordinary people were capable of such complex tasks. For instance, Walter Lippmann (1922) famously argued that the success of mass democracy relies not on mass engagement but rather mass *dis*-engagement, which enables technocratic elites to "manufacture consent" for wise policies that a more engaged population might reject. In response, proponents of participatory inclusion such as John Dewey (1927) argued that elites could never comprehensively address the problems facing the broader public without the latter's involvement. Though they recognized the value of scientific expertise as well as the profound challenges facing mass democracy, in short, Pragmatists like Dewey and Jane Addams maintained that the cure was *more* democracy, not less (Addams 1902: 9). If ordinary citizens were incapable of participating wisely in their present condition, this was all the more reason to raise their condition. For one, this meant engaging them more actively in a wider range of open-ended, inclusive, and collaborative processes of will formation and decision-making, through which they would develop the skills and attitudes required for political participation. In addition, they emphasized the importance of a thoroughly democratic form of education—guided by an egalitarian ethos and a fallibilistic, experimental disposition—as well as a broader civic culture that promoted the same democratic values. For a society to make genuinely collective decisions, Pragmatists argued, democracy must become a way of life.

When "realist" challenges were reformulated in the terms of postwar social science (e.g., Arrow 1951; Campbell et al. 1960), subsequent generations of democratic theorists responded in a broadly similar spirit. Readily acknowledging the many shortcomings of mass democracy, for example, participatory democrats such as Carole Pateman (1970), Benjamin Barber (1984), and Jane Mansbridge (1980) sought inspiration outside of electoral politics, highlighting the potential of collaborative discussion and decision-making in workplaces, social movements, local government, and—increasingly—deliberative forums designed specifically to encourage reasonable discourse on equal terms (James Fishkin 1991). And it is here that this specifically American lineage of thinking about participatory inclusion began to converge with parallel traditions emerging from Europe; most notably the critical theory of Jürgen Habermas.

For Habermas, of course, the most salient challenge was not empiricist skepticism but the radical critiques of modernity offered by his mentors in the Frankfurt School—among other Continental thinkers—whose experiences of the early twentieth century had left them profoundly pessimistic about the prospects of any emancipatory democratic project. Embedded in Marxist traditions, such thinkers rejected Stalinism but also despaired of the strong ideological hold of capitalism upon mass consciousness in the democratic West. In reply, Habermas (1984, 1987) conceded that consumerism, ideology, and instrumental reason were powerful forces that posed serious challenges to genuine collective self-rule under modern conditions of capitalist power relations and technological development. Yet like other advocates of participatory inclusion, Habermas doubled down on widespread popular engagement as the most promising solution.

Drawing on Kant, more specifically, he argued that the internal logic of discourse—the "forceless force of the better argument" (1975: 108)—was the most potent counter-force available to those with emancipatory goals, enabling citizens to unshackle themselves from ideology and form a genuinely autonomous collective will (1990, 1996). As such, he and his successors—alongside neo-Kantian fellow travelers inspired more directly by the later work of John Rawls (1993)—concluded that democracy is fundamentally about reason-giving, and that making it better is thus largely about expanding participation in deliberative practices.

As a result of these convergent perspectives, a remarkable degree of consensus emerged among leading political theorists and philosophers—cresting, perhaps, in the late 1990s—about the centrality of widespread deliberative participation to any democratizing agenda (Benhabib 1996; S. Chambers 1996; Gutmann and Thompson 1996; Macedo 1999). Perhaps even more remarkable than the degree of consensus among philosophers about the democratic imperative of participatory inclusion, however—and even more unusual in the modern world—is the extent to which that imperative has been taken up by political actors around the globe (Bohman 1998; Neblo 2015). It is difficult to pinpoint the precise causal role played by these ideas in the proliferation of deliberative and participatory practices around the globe. What we can say, however, is that as the intellectual foundations of participatory inclusion were being formulated and popularized during the second half of the twentieth century, participatory practices began to dominate the agenda of democratic action and reform as well.

3.2 Participatory inclusion as a program for democratic action and reform

Reflecting the influence of Progressives and Pragmatists in the US, for one, participatory requirements were built into New Deal policies such as the

Tennessee Valley Authority and Agricultural Adjustment Administration as early as the 1930s (Emerson 2019: 118–130). The focus on participatory inclusion really took off in the postwar era, however, with laws such as the landmark Administrative Procedures Act (APA) of 1946, which required agencies to invite public input during a "notice and comment" period before implementing new rules. In 1969, the National Environmental Policy Act (NEPA) greatly expanded this formal participatory requirement, mandating that agencies *actively* seek input from communities who were likely to be affected by their decisions. Meanwhile, many of the policies tackling poverty and racial inequality throughout the 1960s also included strong participatory components—in one case famously mandating "maximum feasible participation" by recipients (Rubin 1969).

Though these requirements were surely motivated by more than high-minded Progressive idealism, they do reflect a core theoretical commitment of participatory inclusion: i.e., that the best way to manage conflict and disagreement is to engage a wide range of stakeholders in collaborative processes of discussion and decision-making. In the case of the NEPA, for instance, it was thought that inviting interested parties to register objections at the planning stage would allow agencies to accommodate their concerns and get them on board, preventing costly lawsuits and other forms of open confrontation later on (Coglianese 1996). Similarly, it was the high-profile conflict surrounding their 1968 Convention—which contributed to their historic defeat in the subsequent general election—that motivated leaders of the US Democratic Party to invite greater input from ordinary citizens in their internal party decisions.

Of course, the US is hardly alone in adopting participatory institutions to supplement its basic electoral framework. Over the past half century, for one, many governments around the world have implemented participatory procedures for administrative rulemaking—often using US legislation as a model—and the NEPA in particular is widely regarded as the gold standard for environmental governance (Yang 2019). Far beyond bureaucratic agencies, meanwhile, a much wider set of political actors has embraced the idea of using participatory inclusion to manage tensions and prevent open conflict, such that "best practices" in many policy areas now includes some form of "participatory governance" (Fung and Wright 2003), "new governance" (Bingham, Nabatchi, and O'Leary 2005), or "negotiated rulemaking" (Susskind and McMahon 1985). Following the example set by US parties, similarly, European parties from across the political spectrum have sought to "democratize" their internal decision-making, as a way of appealing to voters who are increasingly disaffected with traditional party systems.

Nor is the US the only source of innovation. Switzerland has long been distinguished by its extensive use of direct democracy—including referendums and initiatives characterized by low-intensity mass participation, as well as more intensive local practices that more fully reflect the model of participatory inclusion. Since the democratic transitions of the 1980s, meanwhile, countries across Latin America have developed a rich and distinctive tradition of participatory experimentation (Mayka 2019; Pogrebinschi 2023). Perhaps the most famous example is the process of participatory budgeting pioneered in 1989 in Porto Alegre, Brazil, which has since been adopted by thousands of municipalities worldwide (Baiocchi 2001; Baiocchi and Ganuza 2014). As Thamy Pogrebinschi (2023) documents, however, this prominent case is only the tip of the iceberg: participatory innovation has been such a consistent priority across the region that one can speak of a distinctive "Latin American model" of democracy, characterized by continuous pragmatic experimentation with a wide range of participatory devices.

Like many of the practices discussed so far, of course, participatory budgeting and related practices rely primarily on self-selected participants. A concurrent set of innovations, however, makes use of lottery selection to elicit participatory engagement from a more representative sample of the broader public (Fung 2003). At first, assemblies composed of randomly selected ordinary citizens were employed in a purely consultative capacity. Explicitly inspired by the deliberative ideals of Habermas and others, those who created such descriptively representative "mini-publics" sought to discover "what the electorate *would* think if, hypothetically, all voters had the same opportunities that are offered to those in the deliberative opinion poll" (James Fishkin 1991: 4). In recent years, though, the idea of giving randomly selected citizens real power—as in several ancient and medieval polities (Dowlen 2008)—has become increasingly popular (Sintomer 2018). Across Europe and Canada, a growing number of local, regional, and national governments have granted formal power to ordinary citizens selected by lot, while activists with movements like Extinction Rebellion have increasingly embraced such "citizens' assemblies" as a viable radical alternative to the "broken" system of electoral politics.

While there is clearly significant diversity among the theoretical ideals and practical reforms that I have gathered under the umbrella of participatory inclusion, they share a number of core features in common, which allow us to understand them as embodying that broader ideal. At a theoretical level, most basically, they all treat *processes of collective will formation and decision-making* as the primary object of democratic concern, and thus reflect the logic of collective self-rule: i.e., that decisions about the use of public power can and should be legitimized by ensuring that the individuals affected by them can contribute equally to the processes by which they are made. Where ideals of responsive representation rely on elections to achieve this sort of citizen control, ideals of participatory inclusion eschew the mediation of representatives and insist that citizens must contribute *directly* to collective decisions. Given the difficulties involved in direct participation on a mass scale, this means that practices of participatory inclusion are typically confined to *small-scale contexts*, aiming to scale up their impact by asking citizens to contribute to *a much wider range of decisions*. (As noted, practices of mass direct democracy, like referendums and initiatives, hybridize the two models.)

Beyond this broad theoretical baseline, the more specific practical reasons for subjecting particular decisions to widespread participation by ordinary citizens may vary by context. One commonly cited function of participatory inclusion, for instance, is to remedy information deficits. On the one hand, participatory inclusion can ensure that elites understand the concerns of ordinary people, and can incorporate their local expertise in making wise and fair decisions. On the other hand, it can also educate citizens by exposing them to the testimony of authorized experts and other diverse perspectives. Especially in the sort of small-scale, face-to-face deliberative contexts imagined by theorists of participatory inclusion, the hope is that a process of mutual reason-giving led by neutral facilitators will enable the progressive resolution of differences, yielding broad-based agreement, compromise, or at least a majority decision that everyone experiences as fair. Not only are the resulting decisions likely to be better—because they incorporate full information and the wisdom of many different perspectives—they are also likely to attract greater allegiance, on the grounds that they reflect a genuinely fair process of co-authorship. And while the virtues of reasonableness and civic-mindedness required for such practices to succeed may initially be scarce, we might expect frequent exposure to deliberative processes to help more and more ordinary citizens develop those virtues over time.

As attested by the convergence of many different traditions upon a roughly similar agenda for reform, the ideal of participatory inclusion has many attractive features. And as with the electoral reforms suggested by the ideal of responsive representation, participatory innovations can often be quite valuable in practice. After all, many political disagreements *are* caused or exacerbated by information deficits or communication failures among people with different perspectives. Decision makers from wealthy and privileged groups are often unaware of the interests and concerns of people from poor or disadvantaged backgrounds, for instance, while ordinary people do frequently fail to grasp the difficult tradeoffs of policymaking. And when our problems have this character, collaborative participation is an appropriate and effective solution, promising to dissolve key tensions, or at least prevent any lingering disagreements from devolving into more destructive forms of social and political conflict.

With such an effective hammer, of course, we may begin to see every problem as a nail. And as the ideal of participatory inclusion has become the leading conception of democratization and democratic reform, unfortunately, this is precisely what has happened. Often, the interests and concerns of ordinary people and disadvantaged groups are ignored not because wealthy and privileged elites are unaware of them, but rather because elites have strong incentives to ignore them. More generally, political disagreement often reflects deep conflicts of interests and vast asymmetries of power, rather than information deficits and communication failures. In such cases, collaborative forms of participatory inclusion are not only *insufficient*; they can often be *counterproductive*—serving to deflect legitimate criticism, forestall healthy contestation, and channel popular energy into symbolic rituals of inclusion rather than meaningful exercises of collective power. Rather than helping to resist state capture, in other words, processes of participatory inclusion can help elites further entrench their power.

3.3 The promises and pitfalls of participatory inclusion

At the most basic level, the challenges facing participatory inclusion are the same as those facing any ideal of collective self-rule that aims to legitimize decisions about public power by ensuring that they are made collectively, through a process that treats all individuals fairly. As I demonstrated in my discussion of responsive representation in the previous chapter, for one, there is often simply no such thing as a true collective will or genuinely equal control. On any given question of policy, rather, there are often many possible majority "wills," such that the decision reached by any given social choice mechanism will reflect arbitrary features of that mechanism—including how the question is framed, how answers are measured and counted, and so on. Powerful groups can then exploit this ambiguity, employing their outsized private power and organizational capacity before and after a decision procedure itself, to ensure that choices are constructed and implemented in ways that protect their interests.

As I acknowledged, this "collective" indeterminacy can be avoided whenever citizens have single-peaked preferences that vary along a single dimension, and some claim that this is often the case in contemporary politics. Even if and when there is neutral way to generate a coherent collective will by aggregating individual preferences, however, those preferences are themselves indeterminate in a way that leaves them similarly susceptible to elite manipulation. Simply put, most people do not have strong, well informed, and independently formulated views on most political issues: instead, most of our political preferences are heavily shaped by arbitrary features of our immediate context, like the weather or the last conversation we had, as well as (more significantly) by our social identities. And while our social identities are hardly arbitrary—they certainly *can* help vulnerable groups act in ways that protect their interests, for instance (Lepoutre 2020)—powerful groups have outsized capacity to shape which identities we find salient, and how we interpret those identities politically.

As I showed in the previous chapter, these two forms of indeterminacy—and the forms of elite manipulation enabled by them—should lead us to reject responsive representation as an ideal of democracy. In this chapter, of course, I have emphasized that ideals of participatory inclusion were developed at least partly in response to the failure of that commonsense ideal. And indeed, practices of participatory inclusion *do* mitigate the severity of these challenges. This is not primarily because of their reliance on direct participation rather than representation: in fact, reforms that invite direct participation at a mass scale—like referendums—seem to reliably *increase* manipulability overall (Weale 2018). This is not the case, however, with core practices of participatory inclusion that reduce the scale of decision-making. On the one hand, smaller processes involve fewer individuals and bundle fewer decisions together, reducing the severity of collective indeterminacy. On the other hand, they also engage participants more intensively, within environments designed to counter misinformation and promote mutual understanding. Under such conditions, participants may form preferences that are relatively better informed, more independent, and less subject to bias and motivated reasoning.

In my view, indeed, it is largely these two advantages over large-scale decision-making processes that enable certain practices of participatory inclusion, under certain conditions, to provide further insulation against capture by powerful groups, beyond that provided by elections alone. All too often, however, they fail to serve this democratic goal—and in some cases even *facilitate* elite capture. Unfortunately, ideals of participatory inclusion that view collective decision-making as the core meaning and purpose of democracy are of little help in distinguishing between the two types of cases. In setting an agenda for democratization through popular participation, more specifically, they are at once over-inclusive—treating cooperative decision-making procedures as presumptively democratic—and under-inclusive—obscuring the need for oppositional contestation and long-term group-based organizing.

Put simply, advocates of participatory inclusion understand "democratization" to mean inviting ordinary people to participate, as individuals, in the procedures by which certain decisions are made—typically including a discussion period allowing them to raise concerns, share information, air disagreements, and cooperatively determine the best solution to shared problems. Most readily acknowledge that such collaborative decision-making procedures could be distorted by background inequalities or co-opted by elites, under nonideal conditions, and many even recognize the necessity of sustained contestation by organized groups in responding to such conditions. Yet cooperative decision-making among equal individuals remains at the center of their agenda for democratization, while more organized and oppositional methods are justifiable only as a last resort, and only with reference to their function within some broader scheme of collaborative decision-making (e.g., Fung 2005; Mansbridge et al. 2012).[2]

A critical realist approach informed by the convergent insights of realist skeptics and radical critics yields almost the opposite conclusions. Rather than giving participatory practices the benefit of the doubt, such an approach presumes that in societies like ours—characterized by pervasive asymmetries in private power and organizational capacity—elite co-optation will be the rule, not the exception. The contexts in which co-optation is least likely, moreover, will be those where deeper democratization is *least* urgent—i.e., those where participants genuinely face common problems, rather than deep conflicts of interest, and already relate on roughly equal terms. In societies like ours, by contrast, popular participation is most urgently needed to resist the dominance of elite interests over those of ordinary people, not to enable cooperation between equally situated groups who share most of their interests in common. And as I argue in subsequent chapters, this broad imperative generates two specific models of popular participation that must often take priority over generically collaborative forms of participatory inclusion. First, ordinary people can defend a broad public interest as neutral arbiters among

---

[2] For a detailed summary and critique of this move, see Medearis (2005, 2015). For a broader critique of the "paradox" involved in participatory theory—namely, the fact enormous top-down changes in policy would be required to achieve the conditions in which participation can occur on equal terms—see Parvin (2021).

competing elite factions within a range of contestatory oversight institutions. Second, and more importantly, they can defend their own partial interests by constructing enduring sources of oppositional power to effectively counter the organizational capacity of hegemonic groups.

Before we move on to my alternative agenda for democratization, however, we should first examine the limits of predominant approaches more carefully. As I have emphasized, wealthy elites and other powerful groups have an outsized impact on the cultural assumptions, social structure, and media environment in which everyone formulates their beliefs and attitudes. Yet these generic background advantages pose challenges for *any* strategy of democratization that aims to distribute power more equally, including those I will defend as most promising. Why might we think that the sort of cooperative, inclusive, and formally neutral practices favored by ideals of participatory inclusion are *especially* susceptible to co-optation by elites?

There are at least four reasons. First, the inclusive and formally neutral character of those practices ensures that background inequalities in private power and organizational capacity will be reflected in who shows up to participate, as well as how their interactions go. Second, the orientation towards specific decision nodes, considered independently from one another as well as the broader context, enables powerful groups to covertly shape the agenda and scope of participatory processes in ways that favor their interests. Third, the collaborative spirit of such processes is itself a kind of institutional bias, serving to conceal and entrench deeper conflicts of interest and power asymmetries—both by framing disagreements as communication failures among equals, and by delegitimizing the agonistic means ordinary people could use to bring conflicts into the open and contest asymmetries directly. Finally, their claim to present a neutral method for reaching mutually agreeable solutions exaggerates the finality and legitimacy to their results—enabling elites to stifle ongoing controversy, deflect criticism, and demobilize or co-opt potential opponents. As we will see, the forms of popular participation I defend in later chapters are more promising because they relinquish some if not all of these traits.

A paradigmatic illustration of the first of these problems is found in the public consultations held by many government agencies. Since the Administrative Procedure Act (APA) of 1946, for instance, US administrative agencies have been required to give public notice of proposed rules, invite public commentary, and respond in writing to all comments—a process known as "notice and comment" that has been imitated by many regulatory and bureaucratic agencies around the world. Though this and other forms of consultation are ostensibly intended to enable participation by ordinary people, it is a rare "ordinary" person who will, of their own accord, investigate and comment upon arcane administrative rule changes. By contrast, industry actors typically have much stronger incentives to monitor such changes than any private individual, as well as far greater capacity to act on those incentives. When ordinary people do get involved, it is almost always through the mediation of well-organized community groups—and while such groups do have an impact in certain cases, they are still at a great disadvantage, on the whole, compared to well-resourced business interests. As a result, the vast majority of the "public" commentary received through APA procedures actually comes from actors with ties to industry (Cuellar 2005; Wagner, Barnes, and Peters 2011; Yackee 2013).

To be sure, not all forms of participatory inclusion exhibit such complacency about the representativeness of participants. Learning from the APA's shortcomings, for instance, the National Environmental Policy Act (NEPA) of 1969 required agencies to actively seek out input from affected communities. Similarly, participatory budgeting programs are sometimes bundled with significant community outreach efforts. Even so, systematic evidence suggests that NEPA consultative processes remain opaque to most people, and that outcomes still reliably favor industry interests (Eckerd 2017). Similarly, participatory budgeting processes tend to favor existing organized interests in much the same ways as the traditional political procedures they replace. Regardless of who participates, after all, it is groups with significant pre-existing organizational capacity within a given social context or political jurisdiction that will best be able to influence how participatory processes unfold within that context.

A more aggressive strategy for ensuring that participants are representative is to select them randomly—as with deliberative mini-publics and citizens' assemblies—rather than relying on self-selection. And as I explore in Chapter 9, bodies of randomly selected citizens can play an important role in democratic reform. Still, random selection is hardly the silver bullet that certain idealistic reformers believe it to be (Bagg 2022c; Landa and Pevnick 2021). As skeptics have pointed out, for one, mini-publics and other "shortcuts" employing random selection seek top-down transformation without involving the mass citizenry, which is criticized as both unstable and undemocratic (Lafont 2019). Meanwhile, even when participants are demographically diverse and included on formally equal terms, background inequalities between groups will inevitably intervene (Fraser 1990; Sanders 1997). For instance, extensive evidence from mini-publics and similar institutions suggests that those who participate most actively and effectively are usually those with advantages in wealth, education, and social privilege

(Beauvais 2019; Holdo and Sagrelius 2020; Mendelberg and Oleske 2000). While facilitation techniques can mitigate these problems (Afsahi 2021), they cannot be eliminated—and when there is significant power at stake, it is difficult to ensure that facilitators use these techniques neutrally.

Perhaps even more important than how people interact *within* the terms of a participatory process, however, is how those terms are defined to begin with—and as noted, this is a second arena in which groups with outsized organizational capacity will enjoy distinct advantages. Simply put, when ordinary people participate in the process of making a particular decision at a fixed point in a broader policymaking process, they may *feel* like they are helping to shape outcomes, even if the range of possible outcomes has been carefully circumscribed in advance by elites. By focusing our limited political attention on those predetermined decision nodes where ordinary people have been invited to weigh in, ideals of participatory inclusion obscure everything else that contributes to the final outcome, including the many covert tools elites may have used to ensure favorable results. The participatory procedures favored most prominently by such ideals, in other words, enable powerful groups to conceal their capture of state power behind a veil of popular participation, while providing few opportunities or incentives for other groups to develop standing reserves of countervailing organizational capacity over time.

Consider the "active consultation" with affected groups that is required by the NEPA (as well as many similar environmental statutes around the world). In theory, this process allows communities to register their concerns about the potential environmental impact of agency rulings—about whether to allow a proposed development or extraction project to go forward, for instance—which the agency is then supposed to account for in determining its ruling. By the time agencies actually solicit community input, however, they have typically invested significant time and energy into the project in question, often working alongside partners in the private sector who stand to profit. Whether or not they are actually captured by those private actors, therefore, agency officials are hardly neutral on the question of whether that project should go forward (Eckerd 2017). Rather than making a genuine effort to respond to community input, therefore, officials and their private sector partners more often use the obligatory consultations to gather information about potential adversaries, buy them off if possible, and build a paper trail to insure against future litigation (Coglianese 1996).

Far from enabling participants to determine the rules that govern their lives, in short, such participatory rituals transform them into compliant subjects, reconciling them to outcomes that are largely predetermined

(Agrawal 2005; Johnson 2019). By highlighting certain questions as open for discussion—like where to dump the waste products of resource extraction—those who set the agenda and scope of participatory procedures can use those procedures to preempt other questions—such as whether the project should go forward at all, or how its profits should be distributed. Participants are conscripted into narratives and framings that ultimately serve elite interests, taking certain "shared" problems for granted as the salient topics for discussion, and emphasizing the collectively authorized character of the solutions. And this brings us to the third danger inherent to practices of participatory inclusion that I noted above: i.e., that this "collaborative" framing can serve to disguise real conflicts of interest among highly unequal groups as disagreements among equals, while also delegitimizing the oppositional methods through which those conflicts and inequalities might be exposed and effectively contested.

The treatment of Indigenous groups by settler states provides some especially egregious illustrations of this danger. The UN Declaration on the Rights of Indigenous Peoples—adopted in 2007—requires that "free, prior and informed consent" be given by Indigenous groups for certain decisions that affect their interests, which has been interpreted by many settler states as mandating procedures of participatory inclusion. As Jaskiran Dhillon (2017: 14) notes in her analysis of how this has worked in Canada, however, such participation "does not exist in a neutral, suspended space, empty of power and history." Given that "the terms and form of political engagement are mediated by a settler nation state" that was "created through colonial dominance," rather, the "inclusionary governance" practiced by the Canadian state "is fundamentally a reassertion of asymmetrical power relations" (14). In particular, participation in projects whose mandate is defined by the white settler state can serve to "recreate urban Indigenous youth subjectivity" in ways that are aligned with the goals of that state (134).

In this context—as in many others—participatory inclusion "takes what is rightly a political problem and repositions it in the neutralized space of 'blended interests,' where colonial goals are masked under the cloak of neutrality" (136). As Dhillon explains, "the invocation of participation suggests … a consensus between collaborative partners … around the roots and construction of the social problem that is the focus of cooperative efforts, thereby facilitating an agreement about the types of solutions, programs, or policies that are generated to rectify these social conditions." (142) At the same time, this orientation obscures the history of colonial aggression that created these conflicting interests, which is figured not as a historical trauma caused by pervasive power asymmetries, but as "a reflection of 'bad listening skills'" (141) that may be straightforwardly rectified by ceasing explicit forms of exclusion.

In sum, Dhillon argues, "the shift to discourses of collaboration ... paves the way for settler colonialism to be instantiated as a more responsive form of governance, as a superior kind of governing actor that learns and bends with Indigenous input" (156). The state is presented as a co-creation of white settlers and Indigenous peoples, rather than an imposition upon the latter by the former. Indigenous youth are encouraged to feel ownership over the state, as equal co-authors of its laws, and thus to accept its institutions as legitimate. Meanwhile, any remaining problems are located "within the bodies, minds, and spirits of Indigenous youth themselves" (154). Rather than organizing them around opposition to colonial aggression (e.g., Coulthard 2014), participatory inclusion diverts their limited material and motivational resources towards largely symbolic rituals whose scope is firmly circumscribed by the state.

In this way, Dhillon's analysis also provides a potent illustration of the fourth danger of participatory inclusion: namely, its tendency to present ongoing controversies as having been settled, inflating the legitimacy of the status quo, and enabling elites to deflect criticism or demobilize opposition. And while the process may be clearest in Indigenous–settler relations, we can observe roughly similar dynamics in other contexts. Under the NEPA and comparable schemes, for instance, agencies and their private sector allies can use participatory forums both as pressure release valves—tying up opponents in complex, time-consuming, and ultimately toothless consultative procedures—and as exculpatory narratives. If and when community members do finally raise organized opposition to a particular project, that is, its defenders can claim that it has already survived popular scrutiny, and is therefore democratically legitimate. In addition to providing a legal defense in case of formal litigation, this can also undercut the claims of those who may contest the resulting *fait accompli* before the court of public opinion.

Again, this technique is hardly limited to North America. In the Introduction, for instance, I documented how French President Emmanuel Macron has deployed a range of participatory mechanisms to redirect unruly forms of opposition into more manageable collaborative forums (Sintomer 2020). Indeed, the rapid spread of participatory inclusion around the world in recent decades can largely be attributed to the growing recognition by technocratic elites that it ultimately serves their interests; allowing them to gather valuable information from participants while deflecting responsibility for unpopular decisions and sapping political energy from more threatening forms of opposition (Baiocchi and Ganuza 2016; Lee 2014; Lee, McQuarrie, and

Walker 2015). Such tactics have even been deployed by autocrats such as the Chinese Communist Party, whose increasing use of local participatory institutions is quite straightforwardly geared towards assessing, managing, and ultimately stifling more challenging forms of dissent (Woo 2023); as well as corporate managers, who invite feedback as a way of sustaining loyalty among workers and customers, and thus heading off more threatening calls for unionization, strikes, or boycotts (Walker 2015).

It goes without saying, of course, that practices of participatory inclusion are not *always* deployed for such cynical and anti-democratic ends. Rather, participatory procedures can be understood as occupying different rungs on a "ladder of citizen participation"—in Sherry Arnstein (1969) influential formulation—ranging from those that are entirely co-opted by elites at the bottom, to those that enable genuine citizen control at the top. As such, the observation that some collaborative decision procedures are co-opted by elites need not impugn the ideal of participatory inclusion as such. Indeed, its advocates are often the fiercest critics of such cynical manipulations of the ideal, and have gone to great lengths to distinguish genuinely empowering practices from those that simply provide cover for elite rule (e.g., G. Smith 2009).

In casting doubt on the democratic merits of participatory inclusion, therefore, it is crucial to clarify that many of my concerns apply not only to practices that occupy the lower rungs of Arnstein's ladder, but also to those that have ascended to its higher rungs as well. Like the examples I have just discussed, most real-world practices of participatory inclusion fail to live up to the ideal visions of citizen control promoted by theorists like Arnstein. And if our efforts to achieve an ideal repeatedly yield such disappointing results, we might reasonably criticize that ideal for being overly ambitious or impractical. In this case, however, that is not my only—or even primary—concern. Even those practices that fully reflect the ideal of participatory inclusion will fail to effectively protect and deepen democracy—at least in the thick sense we should care about. If anything, indeed, the real problem with this ideal is that the small-scale collaborative procedures of decision-making it favors are not nearly ambitious *enough*, in the face of the profound challenges afflicting contemporary democracies.

Arnstein's own discussion of community-run development corporations (CDCs), which she heralds as the pinnacle of community control, is a case in point. Like more recent participatory budgeting programs—also frequently hailed as exemplary (Wright 2010)—the purpose of CDCs is to give members of underserved communities more control over the allocation of funds that have been earmarked for their benefit. Yet as Arnstein herself readily acknowledges, localizing control in this way could trigger the "balkanization of public services"—ultimately *depriving* underserved populations of access to broader pools of resources—while enabling local elites to be "just as opportunistic" as more distant peers (Arnstein 1969: 224).

Unfortunately, these are not trivial concerns. Even if it is true, as Arnstein shrugs in response, that many previous attempts to improve the lot of such communities had failed, this is not enough to vindicate the broader democratic value of CDCs or any other form of direct citizen control. Whenever they do in fact lead to the balkanization of public services and capture by local elites, such localizing reforms will not merely fail to improve the status quo; they will likely make it worse, by exacerbating inequalities among different groups of people—both in terms of their material resources and, by extension, in terms of their access to political power on a broader scale. And as it turns out, this is exactly what we see in practice: municipal decentralization in the name of "citizen control" by "local" communities is a consistent driver of inter-group inequality (Mattiuzzi and Weir 2019). Meanwhile, evidence from more recent participatory budgeting initiatives (which reflect a similar logic) reveals that they often allocate funds to "pork" projects with major benefits for small constituencies (Annunziata 2015)—rather than genuinely public goods—while diverting resources and energy from unions, parties, and other groups with long-term, large-scale ambitions (Baiocchi 2005: 153).

However unintended they may be, crucially, these consequences are not merely regrettable in some general sense: they are detrimental to *democracy* in particular. Even when a procedure fully realizes the ideal of participatory inclusion, in other words—bringing about a particular form of collective control, over a certain set of decisions, among a specific group of people—this is no guarantee that the procedure advances *democracy*, writ large. Democracy is simply too weighty and complex an ideal to be identified with *any* specific set of procedures for making *any* particular set of decisions. That is the key mistake of responsive representation and participatory inclusion, along with any other ideal that aims to spell out the concrete demands of collective self-rule by specifying which decisions must be subjected to collective control, and how that control can be made *truly* collective.

Here we come to the crux of my argument in this chapter. Advocates of participatory inclusion are right to highlight the profound shortcomings of representative institutions, and to insist that democracy requires more than periodic mass elections. By placing their faith in a different set of decision procedures, however—framed as a more faithful method of realizing "citizen control"—they trade one overly narrow conception of democracy for another, yielding a similarly distorted sense of democratic priorities. By framing direct popular participation in a wider range of collective decisions as both means and end of deeper democratization, in sum, ideals of participatory inclusion crucially *overstate* the importance of small-scale collaborative procedures, and *understate* the urgency of adversarial methods and long-term organization.

While practices of participatory inclusion can help to resolve information deficits and communication failures among equally situated actors with broadly shared interests, they will do little to challenge deep conflicts of interest and asymmetries of power, and at times may even exacerbate such problems. To be sure, this danger of co-optation is greatest for procedures at the lowest rungs of Arnstein's ladder. Yet even those that realize genuine citizen control will rarely pose a serious threat to the interests of wealthy elites. When hegemonic groups enjoy vast advantages in organizational capacity, the core democratic priority must be to undermine those advantages. And once we adopt that targeted goal, an alternative agenda emerges: one favoring contestation over cooperation, effective representation of group interests over unique individual contributions, and ongoing organizational capacity over serial decision procedures.

To be clear, no institutions are entirely resilient to co-optation, and no reform could ever hope to eliminate capture entirely. Where collaborative decision-making procedures tend to suppress conflict and conceal background asymmetries, however, participatory practices that foreground open contestation are *relatively* less susceptible to manipulation—and thus more reliable as tools of deeper democratization. For instance, the citizen oversight juries I defend in Chapter 9 retain a focus on specific decision nodes, but their adversarial structure ensures that underlying conflicts are exposed rather than concealed, and their limited scope minimizes the impact of elite agenda-setting (see also Bagg 2022c). Meanwhile, unions, parties, and social movements are hardly immune to capture, but as I show in Chapter 10, their basis in concrete struggles with clear opponents—along with certain *targeted* forms of internal democracy—makes complete co-optation more difficult. In a world of pervasive capture, these modest advantages are sufficient to make these practices crucial democratic priorities.

3.4 Idealizing participatory inclusion: Deliberative systems and political equality

Even if they accept everything I have said so far, sophisticated advocates of collective self-rule may remain unpersuaded that a radical rethinking of democracy is required. Responsive representation and participatory inclusion may be the most practically significant versions of collective self-rule, but they are not the only ones—and as I acknowledged in Chapter 1, in fact, prominent trends in contemporary democratic theory have already taken these criticisms on board. Instead of abandoning collective self-rule altogether, however, they aim to reformulate it.

First, deliberative theorists have increasingly recast reasonable deliberation as the overall or long-term *goal* of democracy, rather than as a privileged *method* for achieving that goal. Nondeliberative methods may be justified with reference to future deliberation, for instance—because they help bring about conditions in which ideal deliberation is possible (Mansbridge et al. 2010)—or hypothetical deliberation—because their results *could* be the outcome of ideal deliberation (Gutmann and Thompson 2004). Perhaps most commonly, nondeliberative methods are justified with reference to the *function* they serve within the broader "deliberative systems" of society (Mansbridge et al. 2012). In each case, recent work in deliberative theory has largely retreated from any practical commitment to prioritizing deliberative practices of participatory inclusion in democratic action and reform.

Second, analytic philosophers have increasingly converged on the view that democratic legitimacy depends on a very demanding form of political equality—rejecting prior accounts that rested instead on freedom or simple procedural equality. Drawing on some of the same concerns I have raised, for one, they reject Rousseau's supposition that we can remain free, despite the chains that inevitably bind all social creatures, if we choose those chains via democratic procedures (e.g., Beitz 1989; Christiano 1996). If such procedures are legitimate, therefore, this cannot be because they preserve our autonomy, but instead because they realize a valuable form of political equality. Yet as most contemporary democratic theorists recognize, simple majoritarian procedures are not sufficient to confer genuinely equal political status, and thus to legitimize the resulting decisions as genuinely collective. Instead, the most prominent recent accounts have posited a far more demanding conception of what is required for genuine political equality—and thus for democratic legitimacy. Though details vary, for instance, most conceptions include a range of rights and opportunities as prerequisites, as well as substantial material equality (Christiano 2008; Kolodny 2014a; Viehoff 2014; J. Wilson 2019).

Just like deliberative democrats, in other words, analytic political philosophers have largely retreated from strong claims about the practical priority of any particular decision-making procedures, instead recognizing the enormous complexity of democratic ends, and often emphasizing the democratic urgency of equalizing social and economic power relations. And this raises a crucial question: if two of the most important developments in contemporary democratic theory have already incorporated the concerns I have articulated in Part One of this book, do we really need the novel account of democracy that follows in Parts Two and Three?

My answer, unsurprisingly, is yes: we do. As explored in Chapter 1, to begin with, the ideal of resisting state capture is not *necessarily* in tension with the logic of collective self-rule. If we conceive the ideal of collective self-rule in highly abstract terms, rather, my account can be understood as complementary to it, filling in the concrete details of its practical demands rather than replacing it entirely (see §1.3–4). If so, however, it is a *necessary* complement—at least for anyone trying to make concrete judgments.

The most promising interpretations of collective self-rule—including systemic theories of deliberative democracy, as well as expansive accounts of political equality—are plausible precisely because they have retreated from the concrete implications traditionally associated with such ideals; remaining instead at a higher level of abstraction. And while their disavowal of misleading priorities is a step in the right direction, neither tradition has provided a clear set of alternative priorities for democratic action and reform. The guidance they offer democratic actors is unobjectionable: roughly, "take those actions and enact those reforms that are most likely to bring about conditions in which everyone can engage in mutual reason-giving and contribute to collective decisions on genuinely equal terms." Because these conditions are very distant from reality, however, this guidance is too vague to be useful in concrete judgments.

If genuine democratic legitimacy is possible only in ideal conditions that are nowhere close to realization, for instance, we might think that the most promising path from here to there lies not in continuing along the decidedly uninspiring trajectory of existing democracies, but instead in violent revolution or temporary dictatorship. Indeed, this is precisely the logic that motivated legions of twentieth-century revolutionaries—and if their goal was to create an ideal democratic society characterized by genuine deliberation and political equality, it is not entirely clear that they were wrong to abandon the parliamentary road. No actual communist revolution has successfully created such a society, but neither has any actual electoral democracy—and as I show in the next chapter (§4.5), the trend lines are not even going in the right direction. These days, of course, a far more common response to such difficult transitional questions is to avoid them altogether. But in practice, this often means defaulting to methods that are isomorphic with the ideal ends of deliberation and political equality—participatory inclusion and majority rule, respectively—thereby replicating the mistakes of prior accounts.

The rest of this book provides a different way of evaluating democratic practices—and however we think about its relationship to ideals of collective self-rule that account is its core contribution. Either way, moreover, it must ultimately stand or fall on its own merits.

PART TWO
DEMOCRATIC PRINCIPLES

Down with the power of the despot
Wherever his strongholds may be
—**Hutchinson Family Singers, "Lincoln and Liberty" (1860)**

4
What Is State Capture?

Under modern conditions, sovereign states set the basic terms of social life, conditioning or mediating nearly all human activity. The overarching goal of modern politics must therefore be to ensure that states use their distinctive public power to serve broad public interests. Yet give significant uncertainty about exactly what the "public interest" actually is, this goal is not best pursued directly: rather, the trick is to design social and political institutions so that they are maximally likely to pursue the public interest, whatever it turns out to be. And as a wide variety of liberal and democratic thinkers have recognized, this requires ensuring that members of the relevant public have roughly equal influence over public power.

As I have argued in the past several chapters, however, it is a mistake to entrust this task to any particular set of procedures for collective will formation and decision-making—none of which are immune from the efforts of powerful groups to bias the results in their favor. Rather than identifying it with a specific logic of decision-making, I define democracy negatively, as the set of institutions and practices that best protect public power from capture by any particular partial faction or private interest. Instead of pursuing a precise ideal vision of the public interest or the requirements of collective decision-making, accordingly, I argue that democratic actors should study the diverse array of concrete methods used to capture public power, and deploy whatever tactics are most reliably effective in contesting them. They should respond pragmatically to the most pressing threats at a given time, without losing sight of background dangers and long-term goals. The resulting ideal conceives democracy as a complex ecology of diverse practices and institutions, which evolves in response to changing threats.

Elaborating and defending this ideal requires a great deal of further inquiry—both empirical and normative in nature—and this will occupy us for the rest of the book. This chapter begins the first phase of that project, by investigating the extraordinary variety of tools that powerful actors and groups employ to ensure that public power serves their partial or private interests, thus diverting it from the public purposes it ought to serve. Its mission, in other words, is to explore the concept of "state capture" against which the democratic ideal is defined, by examining the various concrete threats that democratic practices must fight.

4.1 State capture, democracy, and the public interest

The phrase itself—"state capture"—is relatively new to the political lexicon. According to John Crabtree and Francisco Durand (2017: 2), it was first widely used in the early 1990s, to describe the "small corrupt groups" who used their influence over post-Soviet governments to accumulate wealth. More recently, it has become a catchphrase for South Africans seeking to expose and contest the political influence of certain prominent oligarchs (Alence and Pitcher 2019), while Alex Hertel-Fernandez (2019) has used it to describe the influence of billionaire-funded lobby groups over US state legislatures (see also Táíwò 2022a). Yet despite the recent origins of the term, the political dynamics it aptly describes are as old as politics itself.

On my deliberately expansive account, state capture refers to a diverse range of ways that state power can be used to advance the partial or private interests of a faction or group, at the expense of a broader public interest or common good. This definition allows great variation in terms of whose interests are favored, how that preferential treatment is secured, how pervasive it is across different state institutions, and how severe its consequences are. Additionally, it does not require that members of the favored group act intentionally to secure their preferential treatment—though of course they often do so. State capture thus serves as something of a catch-all term for a wide variety of political ills that arise from illicit links between state power and private or factional interests, including not just oligarchy and corruption but also tyranny and authoritarianism, clientelism and regulatory capture, as well as the way that state power is used to sustain group-based hierarchies of race, caste, ethnicity, religion, gender, and so on.

At first, it may sound strange to describe these latter problems in the language of capture—and indeed, the methods used by a cabal of elites to ensure that state power serves their private interests are different from the mechanisms by which state power entrenches the advantages of large social groups. A major aim of this chapter, however, is to explore how these kinds of phenomena are in fact deeply connected—both in theory and in practice—and thus to vindicate their inclusion under the broader umbrella concept of "state capture."

Another common worry about this concept of state capture is that it is underdetermined, given my studied refusal to define the public interest. Even if nearly everyone hopes to prevent the state from being captured by a cabal of self-interested elites, after all, we may still disagree strongly about which one to fear most—or even what counts as a cabal in the first place. Financial firms and labor unions both lobby for policies that favor their interests, and unless we know more about the content of the public interest, we cannot know whose advocacy presents a greater threat to it. Given that every state policy has distributive consequences, in fact, no policy can ever be entirely neutral between all groups. Absent an account of the public interest, then, we might wonder whether the concept of state capture means anything at all.

This worry is well founded: we cannot get the idea of state capture off the ground—not to mention the ideal of democracy as resisting state capture—without making certain assumptions about the public interest. As explored in Chapter 1, however, we need not define the public interest in a precise or comprehensive way. For our purposes, in fact, it is best to leave our working conception(s) of the public interest implicit and underspecified. Similarly, that fact that no state can be entirely free of capture, on this account, does not prevent us from making judgments about relative degrees of capture—and for our purposes, again, this is a good thing. We should presume that capture is the default condition of modern states, which can never be fully eliminated. And as a result, we should conceive of democracy as a constantly evolving struggle against capture's many manifestations, rather than as an ideal state of affairs.

Let me explain. My aim in this book, recall, is to provide reliable heuristics for democratic thought, action, and reform: i.e., to explain how we can best advance democratic ends. What this requires is not that we pursue the public interest directly, but that we pursue those practices that will best protect state power from various concrete deviations from the public interest. How can we achieve this aim without precisely identifying the public interest? There are two important parts here.

First, we can often reliably identify concrete deviations from the public interest without being able to specify precisely what the perfect public interest outcome would be. For instance: even if we do not know exactly which method of building a railway line would maximize the public interest, we can be reasonably certain that something has gone wrong when the state official in charge of the project diverts the funds to unqualified cronies after receiving a bribe. Even if we are unsure about the best way for the state to promote racial equality, more broadly, we can be certain that an apartheid state does not advance broad public interests.

In making such judgments, of course, we must presume a vague and implicit conception of the public interest. As explored in Chapter 1, however, that conception can remain vague and implicit. We may have a sense that it lies within a certain range, for instance, yet be unable (or unwilling, in the face of real uncertainty) to say exactly where it lies within that range. Nevertheless, if the outcome we observe lies far outside that range, we can still say confidently that it deviates from the public interest. We can thus identify concrete cases of capture without a precise account of the public interest—either in general or in the particular case in question.

More specifically, there are two key indicators we can rely on in identifying capture. On the one hand, we should see a pattern of outcomes that clearly favors one group at the expense of others, such as the massive profits of a construction firm that has failed to build a functional railway line, or large and persistent disparities across groups in terms of wealth, income, health, education, and so on. On the other hand, we should be able to point to a set of mechanisms that could plausibly have generated these advantages, in noninnocuous ways, and which involve the use of state power on some level—ranging from outright bribery of particular officials to subtle systemic biases in the legal system that no one in particular has intentionally created. In the clearest cases of capture, both the biased outcomes and the biasing mechanisms can easily be identified, and in discussing concrete cases of capture in the rest of this chapter, I rely as far as possible on both indicators. If the evidence on one front is especially strong, however, we can make do with merely suggestive or incomplete evidence on the other.

Even when we cannot confidently identify such concrete cases of capture, meanwhile, we can often still identify the practices and institutions that will most reliably protect public power, on the whole, from the efforts of powerful groups to twist it to their private or factional ends. For instance: even if we have no special reason to suspect bribery or corruption when a public contract is awarded through a secretive no-bid process—and even if we acknowledge that such processes can sometimes generate good outcomes—we can nevertheless say with confidence that public funds are generally less likely to be diverted to private hands when procurement processes are transparent and involve open competition. On a larger scale, similarly, we can be reasonably certain that the public interest is not best served by allowing members of the same family, race, caste, or ethnicity to unilaterally control public resources in perpetuity, with no input from other groups. And once again, crucially, we can be confident of this even if we think that some specific ruling elite, in some specific instance, has ruled in the public interest—in other words, even if they have not (yet) perpetrated capture, as I define it. Of course, these are toy examples, designed to be minimally controversial, and it must be acknowledged that many of our efforts to identify democratic practices will be more contentious. Given the accumulated knowledge of history and social science, however, I believe we can say a great deal—with at least some degree of confidence—about the practices and institutions that most reliably protect public power from capture. That is the task I take up in the rest of the book.

What all of this means, in sum, is that we cannot map terms like "capture" and "democracy" onto real-world phenomena strictly on the basis of the definitions I have given. As with most of the complex, value-laden terms we use in political theory, applying them in practice requires making judgments that are contestable on both empirical and normative grounds. This should not be cause for alarm. In the absence of any claim to proceed on the basis of revealed authority or transcendent logical truths, the best we can hope for in political theory is to persuade one another—or at least clarify our disagreements—by being transparent about which judgments we rely upon, and ensuring they are as well grounded (and widely shared) as possible. For those who do share many of my initial intuitions about which threats to the public interest are most concerning, then, my hope is that the concept of state capture elaborated in this chapter will help to make sense of those intuitions. For others, meanwhile, my hope is that the general framework might still help them organize their own commitments in a useful way. If so, this chapter can help to pinpoint which judgments are responsible for our divergent conclusions.

4.2 Varieties of state capture: Regulation, corruption, tyranny, and beyond

The concept of "regulatory capture" is largely responsible for popularizing the language of capture, and is thus a natural place to begin our examination of the broader umbrella concept of state capture. In the classic formulation, regulatory capture occurs when an incumbent firm induces the government to erect legal "barriers to entry" in their industry (Stigler 1971). For example, an aerospace manufacturer may lobby for certain "safety" regulations that would be very difficult for newer and smaller firms to comply with. By making it difficult for competitors to enter the market, such barriers enable incumbent firms to earn profits in excess of what they would otherwise earn—often called "rents" (Lindsey and Teles 2017: 16). Rents are not always bad: patents grant temporary monopolies, for instance, and are often thought to incentivize innovation in ways that have positive-sum benefits for everyone. Yet many rents are negative sum, meaning that any benefits for those who collect them are outweighed by harms to others.

As Adam Smith famously argued, for instance, the trading monopolies that European monarchs often granted as a routine tool of statecraft were highly inefficient—bringing massive profits to their holders while imposing serious costs on everyone else. As he also recognized, of course, merely demonstrating the costs of monopolies and other barriers to entry would not stop people from trying to create them: "people of the same trade seldom meet together," he observed, "but the conversation ends in a conspiracy against the public" (A. Smith 1904: 130). More specifically, they will always have strong incentives to influence public officials to erect barriers to entry—perhaps by inviting those officials to share in the rents. The primary solution Smith identified was thus to limit government "intervention" in the economy altogether.

In the 1970s, libertarian economists began deploying a version of this argument to buttress their skepticism of the welfare state. George Stigler (1971), for instance, posited that most government regulation is demanded by industry, in order to raise entry costs and limit competition. Similarly, James Buchanan lamented the "rent-seeking society" in which people sought negative-sum rents through preferential state policy rather than generating positive-sum profits through productive innovation (Buchanan, Tollison, and Tullock 1980). Both concluded that much of the administrative state was a ploy by private actors to enrich themselves at public expense, and that getting rid of it was the only solution (see also M. Olson 1965; Wilson 1980).

There is no necessary connection, however, between a focus on capture and libertarian politics. As recent scholarship demonstrates, for one, Adam Smith himself was at least as wary of concentrated economic power as of government intervention: in fact, it was largely the dangers posed by the former that motivated his hostility to the latter. As Paul Sagar writes, Smith's true aim was "not to draw attention to the problem of state intervention, but of state *capture*" (Sagar 2018b, emphasis original; see also 2018a). And as subsequent scholarship has demonstrated, regulatory capture is a prominent vector by which wealthy elites perpetuate their power—meaning that those on the left have ample reason to be concerned with it as well.

Employing Stigler's classic model, for instance—whereby regulations are demanded by industry actors—Lindsey and Teles (2017) have shown that regulatory capture in realms such as finance, intellectual property, occupational licensing, and municipal land use policies all enrich the wealthiest 1 percent. Meanwhile, Carpenter (2013) has argued that many regulations do benefit the public interest, while industry actors demand (and benefit from) deregulation and privatization. In such contexts, industry capture is reflected not in the imposition of regulation but its removal (see also Michaels 2017). Regulatory capture does not always follow the classic model of Stiglerian entry barriers and subsidies, that is—and indeed, deregulatory capture is likely far more pervasive. Either way, eliminating regulation altogether is rarely if ever the best response.

Revisionists like Carpenter also contest narrowly economistic conceptions of the public interest as constituted by competitive market outcomes—such that the public costs of capture can be calculated by measuring a firm's actual rents against an estimate of what it would have earned under more competitive conditions. Looking beyond material incentives in identifying mechanisms of capture, similarly, others highlight problems of "information capture" (Wagner 2010), whereby regulators rely on industry actors for expert knowledge, and "cultural capture" (Kwak 2013), whereby industries sway policymakers through a range of nonmaterial and unconscious inducements. Rather than exerting influence via campaign contributions or the promise of a lucrative second career, that is, industry actors may simply employ informational advantages, high status, and social relationships with policymakers. And they may do so, notably, without intentionally corrupting or manipulating the legislators and regulators involved.

Finally, historical work shows that something like capture has long been a major concern across the political spectrum. As we shall see in later chapters, for instance, US Progressives were acutely aware of the danger that powerful private actors could use state power to entrench their position (Emerson 2019; Rahman 2016)—and they were hardly alone. From the founding through the early twentieth century, in fact, Novak (2013: 40) notes that "concern about private interests or factions capturing public governing institutions and bending them toward selfish ends rather than general benefits was a well-developed (indeed perhaps the central) trope in American political and economic commentary." Two key things differentiate this discourse, however, from recent concerns about regulatory capture. The threat posed by private power to public interests was conceived in much broader terms. And it went by the name of corruption.

Many today—including the US Supreme Court, for instance—conceive corruption quite narrowly in terms of quid pro quo exchange (Teachout 2016). Yet earlier thinkers often defined it much more broadly, in terms of the use of public power for private ends. According to Aristotle's political typology, for instance, this was the key difference between "true" regimes like kingship and aristocracy—where the ruler or ruling faction pursues the common good—and "corrupted" regimes like tyranny and oligarchy—where they pursue their partial interests instead. In Aristotle's influential framing, in other words, tyranny and oligarchy are both forms of corruption, in the sense of using state power to pursue private or factional interests.

Leaving oligarchy aside for now—see §4.5—we can note that tyranny and corruption still had similar connotations when they became major concerns for eighteenth-century reformers. James Madison, for instance, was famously vexed by the danger of "factions": i.e., groups animated by a partial interest adverse to the "public good" or "permanent and aggregate interests of the community." Drawing on more recent thinkers like Montesquieu and Hume, he eschewed Aristotle's "true" regimes in favor of a mixed regime built on the proliferation of factions and the separation of powers. Still, his conception of the underlying dangers shares much with Aristotle, and he was hardly alone in using terms like corruption and tyranny to describe them.

Popular connotations and the US Supreme Court notwithstanding, meanwhile, recent scholarship on corruption typically shares the breadth of earlier conceptions (Blau 2018; Issacharoff 2010; Lessig 2011; Teachout 2016; Vergara 2020; Warren 2004). Michael Johnston (2005, 2013), for instance, defines corruption quite expansively as "the abuse of public roles or resources for private benefits" (2013: 9), and emphasizes that it is endemic to all forms of political life. Instead of measuring the overall level of corruption across different societies, therefore, he prefers to analyze its multifarious forms.

In contexts with weak institutions and fragmented power, for instance—such as Mexico or the Philippines, at the time of Johnston's analysis—contentious elites and their personal client networks alternately use bribery and violence to build temporary coalitions that advance their private and factional interests. Where control is more centralized yet state capacity remains relatively low and opposition is not institutionalized—Kenya or Suharto's Indonesia—personal loyalty is still the currency of advancement, but it is channeled through a state or party structure. Where state capacity is greater and competitive markets better developed—as in Italy, South Korea, or Botswana, on Johnston's account—state institutions may become the focus of "high-level, collusive networks" enabling elites to stifle competition and entrench their position.

Where markets and democratic politics are fully impersonal and institutionalized by a high-capacity state, finally—as in the United States, Japan, and Germany—open bribery is usually inaccessible, and personal networks lose the central importance they have in other contexts. Instead of disappearing, however, corruption changes shape, taking the form of "influence markets" where "private wealth interests seek influence over specific processes and decisions" (2013: 16) within impersonal democratic public institutions. And though more blatant forms of bribery are easier to identify, influence markets may be equally effective at entrenching elite power—perhaps in part because of their obscurity. As a result, Johnston prefers an expansive conception of corruption as a diverse phenomenon that changes form in different contexts—a conception that converges with my own definition of capture.

A similar recognition of continuity also characterizes recent work on authoritarianism—i.e., what earlier thinkers might have called tyranny—which has largely rejected Cold War binaries between dictatorship and democracy. As incumbent elites around the world have faced growing pressure to democratize, they have increasingly sought to employ democratic forms while entrenching their power by tilting the electoral playing field to their advantage (Levitsky and Way 2010). Elected officials in such "hybrid" regimes may openly manipulate elections, curtail civil liberties, and pack the courts with loyalists, for instance, or they may simply target opponents' material support and media access (Levitsky and Ziblatt 2018: 72–96). Yet opposition parties can still operate openly, and generally see elections as their best shot at power. Electoral competitiveness and uncertainty thus emerges as a key regime classification, whereby "full" electoral democracies are characterized by an even playing field and significant electoral uncertainty, nondemocracies by a lack of real competition, and hybrid regimes by a skewed field that nevertheless retains some uncertainty (Levitsky and Way 2010: 5–16).

Once again, all of these phenomena are readily understood in terms of state capture. By undermining civil liberties and the rule of law, incumbents expand their ability to use public power for their own purposes. By limiting electoral competitiveness, meanwhile, they secure control and reduce their incentive to respect remaining constraints—thus giving them a freer hand in using state power to achieve private ends. The result is a self-reinforcing authoritarian spiral, as each case of self-dealing begets further capture and corruption.

Indeed, authoritarian practices are not only conceptually related to corruption; they are also closely linked in practice—and another key part of this toolkit is the equally ancient practice of clientelism. Also called patronage or machine politics, clientelism is as an arrangement in which wealthy and powerful "patrons" offer contingent, particularistic favors to poorer and less powerful "clients"—sometimes through brokers, intermediaries, or a party structure—in exchange for political support (Hicken 2011). The first-order problem here is simple: both patron and client deploy personal relationships to turn public power to private use. Even more concerning, however, are the second-order effects on the political system.

On Susan Stokes' (2005) classic account, clientelism generates a kind of "perverse accountability": instead of voters rewarding or punishing politicians for their behavior in office, politicians may reward or punish voters for their behavior at the polls. As more recent work points out, the reality on the ground is often more complex than Stokes' model suggests (Aspinall and Berenschot 2019; Piliavsky 2014; Szwarcberg 2015). Clientelistic relationships can often have concrete benefits for poor citizens—at least in the short term—and some have even defended them as a path towards lasting countervailing power (Auyero 2001; Golway 2014; Hersh 2020). We should thus be wary of condemning them universally, or eliminating them prematurely (Bagg and Bhatia 2021.). Nevertheless, the overall, long-term effect of particularistic politics—including the forms of pork-barrel politics common in "advanced" democracies (Sidman 2019)—is to exacerbate troubling asymmetries of power. If an incumbent's electoral fortunes depend on particularistic networks divorced from programmatic policy, they will have fewer incentives to pursue the public interest, and a freer hand in using public power for their own purposes. Since the support of poor voters is cheaper to buy through particularistic exchanges external to the policymaking process, moreover, it is their interests that are most likely to be ignored in that process. In addition to facilitating direct quid pro quo exchanges, in sum, clientelism also indirectly increases risks of capture by entrenching the power of incumbents and the disadvantages of the poor.

4.3 Integrative perspectives: State capture and extractive institutions

Despite many shared concerns, scholarly work on capture, corruption, authoritarianism, and clientelism proceeds largely on parallel tracks. Part of my purpose here is to integrate these literatures, and in doing so, it will be useful to draw on two ambitious and influential analytical frameworks that have emerged from political economy in recent years. One is articulated by Douglass North, John Wallis, and Barry Weingast (2009) (henceforth NWW), and the other by Daron Acemoglu and James Robinson (2012) (henceforth A&R). Both feature a core contrast between "extractive" (A&R) or "limited-access" (NWW) institutions—under which a narrow elite monopolizes political and economic power at the expense of everyone else—and "inclusive" (A&R) or "open-access" (NWW) institutions—under which power is more widely dispersed, creating political freedom as well as economic prosperity.

Both accounts begin with the observation that good outcomes in terms of income, health, education, and so on, depend on inclusive economic institutions enabling everyone to engage freely in all kinds of activity. Because anyone can change jobs, start a business, migrate, and buy or sell what they please, with few restrictions and minimal hassle, inefficient technologies and maladaptive social forms are displaced by new competitors in a dynamic process known as creative destruction, which enables societies to adapt effectively in response to shocks. The trouble is that because creative destruction threatens the status quo institutions from which they derive power, elites have strong incentives to prevent it. This explains why elites throughout history have been so keen to suppress economic dynamism, despite the fact that doing so harms their societies over the long run. And as A&R are especially keen to insist, this means that inclusive political institutions are a necessary prerequisite for inclusive economic institutions and the positive outcomes they bring, for it is only under inclusive political institutions that elites can be forced to accept the uncertainty of creative destruction.

As NWW are especially keen to emphasize, meanwhile, open-access political institutions are equally dependent on open-access economic institutions. To see why, however, we must back up a step. Rather than beginning their analysis with an unified ruling elite that aims to protect their privileges by wielding state power, as A&R do, NWW ask how the stable, unified, and relatively peaceful order that characterizes successful states is created in the first place. After all, the way in which rival elites are induced to lay down their arms and participate in a ruling coalition can profoundly shape the way those coalitions rule. On NWW's account, then, the fundamental unit of society is not the state but the organization—a category that includes military units, corporations, religious groups, and any other structure allowing coordinated action—while the state itself is simply an organization of organizations.

For most of history, the only way that the elites who controlled these organizations were able to maintain enough peace among themselves to constitute a state is by carefully allocating various economic rents and sociolegal privileges among themselves. So long as one of these privileges was the ability to form and lead organizations, elites maintained sufficient access to organized violence and other forms of power that they could defect from the ruling coalition if its terms no longer suited them—and could thus feel secure in joining that coalition. So long as rents were allocated and adjusted over time to reflect the relative power of each member, this coalition could generate a self-enforcing—and extractive—political order.

Under modern conditions, however, a different sort of logic has also proven capable of supporting a relatively stable, peaceful, and unified form of political rule. Rather than holding a coalition of elites together through the distribution of personalized rents and privileges in the shadow of factional violence, open-access orders achieve this feat by placing military and police firmly under the control of a civilian authority that is constrained in its use of violence and responsive to broad interests. Meanwhile, impersonal markets underwrite open political competition, which in turn incentivizes obedience to limits on self-dealing, ensures a modicum of responsiveness, and protects consolidated civilian control of violence. Absent any of these pieces, the system will collapse into a limited-access equilibrium, but once they are all in place, NWW argue, societies move to a different self-enforcing equilibrium.

The key innovation of NWW is the recognition that limited-access orders remain hostage to an implicit threat of violence that lurks in the background. As a result, the motivation for elites to implement "extractive" economic institutions is not simply to "maximize the wealth and power of elites," considered as a monolithic class, but more specifically to avoid violent breakdowns by "allocating rents and privileges" in proportion to the relative power of coalition members (NWW 275). More broadly, in fact, elites are "constrained in their ability to act as a unified group by the dynamic relationships among elite groups" (NWW 274). The upshot is that a dynamic economy not only enables outsiders to accumulate power and ultimately pose external challenges to the coalition—a process that could conceivably be slowed or stopped by a sufficiently unified coalition. It also destabilizes that coalition from within, by redistributing relative power among members in ways that cannot be predicted or managed. To protect their position, then, political elites must limit economic openness, inclusiveness, and dynamism.

The key takeaway of both approaches, more broadly, is that economic and political power are tightly linked. In order to maintain their position, members of an elite ruling coalition must monopolize economic and political power simultaneously. On the one hand, they must hoard political power in order to prevent potential economic rivals from changing the structure of wealth accumulation, and thereby eroding or redistributing the extractive rents on which the coalition is built. On the other hand, they must hoard economic power in order to prevent potential political opponents from generating enough material resources to mount a serious challenge. They must rig the rules that govern the acquisition of both public and private power—or, in other words, they must capture the state.

Indeed, that is what links the tactics of ancient tyrants to those of contemporary oil autocrats and crony capitalists, as well as the clientelistic corruption and authoritarian machinations used by elected incumbents across much of the world to maintain their grip on power. In each case, these tactics enable a relatively small coalition of ruling elites to protect their private, factional interests at the expense of everyone else. Conversely, these frameworks also clarify the logic shared by many of the universal rules and neutral, impersonal institutions that characterize modern democracies. These structures ensure political and economic competition among a broad enough sector of society that rents in either domain are gradually dissipated, making it more difficult for elites to entrench themselves in power by rigging the game in their favor. In other words, universal rules and neutral, impersonal institutions help to resist state capture.

The convergent insights of A&R and NWW are thus crucial to my arguments in Chapter 5, where I explore the basic "liberal" demands of democracy. At the same time, however, these two frameworks also share similar limitations, which give rise to the "radical" demands I elaborate in Chapter 6. At bottom, these limitations arise from the stark binary they draw between a virtuous circle of ever-expanding inclusion and a vicious spiral of extraction. Both acknowledge that extraction continues even in open-access societies characterized by universal rules and neutral, impersonal institutions, but such cases are framed as exceptions, which will presumably be worn down over time by the self-reinforcing logic of those inclusive structures.

Unfortunately, the situation of open-access orders is more like a hydraulic system than a virtuous circle (Issacharoff and Karlan 1999). Instead of halting the flow of elite influence, that is, closing off certain pathways for capture often simply forces that influence to flow through other channels. As scholarship on corruption and regulatory capture shows, for instance, public power is frequently used for private ends even in wealthy liberal democracies. More broadly, A&R and NWW obscure the ways that apparently inclusive institutions may serve the unified interests of entire categories of people, such as oligarchs, white people, or men. Although they are right that competition among elites can seriously mitigate capture—and that this helps to explain the value of many familiar liberal and democratic practices—it does not eliminate all disparities of private power, and at times can even facilitate them.

4.4 Persistent capture in inclusive societies (I): Categorical inequalities

Let us begin with the obvious. Throughout history, apparently "democratic" states have routinely privileged the interests of certain racial, ethnic, religious, and cultural groups at the expense of others. From ancient Athens to modern settler democracies like the United States, South Africa, and Australia, in fact, a fierce devotion to freedom and equality for insiders has often been premised on the enslavement and/or displacement of outsiders (Rana 2014; Stovall 2021). In light of these glaring contradiction, it is tempting to draw a stark binary between such "imposter" democracies and the "true" democracies we have now, which have eliminated these exclusions. As was obvious to everyone from Alexis de Tocqueville to Frederick Douglass, however, there was something distinctively democratic about the early United States and other settler democracies, despite the glaring exclusions on which they were founded.[1] Meanwhile, eliminating these formal exclusions has hardly ensured that state power no longer favors the interests of white majorities. For both reasons, it is seriously misleading to make a strict demarcation between the bad old days and the fully democratic present.

Nevertheless, the history of settler democracies like the US may still be thought to count in favor of the virtuous circle thesis upheld by NWW and A&R. They do not predict an immediate transition to utopia following the adoption of open-access institutions, but rather a self-reinforcing cycle of gradually increasing inclusivity. Have not the worst forms of exclusion, extraction, and state-sanctioned privilege been transcended, as their accounts would predict? And can we not expect this progress to continue, if perhaps more slowly than we would like?

While there may be some truth to the first claim, the second is unfortunately very doubtful. Again, the metaphor of a hydraulic system is more apt than that of a virtuous circle. As certain modes of exclusion and extraction have been closed off, the perpetuation of privilege and inequality has often been diverted to other channels. Indeed, the evolution of racial hierarchy in the United States since the Civil Rights era offers a textbook illustration of how categorical inequalities more generally—i.e., asymmetries in wealth and power between different groups of people, along lines of race, ethnicity, caste, religion, social class, gender, and so on—can be upheld and even entrenched through policies that are officially neutral between those groups.

Although legalized racial segregation gradually declined in the decades after Brown v. Board, for instance, US schools are now more racially segregated than they were in 1970 (Reardon and Owens 2014). While Blacks are no longer barred from certain neighborhoods, jobs, and public spaces, meanwhile—and in some cases may be actively recruited as tokens of

---

[1] The basic logic of NWW and A&R—like that of Schumpeter (1942)—has no necessary connection to universal suffrage: it is competition among elites that dissipates rents, and this may be perfectly compatible with the exclusion of certain nonelites from membership. This helps us explain what was actually democratic about those societies, while at the same time underscoring my claim that such frameworks are radically incomplete.

"diversity"—the percentage of national wealth owned by Black people has barely budged since the Emancipation Proclamation was issued in 1863 (Baradaran 2017; Conley 1999; Lui et al. 2006). Though there are more Black politicians, attorneys, and police officers than ever, finally, the criminal justice system still disproportionately targets Black people, and in absolute terms, more Black men are ensnared by it than were enslaved in 1850 (Alexander 2010).

What explains these striking facts? We have identified a pattern of outcomes that clearly favors some at the expense of others, but can we also point to mechanisms that could plausibly have generated these advantages, at least partly through state institutions, in noninnocuous ways? As demonstrated by a veritable ocean of scholarship on the subject, the answer is an emphatic "yes." Above all, the core lesson of this work is that rather than being encoded explicitly and directly into law, racial hierarchy in the United States is now upheld tacitly and indirectly, through the enforcement of laws that are officially colorblind. On the one hand, racial bias still pervades decisions about employment, housing, policing, education, environmental policy, and so on, even if the bias is now more likely to be "implicit," and even if those reproducing racist structures are now more likely to be members of racialized groups themselves (Bonilla-Silva 1997, 2003; Flynn et al. 2017; Roithmayr 2021). Given how deeply racial hierarchy has been written into the physical infrastructure of American life, on the other hand, much of the structure of racial inequality in the US would likely remain intact even in the absence of any implicit racial discrimination (Hayward 2013; Nall 2018; Trounstine 2018). Even if race were rendered invisible tomorrow, in other words, that would not eliminate the vast racial disparities in, say, median family wealth (D. A. Brown 2022; T. M. Shapiro and Oliver 1995), or education funding (Kozol 1992), or neighborhood security (Peterson and Krivo 2010), or environmental quality (Bullard 1990), or access to nutrition (Walker, Keane, and Burke 2010).

While I have focused my attention on the case of the United States, finally—where the dynamics of racial hierarchy under conditions of formal equality have been studied most extensively—it is important to emphasize that these dynamics are hardly unusual in the broader global context. If anything, the situation is even worse for Black populations in other settler democracies such as Brazil—where colorblindness has been official policy since the 1930s, yet wealth disparities are even worse than they are in the US—and South Africa—where Black men are incarcerated at higher rates today than under the brutally repressive apartheid regime. Meanwhile, racialized groups, minority ethnicities, and subordinate castes or classes in many other contemporary democracies face a roughly similar set of conditions—i.e., formal legal equality and sporadic efforts at "inclusion," alongside a dizzying array of informal exclusions and structural disadvantages. This includes Indigenous communities across the Americas and Australasia, for instance, as well as scheduled castes in South Asia, and ethnic minorities with a "migration background" in much of Europe. As in the US, in other words, racial and ethnic hierarchies have not disappeared; it is just that the burden of maintaining them has shifted from intentional action to structural forces; and from the avowedly public realm of explicitly racist policy to the apparently private realm of decentralized social and economic interaction.

Crucially, this shift in mechanisms does not absolve states of responsibility. Even where it is upheld through officially colorblind policies, in other words, racial and ethnic hierarchy in all of these contexts still reflects state capture. It may be easiest to diagnose capture when it is the result of state officials taking active steps to directly advance the interests of a particular group—as with a regulatory barrier that benefits incumbent firms, perhaps, or a law barring Black people from holding certain jobs. As we saw in the regulatory context, however, failure to act can also indicate capture—as when an environmental agency is induced by industry actors not to make a rule limiting the emission of known toxic substances. And the same is true of a failure to act against enduring categorical inequalities. In both cases, what may seem like innocuous noninterference is in fact a consequential, partisan use of state power. Given that all democratic states enforce basic private law—and especially given that most have a history of explicit racist policies—official neutrality enables a partial faction to promote its interests at others' expense.

To illustrate why, let us return to the case of racial hierarchy in the United States. For most of its history, the US government has upheld the brutalization, dispossession, and general mistreatment of Black people, in ways that are obviously and directly responsible for their pervasive and continuing disadvantages (Katznelson 2005). Along with various subordinate state and local entities, more importantly, it continues to use immense coercive force to protect and entrench the vast racial disparities its prior actions had created (Rothstein 2017). Thus, continuing to enforce that extremely unequal social and economic order in a "colourblind" fashion—while failing to take action that would disrupt and mitigate the reliable reproduction of racial hierarchy within it—should be understood as an exemplary case of state capture along lines of categorical group identity. Even if white people do not generally intend or even endorse this state of affairs, in practice the power of the US state reliably privileges their interests over those of other groups. On the expansive sense of "capture" that I have developed in this chapter, therefore, we should understand the state as captured by them to some degree.

At times, of course, both federal and state governments have taken certain active steps to remedy racial inequality, such as affirmative action programs, and to the extent that such efforts successfully reduce Black disadvantage, they also reduce the overall severity of this form of racialized capture. As a general rule, however, these steps have been extremely feeble, relative to the overall impact of government action—and at times have even been actively counterproductive. In a process that Keeanga-Yahmatta Taylor (2019) has called "predatory inclusion," for instance, Black people in the US have been actively recruited into practices and institutions from which they had previously been excluded—such as state-subsidized home loans—but on terms so unfavorable that their "inclusion" only exacerbates their disadvantages. Taken as a whole, then, the use of state power overwhelmingly favors the interests of white Americans—whose median family wealth, to take only the simplest example, is roughly eight times that of Black Americans. And in this context, the demand for state "neutrality"—such as that enforced by the US Supreme Court in its decisions on affirmative action—is in fact anything but neutral. The message of state "neutrality" under such conditions, in Derrick Bell's (1992: 376) words, is that "existing power relations in the real world are by definition legitimate and must go unchallenged," and it thus represents a potent tool of capture by dominant groups.

Again, it is important to emphasize that these arguments are relevant far beyond the case of racial hierarchy in the US. Given the profound legacy of European colonialism on nearly all modern states, for one, state enforcement and facilitation of racial hierarchy is an especially widespread and important form of state capture across the globe, and fighting it must be a central priority in many contemporary democracies (see J. Olson 2004). At the same time, I have focused on the case of racial hierarchy not because its nature and significance are entirely unique, but rather because it offers an especially clear illustration of a much broader set of related dynamics. For instance, ethnicity, caste, religion, and social class are frequently deployed in similar ways to distribute advantages and disadvantages across groups—and in many contexts, these forms of inter-group difference are more salient than race. Meanwhile, similar mechanisms also facilitate the perpetuation of hierarchies based on gender, sexuality, ability, and other forms of intra-group difference as well.

Despite the differences between them, all of these systems of advantage and disadvantage can be understood as forms of "categorical inequality" (Tilly 1999), whereby certain social differences are weaponized by a dominant group—if not created out of whole cloth—in order to enable that dominant group to hoard various resources, privileges, and opportunities for themselves (see also Darity et al. 2017; O'Connor 2019; Reeves 2017; Roithmayr 2010). And as with racial hierarchy in the US, all of these systems have stubbornly outlasted the transition from explicit preferential treatment to formal equality. Even under broadly inclusive, open-access institutions, that is—and even where few if any members of the dominant group actively intend this outcome—decentralized "private" interaction continues to reproduce categorical inequalities (C. Chambers 2008). In each case, moreover, ostensibly neutral state institutions serve at the very least to protect and enable such systems of advantage, and often to covertly promote them (Mahmood 2015). As Catherine MacKinnon (1989: 163) argues powerfully in the case of gender, for instance,

> The foundation for [the state's] neutrality is the pervasive assumption ... that sex inequality does not really exist in society ... the strategy is first to constitute society unequally prior to law; then to design the constitution, including the law of equality, so that its guarantees apply only to those values that are taken away by law; then to construct legitimating norms so that the state legitimates itself through noninterference with the status quo. Then, so long as male dominance is so effective in society that it is unnecessary to impose sex inequality through law ... not even a legal guarantee of sex equality will produce social equality.

What MacKinnon is describing, in short, is the capture of state power in service of patriarchy, which ensures that the use of state power privileges the interests of men.

What then is the lesson of this discussion? For the most part, the basic insights of NWW and A&R—about the capture-resisting effects of political and economic competition—remain intact. What this section demonstrates is not that their broadly liberal perspective is wrong, but that it is crucially incomplete. The problem, in short, is that this perspective ignores the extent to which formally neutral and impersonal structures can sometimes serve the interests of certain privileged groups—and are thus not only consistent with capture by those groups, but may even facilitate it. Protecting the state from capture thus requires a good dose of universality and neutrality, as I elaborate in Chapter 5, but it also requires corrective partiality in certain contexts as well. To put it simply, democracy has enemies—the powerful actors and hegemonic groups whose interests are most often favored by state power—and as I explore in Chapter 6, its advocates must, at times, openly embrace the fight against those adversaries.

Before we explore what this fight will require, however, we must first examine the other primary sort of adversary I am concerned with in this book. In addition to the beneficiaries of categorical inequality, in short, the other hegemonic group whose interests are privileged across all modern democracies consists of those with highly concentrated wealth.

4.5 Persistent capture in inclusive societies (II): Concentrated wealth

The transition from poor autocracy to prosperous liberal democracy, which many societies have undergone over the course of the last few centuries, is usually understood as a dramatic historical discontinuity. According to NWW and A&R, for instance, it represents the wholesale replacement of a pathological equilibrium with a much healthier one—and as I've said, there is clearly something right about this narrative. Even where categorical inequalities persist after decades of formal equality, there has typically been some limited progress on certain fronts. In one key respect, however, very little has changed at all: the protection of concentrated wealth.

We know now that democratization was not accompanied by massive expropriations of wealth, or the end of private property, and in Chapter 2, we began to see some of the reasons why. However, we should not let hindsight blind us to the fact that, on an intuitive level, it is quite surprising that things did not turn out as the wealthy had always feared—i.e., that the poor did not simply expropriate the wealthy as soon as they gained power. Along with the many unique features of modern democracies, and the real historical discontinuities associated with them, we must also account for this equally momentous continuity.

The nature and scope of this continuity is powerfully articulated by Jeffrey Winters (2011, 2017). As Winters tells it, in short, nearly all forms of complex social organization have served one purpose above all others—protecting the extremely concentrated wealth of a tiny coterie of elites—and liberal democracy is no exception. Echoing Johnston and other corruption scholars, Winters contends that this basic imperative of wealth defense is constant throughout most of recorded history, varying only in the methods oligarchs have used to achieve it. Where Johnston addresses the influence of diverse elites upon a wide range of policies, however, Winters is concerned with a smaller class of genuine oligarchs—roughly speaking, the top 0.1 percent of the income distribution—and a narrower set of policies—namely, those governing the accumulation and defense of wealth. In other policy areas, the interests of different elites may come into conflict, enabling other actors and groups to make gains by playing those elites off of one another. In this area, however, the interests of oligarchs are fully unified—and as a result, Winters argues, their combined material power will almost always enable them to get their way, no matter what political system happens to be in place.

In one important sense, in fact, liberal democracy actually simplifies their task: unlike Roman senators, he notes, "oligarchs in America enjoy strong property rights enforced by others, and thus do not need to rule to pursue their core interests" (2011: xi). This entails submitting to the rule of law, which admittedly has significant downsides for them: unlike most oligarchs throughout history, they become vulnerable to the law, which in theory is subject to unpredictable democratic majorities (2011: 209). Yet the transition to what Winters calls "civil oligarchy" also solidifies their position, as the character of property ownership is transformed from a system of "claims" that must be actively enforced by the oligarchs themselves, through direct political or military action, into a system of "rights" that oligarchs can trust the state to enforce on their behalf.[2] Property is still protected through systematic coercion, but the job has been outsourced to an impersonal—and ostensibly neutral—state.

Under other forms of social organization, extreme accumulations of property and wealth are constantly under threat—most often from rival oligarchs, as NWW also emphasize, but at times from popular movements as well. Since this threat only grows more serious as the amount of wealth available for expropriation grows, moreover, the cost of protecting a fortune will rise in proportion to its size. Under the open-access institutions of modern democracy, by contrast, extreme concentrations of wealth receive material protection and ideological legitimacy, entirely irrespective of their size. Today's billionaires may hire private security to prevent petty burglaries and ensure their personal safety, but they expend virtually no resources to protect their major assets, which are nevertheless more secure than any other oligarchic fortunes in history. Indeed, modern democracies are home

---

[2] In most pre-modern social orders, Winters explains, wealthy individuals had to defend their property claims by deploying coercive force themselves, either as warlords in a "warring" oligarchy, or through the institutions of a "ruling" oligarchy such as ancient Rome or medieval Venice, whereby oligarchs pool coercive resources to ward off common threats while retaining the ability to use them individually if necessary. With the consolidation of coercive power under the modern state, oligarchs give up personal access to coercive resources in exchange for centralized protection of property, thus relieving them of the necessity of directly in political or military rule in order to defend their wealth. In certain systems, however—"sultanistic" oligarchies like Suharto's Indonesia—their wealth is still subject to selective expropriation, and they must still defend property claims directly through personalistic favors to state officials. Of the four varieties of oligarchy outlined by Winters, it is only in "civil" oligarchies such as the United States and Singapore that individuals with extreme wealth fully submit to strong and impersonal systems of law. Compare to the categories of Johnston (2013).

to some of the wealthiest individuals the world has ever seen—not only in absolute terms, but also relative to average members of their societies. Liberal democracy, it seems, is the highest form of oligarchy.

Oligarchs do face some taxation in modern democracies, of course, but as Winters shows, those with truly stratospheric fortunes are reliably able to minimize this threat as well, often by shifting the burden towards those who are merely wealthy—roughly, the rest of the top 10 percent. For one, the fact that modern states almost exclusively target income rather than wealth for taxation represents one of the most important victories of the fully oligarchic 0.1 percent, whose vast troves of accumulated wealth are thus largely immune from taxation to begin with (Piketty 2014; Saez and Zucman 2019). While those who are merely wealthy submit to relatively high taxes under progressive tax schedules, meanwhile, those whose wealth reaches truly oligarchic proportions rely on a massive income defense industry to ensure that they pay an effective tax rate lower than that paid by firefighters and schoolteachers (Tait 2019). Although the various legal and illegal methods of tax avoidance peddled by this industry represent a massive theft of revenue from state coffers, no modern democracy has ever done much to prevent it.

Despite all of this, the broad historical narrative and regime typology that Winters articulates are quite similar to the others we have considered. Indeed, he readily concedes that most people are better off under "civil oligarchies" like the US, as compared to "warring" or "ruling" oligarchies, where untamed oligarchs directly enforce their property claims through violence. By focusing on the continuity of oligarchic wealth protection across these otherwise divergent regimes, however, Winters highlights a dramatic flaw in the "good equilibrium" of liberal democracy. And in fact, it is partly because his historical scope and theoretical ambition matches that of NWW and A&R that his account poses an especially stark challenge to their progressive narrative—identifying a hugely significant form of state capture that not only refuses to go away, but actually appears to be getting worse over time. Inclusive institutions may help to resist capture by opening rents to competitive pressure under most circumstances, but Winters shows that this mechanism will fail when those with highly concentrated material power have strong interests in common—as they do when it comes to defending their fortunes.

That said, Winters is hardly the only person to notice that modern democracies reliably serve the interests of wealthy elites, and we can add further detail and complexity to our narrative by examining some of these other accounts of how, why, and to what extent they do so. To begin with, there is a long tradition of Marxist thought that aims to justify, elaborate, qualify, and explain Marx and Engels' famous claim that the state represents nothing more than "a committee for managing the common affairs of the whole bourgeoisie." Though it applies only to capitalist states, taking "capitalists" rather than "oligarchs" as its central category, this tradition makes even stronger claims about the dominance of extremely wealthy elites within modern democracies. According to Marxists, for instance, the interests of capitalists are served not only by policies directly relevant to wealth defense, like taxation and capital controls, but by much of the rest of the state apparatus as well—including functions as diverse as public education, the military, and social insurance. Even when these policies require high taxes and serve an ostensibly redistributive function, many Marxists suspect that they ultimately serve the interests of capital, perhaps by "buying off" the working class (Stinchcombe 1985).

Relatedly, the tradition of Marxist state theory also entertains a wider range of explanations for the state's adherence to the interests of capital (Barrow 1993). Some classic accounts sought to demonstrate that particular capitalists consciously and successfully pursue state policies that serve their interests, thus employing what is sometimes called instrumental power (Domhoff 1967; Miliband 1969; Mills 1956). Others, however, have placed greater emphasis on the structural power of capital (Poulantzas 1969), highlighting the limitations on state autonomy imposed by the threat of capital flight (Lindblom 1982; Przeworski and Wallerstein 1982), or the reproduction of market values through public schools and family law (Bowles and Gintis 1976; Fraser 2013). A third model, intertwined with both, has stressed the role of ideological power in ensuring capitalist hegemony (Althusser 1971; Gramsci 1971; Lukes 1974).

Most contemporary scholars are skeptical of the most ambitious and categorical claims of classical Marxist state theory, which have proved difficult to nail down and test empirically. This does not mean that these claims are necessarily false, but there are good reasons to suspect that they are overstated (Skocpol 1985). If they are true, most obviously, it is difficult to explain why business interests do not simply get their way in every conflict (M. Smith 2000; Vogel 1983, 1987). Yet as inequality has climbed to levels not seen in a century—and as our measures of it have grown more precise (Atkinson, Piketty, and Saez 2011)—it has become equally obvious that something is profoundly awry. To be sure: there is variation in the scale of inequality across democracies, and it is most extreme in places like the US, Brazil, and South Africa—not incidentally, the same places where racialized inequalities are also most severe. Since the anomalous decades of the mid-twentieth century, however, inequality has been high and growing in nearly all democracies (Zucman 2019)—including those seen as paragons of social democracy (Hansen and Toft 2021). In every democracy, meanwhile, there are also countless relatively obscure aspects of the sociolegal order that disproportionately benefit the wealthy—ranging from monetary policy (Dietsch, Claveau, and Fontan 2018) to the protection of platform power (Culpepper and Thelen 2020; Srnicek 2016) to the distribution of risk (Streeck 2014); from natural resource ownership (Wenar 2016) to market coordination rights (Paul 2020; Vaheesan 2020) to intellectual property law (Kapczynski 2011, 2020). In all modern democracies, that is, nearly every area of private law entrenches inequality in a host of subtle ways that are inscrutable to average citizens, yet crucial for the reproduction of wealth (Adkins, Cooper, and Konings 2020; Berman 2023; Christophers 2020; Pistor 2019).

Of course, "the wealthy" do not always constitute a singular group with unified interests. Winters' account is especially powerful in part because it focuses on those specific areas where the interests of those with extreme wealth do converge, but in many areas, different subsets of the wealthy will have diverging interests. Still, it is usually some group of wealthy elites that ends up on top, even if their victory comes at least partially at the expense of some other subsets of the wealthy. Whether state policy in a particular area disproportionately serves the interests of pharmaceutical giants (G. Posner 2020), insurers (Brill 2015), or doctors (Chapin 2015); military contractors (Hartung 2012) or financial elites (Connaughton 2012; Krippner 2011; McCarty, Poole, and Rosenthal 2013; Morgenson 2012); factory farms (Pachirat 2013) or fossil fuel companies (Brulle 2018; Mildenberger 2020); tech monopolies (Khan 2016) or real-estate developers (Goetz 2013); the individuals who benefit most reliably from diverse forms of state capture in modern democracies are those who already possess highly concentrated wealth. The qualitative details and overall severity of capture by wealthy elites may differ from country to country, in sum, but the basic pattern of outcomes across all modern democracies clearly and pervasively favors the interests of concentrated wealth. On any plausible reading of the evidence, a diagnosis of widespread capture is unavoidable.

Still, we cannot escape the question that has long perplexed Marxist state theorists: i.e., how do the wealthy achieve such favorable outcomes in so many democratic states, given that nonwealthy voters always constitute a vast majority? Or in other words, which mechanisms of capture are responsible for the pattern of outcomes we observe?

I began to answer this question in Chapter 2. Due to the structure of collective decision-making and individual preference formation, in short, I argued that any democratic process will furnish opportunities for capture by groups with outsized private power and organizational capacity—i.e., those best positioned to exert influence through informal channels over the framing and implementation of decisions. As Pepper Culpepper (2010) shows in a comparative study of France, Germany, Japan, and the Netherlands, business interests are most likely to win in conflicts with labor and other competing interests when issue salience is low and decision-making is less formalized—in other words, where the scope for informal influence is highest. This does mean that business sometimes loses, especially when the attention of the broader public is focused intensely on a topic. Crucially, however, salience is a strictly limited resource: only a few issues can hold the public's attention at once, and it inevitably fades over time. Meanwhile, groups with outsized private power and organizational capacity are better equipped to wait it out and shift to more favorable, informal forums once the heat of public attention has been lifted (Culpepper 2010: 190). While business interests do not always win, therefore, it is reasonable to expect that the overall pattern of outcomes will favor them.

As I noted in Chapter 2, some evidence of this general bias towards the interests of wealthy elites is provided by recent studies of unequal responsiveness, which demonstrate that the preferences of the wealthy are disproportionately reflected by state policy in a wide range of democracies (e.g., Gilens and Page 2014; Lupu and Warner 2021). Yet this responsiveness-based approach also obscures the fact that wealthy elites get their way in part by shaping the beliefs and preferences of ordinary people, and thus almost certainly understates the full extent of capture. At times, there appears to be broad support for policies that favor the wealthy. More often, the policies that entrench wealthy interests most effectively—from arcane features of the tax code to the structure of intellectual property law—are simply unknown to most voters. In addition, of course, studies of responsiveness still do not identify the mechanisms of capture. I have shown that the structure of decision-making and preference formation provides ample opportunities for wealthy elites to exert informal, behind-the-scenes influence, and that this is most effective when issue salience is low. But what does this influence look like in practice?

As we have already seen, scholars of regulatory capture and corruption have identified a range of diverse mechanisms through which private actors induce favorable outcomes from officials. These broadly instrumental methods run the gamut from explicit bribery of the relevant officials, to the implicit offer of a "golden parachute"—i.e., a lucrative second career in industry, once officials leave government—to a much subtler set of cognitive, informational, and cultural influences. While this research focuses primarily on appointed administrative officials, an equally voluminous literature on money in politics documents how organized groups use these and other tactics to shape the behavior of elected legislators—including everything from direct funding of electoral campaigns (e.g., McKay 2018) to subtle "legislative subsidies" (e.g., Hall and Deardorff 2006). And while views differ on the relative effectiveness of these tactics, it is hard to believe that none have any biasing effect whatsoever.

The scale of money in politics is perhaps most extreme—and is certainly best studied—in the United States. In addition to providing extensive evidence of the unequal representation of wealthy interests in a general sense (e.g., Bartels 2009; Hacker and Pierson 2011; Kelly 2020; Schlozman, Brady, and Verba 2018), scholars of US politics have also carefully documented the extraordinary influence of particular billionaire-funded groups on policy outcomes (Hasen 2016; Page, Seawright, and Lacombe 2018; Skocpol and Hertel-Fernandez 2016)—especially at the state level, which is subject to less scrutiny in an era of increasingly nationalized politics (Grumbach 2022; Hertel-Fernandez 2019). Yet similar techniques are deployed in many other democracies, such as India (Jaffrelot, Kohli, and Murali 2019) and Brazil (Samuels 2001). And even where the impact of campaign donations and other obvious forms of influence has been limited—as in European democracies with public financing of elections, for instance—the image of a hydraulic system is once again apt: money (and influence) simply finds alternative pathways (Cagé 2020; Weschle 2022). In many countries with the sort of campaign finance laws that US reformers dream of, in fact, those policies have led to the growth of "cartel parties" that limit conflict, ultimately serving wealthy interests by other means (Katz and Mair 2018).

All of that said, this sort of instrumental power is only one of the ways that state power can be induced to serve the interests of those with concentrated wealth. Such methods allow wealthy elites to shape the priorities and judgments of various state actors, but there are limits to this power. Given that elected legislators must also care about voter preferences, the wealthy can only rely on back-channel influence to get their way on an issue when a majority of voters either: (a) are unaware of the issue; (b) endorse the policy that favors the wealthy; or (c) do not care enough about it to make it a salient political issue (Ingham 2019). And another important way the wealthy protect their interests is by using ideological power to ensure that when it comes to the issues they care most about, voters are likely to fall into one of these categories.

Perhaps the most obvious way of shaping the beliefs and preferences of ordinary voters in a favorable direction—other than through the process of electoral campaigns themselves—is through the control of media institutions. And indeed, research on the effects of Fox News in the US, along with the much broader media empire owned by billionaire Rupert Murdoch, demonstrates the effectiveness of such methods in shifting voter preferences (DellaVigna and Kaplan 2007; Martin and Yurukoglu 2017; Peck 2019). On a different note, personal control of media has been crucial to the career of certain wealthy politicians like Silvio Berlusconi. More indirectly, wealthy elites may also seek to generate a favorable ideological climate via donations to think tanks, universities, and other nonprofits (Giridharadas 2018; Leonard 2019; MacLean 2017; J. Mayer 2016; McGoey 2015; Page, Seawright, and Lacombe 2018). And again, such efforts can have dramatic ideological and behavioral effects—especially when they target specific groups, such as federal judges (Ash, Chen, and Naidu 2022; Teles 2012).

It must be acknowledged, however, that many media outlets, think tanks, and universities are not controlled directly by wealthy elites; and that—despite real biases (Usher 2021)—most of these institutions do not advance wealthy interests in such a direct way. As analysts of ideology have always insisted, rather, ideological power is rarely so straightforward. As I have emphasized in Chapter 2, our beliefs and preferences are intimately tied up with our social identities, which in turn are shaped by a deeply complex set of social cues and developmental processes. Wealthy elites do have outsized ability to shape those processes in ways that serve their interests, but their influence is not usually reflected in such crude interventions, and at times may not even be intentional. Careful study of specific cases can illuminate how particular people are induced to adopt beliefs and preferences that favor the interests of wealthy elites (e.g., Gaventa 1980; Hayward 2000), but it is difficult to generalize from those cases. Although ideological power is surely an important part of how wealthy elites ensure that state power serves their interests, therefore, I do not rely too heavily on any particular account of it.

In addition to these instrumental and ideological forms of power, finally, recent scholarship has also vindicated certain Marxist claims about the structural power possessed by those with highly concentrated wealth. Where earlier theorists posited implausibly uniform levels of structural power across all sectors and firms, however, more recent analysts typically aim to document variation in structural power, zeroing in on the specific contextual factors that generate structural power for certain businesses and firms but not others (Culpepper 2015). For instance, Hacker and Pierson (2002) have argued that the success of businesses in influencing social policy during the New Deal era depended on their relative capacity to make credible threats of exit—which varied between states at the start of the era, and declined sharply across the board as social policy transitioned from the state to the federal level. As the global mobility of capital has grown over the past half century, conversely, firms and even individuals have begun to make credible threats of exit from national states. This constitutes an increasingly important form of structural power, forcing governments to cater to the interests of extremely wealthy global elites through lax regulation and favorable tax policies (Dietsch 2015).

Short of leaving the country altogether, of course, those with access to concentrated wealth can also just withdraw investment capital from circulation, in response to government actions they dislike. Whether this sort of "capital strike" is understood as an explicit punishment or as a natural reaction from profit-oriented firms to an unfavorable business environment, it can be catastrophic for governments, and the credible threat of coordinated disinvestment can thus exert coercive pressure on governments. According to Young, Banerjee, and Schwartz (2018), in fact, such threats were actively deployed by financial interests in the wake of the 2008 crisis to ensure relatively favorable treatment from the Obama administration.

Beyond their ability to threaten withdrawal and exit, recent analysts have pointed to several other structural advantages possessed by the financial industry. According to Hindmoor and McGeechan (2013), for instance, banks considered "too big to fail" have an important form of structural power: because states are likely to bail them out rather than allowing them to go bankrupt, they are effectively insured against risk. Meanwhile, Larry Jacobs and Desmond King (2017) show that the US Federal Reserve Bank's tendency to privilege the interests of finance capital comes less from the instrumental efforts of particular actors, and more from the structural interests of the Fed itself, which depend upon a flourishing financial industry.

Though it is useful to analyze instrumental, ideological, and structural forms of power separately, the three are often tightly intertwined in practice. Instrumental power is used to promote certain ideologies, which in turn serve to protect instrumental power from challenge—and both can be deployed to create situations in which wealthy actors enjoy structural power. Weaving all three approaches together, for instance, Quinn Slobodian (2018) presents the global rise of neoliberalism as the result of a concerted effort by wealthy elites—with support from libertarian intellectuals—to prevent states from implementing capital controls and other policies that would weaken the structural power of capital. Their strategy, in short, was to evade democratic demands for such policies by moving rule-making to international institutions like the European Union, where capital-friendly policies could be made without direct democratic oversight, and then enforced by global superpowers (J. W. Mason 2018). Drawing freely upon the tools of both instrumental and ideological power, in other words, they successfully limited the ability of democratic states to make policies that would challenge the interests of capital owners, for instance by limiting capital mobility. And in doing so, they bolstered the structural power of those with concentrated wealth (see also Benvenisti 2016; Mattli and Buthe 2013).

What should we conclude from all this? In short, I argue that we should accept a moderated version of the claim made by Marxist state theorists: namely, that the social order anchored by modern democratic states decisively favors those with highly concentrated wealth. Though the severity of the problem varies, in other words, state capture by wealthy elites is a core problem facing all modern democracies—and fighting it should thus be a core priority everywhere.

Like all of the claims I make, this one is contestable. My own confidence in it, however, is as secure as anything I claim in this book. In terms of both the pattern of outcomes, and the range of mechanisms that could plausibly have generated them, the evidence of pervasive capture by wealthy elites is absolutely overwhelming. It is just too implausible to suppose that it somehow serves the public interest for a tiny global elite to command such astronomical fortunes while billions live in poverty and/or precarity. The more we examine the rules that structure the creation and preservation of that wealth, meanwhile, the clearer the diagnosis becomes. Whatever the best system might look like, we can say with absolute confidence that it is not the one we have: i.e., that the existing rules deviate severely from the genuine public interest. And while we may not know for certain which noninnocuous mechanisms are responsible for which deviations, there are more than enough plausible candidates that fit the bill.

Beyond affirming the existence of severe and pervasive capture by wealthy elites, however, I also draw a further inference from the evidence I have presented: namely, that without serious course corrections, things will only get worse. Against the expectation of gradually improving conditions set by NWW and A&R, that is, it appears that material inequality inaugurates a self-reinforcing downward spiral. As their material power continues to grow, that is, wealthy elites will be able to buy ever more political influence, which they will use to enact policies that further exacerbate inequality. And that is before we account for advances in automation and economies of scale (Cowen 2013), or the increasing prevalence of "winner-take-all" markets (Cook and Frank 2010), or the unequal distribution of climate burdens (Islam and Winkel 2017), or trends in the relative rates of interest and growth (Piketty 2014)—all of which will further exacerbate inequality. Some of these projections may turn out to be false, and there may be countervailing trends I have ignored, but on the whole, it seems clear that state capture by wealthy elites is not going anywhere—and, in all likelihood, is getting worse.

Still, this conclusion is importantly distinct from the more categorical claim of orthodox Marxist state theory: i.e., that modern states always and exclusively serve the interests of capital. This assertion not only fails to reckon with the fact that capitalists sometimes lose; it also creates an unhelpful binary between resignation and revolution, neither of which is very promising. We should not underestimate the difficulty of defeating concentrated wealth through democratic means, but as I illustrate in the chapters to follow, history shows us that it is not impossible. Recreating these victories under current conditions is perhaps the central imperative of our time.

5
Structuring Public Power
The Liberal Demands of Democracy

According to a common-sense, civics-class understanding of modern liberal democracy, its core institutions work together towards a common goal: enabling free and equal citizens to rule themselves on free and equal terms (Waldron 1987). The point of elections is to ensure that governments enact the will of the people, and the point of constitutional rules and procedures is to structure these decisions fairly. In particular, an array of liberal rights—including free speech, assembly, and so on—guarantee certain core individual freedoms, without which the resulting decisions could not be considered genuinely collective (Brettschneider 2010).

Other accounts, by contrast, stress the tensions between liberal and democratic principles (Mounk 2018). Where liberalism aspires to impartial governance by experts (Nichols 2017), prioritizing the protection of minority rights via constitutional limits on state power (Dworkin 1996), democracy valorizes popular participation and the wisdom of crowds (Landemore 2012, 2020), prioritizing the ability of majorities to implement popular policies (I. Shapiro 2016b). Where a depoliticizing liberalism may tend to generate elitism and inequality (A. Taylor 2020), on such accounts, democracy threatens to politicize too much (Jones 2020; Talisse 2019), inviting populism and majority tyranny (Galston 2018). While some take these tensions as an argument for prioritizing one of liberal democracy's two core components, others insist that the best system lies in a compromise—though it may be a fragile one—between the two.

This chapter presents a different view of the relation between liberalism and democracy, which in turn is grounded in a distinctive justification of the practices traditionally associated with each ideal. While acknowledging that there can be serious tensions in practice, on the one hand, I insist that the core demands of liberalism and democracy share the same underlying logic and purpose, and should not be seen as fundamentally contradictory impulses. Yet instead of conceiving their common aim in terms of self-rule, on the other hand, I argue that the value of many familiar liberal and democratic practices lies in their tendency to promote the public interest by protecting

The Dispersion of Power. Samuel Ely Bagg, Oxford University Press. © Samuel Ely Bagg (2024).
DOI: 10.1093/oso/9780192848826.003.0006

public power from capture. Insofar as they serve this goal, I endorse all such practices, incorporating them in a broader ideal of democracy as resisting state capture.

The concept of "state capture" incorporates an enormous range of different problems, and so our democratic toolkit—the practices we use to resist capture—must be similarly diverse. The rest of Part Two gives shape to this field of possibilities, elaborating six basic principles suggested by the imperative to resist state capture, and then outlining the distinctive ideal of democracy that emerges from combining them. This chapter explores three of these democratic demands—constitutionalism, competition, and universalism—that are often seen as "liberal," and are at least partly realized by many contemporary democracies. Chapter 6 turns to three more "radical" demands—anti-monopoly, countervailing power, and systemic redistribution—which are less commonly understood as requirements of democracy, and even more rarely realized in practice. Both sets of demands are summarized in Table 6.1, at the end of Chapter 6. Of course, nearly all of the practices I endorse in what follows have also been defended on other grounds, and it is not my intention to undermine all possible alternative justifications. Nevertheless, recasting these otherwise diverse practices as strategies for resisting state capture allows us to see them in a new and generative light. As I explore in Chapter 7, more specifically, what emerges is a distinctive political orientation that blends the most compelling elements of liberal and radical political thought—one that revolves around egalitarian competition as the most reliable method for resisting capture, and the dispersion of social and economic power as the most critical priority within existing liberal democracies.

5.1 Constitutionalism as a weapon against tyranny and domination

The political tradition that is perhaps most obviously and directly concerned with resisting the capture of state power is constitutionalism. On Sartori's (1962: 855) influential account, for instance, the aim of modern constitutions is to "restrict arbitrary power and ensure a 'limited government.'" A constitution's most direct concern must therefore be to limit abuse of public power, most prominently by subjecting officials to the rule of law and prohibiting certain tools of repression. If legal rules are known to everyone and apply equally to all, state actors will find it harder to manipulate the legal system to their benefit (Gowder 2016; Lovett 2016). Similarly, protections for freedom of speech, religion, assembly, and the press—as well as procedural legal rights—prevent politicians from using certain tactics that might help them entrench their rule (Levitsky and Ziblatt 2018). Yet clearly, such formal prohibitions against tyranny are only as good as the mechanisms by which they are enforced. In addition to its first-order concern with limiting the abuse of public power, then, the real core of constitutionalism is actually a second-order concern with structuring political, social, and economic power in ways that facilitate and incentivize this enforcement.

At minimum, a successful constitution must serve as a coordination device. When state actors try to overstep their bounds, in short, a sufficient number of people must be able to agree that a violation has occurred and settle on an appropriate response. By establishing certain legal norms and procedures as foundational, constitutions facilitate such coordination. Writing these rules down can make that easier, but it is not a necessary condition for an effective constitution: what matters is that everyone involved knows and accepts the same rules. To that end, a constitution's longevity and cultural embeddedness are crucial to its success—meaning that volatility tends to undermine the effectiveness of any constitution, and that even salutary changes to fundamental laws must be undertaken only with a substantial degree of caution.

That said, of course, mere coordination is not sufficient. In order to have democratic value, the norms and procedures entrenched by a constitution must actually serve to prevent tyranny and other forms of state capture. Yet constitutions can also have the opposite effect, serving to entrench the power of certain groups and factions over others. Especially notorious examples are the Chilean Constitution of 1980—designed by allies of the outgoing Pinochet dictatorship to protect the interests of wealthy elites—and the US Constitution—designed in part to protect the interests of Southern slaveholders. Even where constitutions are not intentionally designed to do so, however, they often end up favoring certain status quo interests. In addition to the reasons it gives us to be wary of reducing a constitution's effectiveness by revising it too often, in other words, the principle of constitutionalism also gives us reasons to revise those norms and procedures that clearly serve some factions and interests over others. Which of these reasons predominate in any particular case will be a matter of contextual judgment.

On my account, more broadly, the ultimate goal of constitutionalism is not to minimize state power, or otherwise preclude decisive action by public officials, as libertarians have sometimes claimed. Rather, the point of subjecting officials to the rule of law and other constraints is to enable pursuit of the public interest, by blocking the tools that powerful elites most often use to steer it off course. Similarly, the point of dividing power among different actors is not to frustrate the state's ability to act in a general way, but to ensure that these constraints on specific forms of abuse have force—and thereby, again, to facilitate publicly interested policy.

In the modern era, constitutional designers have typically sought to block the accumulation and abuse of concentrated power through political structures that divide power among different officials, ensuring that any given individual or institution can be "checked" by other formally institutionalized forces. Perhaps the archetypal practice of modern liberal constitutionalism, for instance, is the "separation of powers" among different branches of the government—usually legislative, administrative, and adjudicative (Calabresi, Berghausen, and Albertson 2012). Advanced by Enlightenment thinkers like Locke and Montesquieu, this division was embraced as key weapon against tyranny and arbitrary power by many subsequent reformers. Perhaps most influentially, James Madison argued that public officials in each branch would become attached to it, and thus guard its power jealously against encroachments from others.

Many critics have challenged this view. Given that Westminster systems seem to limit the abuse of public power despite combining legislative and administrative powers, for one, Philip Pettit (2013: 221) argues that the canonical accounts of Madison and others are overly cautious in demanding the separation of these functions. At the same time, he observes, they are likely not cautious enough in other respects: for instance, in their failure to demand the "separation of different branches of the armed and police forces … of secular from religious authorities, and … of political power from those in control of commerce and business" (2013: 222).

As Levinson and Pildes (2006) point out, meanwhile, Madison's influential account of how the separation of powers constrains public officials is also unpersuasive. In short, they argue, institutional loyalty may exert some sway over the actions of public officials, but it will often be outweighed by partisanship and other factional motivations. As such, they will be far less likely to check the excesses of those with whom they share partisan or factional goals. To the extent that separation of powers does seem to serve as a check on powerful officials, therefore, this is largely because it facilitates the distribution of state power among different parties or factions. And as parliamentary systems demonstrate, this "separation of parties" may be institutionalized in many ways: for instance, by carving out official positions for members of opposition groups in institutions such as the legislature, the courts, the military, and the bureaucracy.

In addition to the political structures emphasized by modern constitutionalists, finally, many pre-modern thinkers understood social and economic structures as central concerns of constitutionalism, and as crucial to the ability of a constitutional scheme to successfully limit tyrannical abuses of power. As Camila Vergara (2020) shows, for instance, many ancient and medieval thinkers advanced a "materialist" form of constitutionalism, according to which different branches of government would be associated with and accountable to different social classes. Because each class had its own distinct material interests, they argued, the frictional tensions between them would motivate resistance to the tyranny of any particular faction.

Indeed, these materialist assumptions were still dominant in constitutional thinking through the time of Montesquieu. It is only with later reformers like Madison—who sought to make all branches accountable to the same generic body of "the people"—that the formal separation of powers shed its substantive, material basis in class interests (see also MacGilvray 2021; Wootton 2006). Madison's dictum that "ambition must be made to counteract ambition" is thus importantly distinct from Montesquieu's formula that "power must check power": only the latter implies a balance of substantive interests or material powers.

How might such a substantive balance of powers, grounded in shared interests rather than formal institutional allegiances, be attained in a contemporary context? Vergara and others have advocated a return to explicitly materialist forms of constitutionalism, through class-based institutions modeled on pre-modern exemplars like the Roman tribunate (Hamilton 2014; McCormick 2011), or more modern analogues such as workers' councils (Muldoon 2018, 2020). Many of these proposals are intriguing, and as we shall see, they have inspired my own thinking about institutional reform. Under modern conditions of constantly evolving economic structures, however, it seems to me that enshrining fixed class distinctions in fundamental law is not the best way to create balance between contending interests (see Bagg 2022a).

In a sense, much of the rest of this book is an attempt to outline a more promising set of strategies for achieving this goal. And it begins with the insight that it is not separation of powers, per se, which enables constitutions to resist state capture, but rather competition between relatively equally situated powers, each of which is reliably invested in checking its rivals' power. In other words, the best way to encourage coordination on a system of rules that constrain the concentration and abuse of public power is to facilitate vigorous competition between comparably powerful coalitions with interests in sustaining that system of mutual constraint. As such, competition is the second of the six core democratic principles I discuss, and it plays a crucial role in the rest of my analysis.

5.2 Competition as a weapon against concentration and entrenchment

Competitive practices are democratically valuable—when they are—because they tend to undermine the concentration and entrenchment of political, social, and economic power. Most basically, well-structured competitive environments ensure that dominant actors within a given realm are subject to open contestation from forces with the capacity and incentive to oppose them. This prevents those dominant actors from further entrenching their power in illegitimate ways—by concealing genuine conflicts, for instance, or by undermining potential opponents. It thereby ensures that their ability to maintain their position is at least somewhat contingent upon their willingness to use that position in service of genuine public interests.

Most obviously, this is what explains the value of electoral competition between organized political parties, which is widely recognized as an indispensable element of modern democracy. Though each of these competing parties might prefer to rule without constraint, in short, functioning democratic systems are characterized by an equilibrium in which no party seriously attempts to do so (Przeworski 2005, 2018). Given the institutionalized uncertainty provided by regular elections and well-organized opposition parties, that is, no ruling party will be able to guarantee success in a hypothetical attempt to grab unilateral power. So long as their opponents will face the same incentives when they come to power, therefore, all parties can credibly commit to respect election results and abide by other constraints.

Chapter 8 explores this argument, and its limitations, in greater depth. For now, however, let us accept that political competition between well-balanced parties or coalitions can often sustain broad allegiance to constraints on the concentration and abuse of state power. In addition, of course, many have argued that it can also incentivize leaders to serve the public interest through their policy choices (I. Shapiro 2016b). So long as they must compete for the political allegiance and social backing of ordinary people, incumbent elites will never be secure. Facing challenges to their power from opponents with strong incentives to expose their misdeeds, the theory goes, they will offer public goods and minimize extraction.

As I have shown in previous chapters, this pluralist narrative has serious flaws. Especially on low-salience issues, wealthy elites will reliably be able to use their outsized private power and organizational capacity to ensure states favor their interests. Similarly, elite competition does little to erode privileges based on categorical differences and perpetuated by decentralized means—including those of race, caste, ethnicity, gender, and so on. Still, the pluralists are not all wrong: even resolute skeptics like Achen and Bartels (2016) acknowledge that electoral competitiveness has some effect on the behavior of officials.

Meanwhile, elections are not the only form of political competition that can help to prevent state capture. Competition between jurisdictions, for instance, enables people to discipline leaders through explicit or implicit threats of "exit" (Warren 2011). As noted in the previous chapter, the outsized ability of wealthy elites to employ this tool—by threatening to withdraw capital if their demands are not met—is a key example of their "structural" power. When wielded by disempowered groups or a broader public, however, threats of mass exit can also discipline state actors in countervailing ways, helping to keep state action tethered to genuine public interests. In the United States, for instance, federalism has clearly supported white supremacy on balance (Mickey 2015; Robertson 2012), but it has also facilitated certain countervailing trends, such as Black outmigration from Southern states (Somin 2020). While the fractionalization of metropolitan governance is a key mechanism for the perpetuation of race and class inequality, similarly, it is also true that—under the right conditions—competition between jurisdictions can induce public officials to attract resources and migrants to their community by providing public goods (R. S. Taylor 2017). Thus, political "decentralization" can neither be celebrated nor condemned universally (see also Levy 2007).

Indeed, the same is true of all forms of competition. In particular, two key factors determine whether competition will serve to prevent or facilitate state capture: (a) whether its stakes and methods are reliably limited; and (b) whether it is conducted on relatively egalitarian terms.

First, there must be reliable constraints on both the stakes of competition and the adversarial methods that are employed, so as to prevent the sort of destructive arms races—both figurative and literal—that can ultimately undermine competitive practices themselves. Competition is the *raison d'être* of sports, for instance, but if there were no rules against doping and other dangerous adversarial behaviors, it would be impossible for participants to remain competitive without engaging in them, and the result would be a "race to the bottom" that is harmful to all. Similarly, adversarial tactics in the electoral sphere are democratically valuable only when they remain within certain bounds (Bagg and Tranvik 2019; Schedler 2021). At the limit, violent conflict tends to leave the victorious party with unlimited power over the losers, and so the descent of political competition into political violence is almost always harmful to broader democratic goals (Frazer and Hutchings 2019). Indeed, overstepping such limits on acceptable adversarial tactics can often weaken or eliminate competitive practices altogether—meaning that without those limits, competitive practices may become self-undermining.

Second, there must be relative parity among the competitors themselves, as well as among the relevant judges—i.e., the third parties empowered to determine the "winners," whose favor participants must attract. If some competitors have permanent, decisive advantages, on the one hand, adversarial processes will not check their accumulation of power, and may become self-undermining. When an elected party uses power achieved through fair competition to rewrite the rules in ways that entrench its control over political institutions, for instance, it limits the competitiveness of those institutions, and weakens their tendency to resist capture (Issacharoff 2010; Issacharoff and Pildes 1998; Pildes 1999). If certain groups are better able to influence the outcome and determine which competitors are victorious, on the other hand, the results will be reliably biased in their favor, rather than reflecting a broad or pluralistic public interest. The benefits of electoral competition are undermined, for instance, if suffrage is limited to certain categories of people, and the results of jurisdictional competition will favor those with more resources for withdrawal or relocation. Competition may not be immediately or directly self-undermining in such cases, but its benefits will be distributed unequally—and this, we shall see, may contribute indirectly to the attenuation of competition over time.

These same conditions apply when evaluating competitive practices outside of the political realm. By ensuring that both sides in a dispute are represented by qualified advocates with strong incentives to present the best possible legal arguments for their side, for instance, the adversarial structure of civil and criminal trials in Anglo-American legal systems is often thought to minimize certain pathologies associated with inquisitorial systems (Fuller 1978; Luban 1988: 67–103). As a general matter, this logic is sound: as I argued in Chapter 3's discussion of participatory inclusion, open contestation is often the best way to guard against biases that are concealed by more deliberative or consensual approaches (see also Medearis 2015; Mouffe 2000). Indeed, I draw upon similar concerns below to suggest that adversarial processes could help prevent capture and corruption in the administrative state (see also Cain 2011; Rahman 2016). In either context, however, competition will fail to achieve its democratic aims if there are great disparities between adversaries (Agmon 2021; Stark 2019; Wertheimer 1988), or if certain groups have outsized power to determine the outcome (Wagner 2013).

As is widely acknowledged, similarly, a pluralistic civil society—featuring a diverse range of voluntary organizations, media outlets, academic institutions, social groupings, and religious denominations—seems to be a crucial background condition for the enforcement of limitations on the accumulation and abuse of concentrated power (Levy 2015). Indeed, its importance goes far beyond facilitating the proverbial "marketplace of ideas": a flourishing and pluralistic civil society is perhaps even more crucial for its material role in ensuring that opposition groups have access to a variety of independent organizational resources in coordinating resistance to incumbent abuses (Levitsky and Ziblatt 2018; Shklar 1989). More broadly, it constrains the ability of dominant political and economic forces to fully control social and cultural narratives, and helps citizens develop habits of participation and collective action that are transferable to more explicitly political contexts (Havel 1985). Yet if certain groups can set the terms of this pluralistic competition—due either to their dominant position among competitors, or their outsized ability to determine the results—this will limit its genuine democratic potential.

Especially critical to my account, finally, is the complex democratic role of markets. The most common justifications for economic competition tend to argue that it is necessary to generate rising living standards, scientific progress, social development, and other "first-order" goals. Given my focus on "second-order" structural concerns, however, I set those arguments aside. Instead, I argue, the most powerful democratic argument for relatively open markets has to do with their unpredictable effects on elite fortunes, as explained in Chapter 4.

Simply put, there is a great deal of evidence that when the major productive assets in an economy remain fixed, the conditions are ripe for a small coterie of elites to monopolize nearly all economic and political power. This includes economies based on land—the most important economic resource in most pre-capitalist economies—as well as those based on oil and other natural resources, which have long been associated with authoritarian government (Robinson, Torvik, and Verdier 2006; Wenar 2016). In such contexts, we have seen, elites are typically able to capture the vast majority of economic rents, distribute them as necessary to ensure the support of a ruling coalition, and prevent anyone else from amassing enough independent power to pose a challenge from the outside (North, Wallis, and Weingast 2009).

By contrast, open and dynamic economies cannot be managed so easily, because creative destruction redistributes economic rents in unpredictable ways. This disruption can destabilize elite coalitions and shift significant economic power to novel challengers, who then have both means and motivation to contest any social, religious, and political distinctions that reinforce the dominance of the ruling coalition. Classically, for instance, the commercial bourgeoisie played a crucial role in the liberalizing revolutions of the eighteenth and nineteenth centuries (Hobsbawm 1962)—using its newfound economic might to demand the eradication of feudal hierarchies—and is often credited with driving democratization more generally (Ansell and Samuels 2014; Moore 1966). And the lessons of this well-known case can easily be generalized: in an open and dynamic economy, the distribution of power is never entirely fixed or predictable, and this creates opportunities for political dynamism as well. Where stasis nearly always favors existing elites, rapid social and economic change creates critical junctures of open-ended possibility.

As in other realms, however, this endorsement of economic competition must be seriously qualified. A significant degree of market competition is necessary for sustaining a dynamic economic system, and thus for preventing certain actors and groups from monopolizing control over all of the important levers of power in society. To the extent that competitors violate certain rules or exploit pervasive structural advantages, however, market competition will fail to generate democratic consequences, and may even prove self-undermining over the long run. As actors and groups with greater resources find ways to burden their less fortunate competitors or lock them out entirely, they will reduce the intensity of market discipline, and will face fewer checks on their attempts to accumulate power. Unless they are prevented from doing so by forces external to "the market"—which is, of course, always constructed by "external" forces in the first place (Hale 1952; Polanyi 1944)—those with concentrated economic power will reliably attempt to strangle open competition; using their outsized resources to skew the playing field for subsequent competition in their favor. No less than other forms of competition, then, economic markets must be carefully structured in order to serve democratic ends.

Where constitutionalism is concerned with limiting opportunities for abuse of power, in sum, competition is essential for sustaining and enforcing these limits. Across political, legal, social, and economic realms, practices of constrained and egalitarian competition can obstruct the concentration of power and the entrenchment of advantage, and they belong at the center of our democratic imagination. Yet competition is not always constrained and egalitarian, and even when it starts off that way, these features often degrade over time. Just as competition was required to sustain constitutionalism, therefore, additional tools are required to ensure that competition serves democratic ends. In fact, this search for effective restraints on competition gives rise to all four of the remaining democratic demands that fill out the ideal of resisting state capture—including universalism, the last of the traditionally "liberal" demands discussed in this chapter, as well as all three of the more "radical" demands discussed in the next. As I explore in Chapter 7, indeed, the overarching theme of these democratic demands is the pursuit and maintenance of egalitarian competition, as the surest method for resisting capture.

5.3 Universalism as a weapon against exclusion and manipulation

The most basic assumption of a great deal of modern moral and political theory is that all humans possess some form of rational agency, moral autonomy, or dignity, which renders them deserving of equal moral concern, equal political respect, equal social recognition, and various other forms of equal treatment (Waldron 1987). Depending on what is conceived as essential to the human "agent" or "subject," these common characteristics are said to ground many of the universalist practices of egalitarian liberalism—including the universalization of legal and political rights that used to belong to a privileged few, as well as the commitment to procedural neutrality embodied in ideals of secularism, meritocracy, public deliberation, and beyond.

Despite the undeniable moral progress that is reflected in the adoption of these universalist practices, however, diverse forms of social and humanistic inquiry have illustrated that they are not always benign—especially when they are justified with reference to a specific account of human agency or subjectivity. For centuries, such accounts were used to justify the exclusion of women, racial minorities, the disabled, and many other groups, on the grounds that they lacked this essential human capacity (Phillips 2021). Even as such groups have gradually been admitted to the ranks of those deserving equal treatment, meanwhile, the ostensibly neutral practices they gain access to—which are still commonly justified with reference to the same specific accounts of human agency or subjectivity—have functioned in subtler ways to maintain their subordination (I. M. Young 1990). Most fundamentally, critics have long raised doubts about the very existence of a universal form of human agency or subjectivity—of the sort that could offer ontological grounding for universalist practices—and in recent years, these doubts have received substantial support from convergent developments in the biological sciences (Bagg 2018b, 2021a; see also Connolly 2002; Frost 2016; Meehan 2017; Thiele 2006).

Following up these claims would take us much too far afield for our purposes in this book, and one need not accept them in order to follow my arguments here. The reason for bringing them up is simply to highlight that the justification of universalist practices I provide in this section is distinct from such traditional accounts, and thus not vulnerable to the same critiques. For one, I argue, universal rights and guarantees can serve to obstruct dangerous forms of political manipulation that elites could otherwise use to entrench their power. Even if we doubt that they can be grounded in a universal account of human agency or subjectivity, then, many rights still deserve robust endorsement on democratic grounds. Even if complete neutrality is impossible, similarly, I argue that universalist aspirations for impartiality—as reflected in practices like public deliberation and bureaucratic independence, as well as the standards of reason, merit, truth, and efficiency such practices require—can nonetheless limit particularistic abuses of public power in many contexts. Rather than depicting universalist practices as absolute moral requirements arising from an essentialist conception of human agency, in short, my account frames them as pragmatic tools for resisting specific forms of state capture (see Bagg 2021a for more discussion).

Perhaps the most obvious way that universalist practices protect public power from capture is by removing certain levers of manipulation from the toolkit of elites (see also Sabl 2017). In societies without the sort of universal rights and guarantees associated with liberal democracy, elites can use their discretion over the distribution of important resources and opportunities to entrench their power in dangerous ways—either by hoarding such resources for themselves and their allies, or by distributing them conditionally to create dependent clients. In this context, the most important function of universal rights and guarantees is to eliminate this discretionary power, and thus limit the ability of elites to secure their position through particularistic favors. Where "extractive" institutions enable elites to apportion rents among cronies and allies, in short, "inclusive" institutions take away this discretion by guaranteeing certain public goods to all.

This logic is at the core of Chapter 8, where I articulate the real but limited value of basic electoral institutions, in dialogue with various critiques and alternatives. Perhaps most prominent among these interlocutors is a group of "epistocrats" who have defended epistemic qualifications on the franchise, on the grounds that they would lead to better decisions (D. A. Bell 2015; Brennan 2016; López-Guerra 2014). Most defenders of democracy have responded by denying one of the epistocrats' two key premises: i.e., that suffrage restrictions could produce better decisions (Bhatia 2020; Landemore 2012), and that such instrumental concerns should carry the day (Christiano 2008; Kolodny

2014b; Viehoff 2014). By contrast, I accept both premises, relying instead on pragmatic concerns about the dangers of elite manipulation.

Even if certain deviations from a universality rule could conceivably bring about better decisions, in short, I argue that the risks of allowing such deviations are too high. Some age restriction is probably inevitable, but insofar as any adult citizens are denied the franchise, the criteria for doing so will reliably be manipulated by incumbents in ways that entrench their power. This, in turn, will facilitate the evasion of other constraints, and ultimately pave the way for more extreme forms of capture, tyranny, and domination. Crude as it is, a hard-and-fast universality rule is the only way to eliminate these dangers, and thus to ensure the long-term stability of the practices of constitutionalism and competition I have already examined.

As noted, I will address the nuances and implications of this argument in Chapter 8, where I examine it in greater detail. For now, we can simply note that similar concerns apply rather straightforwardly to other legal and political rights, such as the right to a fair trial, or rights to speech and assembly. To the extent that any deviations from universality are allowed in determining the distribution and application of these rights, some elite faction will inevitably use this leeway to burden opponents and entrench their power. And again, the only way to prevent this is a simple universality rule that guarantees political rights to all adult citizens.

With some qualifications, a similar logic can even be extended to a much broader range of social rights and public services. In particular, universal public provision of services such as education and healthcare reduces the ability of elites to use them as bargaining chips, inducing dependence from clients. When distributing goods and services, of course, there may be very good reasons to target the people who need them most—and the dangers of doing so are likely less severe. Meanwhile, universality cannot prevent manipulation entirely: the management of public services like education and healthcare requires significant discretion, and will therefore be susceptible to some degree of capture wherever they exist. Unlike with political rights, therefore, targeted (rather than universal) provision of public goods and services may be the best available option in certain cases. Nevertheless, giving public officials discretion over recipients always creates risks of clientelism and corruption. All else equal, then, universality is preferable: not because everyone always deserves equal allocations, but—as with suffrage—because a hard-and-fast universality rule limits opportunities for political manipulation. And as I explore in Chapter 9, the overall benefits of universal provision will often outweigh the costs.

Generalizing even further, the democratic function of universality rules extends far beyond the distribution of rights and privileges by the state: a similar logic also justifies many practices aspiring to publicity and impartiality. In previous chapters, I have shown how many ostensibly "neutral" procedures—including deliberative reason-giving—can serve in practice to conceal capture by hegemonic groups. When recast as tools for resisting specific types of particularistic manipulation, however, such practices have important roles to play in a democratic ecology.

Even if public discourse can never be fully neutral, reasonable, or free of power relations, for one, effective enforcement of deliberative norms can still limit the ability of powerful actors to conceal self-interested motivations or bend the truth to suit their aims. By subjecting political claims to robust public scrutiny according to certain universalist norms of discourse, therefore, a healthy public sphere (or "deliberative system") can obstruct certain prominent mechanisms for achieving and legitimizing state capture (Elster 1999; Hayward 2021; Schimmelfennig 2001). As I explore in Chapter 9, meanwhile, carefully structured mini-publics using similar standards can generate judgments about certain issues that are relatively free from certain biases—especially when participants are chosen at random.

Even if there is no such thing as a purely impartial interpretation of historical events, legal doctrine, administrative policy, or a candidate's qualifications for office, similarly, widespread adherence to common standards can still serve to limit the scope for self-serving manipulation in all of these domains. More specifically, norms developed by independent communities of journalists, scholars, lawyers, and other professionals can limit the flexibility possessed by public officials in narrating events, applying the law, and staffing ostensibly independent institutions like the judiciary and bureaucracy. When these norms are well enforced, therefore, public officials will have fewer tools for entrenching their power by structuring political, social, and economic competition in ways that favor their private or factional interests. In sum, judicial and bureaucratic independence—along with the professional standards necessary to sustain that independence—can facilitate the implementation of procedurally legitimate public aims.

As we saw with constitutional rules, achieving coordination on shared standards of any kind serves to constrain public officials, and doing so has democratic value for that reason alone. As with constitutional rules, however, any such standards also privilege certain interests over others, and must therefore be subject to contestation. For instance, deliberation is at least aspirationally governed by norms of impartiality and public reason that have long been criticized by theorists of race, gender, and multiculturalism for multiplying the advantages of certain privileged worldviews and subject positions (Sanders 1997; C. Taylor 1992; I. M. Young 1990). In many contexts, similarly, legal interpretation and policy implementation are driven by ostensibly neutral standards of efficiency, which in fact grant disproportionate weight to wealthy interests (Berman 2023; Britton-Purdy et al. 2020; Kapczynski 2011; Liscow 2018).

Even as we recognize the very real biases embedded in these standards, however, we should not forget that those who are most disadvantaged by them would likely be even worse off if officials were not accountable to any common standards whatsoever. Given the flexibility this would grant powerful actors in their efforts to interpret and shape the world to their advantage, we have at least some reason to be wary of undermining well-enforced public norms of any kind. Yet neither can we afford to keep systematically biased standards closed to contestation. Rather, those who seek to advance democratic goals should aim to diminish whichever biases appear most pressing, while simultaneously remaining alert to the dangers of completely destabilizing all common standards, and eschewing any claim to final or complete neutrality.

As with all of the democratic demands I articulate, in other words, applying the principle of universalism in practice will require a healthy dose of contextual judgment. What I have shown, however, is that despite the real biases unearthed by critics of liberal universalism, many universalistic practices can serve to obstruct particularistic manipulation, and thus belong in the democratic toolkit. In the context of this chapter, meanwhile, I have shown that the demands of constitutionalism and competition must be supplemented by those of universalism for precisely the same reason they are valuable in the first place: under the right circumstances, that is, all work together to protect public power from capture by various factions and elites.

At the same time as it allows us to appreciate the genuine democratic value of these three core liberal principles, however, the framework of resisting state capture also gives us the resources we need to recognize their limitations. In particular, universalist practices such as equal suffrage and bureaucratic independence can limit the contamination of public life by asymmetries in private power—as liberals such as Michael Walzer (1983, 1984) have argued—and are valuable for that reason. Yet they cannot prevent such contamination altogether. As long as some groups retain outsized private power and organizational capacity, they will always find ways to influence public power to their advantage. While liberal strategies for containing the public impact of private inequalities are a crucial part of the democratic toolkit, therefore, they do not exhaust it: we must also find ways to undermine those inequalities more directly.

In a word, that is my principal objection to standard liberal views of democracy. Such views suggest three core principles for structuring public power—constitutionalism, competition, and universalism—and contrary to what certain radicals have suggested, all three of them really are necessary for democracy. Yet they are also insufficient, on their own, for resisting the many forms of state capture that are enabled by vast background inequalities in private power, and at times can even be deployed in ways that exacerbate those inequalities. If the competition for public power that is constitutive of modern politics is to serve the public interest, it must not only be confined to certain peaceful and regulated channels, it must also take place on genuinely egalitarian terms. In order to articulate a truly comprehensive democratic ideal, therefore—one that protects public power from all forms of capture— we must supplement a liberal commitment to fair structures of public power with a coequal commitment to more radical methods of dispersing private power. In addition to the impartial tools of universalism, that is, making competition genuinely egalitarian also requires certain tools of corrective partiality. That is the explicit goal of the practices of anti-monopoly, countervailing power, and systemic redistribution, which I explore in the next chapter.

6
Dispersing Private Power
The Radical Demands of Democracy

Liberal democracies blessed with robust constitutionalism, vigorous electoral competition, and universal inclusion in impartial procedures have achieved something distinctly valuable and impressive. In short, they have tamed the competition for public power that is constitutive of modern politics—forcing it into constrained and formally egalitarian institutions, and thus limiting the most destructive forms of state capture. Yet celebrating this achievement should not prevent us from recognizing the pervasive forms of capture that remain, and even thrive, in liberal democracies. The problem, quite simply, is that some groups still have overwhelming advantages in private power and organizational capacity, which enables them to exert outsized influence on public power in the diverse ways surveyed in Chapter 4. Though constrained and formally egalitarian, in other words, competition for public power is still conducted on profoundly unequal terms. In addition to the liberal methods of structuring public power explored in the previous chapter, a comprehensive democratic agenda must also include radical strategies of corrective partiality, in order to ensure greater balance in the organizational capacity of different groups.[1] This chapter examines three distinct ways of pursuing this goal.

Through practices of *anti-monopoly*, first, democratic actors must directly constrain the most likely perpetrators of capture—i.e., those actors and groups with the most concentrated private power—by attacking their power resources and undermining their ability to coordinate. Through practices of *countervailing power*, second, democratic actors must also ensure these dangerous actors and groups face well-organized and well-resourced opposition in their efforts to capture public power—most notably by strengthening the organizational capacity of those with the least concentrated private power.

---

[1] Note that this does not entail a demand for *equality* in organizational capacity among all groups—nor even all groups of the same size or type. However we chose to define the appropriate reference class, for one, it is unclear that enforcing precise equality among such groups would be desirable on the whole. Moreover, precise measurements of categories such as private power and organizational capacity are both impossible and unnecessary for making practical judgments. As such, the demand for "some measure of balance" is *negative* and *directional* in character: i.e., the point is to reduce the most severe and consequential inequalities in organizational capacity, not to achieve perfect or precise equality.

The Dispersion of Power. Samuel Ely Bagg, Oxford University Press. © Samuel Ely Bagg (2024).
DOI: 10.1093/oso/9780192848826.003.0006

Third and finally, democratic actors must also enact a more general *systemic redistribution* of private power resources.

To some extent, standard liberal accounts already recognize the need for such correctives. Nearly all democratic theorists support limits on the ability of wealthy actors to spend unlimited amounts of money on elections, for instance, which is a rudimentary form of anti-monopoly. Recognizing the value of countervailing power, meanwhile, nearly all democratic systems institutionalize the power of opposition parties in some way. In the spirit of systemic redistribution, finally, nearly all democracies also enact some form of social insurance and public education in the hope of equalizing opportunities. Yet these standard liberal remedies are profoundly inadequate for addressing the pervasive forms of capture described in Chapter 4. In order to tackle these problems at their root—i.e., in the vast asymmetries of private power that characterize all modern democracies—practices of anti-monopoly, countervailing power, and systemic redistribution must be radically expanded, explicitly tasked with altering the distribution of private power, and regarded as core elements of democracy.

Implementing such corrective partiality entails its own challenges. In particular, policies intended to achieve downwards redistribution of power may be co-opted by the powerful and used to redistribute upwards instead. For instance, antitrust laws designed to undermine the organizational capacity of those with concentrated economic power have often been deployed to obstruct labor organizing and other forms of coordination among subordinate market actors (Paul 2020). Recall, however, that similar risks afflict *all* state policy: in practice, even facially "neutral" laws often serve partial interests. As I explore in Chapter 9, meanwhile, these dangers can be mitigated through careful democratic design. For now, I set such worries aside.

In what follows, I also take for granted my substantive judgment, discussed in Chapter 4, that the most pervasive forms of capture in nearly every democracy are perpetrated either by wealthy elites or the beneficiaries of categorical inequalities. In illustrating what anti-monopoly, countervailing power, and systemic redistribution might look like in practice, therefore, my main examples are practices directed at resisting capture by these groups. As before, however, my hope is that even readers who dissent from this kind of substantive judgment will still find my theoretical framework useful in organizing their own commitments. Though they may disagree about which groups pose the greatest threats of capture, in other words, such readers should recognize that *some* forms of corrective partiality are required for resisting them.

6.1 Anti-monopoly as a weapon against concentrated private power

The term "anti-monopoly" came to prominence in the late nineteenth-century United States, when it served as the unifying slogan for a coalition of scholars, activists, and Progressive politicians—as well as large numbers of ordinary people—who sought to weaken the vice grip of big business on social and political life. In their view, laissez-faire competition alone was unable to whittle away the massive corporate profits and other elite rents that characterized Gilded Age society. Companies like Standard Oil in the US, and Thyssen in Germany, wielded unprecedented power over life and politics in industrialized countries. And far from reining in those excesses, the nascent administrative state seemed to support them: as Progressive observers such as Louis Brandeis noted, in fact, monopolies and oligopolies seemed to be growing more common, more entrenched, and more tightly integrated with state power. Where many critics of concentrated private power turned to state ownership and control as the only hope for a more egalitarian solution, others proposed that a more promising role for the state might be to actively level the playing field (Stoller 2019). Perhaps the most prominent expression of this position was the common demand to break up the largest firms into smaller parts. In two crucial ways, however, the broader spirit of anti-monopoly went beyond what has now become known as antitrust or competition policy.

First, Progressive visions of anti-monopoly implied hostility not just towards market power in the traditional sense—i.e., the ability of a seller to set prices without losing buyers—but also towards many other forms of economic power that firms and other private actors might have.[2] Indeed, many Progressives were suspicious of concentrated private power as such (Rahman 2016). As they observed, anyone who has such power will sooner or later be tempted to use it to entrench their dominant position, by inducing officials to enact favorable policies. If we wait for them to be caught in explicit acts of corruption, it will often be too late to stop them, because they will have already amassed enough power to escape the consequences. We should therefore regard highly concentrated private power as dangerous for democracy, in and of itself.

---

[2] As Suresh Naidu (2020) points out, for instance, firms might have bargaining power—"shares of relationship-specific economic value appropriated by different agents"—and short-side power—the "credible threat of unilaterally terminating" the economic relationship, as well as the various powers afforded directly by wealth.

Notice that many practices of constitutionalism are justified on similar grounds: i.e., that first-order constraints on the abuse of power can only be sustained through second-order limits on the concentration of power more generally. Where modern constitutionalism aims primarily to limit the concentration of *public* power, however, the anti-monopoly tradition follows earlier materialist forms of constitutionalism in viewing the concentration of *private* power as equally dangerous (Andrias 2015; Fishkin and Forbath 2014; Khan 2018). After all, problems of capture arise not from the existence of public power as such, but from its relationship to private interests.

Second, breaking up large firms was not the only way Progressive anti-monopoly advocates sought to constrain concentrated private power. Depending on the industry and other contextual factors, they also endorsed many other regulatory mechanisms for structuring competition to achieve outcomes in the public interest (Novak 2019). In the case of railroads and other firms that provide key infrastructure, for instance, regulators might treat them as common carriers or public utilities, preventing them from exploiting sellers who depend on them to transport goods to market. And while direct state control should not be the default, they argued, it might be the best option in cases where market competition cannot be structured to serve the public interest.

For both of these reasons, the expansive visions of anti-monopoly developed by Progressive thinkers contrast sharply with dominant contemporary approaches to antitrust and competition policy. Like many other areas of law, for instance, antitrust regulation was heavily shaped by the law and economics movement in the late twentieth century (Teles 2012), and the now standard reading holds that its only legitimate purpose is to protect consumers from high prices (Bork 1978; Director and Levi 1956).[3] As long as concentrated market power can be said to benefit consumers in some way, it is thought, regulators have no reason to interfere.

Even by this narrow consumer welfare standard, however, US regulators have likely been underenforcing antitrust law for decades, generating steadily increasing market concentration across many sectors (De Loecker, Eeckhout, and Unger 2020; Elhauge 2016; Philippon 2019; Wollmann 2019). As we have seen, more importantly, consumer welfare as such was never the primary concern of the Progressive architects of antitrust policy to begin with (Leslie 2013). The "curse of bigness" (Brandeis 1913) might sometimes be reflected in inflated prices, of course, but as anti-monopoly

---

[3] My narrative here draws largely from the US case, but a similarly narrow understanding of the purpose of competition law is also dominant in most other jurisdictions around the world (Gerber 2019).

advocates understood, market concentration could also undermine economic dynamism in a variety of less obvious ways. Even more crucially, economic actors with concentrated private power have strong incentives to shape the legal environment in their favor, initiating a vicious cycle of ratcheting political and economic capture (Pitofsky 1978; Schwartz 1979). Under the neoliberal ascendancy of the last half-century, unfortunately, these broader concerns often dropped out of the regulatory picture entirely (Grewal and Purdy 2014).

That said, a broader vision of anti-monopoly has recently received renewed attention from legal scholars (Britton-Purdy et al. 2020), and is even beginning to gain traction among some public officials—both in the United States, where the anti-monopoly tradition has the deepest roots (Klobuchar 2021; Lynn 2011; McCabe 2020), and also, increasingly, in Europe (Fox 2019; Kampourakis 2021). This includes calls to strengthen enforcement of existing antitrust law, but like their Progressive antecedents, recent anti-monopoly advocates have also articulated a much broader menu of policy tools (Khan 2019; Naidu, Posner, and Weyl 2018; Rahman 2016; Teachout 2020; Wu 2017, 2018). Just like railroad companies in the late nineteenth century, for instance, giant technology firms like Amazon, Google, and Facebook now wield nearly absolute control over critical elements of contemporary market infrastructure, serving as "platforms" for a vast number of other firms (Culpepper and Thelen 2020; Khan 2016). And as with the railroads, many argue, regulating them as common carriers or public utilities will often be a more promising way to restore the competitiveness of markets, rather than breaking them up into smaller pieces (Novak 2019; Rahman 2018a, 2018b).

Of course, this revival of Progressive approaches to antitrust and market regulation is only one facet of a much wider contemporary effort to place the problem of concentrated economic power back on the political agenda. Spurred partly by the 2008 financial crisis, concerns about *absolute* poverty have increasingly been supplanted by attention to *relative* inequalities (Moyn 2018: 212–220; Purdy and Grewal 2017)—and especially to the *political* influence of those with highly concentrated wealth. This focus on "plutocrats," "oligarchs," and "the 1 percent" also reflects anti-monopoly thinking in the broad sense—i.e., as a demand for corrective partiality, focused on constraining those at the top—and it suggests another crucial set of anti-monopoly practices.

Where antitrust and other forms of market regulation deal primarily with corporations, the broader principle of anti-monopoly, as I understand it, also entails constraining those *individuals* with the most concentrated private power (see also Robeyns 2017, 2022). Most obviously, this means targeting their material power resources directly, through sharply progressive taxation of income (Avi-Yonah 2002), inheritance, and wealth (Dietsch and Rixen 2016; Piketty 2014; Saez and Zucman 2019)—endeavors whose success depends, in turn, on transparency requirements, capital controls, and other complementary reforms.

In any particular society, meanwhile, there will be a complex maze of context-specific legal rules and social structures that serve to protect extreme concentrations of wealth, which must be addressed through a similarly complex series of context-specific policies—such as limiting the tools of wealth defense (Winters 2017), constraining executive pay (Bebchuk and Fried 2003), and upending the diverse array of regulatory regimes that enact "upward redistribution" (e.g., Lindsey and Teles 2017). At a more abstract level, finally, any reform that lowers the rate of return on capital, relative to the overall level of economic growth, will reduce the advantages of those whose income comes primarily from capital. To the extent that certain kinds of capital are disproportionately held by the wealthiest actors, meanwhile, reducing the relative rates of return on those forms of capital will also limit the advantages of those at the very top.

Of course, the threats posed by very powerful individuals are hardly unique to the modern era, and historically, societies have employed a wide range of mechanisms for mitigating these dangers (Kramm and Robeyns 2020). Prominent among these is the ancient Athenian practice of ostracism—through which ordinary citizens could vote to expel anyone they judged had accumulated too much private power, on the grounds that they posed a threat to the democratic system (Kirshner 2016). Building on Machiavelli, meanwhile, John McCormick (n.d.) has proposed that plutocratic elites could face the death penalty, after a public trial conducted by ordinary citizens, for attempts to corrupt the public purposes of the polity. As the anthropologist Christopher Boehm (1999) has demonstrated, indeed, both ostracism and execution have been used to maintain egalitarian social organization among human groups for millennia.

To be clear, neither of these extreme remedies is remotely justifiable in modern conditions. Nevertheless, these historical practices suggest an important point: because of the special threat they pose to the public interest, those with extremely concentrated wealth should be liable to heightened scrutiny and special sanctions. Given the outsized power they wield, we often hold politicians to higher standards of consistency and transparency than our fellow citizens (J. Green 2009). Similarly, we accept that celebrities forfeit some degree of privacy when they choose to put themselves in the public eye. Yet we typically shrink from applying special rules to those with extreme wealth—even though their outsized influence is neither less significant nor less voluntary. The principle of anti-monopoly suggests that this is a mistake.

One recent suggestion in this vein, for instance, is to employ randomly selected citizen juries to audit the financial practices of extremely wealthy individuals and large multinational corporations (Arlen 2021). If the citizen jurors find evidence of objectionable forms of tax sheltering or other unfair practices, they might expose those practices to the public, or sanction the actors involved—even, controversially, when the practices in question did not technically violate any particular statute. While some might worry that this violates the rule of law, I argue that this concern is overstated. Crucially, the handful of extremely wealthy actors to whom the law applies would know in advance that their activities would be subject to judgment by ordinary citizens, and could plan their activities accordingly. In doing so, moreover, they could refer to the public standards that participants in citizen tax juries would be required to apply. Those standards would be more open-ended than is customary for the tax code, but they would not be *infinitely* pliable. In particular, the definitions of "objectionable" and "unfair" practices would be broad enough to include practices of tax sheltering and evasion that clearly harm the public interest, but not so broad as to make verdicts entirely arbitrary or unpredictable.

To be sure, significant uncertainty would remain about whether certain practices were liable to sanction. Yet this is already commonplace among those with extreme wealth, many of whom invest millions on tax avoidance specialists—whose job is to deprive governments of revenue by exploiting ambiguities in overlapping legal frameworks, and who typically earn their fees many times over. At the same time, crucially, any cautious or scrupulous actors who genuinely sought to avoid all danger of sanction could still easily and reliably do so, by staying clearly within the bounds set by public standards. Citizen tax juries would not create legal uncertainty where it does not already exist, in other words; they would simply shift its burdens onto the oligarchic elites who currently exploit it for personal gain. If the point of the rule of law is to prevent the manipulation of public power for private ends, we may conclude, citizen tax juries are not only compatible with that principle, but may actually represent a significant advance.

A similar logic may also vindicate controversial forms of corrective partiality in a variety of other legal and adjudicatory contexts. In order to preserve the benefits of an adversarial legal system in a context of extreme inequality, for instance, several theorists have suggested placing limits on the amount wealthy parties can spend (Agmon 2021; Wertheimer 1988). By "leveling down" legal resources in this way, we make the adversarial playing field more egalitarian—and thus more likely to serve democratic ends. This represents a radical departure from legal tradition, and may even be thought contrary to basic democratic rights such as free speech. As others have noted in the parallel case of campaign finance (Purdy 2018), however, speech protections and spending limits ultimately serve the same democratic purpose: to obstruct powerful actors from using state power to entrench their position. Practical tensions do exist between these demands, but once we recognize their shared normative foundations, we can no longer suppose that one deserves absolute or categorical priority over the other—and in some cases, at least, the balance clearly weighs in favor of restricting spending.

The pretense of neutrality can advance democratic purposes, more broadly, but there will also be contexts in which it serves on balance to conceal and perpetuate elite advantages—and when it does, corrective partiality is the appropriate democratic response. Given that all legal orders privilege certain groups over others, the principle of anti-monopoly suggests that on the margins, we should shift more of the burdens of sociolegal ordering onto those who are already most advantaged by it. In some cases, that justifies imposing asymmetric burdens on extremely wealthy actors—such as broad discretion in punishment of tax sheltering, for instance, or limits on the amount anyone can spend on political campaigns and legal representation.

All of that said, the outsized organizational capacity of those at the top is only part of the explanation for the pervasive forms of capture documented in previous chapters. Targeting actors and groups with highly concentrated private power is thus only one form that radical efforts to preserve and deepen democracy must take.

6.2 Countervailing power as a counterweight to hegemonic interests

Countervailing power is the natural complement to anti-monopoly. Both demands are set in motion by the insight that capture is most often perpetrated by certain hegemonic actors and groups—i.e., those with the most concentrated private power and organizational capacity—and that protecting the public interest thus entails special attention to those specific forces. Where anti-monopoly entails targeting their resources and organizational capacity directly, however, practices of countervailing power aim to support their opponents. The aim, in other words, is to ensure that whichever interests are hegemonic in a given society face stiff opposition from well-resourced and well-organized *counter*-hegemonic groups.

It is this specificity—i.e., the focus on opposing specific hegemonic groups by bolstering specific counter-hegemonic forces—that differentiates the idea of countervailing power from more generic paeans to civil society and civic virtue. After all, conventional liberal theorists of democracy frequently stress the importance of building civic capacity among ordinary people. Most often, however, their unwavering commitment to the pretense of neutrality prevents them from grappling openly with what is actually required to advance democracy in practice. As I emphasized in Chapter 3, capture most often results not from a generalized deficit of civic virtue or citizen participation, but from severe *inequalities* of organizational capacity between groups. In opposing this specific threat, accordingly, what must be fostered is not civil society as such, but organizations that will reliably and effectively oppose hegemonic interests.

As with anti-monopoly, of course, the general idea of countervailing power does have a long history in political thought. Scott Gordon (1999: 120) has even identified "countervailance" as "the foundation of modern constitutionalism." A key milestone in the development of the term as I employ it, however, was John Kenneth Galbraith's *American Capitalism: The Concept of Countervailing Power* (1952), which argued that the consistent growth and broadly egalitarian distribution of the postwar US economy was a result of the strength of countervailing forces that checked the power of big business—and that the weakness of such forces in prior eras partly explains the tumultuous upheavals and rampant inequalities that characterized late nineteenth- and early twentieth-century capitalism. Most prominent among these was labor unions, but he also noted that the power of large firms could be countervailed by powerful firms in related sectors—monopolistic retailers, for instance, vis-à-vis monopolistic producers. Though he saw some regulation as necessary to ensure this competitive structure served broad public interests, Galbraith was wary of excessive reliance on state action, and thus embraced countervailing power as a middle way between laissez-faire and public ownership (1954: 1).

In certain respects, my account builds on that of Galbraith. I embrace his general aim of balancing economic power, for instance, as well as his specific focus on labor unions as a key instrument for achieving that aim under modern conditions. In my view, however, the relevance of countervailing power extends beyond the economic sphere as well as the concentrated power of particular agents. In the broader understanding of countervailing power I employ, the term refers to any entity that challenges the outsized influence of any hegemonic interest—ranging from wealthy individuals and corporations to the large social groups advantaged by categorical inequalities. Alongside labor unions, then, we should also see political parties, community organizations, and social movements as paradigmatic structures of countervailing power.

Of course, not every union, party, or movement is an instance of countervailing power: they count as such only when they reliably serve the *counter-hegemonic* end of obstructing capture by hegemonic interests. This means that identifying countervailing power in the wild—and deciding how best to encourage it in any particular circumstances—will always require making contestable judgments about which interests are hegemonic in that context. Just because those judgments are contestable, however, does not mean we cannot or should not make them: in Chapter 4, for instance, I argued that wealthy elites and groups advantaged by categorical inequalities are hegemonic across all contemporary democracies. Meanwhile, those who disagree with this assessment can substitute their own judgments about which interests are hegemonic, in order to draw practical inferences.

Either way, many difficult questions remain about the construction of potent counter-hegemonic forces. Which actors or groups occupy structural positions that generate both the capacity and the incentive to effectively oppose hegemonic interests? How can those with democratic ambitions foster the collective identity, solidarity, and motivation required for collective organization among these groups? And which organizational forms will enable them to wield power effectively, while minimizing the risks of backlash, co-optation, and so on?

Different forms of capture require different solutions. Generally speaking, however, the outsized influence of hegemonic groups is due to their superior organizational capacity—i.e., their ability to wield outsized private power resources, in a coordinated fashion, in defense of shared interests. As such, the core challenge of countervailing power is to generate comparable organizational capacity among groups with fewer private power resources. This often means relying on the power of numbers, especially by employing mass collective action to impose costs on hegemonic groups. And this, in turn, requires surmounting the many diverse obstacles that typically stand in the way of such large-scale coordination.

These obstacles may include rules whose express purpose is to prevent mass organization, such as the outright prohibitions on labor unions enacted by nearly all early industrial powers, or the "right-to-work" laws that make organizing difficult in many US states today. They may also include other forms of social engineering, such as "workplace fissuring," whose effect is to increase the physical and social distance between groups that might otherwise discover common interests. At a structural level, more broadly, the interests of various counter-hegemonic constituencies may differ quite widely. Though all could benefit from unifying against the hegemony of wealthy elites, for instance, groups like subsistence farmers, wage laborers, welfare recipients, and students have fundamentally different relationships to one another, to land and other forms of property, to economic and cultural elites, and to the state. Organizing tactics that succeed with one group thus tend to alienate or antagonize others, and it has historically been quite difficult to unify these disparate groups into a single coalition.

No less impactful are divisions of race, gender, caste, nationality, and so on—which have often been fomented by wealthy elites as part of a "divide-and-conquer" strategy (Allen 1994, 1997; Du Bois 1935), and are in any case frequently deployed to that end (Roediger and Esch 2012). Finally, mass collective action may be hindered by cultural norms and ideologies—such as the myth of meritocracy (Frank 2016; McNamee and Miller 2013)—and the increasing atomization and marketization of modern life (W. Brown 2015). Even if such forces are not intentionally created by hegemonic groups, they still obstruct the growth of solidarity and coordination necessary for mass collective action, and thus end up serving hegemonic interests.

The most basic task of those who seek to promote countervailing power, then, is to enable members of counter-hegemonic groups to overcome these persistent obstacles to collective action in defense of their interests. Sometimes, state policy does this indirectly, by structuring the daily lives and political interactions of ordinary people in ways that facilitate certain kinds of concerns and identities over others. For instance, a housing policy regime that subsidizes and incentivizes home ownership will tend to create a large constituency of homeowners who are materially invested in preserving their property values at the expense of broader social and public goods, while a regime that incentivizes renting and prioritizes the creation of attractive public housing will create incentives and identities more conducive to prioritizing public goods (Radford 1997). Similarly, the "policy feedback" (Pierson 1993) effects of universal programs contrast sharply with those of means-tested programs: in the US, for instance, Medicare provides health coverage for everyone over 65, creating a diverse and supportive constituency, while Medicaid provides coverage only to the poor, and is far more divisive. As Lisa Disch (2021) has argued, then, designing social policies that foster broad solidarity is a critical democratic tool.

In addition, many state policies contribute more directly to the formation of countervailing power. Kate Andrias and Benjamin Sachs (2020) present a comprehensive accounting of the myriad visible and invisible ways that law conditions the ability of ordinary people to organize and act collectively.

They outline dozens of policies that would enable the growth of mass membership organizations as a vehicle for collective power, building on a variety of shared interests and identities as sources of solidarity. Again, the paradigm case here is labor unions—whose strength varies widely across different legal regimes—but they also discuss innovative policy tools that might facilitate organizing among other groups with a shared structural position, including tenants, debtors, and recipients of public benefits (see, e.g., Bangs 2018).

Across these different contexts, Andrias and Sachs argue, policies that facilitate the organization of countervailing power will typically "grant collective rights in an explicit and direct way" and guarantee access to "financial, informational, human, and other relevant resources" as well as "spaces … in which movement organization can occur, free from surveillance or control." They will prohibit retaliation against participants and remove material barriers to participation, create "mechanisms for the exercise of real political and economic power"—like the right to participate in certain decisions or bargain directly with certain actors—and protect disruptive methods of contestation such as strikes. Unsurprisingly, then, my account implies that a central democratic priority must be to shift policy in the direction outlined by Andrias and Sachs on multiple fronts.

At the same time, one of the distinctive features of countervailing power as a democratic demand is precisely that it does *not* foreground policy reform as the presumptive vector of all practical change. This is what separates it from many other democratizing agendas—and, indeed, from the other elements of the agenda elaborated here. If the underlying balance of power makes it unlikely that states will implement policies opposed to hegemonic interests, as I have argued, then prospects for deeper democratization can seem quite dim. The development of countervailing power thus offers a unique source of hope. Though its prospects are certainly shaped by the legal environment, countervailing power does not depend on any particular state policy, and thus presents counter-hegemonic groups with a lever of power they can wield at any time, under any conditions (K. A. Young, Banerjee, and Schwartz 2020). Because it acts directly on the balance of power, moreover, using this lever makes others more accessible. If an organization durably enhances the ability of ordinary people to act collectively in defense of shared interests, that in itself reflects a shift in the balance of power, whose impact is presumptively democratic. On my account, then, a key democratic priority for actors outside the state must be to foster the development of organizations that serve this function.

As ever, there are many dangers involved here. There may be tensions between different solidarities. Backlash from hegemonic interests can erode the achievements of countervailing organizations. And whatever its initial goals, any organization that successfully wields power becomes a potential vector of state capture in its own right—either because it is co-opted by existing hegemonic interests, as when labor leaders cozy up to business elites; or because it creates a new hegemony, as when a "revolutionary vanguard" becomes the new ruling elite.

Chapter 10 is addressed to these challenges, asking how countervailing organizations can be built, maintained, and held accountable to the interests of those they purport to represent. A single chapter, however, can only scratch the surface of this complex question, and rather than attempting to articulate a fully comprehensive theory of countervailing power in such a limited space, I have chosen to highlight one particularly promising approach. The more important lesson of this book as a whole, then, is that *this question*—and not, for instance, how to broaden participation in formally neutral processes of collective decision-making—is the central question facing those who aim to protect and enrich democracy in the twenty-first century. For now, let us turn to the final radical demand of democracy.

6.3 Systemic redistribution as a weapon against background inequality

The outsized ability of hegemonic groups to shape state action is largely a result of their advantages in organizational capacity over counter-hegemonic groups—i.e., their superior ability to make coordinated and effective demands on the state. Practices of anti-monopoly and countervailing power promise to protect public power from capture by directly addressing this crucial asymmetry. By mitigating disparities in the ability of groups to coordinate in defense of shared interests, that is, they directly reshape the power structure in a democratic direction, thus tackling the root causes of democratic dysfunction rather than surface-level symptoms.

Still, the outsized ability of any hegemonic group to perpetrate capture is constituted not only by its capacity to coordinate as a group, but also by the disproportionate access to material resources, social connections, cultural capital, and positions of institutional authority possessed by its members. More subtly—though no less profoundly—it is further enabled by the fact that prevailing ideologies, social norms, and cultural narratives structure our collective habits of thought and action in ways favorable to their interests. This is to be expected, given their control over processes of economic, social, and cultural production; as well as the disproportionate influence of their consumption patterns on the incentives facing producers. And as long as these background inequalities of private power are unaddressed, achieving balance in organizational capacity will always be an uphill battle. The principle of *systemic redistribution* thus demands broader efforts to address all underlying material, social, and cultural asymmetries.

The trouble is that dismantling such deep-seated hierarchies—especially those relying on subtle patterns of social and cultural organization—is extraordinarily difficult. Because they are often perpetuated unconsciously, through distributed everyday interactions, addressing them directly would imply deep intrusions into private life. The unequal division of domestic labor is a linchpin of patriarchy, for instance, but it is hard to imagine how we might enforce greater equality without granting enforcers too much discretion. Similarly, sexism in popular culture plays a large role in reproducing patriarchy, but empowering states to enforce strictly egalitarian content standards would inevitably create dangerous structures liable to abuse.

At the same time, more measured policies are simply unable to address problems of this magnitude. Laws banning extreme forms of hate speech may give enforcers less discretion than laws mandating egalitarian values across the board, for instance—and are thus less vulnerable to capture—yet they do nothing to counteract the subtler stereotypes that suffuse the media we consume every day. Similarly, women's shelters and aggressive prosecution of domestic violence can mitigate patriarchal power asymmetries in important ways, but they alone cannot disrupt the toxic norms of masculinity that lead men to become abusers in the first place (hooks 1982: 191). And while anti-discrimination laws and affirmative action programs may help to alleviate certain background asymmetries between certain groups, they often do remarkably little to undermine the broader social hierarchies they are ostensibly intended to address.

On the one hand, then, such conventionally liberal practices are insufficient to dismantle the collective habits of thought and action that sustain systems of oppression and categorical advantage. On the other hand, state policy that would directly tackle those collective habits—such as egalitarian standards for cultural content—is generally too intrusive and dangerous to be a viable democratic tool. As such, the responsibility for undermining oppressive ideologies, norms, and narratives falls largely to decentralized efforts by nonstate actors—ranging from counter-hegemonic cultural production by individual creators, to the enforcement of counter-hegemonic norms by mass social movements. And indeed, I argue, such efforts to transform the cultural landscape must be a central priority for anyone who seeks to advance democracy.

Beyond implying priorities for nonstate actors, finally, my account also has implications for state policy. Though centralized enforcement is ill-suited to the task of dismantling systems of social advantage *directly*, states can and should provide *indirect* support to the nonstate actors and groups aiming to do so. Partly, this means ensuring a favorable legal and institutional environment for the growth of counter-hegemonic organizations and movements, as suggested above. An equally important democratic priority, however, is the more general redistribution of *material* resources through massive and continuous wealth transfers. After all, it is easier to attack the *social* and *cultural* foundations of hierarchical structures when their *economic* basis is weak. And crucially, the mechanism of wealth transfers can be scaled up indefinitely without incurring prohibitive risks of capture—unlike more direct policies such as content standards. It thus presents a uniquely promising tool for cracking open background asymmetries that are otherwise highly resistant to disruption, and the rest of the section is devoted to it.

The mere demand for economic redistribution is hardly novel. As with some of the other familiar practices I have defended in this chapter, however, my justification for it is distinctive. For one, my argument occurs on the terrain of democracy rather than welfare or justice. Wealth transfers are justified not because all people require certain resources in order to live minimally decent lives or be respected as equals, on my account, but rather because pervasive material inequalities reliably produce asymmetries of organizational capacity, which in turn enable advantaged groups to capture state power and threaten the public interest. Meanwhile, the reason I focus on redistributing *wealth* in particular is not because the material sources of inequality are more real or important than its social or cultural sources, but rather because the methods we can use to mitigate material inequalities are relatively safer. Indeed, even if the magnitude of wealth transfers grows quite large—as I argue it should—the centralized state actors who carry them out need not have much discretion over how they are applied or *who* is impacted by them. Crucially, this minimizes opportunities for capture.

One noteworthy feature of this justificatory logic, then, is that it provides no internal limit on the desirable level of wealth transfers. Considered solely in light of the proximate aim of remedying background power asymmetries between different groups, that is, redistribution remains valuable right up to the point where there are no more inequalities left to be remedied. Within any given set of circumstances, of course, *external* concerns of various kinds will likely limit how much redistribution we ought to strive for—concerns grounded in other democratic demands, for instance, or in the public interest itself.[4] Still, it is significant that unlike standard justifications of redistribution, this one provides no *internal* limit on its desirable extent: the implicit assumption is rather that wealth transfers should be scaled up indefinitely.

On a standard welfare state model, for instance, social insurance and certain basic services are provided on the grounds that they establish a floor below which no members of society can sink, thereby enabling everyone to participate meaningfully in core aspects of social, political, and economic life. As valuable as this is, however, the actual *redistributive* effects of such programs are often quite limited. In many cases, their main impact is to smooth income over the life cycle and socialize risk *within* class groups, not to redistribute power *between* categories of people. The wealth transfers implied by the democratic demand of systemic redistribution are far more ambitious, because their purpose is distinct. Rather than providing a minimum level of welfare, capabilities, or democratic agency, in short, they aim to flatten the distribution of power as much as possible (without threatening other valuable goals).

As we have seen, similarly, the standard suite of liberal strategies for addressing pervasive categorical inequalities—such as anti-discrimination laws and affirmative action programs—are woefully inadequate to their task. In cases of profound and enduring asymmetry, such as those arising from the legacy of Atlantic slavery, genuine remedy would require far more direct and ambitious measures such as reparations: i.e., massive wealth transfers to members of the disadvantaged group (Balfour 2003; Coates 2014; Táíwò 2022b). Indeed, my forward-looking justification for such transfers may be more straightforward than traditional backward-looking views.[5] Even if a group's outsized private power cannot be definitively attributed to specific instances of capture, it still gives them greater ability to perpetrate capture in the future, and on my account, that is sufficient to justify redistribution.

---

[4] The key concern is that high taxes and unconditional transfers would alter incentives in ways that reduce economic growth. In public discourse, such concerns are mostly used in bad faith to oppose modest tax-and-transfer schemes that would have little impact on incentives, but there is probably a much higher level at which they would become relevant. In my view, wealth transfers should be scaled up at least to the point where they noticeably impact growth, and—given climate concerns—probably somewhat beyond. Rawls' difference principle may be a useful heuristic, but we need not be precise: my aim is to set a direction, not an endpoint.

[5] A forward-looking approach would also make it easier to identify the proper recipients of reparations. At the same time, clearly, a historical approach also makes many valuable contributions, and the two are not mutually exclusive. Where the fact of pervasive economic inequality along categorical lines provides only *preliminary* evidence that the wealthier group benefits from capture, for instance, a historical story will *strengthen* our initial hypothesis. In some cases, a historical account can also help us tailor our remedial responses to the specific mechanisms that have created and sustained a certain injustice over time: see, for instance ongoing debates about whether integration is the best remedy for racial inequality in the US (Anderson 2010; Shelby 2014).

Where severe inequalities track salient group identities, meanwhile—as in the classic cases giving rise to demands for reparations—direct wealth transfers across groups are likely the most efficient way to address them.[6]

Ultimately, however, the idea of reparations is only a special case of the far more general demand for wealth transfers that emerges from my account. Even if it would be an especially *direct* way to mitigate background asymmetries between groups, meanwhile, I worry that the logic of reparations orients us towards a lost utopia of equal opportunity which, if attained, would obviate the need for further corrective action. By contrast, my account emphasizes that the need for redistribution will never fade: even if all background inequalities were temporarily eliminated, new ones will always arise. And because concentrated private power always poses threats of capture, these new asymmetries will always require remediation—even if they arise in an ideally egalitarian competitive environment, and cannot be attributed to capture. As I have insisted throughout, in other words, democracy should be understood as a never-ending process of opposition to an ever-shifting set of adversaries with outsized private power.

If social insurance and even reparations provide incomplete solutions to the fundamental problem of background inequality, then, what sort of material redistribution should we strive for? The ideal form of systemic redistribution, and the central aspiration I endorse under that umbrella, is a policy I call "unconditional wealth transfers" or UWTs. Like standard welfare programs, UWTs are funded by progressive taxation. Like proposals for "unconditional basic income" or UBI, however, UWTs would distribute flexible transfers of cash—rather than fixed services (like education or healthcare) or vouchers (like food stamps)—which are not means-tested or conditional on age, employment, disability, or family status. As UBI advocates have long pointed out, this minimizes the discretion of state actors at all levels, forestalling various forms of capture.[7] Unconditional cash transfers thus address

---

[6] This does not apply in precisely the same way to categorical distinctions such as gender and sexuality, which do not correlate strongly with spatial distribution, social network clusters, and cultural affinities—and thus tend to cut across classic *group* identities such as race, class, ethnicity, religion, and caste. Redistribution of material resources is often still appropriate, but because the dynamics of subordination are different in these cases, the justification will take a slightly different form—as may the appropriate mechanism.

[7] For instance, redistributive schemes may be manipulated by industry actors—as when soda companies ensure that unhealthy soft drinks are not excluded from food stamp programs (Barnhill and Hutler 2021). More generally, they can be "captured" by groups to perpetuate categorical inequalities—as when Southern Democrats in the US burdened the New Deal with a panoply of racist exclusions (Katznelson 2005). Most broadly of all, finally, welfare states have often served to perpetuate patriarchal gender relations (Abramovitz 1988) and to police the lives of the poor and people of color (Piven 1971; Quadagno 1994).

key critiques of welfare programs from left and right, attracting support from a surprisingly wide range of political actors.[8]

The key question is *how extensive* such programs should be. Center-right UBI advocates propose relatively modest sums as sufficient for "basic" income, and frame it as a replacement for public provision of basic services and other welfare state programs. For left advocates, what counts as a "basic" income is more generous, and it is meant to supplement existing programs, not replace them. Of the two visions, mine shares more with the latter, involving large transfers that coexist with extensive public provision.[9] Recall that on my account, however, the aim of systemic redistribution is not to provide a "basic" level of income in *absolute* terms, but to balance the *relative* power of different groups. This is why I have given my proposal a different name: wealth transfers are not a means to the end of universalizing a certain level of welfare or agency; instead, the flatter distribution of power created by such transfers is an end in itself.

Unlike left UBI advocates, then, I set no lower bound on scale, below which cash transfers are no longer democratically valuable. Presuming their introduction is not conditional on the elimination of other essential programs, UWTs of any size would represent some transfer of private power. Even if they are too small to meet recipients' subsistence needs, they could serve democratic goals on the margins. More importantly, I also set no upper bound: from the perspective of the democratic demand for systemic redistribution, at least, the point is to scale up indefinitely. As noted above, concerns external to this demand—including other democratic demands as well as first-order concerns such as economic efficiency and growth—will speak against eliminating all material inequality. At least as a utopian horizon, however, my account suggests far more redistribution than even the most generous "basic" income proposals, not to mention traditional welfare states.

Such extensive unconditional transfers would also transform many of the other forces that give shape to the underlying distribution of private power. In the economic realm, for one, they would furnish workers with robust "exit

---

[8] Radicals have long seen UBI as a possible route to egalitarian ends that avoids coercive centralization (King 1967; Van der Veen and Van Parijs 1986). Meanwhile, its minimally invasive character has long been attractive to libertarians (Cowen 2013; Murray 2006), while trends of increasing capital mobility (Standing 2011), automation (Ford 2016), and artificial intelligence (Schwab 2017) have led many to see some form of UBI as necessary if not inevitable. Finally, recent research in development economics has tempered resistance from technocratic elites averse to creating dependence, showing that on many conventional measures, direct cash transfers are among the most *effective* interventions available (Hanlon, Barrientos, and Hulme 2010).

[9] The most common arguments against unconditional cash transfers—grounded in microeconomics (e.g., incentives), macroeconomics (e.g., inflation), or culture (e.g., "laziness")—have been capably addressed by others, and I do not discuss them here (Standing 2017; Van Parijs, Cohen, and Rogers 2001; Wright 2006b).

options" (Van Parijs 2006: 10), giving individual employees greater bargaining power vis-à-vis employers, and thus generating more equitable workplace relations (Casassas 2016). Because this happens for all workers simultaneously, moreover, they would also gain bargaining power as a class (Wright 2006a: 95). In the social realm, similarly, a system of unconditional transfers would also facilitate "resourced exit" from abusive or unhealthy personal relationships (R. S. Taylor 2017). And while it clearly helps people of all genders, this feature has been especially attractive to feminists for the way it increases the bargaining power of women relative to men—potentially leading to significant reductions in the gendered division of labor (Zelleke 2008: 1).

As Carole Pateman (2006: 109) points out, meanwhile, a system of unconditional transfers could also support more egalitarian access to participation in the political realm. In my terms, more specifically, wealth transfers would reduce inequalities in the amount of time and money that members of hegemonic and counter-hegemonic groups can devote to political pursuits, thus facilitating greater collective power among the latter. UWTs could reduce inequalities of organizational capacity in less direct ways as well, by transforming the conditions of social and cultural production. On the supply side, they would enable more members of disadvantaged groups to pursue careers in prominent fields with prohibitive entry costs—such as media, law, medicine, scholarship, and the arts—and thus to more effectively contest the ideologies, norms, and narratives that reliably serve hegemonic interests. On the demand side, meanwhile, they would also mitigate the outsized power exerted by hegemonic groups as consumers.

To be clear: wealth transfers would not automatically bring about the elimination of other hierarchical structures. Still, they are enormously important as part of a broader democratic agenda. Given that the organizational capacity of groups is shaped by the material resources available to their members, on the one hand, flattening the overall distribution of wealth will contribute directly to the goal of improving balance between groups, and thereby limiting the ability of any group to perpetrate capture. Given how access to material resources shapes our engagement in economic, political, social, and cultural activities, on the other hand, wealth transfers can also provide critical support for broader efforts to undermine hierarchies in these other realms as well. And this gives us very strong reasons to support them.

With this, we complete our survey of the six core demands of democracy, as summarized in Table 6.1 below. Yet many important questions remain. How do we weigh these demands against one another, when their recommendations come apart? What sort of ideal emerges when we combine them, and

Table 6.1 The Six Demands of Democracy as Resisting State Capture

Tradition	Principle	Subtype	Examples of Practices	Key Tensions
Liberal Basic goal structure public power in ways that minimize opportunities for capture	**Constitutionalism:** prevent dangerous concentrations of political power by any actor or group	**First-order:** formally constrain state actors to limit tyranny and abuse **Second-order:** ensure no one can amass sufficient formal or informal power to violate first-order constraints	Rule of law, procedural rights, freedom of speech, religion, assembly, press, etc… *Formal* (modern/liberal): separation of powers, institutionalized opposition *Material* (ancient/radical): tribunate, worker's councils	The role of constitutions as coordination devices requires limited volatility, but revision is required when existing rules entrench elite power
	Competition: ensure dominant actors and groups face continuous challenges from organized, well-resourced rivals	**Political:** limit stakes and intensity of conflict, promote coordination on rules and norms **Legal:** ensure powerful interests face resourced opposition in key contests **Social:** provide *organizational* basis for resistance to abuse (and contestation broadly) in politics and law **Economic:** provide *material* basis for resistance to abuse (and contestation broadly) in politics, law, and society	Elections (party competition), federalism and subsidiarity (jurisdictional competition) Adversarial trials, public defenders, regulatory contrarians, citizen oversight juries Religious pluralism, "marketplace of ideas," associational freedom, civil society Open markets, competition policy, dynamic economy built on diverse assets with unpredictable returns	Competition may be harmful or self-undermining when: (a) its stakes and methods are not constrained; and/or (b) some competitors (or judges) have systematic advantages over others

Continued

Table 6.1 Continued

Tradition	Principle	Subtype	Examples of Practices	Key Tensions
	Universalism: ensure that all have access to the tools (and benefits) of constitutionalism and competition	**Inclusion:** universality prevents manipulation of access to entrench elite power **Impartiality:** public standards of impartiality and neutrality limit scope for elite manipulation	Universal suffrage, legal equality, universal provision of goods and services Norms of transparency and reason-giving, meritocracy, judicial and bureaucratic independence	The pretense of neutrality can be beneficial, but it can also conceal inequality and the need for corrective partiality
Radical Basic goal: disperse private power among groups to minimize the ability of any one to perpetrate capture	**Anti-monopoly:** constrain wealthy elites and other hegemonic groups	**Economic:** limit the wealth and coordination rights of actors and groups with outsized economic power **Noneconomic:** impose special burdens or limits on actors and groups with outsized private power	Antitrust and regulation, intellectual property reform, wealth and inheritance taxes, salary caps Rules that apply only to the super-rich, citizen tax juries, caps on legal and political spending	Judgments about which actors and groups are hegemonic are always contested, and policies of corrective partiality are always open to abuse
	Countervailing Power: build capacity to exert collective power among counter-hegemonic groups	**Geographic:** solidarity based in local concerns **Material:** solidarity based in structural position **Ascriptive:** solidarity based in ascriptive identity	Community groups (e.g., city, neighborhood, watershed) Unions (e.g., workers, renters, debtors; welfare rights) Movements (e.g., race, gender, ethnicity, religion, caste)	Discipline and hierarchy are required to wield power at scale, but these introduce opportunities for capture; cross-cutting solidarities may clash
	Systemic Redistribution: shift resources top to bottom	**Economic:** redistribute wealth, control of production, bargaining power, consumer power **Noneconomic:** redistribute capacity for (and control over) the creation of culture, knowledge, ideology	*Liberal:* social insurance, education, affirmative action *Radical:* reparations, unconditional wealth transfers *Pre-distribution:* market reforms (e.g., Meidner plan)	Liberal forms are often necessary in the short term, but may undermine long term prospects of radical methods; redistribution and pre-distribution may conflict

Note: The top half of Table 6.1 summarizes Chapter 5, and the bottom half summarizes Chapter 6.

how do we weigh its demands against other values we may have? What should our practical priorities be, if our aim is to protect and enhance democracy in contemporary societies? These questions will concern us for the rest of the book—beginning with an overview of the ideal of resisting state capture in Chapter 7, and continuing with an elaboration of its most important practical implications in Chapters 8, 9, and 10.

7
Resisting State Capture as a Democratic Ideal

In broad strokes, the six core demands of democracy are complementary. Limits on abuse of state power can be sustained only by competition among factions, while healthy competition is possible only if certain rights are guaranteed for participants, and it serves the public interest only if everyone can participate. Because impartial procedures and universal guarantees are still compatible with vast imbalances of private power, meanwhile, these liberal practices must also be supplemented with more direct, radical efforts to level the playing field.

Nevertheless, there are also real tensions between the different demands of resisting state capture. Most basically, liberal demands for universality and impartiality conflict with radical demands for corrective partiality. Meanwhile, tensions also emerge within each set of demands, and even within each demand itself. The liberal principle of constitutionalism suggests limiting the discretionary power of state actors, for example, but pursuing liberal universalist goals requires empowering them in various ways. While the radical demand of anti-monopoly entails a bias *against* the concentration of private power, the radical mandate of countervailing power is to *facilitate* the concentration of power by certain kinds of nonstate organizations. In some cases, finally, protecting one form of competition may require curtailing others—as when limits are placed on certain forms of speech around election time, for instance, in order to protect electoral integrity and ensure a level playing field for political competition.

These tensions—among many others—will arise at a more practical or institutional level as well. Is it better to enable impartial courts to protect minority rights by exercising extensive judicial review of legislation, for instance, or to enable majorities to pass legislation that is not subject to the veto of unelected elites? Is it better to maintain an absolute and exceptionless commitment to freedom of speech, or to deny certain platforms to groups seeking to perpetuate deeply entrenched racial hierarchies? Is it permissible to defend democracy with "militant" means—by denying the vote to avowed anti-democrats, perhaps, or blocking their party from taking power?

Is it justifiable to bend certain procedural rules, mislead voters, or encourage cycles of polarization, in service of valuable "substantive" goals like systemic redistribution?

These are precisely the sorts of questions a democratic theory should help us answer, and this chapter explores three ways the ideal of resisting state capture does so: as a utopian horizon for the distant future, as a political orientation for the medium term, and as a guide to practical judgment. Rather than the common horizons of *ideal deliberation* or *full socialization*, first, I embrace the *dispersion of private power* as the long-term goal of democratic action, and §7.1 explores the implications of this shift. Instead of adopting a conventional orientation towards *equal control over collective decisions*, second, I argue that democratic actors should generally aim to bring about an *egalitarian balance of social forces*, and §7.2 compares my version of this orientation with related views such as agonism, republicanism, and pluralism. By clarifying the overall perspective and priorities implied by the ideal of resisting state capture, these more abstract discussions enable a return to concrete dilemmas in §7.3, which uses the tools I have developed to work through difficult cases of tension between different democratic demands.

7.1 Dispersing private power: Resisting state capture as a utopian horizon

We might wonder why a book claiming to take a realist approach should contain a section on utopian horizons. Whether we like it or not, however, our judgments are often informed by implicit utopian horizons. Rather than trying in vain to eliminate utopian thinking, then, a genuinely realistic approach will seek make it explicit and pursue it wisely, articulating the sort of horizons that are likely to point us in the right direction. Given our epistemic limitations, on the one hand, a detailed picture of the best possible destination is rarely if ever warranted, so a critical realist horizon should be imprecise. On the other hand, these same epistemic limitations should also lead us to presume the persistence of self-interest, conflict, and the predicament of modern politics—not because humans could never transcend these conditions, but because it is too difficult to speak reliably about how societies would function if they did.

With this in mind, let us examine some of the utopian horizons that commonly guide our action already. Ideals of collective self-rule aim to subject decisions about state power to collective control. Their utopian horizons thus tend to involve *more* decisions being made *more* collectively—as in classic socialist visions of the economy, as well as the deliberative ideals central to many recent political imaginaries. And while we can learn a great deal from these ideals, I argue that they orient us towards the distant future in ways that do not always serve us well. The ideal of resisting state capture suggests a more promising sort of horizon.

Consider the classic ideal of socializing the means of production. At the heart of this ideal is a very logical desire to extend collective decision-making from the political sphere, where it is widely accepted, to the economic sphere. As long as society's productive resources remain in private hands, indeed, many socialists claim that "collective" control over political decisions is meaningless. And they are right, I have argued, to think that electoral democracy cannot address the background asymmetries that pervasively structure contemporary societies on its own. As socialists rightly insist, indeed, the project of democracy will be radically incomplete unless private power relations are dramatically transformed. Given my arguments about the slipperiness of collective self-rule, however, I am skeptical that socialization provides a general solution. The horizon of genuinely collective control over economic resources is a mirage, in other words, and it is no accident that its pursuit has so often led to wholesale capture of the political system.

For the reasons articulated in previous chapters, economic competition plays a crucial role in sustaining social pluralism and political competition. As a result, it will always be too risky to centralize economic decision-making while eliminating all independent centers of economic power. In the short term, this will reliably provoke existential resistance that can only be crushed with violence (Levitsky and Way 2022). Even if this challenge could be overcome without creating permanent authoritarian institutions, meanwhile, leaders would still have enormous discretion over economic activity, and would continually be tempted to use it to entrench their position. Because of such concerns, indeed, many contemporary proponents of socialism have retreated from the assumption that it entails fully centralized production. Beyond favoring electoral victory over revolutionary violence, that is, they accept the value of open economic competition in at least some cases—defending "market socialism" (Roemer 1996) and other market-friendly forms of "liberal socialism" (Baum 2007; Crotty 2019), "democratic socialism" (O'Neill 2020), or "socialist republicanism" (O'Shea 2020).

My account shares much more with such hybrid views than with those orthodox versions of socialism that simply equate it with state ownership of the means of production. Yet the broader aspiration to collective self-rule still leads many radical theories astray. For instance, revisionist accounts of what it could mean to socialize the means of production often focus on worker self-management at the firm level, rather than fully nationalized industries (Gourevitch 2015). Since it retains pluralistic competition, this model is far less dangerous, and there is no harm in experimenting with it as part of a broader democratizing agenda. Precisely because self-managed firms would still exist within a competitive market, however, I suspect that the transformative potential of this approach likely remains quite limited (Singer 2018). As with many of the strategies of participatory inclusion examined in Chapter 3, in other words, its focus on expanding access to decision procedures within specific organizations is misplaced, because it fails to address underlying asymmetries of organizational capacity. Efforts to include workers directly in management decisions at specific firms may contribute on the margins to a more democratic society, but on my account, it is more important to build countervailing power among workers, outside of these firms, through large-scale, independent, oppositional organizations like labor unions.

This brings us to the other most prominent form taken by utopian projections of the logic of collective self-rule: deliberative democracy. In short, rather than expanding the reach of collective decision-making into the economic realm—or, perhaps, as a necessary precondition for doing so— theories of deliberative democracy shift our attention to the processes of will formation that precede decision-making. And like the demand to socialize the means of production, the aspiration to make these processes more egalitarian and deliberative is founded in a very real and important insight: namely, that elections and other political decision-making procedures are biased in systematic ways by the broader social conditions in which they exist. Hegemonic groups are systematically advantaged not only by relations of production but also by an array of subtler social norms and cultural narratives, which exert profound influence on the way a "collective" will is formulated. Unless we collectively determine these features of our shared reality as well, democratic decisions will fail to reflect a *genuinely* collective will.

As noted in §3.4, highly abstract versions of the deliberative ideal may be compatible with my account. If all it implies is a utopian horizon where all people can share in the deliberative co-construction of social reality because background asymmetries are continually undermined, the ideal of resisting state capture can be understood as articulating the best way to pursue it: namely, through corrective partiality and oppositional collective action by counter-hegemonic groups. Yet deliberative democrats typically value reasonable and egalitarian deliberation not just as a by-product of broader social, cultural, and economic transformations, or as evidence of a healthy balance of power, but as both quintessential means and ultimate end of democratic reform. That is where the horizon I have in mind diverges from those most often inferred from deliberative ideals. Deliberation can be one important vector for deeper democratization, but it faces sharply diminishing marginal returns (Bagg 2018a). Even in ideal conditions, meanwhile, no deliberative forum can eliminate all bias and manipulation. Thus, corrective partiality and oppositional collective action cannot be seen as remedial tactics that will be unnecessary once ideal conditions have been achieved, but as constitutive elements of our democratic horizon.

More broadly, the horizon implied by the ideal of resisting state capture refuses to frame *any* practice as singularly or paradigmatically democratic. In serving the overarching goal of protecting public power from capture, rather, it relies on a unique combination of liberal and radical practices, all of which are framed as co-equal components of a broader democratic ideal. So long as we remain in the predicament of modern politics, I maintain that top-level leaders should still compete for power within a constitutional system anchored by social and economic pluralism. My claim, however, is that the character of this familiar system would be profoundly transformed by the dramatic expansion of radical practices that redistribute private power.

The most important source of capture in liberal democracies, I have argued, is the outsized organizational capacity of wealthy elites and other hegemonic groups. The core contention of my democratic horizon is that if practices of anti-monopoly, countervailing power, and systemic redistribution were widespread enough to significantly balance organizational capacity and flatten the distribution of private power, this would dramatically reduce the scope and severity of capture. Instead of certain groups enjoying reliable advantages in the struggle to influence public power, in other words, the efforts of different groups under this system would largely balance out, and public power would more often serve broader public interests.

Though the democratic horizon suggested by resisting state capture projects all six demands from the previous two chapters into the long-term future, then, its *utopian* character clearly arises from its three radical demands—not from major changes to collective decision procedures, that is, but from changes to the underlying distribution of power. That is what distinguishes it from the democratic horizons of collective self-rule, which focus on processes of collective choice—either expanding what we make collective decisions about, or changing how we make them.

Like schemes to socialize the means of production, for one, the radical practices I endorse also aim to equalize control over economic resources. Instead of insisting that this control be exerted "collectively," however, they distribute it directly to individuals in the form of wealth, and to counter-hegemonic groups in the form of organizational capacity. Similarly, I argue, we should aim to "democratize" decisions about cultural production not by centralizing them and subjecting them to dubious forms of "collective" control, but rather by placing both the producers and the consumers of culture on less unequal footing in the first place. Finally, they establish the preconditions necessary for egalitarian deliberation to thrive, without implausibly overstating the latter's significance to democracy—either as its essence or its motive force. They therefore preserve much of what is attractive about the horizons implied by collective self-rule, while abandoning troublesome notions of a collective will. Instead, they suggest a distinct orienting principle for democratic action over the long term, which is more likely to point us in the right direction in the present: the *dispersion of private power*.

In many ways, the utopian horizon developed here resembles the ideal of "property-owning democracy" promoted by Rawls (1971)—drawing on earlier work by James Meade (1993)—which has recently attracted renewed attention (Kerr 2019; O'Neill and Williamson 2012; Thomas 2016). For reasons similar to those articulated here, its advocates reject centralized ownership of productive resources in favor of dispersed private ownership and some degree of market competition. Yet they also spurn the welfare state model—which relies on redistributive schemes to reverse the inegalitarian effects of unrestrained market activity—in favor of "pre-distributive" policies that ensure a more egalitarian distribution of property (and bargaining power) *before* taxes and transfers, so that markets yield more equal results in the first place. As should be clear, my turn to the dispersion of private power is motivated by a very similar set of concerns, and the utopian horizon I endorse can fairly be described as a form of property-owning democracy. For several reasons, however, I hesitate to fully embrace that label.

To begin with, property-owning democracy is typically seen as an account of the economic system that best fulfills the specific requirements of certain comprehensive theories of justice—especially that of Rawls. As a result, its justification appears to be far downstream from the Rawlsian system—which views society as a cooperative scheme for mutual advantage, entails a neo-Kantian conception of justice within such societies, and relies on a hierarchically ordered set of principles said to follow from that conception. Much discussion of property-owning democracy thus focuses on whether and how it does in fact realize those abstract principles, such as "the fair value of the political liberties." In my view, frankly, this reliance on Rawlsian jargon threatens to obscure the attractiveness of the dispersion of private power as a utopian horizon, which can be appreciated from a much wider range of theoretical perspectives.

Perhaps because it is conceived primarily as a theory of (economic) justice, meanwhile, theorists of property-owning democracy tend to focus more on the precise structure of capital ownership in the ideal—distinguishing sharply between pre-distribution and redistribution—and less on the transitional strategies of anti-monopoly and countervailing power that would be required to bring any of these ideal policies within reach. Many of their proposals are plausible and inspiring, helping us imagine more concretely what a utopian horizon characterized by the dispersion of private power might look like in practice. For my purposes, however, this level of detail is unnecessary, and may even be distracting. In articulating a utopian horizon, we need only a vague direction of travel, not a precise destination, and in particular, I worry that drawing such a hard boundary between redistribution and pre-distribution will unnecessarily exclude certain tax-and-transfer schemes—including the unconditional wealth transfers I endorse. Still, these are relatively minor differences of emphasis, not major substantive disagreements, and while I remain wary of its terminology, property-owning democracy is probably the closest approximation, among existing approaches, of the utopian horizon I seek to promote.

To some degree, the attractiveness of this horizon must speak for itself. Before moving on, however, it is worth addressing one final set of worries that might be raised by radical critics: namely, that by incorporating certain liberal commitments, this supposedly "utopian" horizon serves to narrow our "political imagination" (Steinmetz-Jenkins and Zamora 2019). It might be charged, for one, that an exclusive focus on the dispersion of *private* power rather than collective decision-making betrays an ideal that is actually essential to democracy. By envisioning a significant role for competitive markets, meanwhile, it fails to transcend the stunted horizon of social democratic welfare states, and their assumption that human beings are driven by greed and self-interest. On a symbolic level, finally, it accepts the individualizing logic of neoliberalism, thereby weakening efforts to build truly collective power (Gourevitch 2016). Perhaps markets have a role as a second-best solution, it might be argued, but as long as we are articulating utopian dreams, why not imagine a community founded instead upon cooperation and good will (G. A. Cohen 2008, 2009)? Is my vision really a utopian horizon, it might be asked, or only an ideological capitulation to capitalism (Hagglund 2019)?

Several responses can be given here. The first is simply to acknowledge that this is not the only kind of utopian thinking worth doing. In some contexts, for instance, it may be valuable to speculate about societies that transcend constraints such as self-interest or the international state system. Yet because of the epistemic obstacles this sort of inquiry faces, it must have a different role in shaping our practical judgments than the sort of democratic horizon I aim to articulate here. Indeed, the vast majority of democratic theorists appear to agree, for they accept most of the same constraints; responding in some way to the predicament of modern politics. While it is not the *only* thing worth doing, this sort of democratic theory is clearly important.

More substantively, we can and should acknowledge that human beings are deeply plastic creatures—constitutively shaped by our social and cultural environments—and that as a result, people raised in a more cooperative and egalitarian culture could very well become much more cooperative and egalitarian. Even then, however, it seems to me that we would still have good reason to retain much of the infrastructure of adversarial competition, which is designed to keep potentially self-interested people accountable to the public interest. Though we are deeply shaped by our cultural environment, after all, we are no more enslaved to it than we are to our genetic material: human agency is a product of deeply complex and unpredictable interactions between culture and biology, and will always exceed the bounds we attempt to set for it (Bagg 2018a). Put simply, then, some people will inevitably be more self-interested than others, and if we eliminate practices designed to channel and control self-interested behavior—trusting entirely in cooperative and egalitarian socialization—these outliers will exploit the system, acquiring greater power and eventually threatening to overturn the cooperative system itself.[1]

Is this horizon a capitalist one? If that term refers to any system that relies on markets and private property to any significant degree—such that the only genuine alternative to capitalism is fully collective ownership and centralized control of production—then the horizon I defend surely counts. At the same time, it would transcend many of the other constitutive features of capitalism, including vast inequalities in relative power, widespread absolute poverty, and the fundamental fact that most people must either work or starve. My contention is that this would profoundly transform the character of those elements of the current system that would remain in place, such that whatever we call it, the resulting horizon deserves to be seen as utopian.

Consider, for instance, how large-scale UWTs would shift the very meaning of production, distribution, and work. Advocates of similar programs

---

[1] This is precisely the insight of the most sophisticated attempts by science fiction authors to imagine a world beyond states, markets, and other familiar institutions. The point is not that we cannot get beyond these systems, just that other practices will inevitably serve structurally similar functions (Byrne 2021; Le Guin 1974).

often suggest they could undermine the "producerist" assumptions central to capitalist ideology as well as the traditional Marxist left (Srnicek and Williams 2015; Weeks 2011)—and in his study of how small-scale unconditional transfer programs in Southern Africa have altered the texture of everyday life, James Ferguson finds support for this hypothesis.[2] On the producerist model—reflected in the saying "give a man a fish, and he eats for a day; teach a man to fish, and he eats for a lifetime"—moral value is attached to productive labor, and success attributed to masculine virtues like independence. As a result, unconditional transfers can only invite immoral and unmanly forms of dependency, treating "the symptoms of poverty" rather than "its underlying causes" (Ferguson 2015: 38). Conditional welfare programs reinforce these assumptions, framing transfers to able-bodied men as shameful and temporary measures aimed at encouraging a swift return to the labor market. Any long-term recipients, meanwhile—including children, the disabled, the elderly, and women—are framed as *naturally* dependent (Pateman 2006: 111).

These are dangerous fictions. All supposedly independent producers are in fact dependent upon many things obscured by producerist ideology, ranging from feminized care work (Tronto 2013) and the "work of nature" (Battistoni 2017) to the role of luck and social privilege in market success (I. M. Young 1990). Thus, any individual's claim to the exclusive enjoyment of the "fruits of their labor" is dubious, and the vaunted independence of male "breadwinners" is a sham—serving only to erase the contributions of those upon whom they actually depend.

Even at the very small scale of the programs he observed in Southern Africa, Ferguson argues, practices of unconditional distribution can begin to undermine this narrative. Instead of assuming that no one deserves a share of the social product unless they engage in activities socially sanctioned as "labor," such programs assert that everyone has a rightful share simply in virtue of their existence. Where a producerist mindset reinscribes structures of domination such as patriarchy and ableism, therefore, a "distributionist" alternative puts all people on a more equal footing, granting social recognition to a much wider range of contributions.

Rather than attributing poverty to failure or dependency, finally, the distributionist logic enacted by unconditional transfers implicates the systemic global forces that coerced them into wage labor, then gradually rendered their

---

[2] As Ferguson notes, the turn towards distributionist logic has been led by countries in the Global South, such as Brazil and South Africa. In recent years, however, many wealthy countries demonstrated openness to this logic as well, when they temporarily adopted unconditional cash transfers to citizens during the COVID-19 pandemic.

labor superfluous, effectively cutting them out of "a distributive deal which used to include them" (2015: 38). As a result,

> getting cut back in to the distributive deal is not treating the "symptom" but goes, in fact, to the very root of the matter: the lack of any distributive entitlement is the underlying cause. Indeed, a distributionist (rather than productionist) analysis might revise the "fish" formula as follows: if the proverbial "man" were to receive neither a fish nor a fishing lesson but instead a binding entitlement to some specified share of the total global production, then (and only then) would he really be fed "for a lifetime."

In a word, that is how we should understand the role of UWTs within this horizon: i.e., as binding entitlements to a share of total production. When conceived in this way, they would be very difficult to dismantle, and could thus provide the sort of bargaining power that advocates of property-owning democracy associate with "pre-disribution" rather than "redistribution." In doing so, moreover, they could also inaugurate even more radical changes to the ideological presuppositions of capitalism. It thus strikes me as irrelevant what we call the resulting society. Whether we see it as a profoundly egalitarian form of democratic capitalism or a vigorously competitive form of democratic socialism, it is a horizon worth striving for.

7.2 Egalitarian competition: Resisting state capture as a political orientation

In addition to a utopian horizon that points us in the right direction over the very long term, democratic ideals also offer a *political orientation* for the medium term—indicating the right stance to take towards existing practices and the right priorities to adopt in improving them. Here too, the ideal of resisting state capture is distinctive for its focus on ensuring egalitarian competition across all spheres of life, rather than scaling up collaborative decision-making. As I have argued throughout this book, politics consists of competition for control of public power among groups of various kinds—be they extremely powerful families and their networks of cronies, factions and interest groups within a wider political elite, or much broader classes and categories of people. Where conventional ideals of collective self-rule strive to minimize or eliminate this conflict—replacing it with a collaborative process for making decisions on equal and reasonable terms—the ideal of resisting state capture seeks rather to channel it towards peaceful forms of competition, while striving to ensure an ever more egalitarian playing field.

Thought it goes against the grain of much democratic thinking, of course, it is hardly the *only* democratic theory to emphasize the centrality of conflict and competition. In particular, certain forms of agonism, republicanism, and pluralism, also place egalitarian competition at the heart of the democratic ideal. To draw out the distinctive features of the political orientation I have in mind, then, it will be useful to compare it to these allied and neighboring frameworks.

To begin with, theorists of "agonistic democracy" such as William Connolly (1991, 1999), Bonnie Honig (1993, 2009), and Chantal Mouffe (2000, 2005) have done important work in highlighting the instability of the claims to neutrality often made by liberal and democratic ideals—and the exclusions such claims inevitably underwrite (Wenman 2013). Against those who would confine democratic conflict and contestation within narrow boundaries of liberal consensus or public reason, they have rightly insisted both that deeper conflict is inevitable, and that more pervasive contestation can often be a desirable reflection of democratic vitality, rather than a blemish on what would otherwise be a fundamentally cooperative enterprise.

In most cases, however, their astute critiques of neutralist ideals—and their vindications of a more oppositional orientation—have not been accompanied by similarly compelling visions of what egalitarian democratic competition requires in practice. As Lois McNay (2014) has observed, indeed, the analysis of agonists and other "radical" democrats is often carried out as such a high level of abstraction that it can obscure the real requirements of collective power—and the real obstacles that so often stand in the way of its development. The ideal of resisting state capture thus builds on many of the foundational assumptions of agonistic theories, while offering more detail about the institutional requirements of democratic competition, as well as the substantive policies and forms of collective power that could make this competition more egalitarian. And in doing so, it draws substantially from republican traditions.

Contemporary republicanism is quite diverse, ranging from broadly liberal thinkers like Philip Pettit (1997, 2013), Frank Lovett (2010, 2016), and Robert Taylor (2017)—often inspired by figures such as Montesquieu and Madison—to radicals such as John McCormick (2011), Alex Gourevitch (2015), and Camila Vergara (2020)—who are more likely to draw from Machiavelli and Marx (Leipold, Nabulsi, and White 2020; Muldoon 2019; O'Shea 2020; Roberts 2016). United by the goal of preventing domination and the means of institutionalized contestation, they disagree about what domination entails and which kinds of institutionalized contestation are most crucial for combating it. Where liberals aim to ensure citizens can contest majority tyranny and public domination by appealing to impartial bodies, for instance, radicals and plebeians emphasize the importance of *collective* institutions—often explicitly organized along class lines—through which disempowered groups can contest domination by elites.

My view has clear affinities with both forms of republicanism, and their shared negative ideal of nondomination.[3] Like me, crucially, most republicans also reject the common view of states as unitary entities with a sovereign decision maker in charge. Instead, they assume that political outcomes emerge from a complex thicket of contradictory tendencies and conflicting intentions. Democracy is thus seen not as popular *rule*—i.e., a creative process of collective decision-making in which the will of a sovereign people is enacted—but as popular *control*—i.e., a primarily reactive process of contestation through which those who do actually make decisions are incentivized to act in the public interest (Ingham 2019; Lovett 2022; Pettit 2013).

When liberal and radical republicans disagree, meanwhile, my sympathies are most often with the latter. Like mine, their preference for collective forms of contestation is rooted in a recognition that the outcomes of this complex, nonsovereign process are powerfully shaped by underlying relations of social and material power—relations that are always skewed toward the wealthy to at least some degree. Where liberal republicans see democratic goals such as the "balance of power" and "civic virtue" in neutral terms, therefore, I embrace the more partisan and materialist vision of democratic demands favored by radicals. In this latter view, for one, the crucial form of balance required by a healthy democracy is not among different branches and levels of government, but rather between *social* groups and *material* forces. Given the inevitable advantages possessed by wealthy elites, this entails constant proactive efforts to undermine their power and foster that of disempowered groups. Accordingly, the central virtue demanded of ordinary citizens is not a generic sense of commitment to the common good, but a specific set of solidaristic dispositions that facilitate collective action against wealthy elites.

That said, nearly all republicans also share two key blind spots. First, neither liberals nor radicals devote serious attention to *electoral* competition: while accepting it as a necessary baseline, most republicans dismiss it

---

[3] The category of state capture focuses on abuse of state power, and does not *directly* incorporate concerns about private domination. As noted in §1.5, however, nearly all private domination is *facilitated* by state policy in one way or another, however, so the ideal of resisting state capture can help us diagnose and respond to nearly all of the same problems.

rather quickly as insufficient, presenting their preferred supplemental institutions (whether liberal or radical) as the solution. As such, they often fail to appreciate the real virtues of elections—and, more importantly, the ways that cross-cutting forms of institutionalized contestation might undermine those virtues. While republicans often pay lip service to civil society organizations as critical to civic virtue, second, few give detailed accounts of what the right sort of organizations look like, how they might be fostered, or how they might interact with state power through elections and other contestatory institutions.

Both blind spots converge in a widespread neglect among republicans of the central vehicle for political competition: i.e., political parties. Republicans rightly recognize that political life is about competition for power among different groups—and that our best response is thus to structure this competition to the benefit of all. Yet in their drive to institutionalize contestation *beyond* the electoral realm, republicans risk entrenching the specific axes of contention around which their preferred extra-electoral bodies are constructed. Despite its many flaws, inter-party competition is much more flexible, allowing shifting coalitions to compete on terms they set themselves. As such, it better accommodates the evolving demands of a dynamic social world.

This motivates Ian Shapiro's (2003, 2016b) neo-Schumpeterian rejoinder to republicans, which adopts the ideal of minimizing domination, but holds that the best way to achieve it is to ensure top-level leaders face sharp competition from strong rival parties in majoritarian elections (see also Rosenbluth and Shapiro 2018). Whatever their designers' intent, he insists, additional constraints on top-level leaders—including practices as diverse as bicameralism, the separation of powers, federalism, and intra-party democracy—will only obscure responsibility for outcomes and introduce new "veto players" (Tsebelis 2002). At best, therefore, the extra-electoral institutions favored by republicans will entrench the status quo. At worst, they will actively privilege wealthy elites, who are better able to take advantage of additional complexity by exerting influence through back channels (2016b: 44–45). Like the agonists, Shapiro holds that impartiality is impossible, and that practices claiming to realize it—such as judicial review, independent central banks, and deliberative bodies—will serve only to conceal the conflicting interests and power relations that truly drive outcomes (1999, 2016a, 2017).

Shapiro is right to be skeptical of apparently impartial expert bodies: rather than allowing citizens to contest public domination, such institutions often serve in practice to entrench elite interests, and are harmful to democracy on balance—notably the US Supreme Court. Amid growing skepticism of electoral politics, meanwhile, he rightly highlights the virtues of sharp competition between strong disciplined parties. Still, his rejection of extra-electoral contestation is too categorical. On the one hand, he understates the barriers to accountability examined in Chapter 2, and thus overstates the ability of electoral mechanisms to minimize domination.[4] On the other hand, he neglects the possibility that contestatory procedures could be designed to favor counter-hegemonic interests, as well as the importance of fostering independent organizations of countervailing power outside of official party structures. Like most republicans—and many other "realist" theorists of democracy (e.g., Maloy 2019)—Shapiro ultimately devotes too much attention to fixing decision-making institutions, and too little to mitigating underlying asymmetries in organizational capacity and private power.

The thinkers most concerned with this latter aim, finally, can be understood as contributing to a *pluralist* tradition in democratic thought. Like republicans, those I call pluralists eschew sovereigntist assumptions and view competition rather than consensus as central to democracy. Yet compared to republicans, pluralists typically focus less on the institutional framework for competition, and more on the relative strength of competing groups—especially as reflected in their organizational capacity outside of formal state and party structures. For pluralists, the health of a democracy is determined largely by the degree of balance between interests. Yet they disagree among themselves about issues of both diagnosis—i.e., whether there is already sufficient balance in existing democracies, and if not, which interests are most in need of better representation—and treatment—i.e., which kinds of nonstate organizations would help to achieve or preserve balance, and how they should be integrated within parties and states.

As I conceive it, then, the category of pluralism does include those most commonly known by that label in political science—i.e., Robert Dahl (1961) and other mid-century thinkers who argued that interest group competition in the US was conducted on roughly egalitarian terms. However, it also includes critics of that tradition—from E. E. Schattschneider (1960) to Lisa Disch (2021)—who also value egalitarian interest representation through nonstate institutions, but disagree that the US (or any other democracy) actually realizes or approximates that ideal.

---

[4] More specifically, Shapiro's faith in the tendency of inter-party competition to serve the interests of the median voter neglects two important realities. First, voters do not simply present a fixed set of preferences which parties can cater to, as assumed by Downsian convergence models. Instead, parties shape the preferences of their supporters; often influencing their conceptions of their interests (Disch 2021). Second, wealthy elites and other concentrated interests can influence the leaders of all viable parties in the same direction simultaneously, effectively keeping certain issues off the table entirely (see Bagg and Bhatia 2022).

In this broad sense, then, the pluralist tradition also includes a range of contemporary non-Kantian liberals—such as Jacob Levy (2015), Andy Sabl (2001, 2017), and Pierre Rosanvallon (2008)—along with their intellectual forebears, from Montesquieu and Tocqueville to Lefort and Shklar. And it includes more radical thinkers as well—such as John Medearis (2015), Marc Stears (2010), Jeffrey Stout (2012), and Deva Woodly (2015, 2021), along with predecessors ranging from GDH Cole and John Dewey to Saul Alinsky and Ella Baker. The key difference is that liberal pluralists see civil society as a generic source of counter-power, whose role is to contest abuse by state actors and capture by special interests, whereas radical pluralists regard demands for balance, under current conditions, as partisan. Given the pervasive asymmetries that characterize all modern democracies, in other words, what deeper democratization requires is not a stronger civil society as such, but specific forms of solidarity and organization to help counter-hegemonic groups contest capture and domination by specific elite interests.

As should be clear, my sympathies lie with the radicals on this point of divergence. Indeed, among all the neighboring approaches examined here, radical pluralists are perhaps my closest allies. Where existing accounts of radical pluralism tend to focus either on specific thinkers or types of political action, however, this book aims to articulate a more comprehensive theory of democracy—and thus to illustrate how the forms of countervailing power defended by radical pluralists fit into a broader ecology that also includes things like constitutional constraints, vigorous market competition, a meritocratic bureaucracy, and aggressive anti-monopoly tactics. The resulting political orientation thus gives us strong reasons to defend the merits of electoral democracy against alternative methods for selecting top-level leaders, *and* to endorse a unique suite of radical practices that will enable us to transcend its limitations.

7.3 Navigating danger: Resisting state capture as a guide to practical judgment

The aim of this chapter, recall, is to clarify how the ideal of resisting state capture functions as a distinctive set of heuristics for democratic judgment. And by elaborating the utopian horizon and political orientation it suggests, we have gone some way towards understanding its overall democratic priorities. What remains, however, is to show how this distinctive view of democratic priorities can be applied to the kinds of difficult concrete dilemmas highlighted at the outset, in which the demands of democracy are in direct tension with one another.

7.3.1 Pitting democracy against itself: Dilemmas of militant democracy

As we have seen, resisting state capture entails a very robust commitment to principles like universal suffrage and free speech. Yet it also makes sense of the intuition that these principles may need to be suspended in defense of broader democratic goals. As militant democrats argue, for instance, it is surely better for democracy to ban the Nazi party than to let the Nazis come to power and eliminate electoral competition entirely (Loewenstein 1937a, 1937b).

Conventional ideals of democracy sometimes struggle to make sense of these demands, or at least to navigate them in sufficiently textured and nuanced ways. For instance, they often depict suffrage and speech as intrinsic rights, owed to all persons in virtue of their agency, and if so, it is easy to conclude that these rights are absolute. Even Nazis deserve a say over the rules that govern their lives, on this account, so disenfranchising them is always impermissible. For others, meanwhile, this logic of desert will offer a tempting rationalization of exclusion. If people exercise their agency in anti-democratic ways—for example, by attempting to deny such rights to others—then perhaps they have forfeited their own claims to have these rights respected. The strategy of grounding rights in an overriding interest in self-rule thus boasts a suspicious level of certainty either way. If the point of upholding universal suffrage and free speech is that doing so helps to prevent state capture, however, a different justificatory logic emerges— grounded in the perspectives of particular actors—which avoids these two extremes.

Consider first the hypothetical perspective of an omniscient being with perfect knowledge of the consequences of action and the proper weighting of various dangers. On this god's-eye view, violating rights of suffrage and speech is democratically acceptable whenever the danger of doing so is eclipsed by the danger of *not* doing so. Just when the danger of a Nazi takeover exceeds the danger posed by banning the party, that is when banning it becomes justifiable. Based on their precise and certain knowledge, this ideal observer could tell military generals, judges, and other well-positioned actors whether they should intervene in any given case—and sometimes, at least, the answer will be yes. Certainly, it is possible to design hypothetical scenarios in which the objective advisability of a "coup for democracy" appears undeniable.

The trouble is, of course, that no one will ever occupy this omniscient perspective. If we examine political dilemmas not from a god's-eye view, but instead from the limited and uncertain perspective of those who might actually face them, our calculus changes quite a bit. For instance, the assassination of Hitler is often cited as a paradigmatically justifiable example of political violence, but as Rob Mayer (n.d.) very cleverly and comprehensively illustrates, it is far from clear whether any *real* actor could ever have had enough certainty about the likely consequences of an attempt on Hitler's life to render the action justifiable *ex ante*, i.e., from their own limited perspective. Certainly the time-traveler's fantasy of killing baby Hitler would have been unethical from the perspective of his contemporaries. Neither was the danger he posed apparent enough to justify assassination when he was the leader of a fringe party in the 1920s. Once the Nazis were in power, finally, removing their oft-blundering Führer could plausibly have *increased* their ability to achieve genocidal goals: indeed, both the UK and the USSR scrapped plans to assassinate Hitler for precisely this reason. As Mayer acknowledges, there are some potential scenarios in which killing Hitler—as part of a broader effort at regime change with a real chance of success—might have been justifiable. Even in this seemingly obvious case, however, the waters are unexpectedly murky.

For similar reasons, Alex Kirshner (2014) also urges caution about preventive interventions to defend existing democracies against anti-democrats. While maintaining that intervention could sometimes be the most democratic option, he insists that this is only in the direst of circumstances, when all other options have been exhausted, and the threat to basic democratic rights is both imminent and undeniably grave. Even then, those behind the intervention must follow strict procedures designed to minimize the democratic costs of their action. And as he shows, most real-world interventions—such as the 1997 coup that removed a controversial religious party from power in Turkey, and was subsequently endorsed as democratically legitimate by the European Court of Human Rights—meet few if any of these criteria.

If we focus more thoroughly on the perspective of particular political actors, indeed, we may go even further in this respect than Kirshner. In the real world, for one, no one has the sort of omniscience that may be freely stipulated in hypothetical examples. What is more, all real political actors are also subject to motivated reasoning and other pervasive cognitive biases that distort their judgment. In short, we human beings want desperately to believe in our own righteousness, which reliably leads us to overestimate the objective merits of the choices we *want* to make for self-serving reasons (Bagg 2018a; Galeotti 2018). As such, political leaders have very powerful reasons to refrain from actions that entrench their own power, even when it genuinely seems to them that doing so would help to resist some other form of state capture.

In particular, it strikes me as highly unlikely that military generals will *ever* have enough certainty about the results of unseating elected leaders to render this action justifiable. Given the difficulties involved in plotting a successful coup and ensuring that power returns to democratically elected leaders in the aftermath—not to mention the danger of licensing further authoritarianism if the coup fails—it is probably best to place this strategy off-limits altogether. On these thoroughly pragmatic grounds, that is, we can justify a categorical prohibition. In this way, the prospect of a "coup for democracy" is analogous to the specter of the "benevolent despot" that has long haunted democratic theory, motivating many theorists to abandon instrumentalist approaches and defend the intrinsic value of collective self-rule. If we instead abandon the conceit of an omniscient perspective—considering dilemmas from the perspective of those who actually face them—we need not turn to intrinsic accounts in order to defend robust commitment to principles like universal suffrage and freedom of speech. Epistemic humility does the trick just as well. The ideal of resisting state capture thus recommends even greater caution about many interventions than Kirshner and other admirably cautious analysts of the dilemmas of militant democracy.

For two reasons, however, there are also certain cases in which the ideal of resisting state capture will suggest a *more* aggressive approach to promoting democracy than is typical among militant democrats. Because it considers dilemmas as they are actually faced by political actors, for one, my account recognizes important asymmetries between situations where the actors in question would be the first to cross certain dangerous lines, and situations where those lines have already been crossed. Most conventional accounts make no such distinction, given their view of democratic demands as intrinsic requirements of political equality or self-rule, rather than pragmatic requirements of resisting capture. Because it includes radical demands normally seen as "substantive," meanwhile—in addition to the standard liberal procedures typically emphasized by contemporary militant democrats—it conceivably licenses certain "procedural" sacrifices in the name of sufficiently large "substantive" gains. Again, this possibility is rarely countenanced on standard approaches that focus more exclusively on procedural rights.

7.3.2 The substantive sources of liberal procedures: Moderate vs. radical Reconstruction

To illustrate both of these distinctive features of my account, let us consider Kirshner's analysis of the dilemmas facing the US Congress in the aftermath of the Civil War from 1867 to 1876. At the beginning of this period, known as "Reconstruction," former Confederate rebels were not yet allowed to vote or hold national political office. As such, Congress was dominated by Northern Republicans, who had to decide when and how to re-enfranchise the former rebels. Moderate Republicans argued that this should happen as soon as possible, subject to former Confederates officially accepting Black suffrage and other basic principles. By contrast, radical Republicans like Charles Sumner and Thaddeus Stevens sought a much broader mandate for Reconstruction—including land redistribution from plantation owners to their former slaves—which would require excluding Confederates for a longer period, until this was accomplished.

While Kirshner admires the egalitarian vision of the radical Republicans, he argues that it would have made the South into a "quasi-permanent vassal territory" and was "irreconcilable with the principle that all citizens possess basic interests in participation." As a result, he ultimately faults radicals for pursuing "utopian" visions of "political paradise" through "exclusionary policies," and praises moderates for adopting the more reasonable aim of "legitimacy" or "democracy" (149). And though I otherwise endorse Kirshner's reasoning, my intuitions differ quite strongly here. It seems to me, rather—and I am hardly alone in this—that the failure of the radical Republican vision of Reconstruction is among the great tragedies of US history. If the radicals had succeeded, rather than the moderates, that is, it is quite plausible to suppose that US history would have turned out very differently—and very much to the *benefit* of any plausible definition of democracy (Balfour 2003; Du Bois 1935).

Indeed, Kirshner himself acknowledges that his conclusion seems counterintuitive—and even allows that the radicals' plan was more *just* than that of the moderates. Whatever the best response overall might have been, however, he maintains that the moderates' plan was more *democratic*, where "democracy" is conceived in minimalist terms as consisting of participatory rights for all citizens. He writes, for instance, that "members of the Reconstruction Congress faced a tragic choice: they could pursue democracy by finding ways to allow Southern antidemocrats to participate or they could pursue justice by excluding those antidemocrats. But they could not pursue both" (24). Throughout, he emphasizes a "tragic fault line between the duty to give people what they are due and the duty to act democratically" (152, 159–162).

Even if we accept his definition of democracy in terms of participatory rights for all, however, a longer historical perspective casts doubt on Kirshner's inference that the moderate plan better served its demands. After Reconstruction ended in 1876, due to the flagging resolve of Republicans, the participatory rights of southern Black people were eviscerated for nearly a century. Based solely on the criterion of participatory rights, then, the moderate plan of immediate readmission turned out disastrously for democracy over the long term—in ways that were predicted by many at the time. Somewhat oddly, however, Kirshner treats the failure of moderate Reconstruction as further evidence that it was the best plan, arguing that the radical plan "would have required far more determination" (150) and would thus have fared even worse. Yet this is hardly the only inference we might draw. Given how Reconstruction actually ended, in fact, we might reasonably think that delaying readmission of former Confederates until Black suffrage was more securely entrenched was the only thing that could have *saved* it.

After all, the deadlocked 1876 presidential election that ended Reconstruction by forcing a deal with white Southerners was deadlocked at least partly thanks to the political participation of former Confederates who would not have regained participatory rights so quickly on the radical plan. Though we can never be certain about such counterfactual conjectures, therefore, it is not implausible to suppose that if the radical plan had been enacted, Reconstruction might not have ended so quickly or disastrously. Even assuming that participatory rights must be categorically prioritized above other concerns, that is, a more dynamic historical perspective suggests that the radical plan might actually have been *less* utopian—requiring *less* sustained commitment to upholding Black political rights—than that of the moderates.

In this respect, it is important to recognize the role played by land redistribution, alongside education and other social reforms, in the radical plan. As the radical Republicans understood, Black political rights could only be guaranteed if they were grounded in secure access to social and economic power resources—and, through them, the ability to organize collective power amongst themselves (Du Bois 1935: 585–591). The radical plan was precisely *not* for the North to maintain the South as a vassal territory through a permanent military occupation—as has been charged ever since by Southern critics, even in reference to the moderate plan that was actually enacted. Instead, the real radical plan was to create the sort of social and economic conditions that would sustainably support Black political rights once the military occupation inevitably came to an end—i.e., conditions in which Black people enjoyed a stable base of power from which to defend their political rights against the inevitable onslaught from former Confederates who would then be readmitted to political participation. In Du Bois' (1935: 586) words, achieving a sustainable democracy would have required that Black people have both "permanent organization" and "savings to sustain it" in this fight—resources the radical plan would have given them, but the moderate plan did not. Or in the terms I have been using, rather, the radical plan was to ensure that Black people had sufficient *organizational capacity* and *private power* to match that of the white planter class, thereby creating the sort of *balance of social forces* that could realistically support electoral competition on equal terms.

Would this plan have worked? We can never know for sure. It would certainly have carried great risks, and could have been thwarted at many points. This is why a similar plan would never even be worth considering, in almost any set of circumstances *other* than the aftermath of a bloody civil war. No matter how valuable the consequences of such an egalitarian program might be in theory, that is—i.e., if its success could be guaranteed, from a god's-eye view—it will always a terrible idea for the government of one country to unilaterally impose a program of land redistribution and social uplift upon another country or region with which it was initially at peace, through the means of violent conquest and military occupation. We can state this categorically. Crucially, however, this was not the situation facing the Republican-dominated Congress in 1867, which had no democratic status quo to protect, and no further escalation to prevent. Given that Confederates had already been disenfranchised by secession and war, in other words, the main damage to democracy had already been done, and re-enfranchisement could have been delayed quite a bit longer without incurring significant *further* risks of capture.

For Kirshner, whose account is grounded in the intrinsic value of participatory rights, the situation of the Reconstruction Congress was not meaningfully different from that of generals considering a coup to prevent an anti-democratic party from taking power in a country with established electoral institutions: in both cases, anti-democrats have indefeasible participatory rights, which may be violated only when failing to do so would immediately threaten minimal democratic requirements. Just as *preventive* intervention is acceptable only when there is an imminent and grave threat to basic rights—if at all—*keeping* Confederates disenfranchised was acceptable only as long as it took to formally enfranchise Black men, and no longer.

By contrast, my approach recognizes a key asymmetry between these two situations. The participatory rights of Confederates would have to be restored eventually, in my view, but in deciding when and how to do so, I argue that the victorious Union could have used their temporarily inflated power—bought at the expense of hundreds of thousands of lives—to foster a more robust democracy over the long term, rather than rushing to restore a status quo that had already been destroyed. That is precisely what the radicals proposed, of course, in seeking to redistribute land to formerly enslaved Black people, and thereby to give them a base of social and economic power from which they could then build further collective power.

After all, the Reconstruction Congress rightly used this opportunity to impose several Constitutional Amendments on Southern states, among many other laws and requirements that were widely perceived as noxious by most Southern whites. Pushing this program one step further to include land redistribution and a somewhat longer period of exclusion would not have imposed significant *further* risks on democracy. Whatever would have happened, it is difficult to believe that the US South would have been a *less* democratic place in 1910, or 1960, or 2020, if former Confederates had been excluded from participation for a few more years, as freedmen received the requisite land and social resources to solidify their power. As Du Bois saw a century ago, indeed, the real tragedy of Reconstruction is that the Radical Republicans lost their fight against the moderates, and were not able to see their plan through to fruition.

The reasons for our regret, importantly, cannot be limited to concerns about justice, insofar as that is seen as something distinct from democracy. Even on a minimalist account defining it in terms of participatory rights, I have emphasized, the success of the moderate plan was a disaster for *democracy,* not only justice. In order to stand a realistic chance of maintaining their participatory rights in the South over the long term, Black people would have needed a stronger base in economic and social power than they had managed to win for themselves by the end of moderate Reconstruction. Even if we do not include radical demands for egalitarian distribution of social and economic power within our *definition* of democracy, therefore, the case of Reconstruction provides a particularly clear illustration of why those demands are an integral part of the broader democratic *project*. And once we accept this point, we might as well include it in our definition as well—as does the thick ideal of democracy as resisting state capture.

Kirshner's choice to define democracy in minimal terms, and frame its procedural demands as opposed to the substantive demands of justice, is quite common in debates about militant democracy. In my view, however, the case of Reconstruction nicely illustrates the importance of incorporating both kinds of demands within a broader ideal of democracy. This alternative framing preserves the insight that there are genuine tensions between different sets of demands, while emphasizing that both sets ultimately serve the same end, and suggesting that neither can be given absolute priority over the other. On my account, more specifically, ensuring a stable base of social and economic power for formerly enslaved Black people is not properly seen as a "utopian" demand of justice, which tragically conflicts with the more "basic" demands of democracy. Given the tight connection between public and private power, rather, it should have been seen as an essential condition for achieving even the most basic procedural goals.

7.3.3 Liberal procedure vs. radical substance: Dilemmas of redistributive populism

Indeed, a similar logic applies to all six of the basic strategies for resisting state capture—such that neglecting any one of them will eventually degrade the effectiveness of the others. And this has broader implications about fending off threats to democracy. The most obvious manifestations of proto-authoritarian incursions can often be seen in violations of impartiality and universality within formal political institutions, for instance, but my account insists that such threats typically reflect deeper pathologies in the underlying power structure, and that effectively defending democracy thus requires much more than simply restoring the formal status quo. In response to contemporary democratic challenges from authoritarian populists, more specifically, an important priority must be to reinstate practices of impartiality and universality within formal political institutions. Just as important, however, are efforts to make competition more egalitarian by fostering the growth of countervailing power—indeed, the latter may be required to have any hope of achieving the former. Once a leader decides to use proto-authoritarian tactics, formal constraints are only as strong as the opposition forces who enforce them, so attending to the organizational strength of these forces is paramount.

How far can we take this logic? Are there cases where we should pursue radical substantive priorities even at the expense of respect for liberal procedures? How robust must our support for electoral democracy be, in other words, given all of the vast imbalances of power it sustains, and the resulting biases in democratic outcomes? The tensions between liberal procedures and radical substantive goals—both of which are core demands of democracy, on my account—raise a number of challenging questions about the democratic merits of what I call "redistributive populism." How does the ideal of resisting state capture help us grapple with these dilemmas?

Nearly all democratic theorists readily condemn the authoritarian populists of the right and center, like Hungary's Viktor Orbán and Turkey's Recep Tayyip Erdoğan, who use electoral victories as an excuse to dismantle constraints on their power. Yet some have greater sympathy for figures on the ideological left, like Venezuela's Hugo Chávez and Bolivia's Evo Morales. Indeed, a framework such as mine—which incorporates liberal and radical demands within the same ideal of democracy, and thus puts them on the same level—might seem to lend support to one of the core justifications offered by populist leaders in their efforts to circumvent established procedures and maintain power: namely, that certain constraints on their power represent the interests of a wealthy elite, and that advancing democracy requires radical action against these elites, even when that means circumventing liberal procedures.

These claims characterize right and left populisms alike, and ring false in the mouths of Orbán or Erdoğan. Yet broadly similar claims are sometimes quite plausible. Perhaps the most significant impact of many constraints on central government authority in the US, for instance—including "states' rights' as well as certain Madisonian "checks and balances" at the federal level—has been to entrench the interests of a relatively small group of white elites at the expense of nearly everyone else. In the infamous "Lochner" era between 1897 and 1937, similarly, the US Supreme Court repeatedly overturned redistributive legislation favored by wide majorities, thus protecting wealthy elites at the expense of the broader public (Sunstein 1987). Those who sought to dismantle these obstacles to enable sweeping egalitarian reforms—such as Abraham Lincoln, Franklin Roosevelt, and Lyndon Johnson—were routinely branded by opponents as tyrants, but most now recognize their acts as major democratic achievements.

As such, democratic actors cannot dismiss genuinely *redistributive* populists out of hand. When democratic demands come into conflict, it is difficult to draw categorical conclusions. By adopting the perspective of real political actors rather than hypothetical omniscient observers, however, we can begin to articulate some provisional guidelines for action.

On the one hand, certain actions should—like military coups—remain off limits entirely. We will always be able to imagine a disaster great enough that averting it would, from a god's-eye view, justify massive violations of foundational democratic commitments. If we could be certain that electoral fraud or executing opponents on trumped-up charges in show trials would avert catastrophic capture on the level of the Nazi regime, for instance, we would have to admit that such actions were probably justifiable. In practice, however, we will never have anything close to certainty in such matters. On the contrary, in fact, those who would benefit from such acts should expect to be routinely overconfident about their predictions in this regard. Meanwhile, show trials and electoral fraud are extremely damaging to the fragile norms and expectations required for electoral democracy to function. Given that we can never attain absolute certainty that such strategies will have the desired effect, therefore, we may conclude that they are never justifiable as means to the democratic end of resisting state capture.

On the other hand, some deviations from democratic procedure may be appropriate under certain circumstances. The rule of law is a central pillar of resisting capture, for example, but illegal protests or strikes will often have democratic benefits—like building countervailing power—that outweigh the costs of weakening respect for law. The costs to the rule of law are significantly higher in the case of a security official leaking sensitive documents, meanwhile, or a judge enacting what she perceives to be a good outcome against her understanding of the best statutory interpretation, but these acts are still plausibly justifiable in certain cases.

In the case of leaders seeking to deepen resistance to capture by dispersing private power, meanwhile, it might be justifiable—within reason—to appoint politically reliable judges or pass laws weakening the financial backing of opposition parties. Especially if the opposition has taken similarly self-serving steps while in power, a certain "arms race" logic can even seem to require it (Bagg and Tranvik 2019). In the US, for instance, both major parties rely on gerrymandering to entrench their power, and unilateral disarmament by either party would likely give the other such a comfortable advantage that it would *aggravate* problems of state capture. Given the unilateral steps taken by the Republican Party to entrench minority rule over the past three decades (Hacker and Pierson 2011; Hertel-Fernandez 2019; Levitsky and Ziblatt 2018), meanwhile, some commentators have plausibly argued that the Democratic Party must engage in certain reciprocal norm violations—including a "court-packing" scheme—in order to re-establish a viable democratic equilibrium (Faris 2018; Keck 2022).

My account gives us reason to take such proposals seriously. At the same time, however, it gives us equally powerful reasons not to underestimate their dangers. Even the most well-intentioned leaders are likely to err on the self-aggrandizing side, and should try to counteract that tendency by being far more scrupulous than seems necessary. Meanwhile, those with the most concentrated private power will usually be best able to advance their interests by violating procedural norms. By constraining such actors from bending the rules whenever it is useful to them, therefore, stronger procedural norms often serve to protect the disempowered, and those seeking to contest elite capture should be extremely wary of changing them, even in ways that appear beneficial. Even if the status quo norms are mildly favorable to elites, attempts to alter them may trigger escalating arms races of norm erosion that are likely to work out in elites' favor. At the limit, such arms races could even upend the equilibrium of electoral democracy—an event that rarely works out well for anyone in the long run, least of all those at the bottom.

Redistributive populists and others who seek to use radical practices to undermine capture by wealthy and powerful groups thus face an extremely high burden of proof. They cannot take their redistributive ends as an all-purpose excuse to ignore liberal constraints on their power or otherwise weaken the institutions of electoral democracy. Where an arms race has already begun, I have acknowledged, it is sometimes democratically necessary to respond in kind, deviating from certain procedural norms in order to prevent opponents from dangerously entrenching their rule. In doing so, however, partisans of democracy must always explicitly aim to restore a democratic equilibrium with legitimate oppositional institutions and a level playing field, rather than simply ensuring perpetual domination for their own side. More specifically, they must pre-commit themselves to such an aim in materially and politically meaningful ways. As Kirshner (2014) argues in the case of militant democracy, in other words, those aiming to defend and enrich democracy must employ "self-limiting" means.

What can we conclude? Given that the basic liberal procedures of electoral democracy are justified on the same grounds as the substantively redistributive tactics favored by radicals, for one, the former cannot be granted *categorical* priority over the latter. Yet the protection of such procedures deserves very significant *practical* priority over substantive goals of any kind. After Donald Trump won the 2016 US election, for instance, some pundits encouraged members of the electoral college to disobey the wishes of voters in their states. Even though the electoral college is an anti-democratic institution that should be abolished—and even though Trump's presidency did great damage to the procedural and substantive foundations of democracy—this was a terrible idea, which would have vastly accelerated the deterioration of the fragile balance of forces that sustains electoral competition for power.

Out of respect for their own epistemic and cognitive limitations, meanwhile, would-be democratizers should nearly always resist temptations to take actions that would eliminate constraints on their power. Again, however, the reason for this is not principled but pragmatic: i.e., because the likelihood of sustainably redistributing wealth and power *without* electoral procedures is quite low. It is true that the most spectacular episodes of redistribution have been instigated by autocracies (Albertus 2015). Aside from the devastating human costs often incurred along the way, however, egalitarian distributions that result from authoritarian action and violence have proved all but impossible to maintain over time. If incumbents are able to hold on to political power without regularly facing plausible political challenges, after all, they are eventually likely to appropriate more and more of the social product for themselves.

Still, the world is a profoundly complex place, and my account leaves open the possibility that certain temporary and carefully self-limiting deviations from standard liberal procedures might be justifiable in service of radically redistributive ends. This refusal to make categorical pronouncements will undoubtedly be frustrating for some. In my view, however, providing clearer and simpler rules would betray the real normative difficulties involved. Sometimes, we have no choice but to make case-by-case judgments. In certain democratic dilemmas, that is, the most reliable guidance a general theory can offer is simply to draw our attention to a range of potentially relevant concerns, and insist on further inquiry informed by those concerns.

To illustrate this process of inquiry and judgment, it is worth briefly working through one final example, using the tools developed here to examine the divergent impacts of Hugo Chávez in Venezuela and Evo Morales in Bolivia. Both leaders faced political systems dominated by entrenched elites, thanks to pervasive biases in social norms, economic structures, and political institutions that favored the interests of the wealthy. Both rode populist platforms to landslide victories, as part of a broader "pink tide" across Latin America, with mandates to dismantle the oligarchic constitutional orders they inherited, and remake their societies on more egalitarian terms. As a result, both took various steps that transgressed the spirit (if not the letter) of liberal procedures, such as revising constitutional rules in ways that reduced constraints on executive power, and replacing conservative judges who were likely to thwart their plans.

These moves were widely interpreted—by opponents, as well as many outside observers—as threatening to democracy. And the ideal of resisting state capture gives us good reasons to take this concern seriously: any changes to constitutional rules can destabilize a democratic order, especially when they reduce constraints on incumbent power. Yet crucially, it also insists that such changes may be beneficial or even necessary for democracy, in cases where existing rules are heavily biased in favor of certain interests—as they clearly were in both Venezuela and Bolivia, two of the most unequal societies in the world. They thus provide useful test cases for the dilemmas of redistributive populism: were Chávez and Morales really anti-democratic forces, as their critics claim, or did they simply embrace the radical means necessary for advancing democracy under adverse conditions of vast and pervasive inequality?

Of course, no simple, satisfying answer can be given to such a question. Both leaders took some steps that were democracy-enhancing, while both also made many blunders. The overall democratic impact of the two leaders ultimately diverged, however, in a striking and instructive way. Though critics and admirers alike often paint them with the same brush, in short, Chávez's rule was a disaster for democracy, while Morales' legacy is far more positive on balance.

To be clear: Morales violated many democratic norms, and had a worrying tendency to concentrate power into his own hands. Nevertheless, his rule was constrained by a variety of countervailing forces that retained their independence—notably including dissenting elements within his own party (Movement for Socialism, or MAS) and broader ruling coalition (Anria 2016; Faguet 2018). Indeed, the defection of Bolivia's largest trade union confederation from his coalition, in the wake of his decision to run for a fourth term in 2019, played a crucial role in his eventual ouster (Anria and Roberts 2019). Morales prosecuted some of his opponents and appointed loyal allies to official posts (Mainwaring and Pérez-Liñán 2015)—including the Constitutional Tribunal whose controversial ruling, overturning a 2016 referendum, enabled him to run for a fourth term in the first place. At least some of this, however, can be understood as restoring balance to a lopsided system that had been ruled for decades by a narrow, racially homogeneous elite. It is worth noting, meanwhile, that he typically adhered to the letter, if not always the spirit, of legal procedures. Finally and most importantly, Morales never seriously threatened the ability of opposition groups to access organizational resources, media systems, or electoral institutions. Overall, then, his legacy was greater balance of organizational capacity among groups in Bolivian society, rather than a more lopsided distribution of power.

Unfortunately, the opposite is true of Venezuela under Chávez and his successor, Nicolas Maduro. In contrast to Morales, for one—who was consistently held accountable by the multilevel, mass-membership party organization that brought him to power (i.e., MAS)—Chávez's power was grounded from the start in "personalistic" loyalty (Levitsky and Loxton 2013). Even more importantly, Chávez went much further in dismantling the ability of opposition groups to organize, promote their views, and compete for power in the electoral system (Hawkins 2016). It is true that Chávez brought about substantial redistribution and popular mobilization, and also that his opponents bear a considerable portion of the blame for escalating the arms races in which both sides participated—including a failed coup attempt against him in 2002. Nevertheless, the outcome of Chavismo in power has not been a deepened democracy, characterized by greater balance in organizational capacity, but rather a barely competitive autocracy in which nearly all of the organizational capacity is concentrated in the hands of a new Chavista elite.

To be sure: this brief summary barely scratches the surface of the deeply complex questions facing democratic actors in both Bolivia and Venezuela, regarding how they could or should have acted in order to pursue democratic ends most effectively. My own judgment, based on a necessarily incomplete reading of the literature, is that Morales's rule had a net positive impact on the distribution of organizational capacity—and thus on democracy itself—while that of Chávez was damaging to democracy on the whole. Still, there are surely many nuances I have missed. Regardless, I remain confident of the broader point this case study is meant to illustrate: i.e., that there are genuine tensions between democracy's liberal and radical demands, which cannot be resolved as easily as partisans of either set would like to imagine. Dilemmas of redistributive populism pitting them against one another will thus pose recurring and difficult challenges for democratic actors, which cannot be evaded by granting one categorical priority over the other. Difficult and dangerous as it may be, we must work through these challenges.

Thankfully, not all problems are as difficult as the dilemmas of redistributive populism—and in the chapters of Part Three, I explore a wide range of democratic practices we can endorse with greater confidence. I begin with a robust defense of the institutions of electoral democracy in Chapter 8, before proceeding to examine the most promising strategies of policy reform and civic action outside the state in Chapters 9 and 10, respectively. Though nothing is guaranteed in our uncertain world, it is the combination of practices I defend in what follows that is most likely to bring about and sustain greater balance in the power of different groups—thereby limiting the ability of any one group to divert public power from its public purposes. They are the best bet we have, in other words, for advancing the cause of democracy.

PART THREE
DEMOCRATIC PRACTICES

Power concedes nothing without a demand. It never did and it never will.

—Frederick Douglass, "West India Emancipation" (1857)

PART THREE

DEMOCRATIC PRACTICES

8
The Power of the Multitude
A Realistic Defense of Elections

Drawing on a range of realist skeptics and radical critics, this book has sought to unsettle common assumptions about the intrinsic value of electoral democracy. Given the findings of Social Choice Theory (SCT) and Social Identity Theory (SIT) surveyed in Chapter 2, I have argued that elections can only fail to achieve a meaningful form of collective control over public power, and thus cannot authorize or legitimize the actions of democratic states in the distinctive way they are often assumed to do. At the same time, I have also argued that elections force competition for power into peaceful and regulated channels, while enabling resistance to persistent forms of capture, and are therefore indispensable. We might worry, then, about the compatibility of these two claims. More specifically: if electoral responsiveness is really as limited as I have suggested—and if voter behavior is really so tribal and uninformed—why should we accept that a system of competitive elections with universal suffrage is the best way to promote the public interest?

This chapter answers these questions, offering a robust and realistic defense of elections that nevertheless refrains from inflating the legitimacy or authority of their results. Its primary task is to explain why electoral democracy deserves robust support, despite its many flaws—which it does, in the first four sections, via an extended engagement with the most prominent contemporary alternatives to competitive elections and universal suffrage. In the final section, then, I show why it matters that we express our enthusiasm for electoral democracy in relatively muted and cautious tones—and explore how this attitude of *measured appreciation* ought to shape our approach to democratization and democratic governance more broadly.

8.1 Epistemic worries and the need for a realistic defense of democracy

Worries about the competence of ordinary citizens to wield political power are as old as Western political philosophy itself—and they come from all ideological corners. Libertarians often lament popular ignorance about economics (Caplan 2007), for instance, while egalitarians worry about the depth of popular commitment to basic rights (Dworkin 1996), and both have suggested curtailing popular power on these grounds. Environmentalists bemoan the impact of short-sighted democratic choices on natural systems (Humphrey 2007), and some have flirted with nondemocratic solutions (Mittiga 2022). Finally, revolutionary socialists have long worried that ideology would prevent ordinary people from recognizing their own interests—leading all too many to embrace authoritarian tactics by a revolutionary vanguard as necessary for liberation.

Since the Second World War, of course, very few political thinkers within the democratic world have favored the abandonment of core practices of electoral democracy. The most that conservative critics have dared to suggest is that populist overreach must be curtailed through constitutional checks and balances. Meanwhile, radicals chastened by the horrors of Stalinism have generally agreed that electoral institutions must be supplemented rather than entirely replaced. In recent years, however—mirroring the broader decline of democratic faith among citizens of democracies around the world (Foa and Mounk 2016)—political thinkers of various stripes have begun to voice more full-throated critiques of electoral democracy on epistemic grounds. Some have even suggested that we might be better off under an alternative system.

In political philosophy, the most prominent of these voices is Jason Brennan (2016: 23), who argues that if people have a right to good government, we cannot be content with universal suffrage—which leaves important decisions in the hands of "ignorant, irrational, misinformed nationalists"—and should instead consider alternatives such as restricted suffrage and plural or weighted voting (see also Caplan 2007; López-Guerra 2014). Pushing even further, Daniel A. Bell (2015) defends a neo-Confucian political meritocracy, loosely modeled on contemporary Singapore and China, which eliminates competitive elections altogether. Both acknowledge the relative instrumental success of electoral democracy (D. A. Bell 2015: 7; Brennan 2016: 8, 195). They rightly observe, however, that elections hardly constitute a *guarantee* of peace, prosperity, and liberal rights—much less a thorough democratization of social life—and that democracies have also done awful things, especially to noncitizens (D. A. Bell 2015: 46–47).

Perhaps electoral democracy has performed better than the alternatives thus far, in other words, but why should we think this trend will continue into perpetuity? Are the defenders of democracy left with nothing more secure than Churchill's quip that democracy is the "worst form of government, except for all the others that have been tried"? The political scientists Christopher Achen and Larry Bartels seem to think so, arguing in their 2016 book *Democracy for Realists* that "*all* of the conventional defenses of democratic government are at odds with demonstrable, centrally important facts of political life." Although they support democracy, based on its record of success relative to the alternatives, it is difficult to square this record with their comprehensive account of the political ignorance and irrationality of ordinary voters.

Alas, this problem is not merely of academic relevance. If Churchillian pessimism is all we have, well-intentioned political actors—most notably the leaders and citizens of nondemocratic countries considering the merits of democratization—might reasonably wonder whether elections with universal suffrage really are the best way to achieve their substantive goals. Might some alternative political system allow them to pursue economic development, political stability, social peace, or redistributive policy—among other worthy ends—more efficiently? Why not grant political power to those with exceptional knowledge or virtue, rather than those best able to satisfy the whims of an uninformed and easily manipulated mass public?

Despite nearly axiomatic faith in democracy, political theorists and philosophers still lack a compelling way to answer these questions in instrumentalist terms.[1] In other words, we lack a plausible account of why some form of "benevolent despotism" would be unable to advance valuable substantive ends more effectively than electoral democracies. And as a result, many democratic theorists have concluded that the only secure justification for democracy must rest on its intrinsic properties (Beitz 1989: 98; Christiano 1996: 16–17, 56; Kolodny 2014a: 202). If instrumentalist reasoning yields only a contingent and defeasible commitment to democratic institutions, that is, committed democrats had better be able to explain their commitment in terms of the intrinsic value of political equality and self-government. And while I disagree that such intrinsic accounts actually do provide a firmer defense of electoral democracy (see Bagg n.d.; Bagg and Chan 2022), I agree that we should be dissatisfied with vague assertions that it is less awful than other systems. We must explain to challengers like Brennan and Bell—and, by proxy, potential reformers around the world—why we should refrain from trying anything else.

---

[1] Instrumentalists have often been more concerned to debunk intrinsic views of democracy than to explain its instrumental value (e.g., Arneson 2004; Wall 2007). In an article from which parts of this chapter are drawn, meanwhile (Bagg 2018b), I demonstrate the insufficiency of the analogies and formal results employed by recent "epistemic" defenses of democracy (e.g., Landemore 2012). Political scientists like Przeworski (1999, 2018) offer more to build on, and have clearly informed my account, yet they are rarely taken seriously in political philosophy. Among the many aims of this book is to remedy that unfortunate oversight.

That is what I do in what follows, examining the most prominent alternatives to electoral democracy in order to demonstrate why each of its core components is essential. In brief, any system lacking either competitive elections—like Bell's meritocracy—or universal suffrage—like Brennan's epistocracy—would grant incumbents and other elites too much latitude to entrench their own power. It would therefore present unacceptable dangers without generating significant compensatory benefits. And though I focus on Bell and Brennan as convenient targets, it is important to note that my arguments apply to any "epistocracy" (Estlund 2008)—i.e., any system that grants political power on the basis of knowledge, wisdom, or virtue—and thus to nearly all nondemocratic systems endorsed by any significant number of contemporary thinkers.[2] Though much capture remains within all electoral democracies, therefore, elections with universal suffrage still resist state capture better than any available alternative—and they do so, crucially, even if citizen behavior exhibits all the pathologies critics have identified.

8.2 Political meritocracy and the need for competitive elections

Daniel A. Bell is a Canadian scholar who has spent most of his academic career in China, comparing Chinese political thought and institutions—often favorably—with their Western counterparts. In a 2015 book called *The China Model*, more specifically, Bell contends that a political order grounded in some form of neo-Confucian meritocracy could provide equal (if not greater) legitimacy, as compared to liberal democracy (see also D. A. Bell 2006). Despite what many assume from the book's title, however, Bell (2015) does not claim that the contemporary Chinese government fulfills this ideal, nor that it outperforms existing electoral democracies (19). Instead, the version of political meritocracy he proposes as a "model" will have eliminated the political repression and corruption characterizing the current CCP regime by implementing independent checks on centralized power (116, 124, 150), a freer press (134, 174), intraparty competition (138), more widespread participation in local affairs (169, 189–191), improved Confucian moral education (124), greater economic equality (132), and diversified methods of meritocratic selection (130, 135, 193–194), among other reforms. At the same time, his model does not involve open elections or widespread suffrage:

---

[2] To my knowledge, the only exception is arguably lottocracy—rule by randomly selected citizens—which may or may not count as democratic. I leave it aside for now, having addressed it in detail elsewhere (Bagg 2022c).

political leaders are selected instead by their predecessors, on the basis of demonstrated capability.

Many of these mechanisms embody the liberal principles for preventing capture outlined in Chapter 5. Indeed, meritocracy itself originated—in both Western and Confucian traditions alike—as a way of constraining the power of the nobility and other privileged elites (65–66). Bell and other epistocrats happily concede that rule by unconstrained, extractive elites is worse than rule by the many: they, too, seek to prevent elite capture through strategies such as constitutionalism and competition. Their strategy is to point out that electoral democracy is hardly free of capture, while insisting that nondemocratic institutions are not *necessarily* unconstrained or tyrannical. The leaders of contemporary China and Singapore are already constrained in various ways, after all, and Bell's reforms would constrain them further.

Bell's account is a valuable reminder not to sacralize elections or exaggerate the differences between democracies and nondemocracies. Nevertheless, I maintain, any long-term, large-scale response to the predicament of modern politics must include open political competition. This is not because elections are intrinsically valuable, nor because they always yield superior outcomes. Instead, the primary reason political meritocracy does not present an attractive alternative to electoral democracy is that it is far more likely to experience the severe forms of capture associated with unconstrained tyranny. Though constraints on centralized power can also be eroded in a system with electoral competition, the *magnitude* of this risk is much greater under political meritocracy—even given highly advantageous conditions—than it is under any ordinary consolidated democracy. The key difference is that meritocratic leaders have much more effective tools for entrenching their power.

In any political system, many forces influence whether incumbent leaders and their factional allies retain power. In both meritocracies and democracies, for instance, the approval of a broad class of economic and cultural elites is an important contributing factor. In both systems, similarly, massive popular discontent bodes poorly for incumbents. In a political meritocracy, however, incumbents have far greater capacity to determine outcomes. Given the significant discretion afforded by the unavoidably ambiguous standard of "merit," leaders can gradually shift the balance of power in their favor, appointing cadres at every level who will support their factional interests, and replacing those who will not. There seems to have been what Xi Jinping did, for instance, with his "anti-corruption" campaign (Hualing 2015; Yuen 2014)—setting the stage for his subsequent moves to consolidate power. Compared with elected democratic politicians, therefore, leaders in a political meritocracy have much greater latitude in shaping the structural conditions supporting their political power, and so much greater capacity to entrench their rule.

Of course, democratic incumbents also use their control over the state apparatus to increase their chances of retaining power through techniques like gerrymandering, appointing factional allies to agency posts, or undermining the economic and organizational support for opposition parties (Levitsky and Ziblatt 2018: 72–96). Yet there are at least three crucial factors restraining such efforts at entrenchment: the uncertainty of electoral outcomes, the organizational strength of the opposition, and independent commitment to the institutional framework of democracy.

Despite their efforts to stack the deck, for one, incumbents know that their opponents may yet come to power and retaliate. Moreover, their attempts may be foiled by independent power centers within the state, such as the judiciary, bureaucratic agencies, subsidiary jurisdictions, and even the military. More generally, rival parties will be able to coordinate opposition to incumbent entrenchment—including through armed rebellion, in the most extreme cases. Given sufficient uncertainty about the results of subsequent elections, and the willingness of other state actors to cooperate, incumbents will generally refrain from trying to seize unilateral power for themselves. The result is a self-enforcing equilibrium in which all incumbents avoid certain self-serving strategies (Przeworski 1991: 2005; I. Shapiro 2016b: 49–50). Indeed, electoral competitiveness and the organizational strength of opposition parties both appear to be key conditions for consolidating democracy (Levitsky and Way 2010: 5–16, 68–70).

Finally, these incentives will be supplemented by some degree of genuine commitment to democracy—especially among those with strong professional socialization such as lawyers and journalists. For one, this commitment will reinforce the incentives opposition officials already have to obstruct incumbent entrenchment. Perhaps more importantly, a strong commitment to democracy among the incumbents' allies may stiffen their nerve, leading them to withdraw support when the incumbents' actions threaten to destabilize a valuable electoral equilibrium. In the absence of principled commitments, then, the sort of material and political incentives we have been discussing would surely be weaker and less reliable. Yet the converse, crucially, is also true: in the absence of strong incentives, the motivational force of principled commitments would be far, far weaker. And under conditions of polarization—in which principled commitments to procedural norms reliably become less salient, relative to strong substantive disagreements with political opponents—they may have little force at all (Ahlquist et al. 2018; Svolik 2019). Given these vulnerabilities, it is unwise to rely entirely on principled commitments, produced by education and socialization, to maintain the integrity of fragile constraints on centralized power.

That is precisely what Bell's political meritocracy would do. Even if the independent power centers he proposes were initially effective, their continued independence would not be supported by electoral uncertainty and organized opposition, and could be relatively easily co-opted by top-level leaders disposed to do so. As Bell concedes (123–124), the stability of constraints on power in a meritocracy ultimately relies on the forbearance of top meritocrats, which he proposes to secure through Confucian moral education. And while I do not deny the efficacy of such principled commitments, I share Andrew Nathan's (2016: 155) doubts that "any political system can be induced to operate on the basis of moral virtue alone" (see also Ong 2016). Without reinforcement from strong incentives—such as those provided by electoral uncertainty and an organized opposition—principled commitment to maintaining independent power centers will eventually succumb to the temptations of political expediency. As a result, requiring incumbents to compete for power against an organized opposition—rather than selecting their own replacements—reduces the likelihood that they will either seek or acquire the sort of unconstrained tyrannical power that nearly everyone agrees is bad.

This danger gives us more than enough reason to abandon the idea of political meritocracy. It is also worth noting, however, that this risk is not offset by great prospective rewards. Even meritocratic leaders who do not actively consolidate power and pursue extractive policies will still be subject to more mundane forms of capture and corruption, and these will erode any major advantages political meritocracy might be supposed to have over electoral democracy.

Consider the strict conditions enabling the progress of natural science—perhaps the most obviously successful meritocracy in existence. Especially within Kuhnian "normal science," standards of merit are relatively uncontroversial. Where disagreement exists, it is usually resolved methodically within structures of open competition, which are themselves supported by a decentralized disciplinary structure. Finally, few scientific questions have significant consequences for the distribution of social power, meaning that scientific institutions are rarely targeted for "capture" by outside interests. (The exceptions to this generalization, meanwhile—such as certain areas of pharmacology and climate science—prove the rule.)

In politics, by contrast, the distributive stakes are far higher. Political meritocracies are the target of intense competition for capture among factions seeking to advance their interests, and given the inevitable limits to open competition under a centralized hierarchy, these factions are forced to displace their conflicts onto the definition and application of meritocratic standards. Yet these standards are far more ambiguous than those of science—due to wider disagreement on the ends to be served—and consequently *less* capable of withstanding such strain. Though scientific meritocracies have enabled remarkable progress through the methodical resolution of disagreements, therefore, this is only in virtue of several features that cannot be replicated by a centralized political meritocracy (see Bagg 2018a: 269–273).

Despite these vastly more favorable conditions, of course, even science is hardly a perfect meritocracy. From its origins to the present, systematic biases and exclusions have profoundly affected its character (Longino 2013; Marks 2009). In other contexts, meanwhile, meritocracy has even less basis in reality, and is often simply used to legitimize vast inequality (Frank 2016; McNamee and Miller 2013). This does not mean the concept of meritocracy is incoherent or inherently reactionary—on the contrary, meritocratic standards are a necessary feature of any modern political system, including electoral democracy. Yet no meritocracy is immune to bias, capture, or corruption (Fricker 2009; Medina 2012), and given the intense strains they must bear, such defects will be especially significant in *political* meritocracies. While meritocracy is necessary, it functions best under democratic conditions that check its pathologies.

That said, we need not deny that political meritocracies *can* govern well—perhaps even outperforming electoral democracies in certain cases. Rather, my claim here is that political meritocracies are unlikely to enjoy either *systematic* or *substantial* advantages over comparably situated electoral democracies in the long run. Given this, the increased risk of authoritarian consolidation easily counts as a decisive argument against political meritocracy. This does not mean that immediate democratization must be the first priority of all nondemocracies. It does mean, however, that any plausible response to the predicament of modern politics must include electoral competition—and, more concretely, that citizens of nondemocratic societies who seek to advance a broad public interest over the long term should generally promote a transition to an electoral system as soon as that can be sustainably achieved.

The same logic also enables us to decisively reject any other proposals that would require eliminating competitive elections for top-level leaders in service of valuable substantive ends—such as Ross Mittiga's (2022) suggestion that authoritarian measures may be justified by the existential threat of climate change. No matter how tempting this sort of epistocratic solution might seem, given the obvious mendacity of those who obstruct climate action, my arguments here give us abundant reason to reject it as well. Even if they could somehow guarantee their own benevolence, in short, even the most well-intentioned climate despot would need to create structures of unconstrained and unaccountable power in order to achieve their aims. And once created, opponents could usurp these power structures to reverse whatever substantive gains have been made. In the case at hand, indeed, it is unlikely that oil and gas magnates would stand idly by while their power and profits are demolished. Rather, any attempt by a "benevolent despot" to stop climate catastrophe by subverting democratic processes would threaten to open the floodgates of political violence—thereby enabling fossil fuel interests to *accelerate* that catastrophe after taking the reins of a powerful, non-democratic state. For all of its many real and maddening flaws, electoral democracy is still the best way of managing power in pursuit of the public interest, under the conditions of modern politics.

8.3 Franchise qualifications and the need for universal suffrage

Unlike Bell's proposed meritocracy, the epistocratic models proposed by Brennan presume a system of elections for top-level leaders, and are thus perfectly consistent with everything I have argued so far. Instead of using epistocratic criteria to select political leaders directly, he advocates using those criteria to select the selectors: i.e., restricting the franchise to those who meet certain minimum epistemic standards (2016: 204–230; see also Caplan 2007: 197–198). He acknowledges that historical restrictions based on morally irrelevant factors—such as race, sex, or property—were unjust. Yet given the epistemic shortcomings of democracy, he asks: why not use morally relevant qualifications instead? Prospective drivers must pass a driving test, and prospective doctors must attend medical school. Why not issue voting licenses in a similar way, through competence testing or educational requirements?

Much more than Bell's case for political meritocracy, Brennan's provocative claims have attracted a great deal of interest from political philosophers. And while most responses have been critical, a significant number have sought to defend some form of epistocracy. Perhaps more importantly, even Brennan's critics have largely accepted key elements of his framing of the problem. In particular, many contest Brennan's assertion that certain people have greater epistemic virtue than others, overall, while accepting his assumption if they did, this would lend at least presumptive justification to arrangements granting them outsized political power. However, this assumption makes sense only if we completely ignore all questions regarding what it would take to realize such arrangements in practice. And it is in this pragmatic domain that Brennan's case for franchise restrictions—like Bell's argument for meritocracy—is weakest of all.

As with Bell, then, my response to Brennan concedes the point that most other critics are at pains to contest: i.e., that, *theoretically*, certain epistemic qualifications could be harmless or even beneficial. Instead, my argument is grounded in the enormous *practical* risks of enabling political leaders to design them. Though perhaps not quite as dangerous as the ability to appoint successors directly, the ability to enact epistemic qualifications would also enable incumbents to entrench their rule by choosing their own voters. Meanwhile, the supposed benefits of such qualifications are even less likely to materialize than those of political meritocracy.

Of course, democracies already enable incumbents to manipulate the pool of eligible voters in various ways. Some restrictions, like those concerning age and residence, are probably inevitable. Others, however—including voter identification requirements, disenfranchisement of felons, and gerrymandering of single-member districts—are routinely used by incumbents to tilt the electoral odds in their favor (Levitsky and Ziblatt 2018: 183–186, 208–211). Such policies are typically justified on other grounds, and some may be valuable on balance, yet in each case, this feature gives us reason to be suspicious (Issacharoff and Pildes 1998; I. Shapiro 2016b: 86–88). By comparison, then, Brennan's proposals would grant politicians far greater leeway in choosing their own voters, and should be regarded as far more dangerous.

Consider the possibility of conditionalizing suffrage on educational attainment. Brennan himself speculates (223) that in the US, Democrats would favor very low or very high qualifications, while Republicans would prefer a mid-range qualification, such as a high school diploma. Yet he fails to recognize what a dramatic effect this could have: for either party, implementing a properly targeted policy would instantly translate a small and temporary majority into a massive and durable electoral advantage. Where traditional gerrymandering faces natural limits, moreover—imposed by the need to distribute a fixed voting population among geographically contiguous districts—"epistemic" gerrymandering could continuously compound incumbent advantages through ever-more-targeted qualifications. Even if their immediate effects were not so extreme, finally, such policies would still give incumbents strong incentives to manipulate educational attainment patterns for partisan ends.

Competence tests present no solution, as incumbents would have similar incentives (and even greater leeway) to manipulate its content. Once established, moreover, parties would scramble to prepare their voters, much as they already conduct registration drives and get-out-the-vote campaigns among pools of likely supporters. The resulting arms race between parties to ensure their own members pass the test can hardly be expected to yield substantial benefits in vote quality. Given the massive expenditures required by parties, however, it would almost certainly intensify their dependence upon concentrated wealth.

Brennan concedes that his proposals could have drawbacks, including the potential for manipulation (222–230). However, he asserts that they also promise vastly superior outcomes. Caricaturing any unwillingness to experiment with epistocracy as a species of Burkean conservatism, he insists that we cannot know in advance whether such tradeoffs will be worthwhile. I disagree. As I have already argued, we know enough about politicians to predict that some would use these tools to entrench their power. Perhaps more importantly, we also know enough about voters to predict that disenfranchising those with low political knowledge would not substantially improve the epistemic quality of electoral results. Thus, even if incumbents (or independent bodies) imposed perfectly benign epistemic qualifications, the benefits Brennan projects would be very unlikely to materialize.

Consider that voters in modern democracies do not choose directly between different *policies*. Instead, they choose between parties or candidates. There is thus substantial distance between a voter's overall level of political knowledge and the quality of her *vote choice*. Yet Brennan makes very little effort to demonstrate that higher political knowledge scores would be associated with greater likelihood of voting for the "correct" party or candidate. Instead, he relies on an intuitive sense that political knowledge *must* raise vote quality.[3]

Perhaps, on the margin, it does. Yet if we accept the insights of social identity theory outlined in Chapter 2—which Brennan himself relies upon throughout his book—this argument falls apart. For one, rational assessment of the arguments for competing policies plays a small role (at best) in vote choice: better information rarely changes our mind, it simply gives us better tools for defending our intuitions. Meanwhile, education primarily alters

---

[3] Brennan does cite two studies correlating high information with a smattering of broadly libertarian preferences that he presumably considers correct (33–4). While these studies control for certain demographic variables, however, other potential confounds remain (e.g., group identities elided by crude demographic controls). More importantly, they do not establish that having such 'superior' policy preferences actually enhances *vote choice*.

our policy preferences indirectly, by changing our social context and identity. Where they exist, then, correlations between political knowledge and vote choice are largely explained by unrelated, nonrational factors—centrally including the set of *identity groups* to which we belong (Achen and Bartels 2016; Lodge and Taber 2013). By far the most significant consequence of disenfranchising those *individuals* with low epistemic qualifications, therefore, would be to disenfranchise the (already disempowered) *groups* to which they disproportionately belong.

Brennan glibly dismisses this "demographic objection." He announces repeatedly, for instance, that by his "objective" standards, Black women are the least "competent" voters in the US, and that his proposals would therefore disenfranchise them in large numbers (33, 132–133, 148, 227–228). Rather than taking this opportunity to re-examine his epistemological premises, however, he assures readers of his excellent implicit bias scores, and asserts that disadvantaged citizens cannot vote in ways that promote their interests "unless they have tremendous social scientific knowledge" (227).[4] Remedying their disadvantages thus requires *disenfranchising* them—and thereby entrusting their interests to better informed voters.[5]

Such claims are, quite frankly, preposterous, and one may be tempted simply to ignore them. Given my own critiques of common assumptions about democracy in Chapter 2, however—drawing on much of the same empirical evidence—it is worth clarifying why Brennan's extreme conclusions do not follow. We may grant, first, that enfranchisement often brings surprisingly *few* benefits to disadvantaged groups. For instance, nineteenth-century socialists and reactionaries both assumed that working-class suffrage would yield far more extensive redistribution than it did (Ansell and Samuels 2014). We may also grant that people typically vote *sociotropically*, aiming to achieve a common good rather than their own self-interest. Yet even Brennan acknowledges that there is clearly *some* connection between enfranchisement and group interests, observing for instance that "if we deprive all black people of the right to vote ... this will help facilitate people of other

---

[4] One might suggest that a more relevant measure of epistemic merit is one's likelihood of voting for a know-nothing authoritarian populist—implying that Black women were the *most* competent demographic group in the 2016 US presidential election, among many others—but I will not pursue that argument here.

[5] On most of Brennan's proposals, this would entail entrusting the interests of the poor, women, and African Americans in the United States to rich white men. To pre-empt the obvious objections, he proposes that worries about fairness could be resolved by giving extra weight to the votes of those demographic minorities who do qualify to vote. Even if we grant that this solves the problem—which is doubtful—it does so only by exacerbating another: clearly, entrusting electoral outcomes to complex algorithms only widens the opportunity and incentive for manipulation.

races in exploiting, dominating, and oppressing blacks" (97–98). Alas, it seems, not everyone votes sociotropically—and even when we do, our views of the "common good" are inevitably biased by our group identities (Bagg 2018a).

More broadly, even the most skeptical reading of the evidence from public opinion and political psychology does not remotely imply that low-knowledge voters would be better off disenfranchised. It does show, in my view, that processes of responsiveness and representation are far from ideally rational and reliable. If "most citizens support a party not because they have carefully calculated that its policy positions are closest to their own, but rather because 'their kind' of person belongs to that party"—as Achen and Bartels summarize (2016: 307)—members of disadvantaged groups may not always vote in ways that promote their interests. This is concerning, if unsurprising. Yet it hardly implies that their voting behavior is *entirely* insensitive to their interests—much less that their interests will be more reliably protected by others. Voters driven by identity rather than policy will effectively promote their interests as long as their identities lead them to support parties whose policies promote their interests.

And while this is not always the case, neither is it especially rare. In fact, some degree of genuine interest representation seems especially likely among groups whose disadvantages render their collective identity salient. In such cases, ordinary group members will often follow the recommendations of respected leaders, many of whom would pass any epistemic qualification Brennan could propose. Because this compliance is largely driven by identity rather than informed and independent consideration of the issues, leaders have latitude to extract rents and engage in various deceptions. Voter ignorance does have real costs. Yet it need not render their votes *counterproductive*, as Brennan suggests.

Just like everyone else, members of disadvantaged groups surely vote in suboptimal ways. As we have seen, however, it is highly unlikely that instituting epistemic conditions on the franchise would reliably and significantly improve average vote quality. It is far more likely that they would be used to entrench the power of incumbents—potentially so effectively as to endanger the competitiveness of elections. Restricting the political rights of low knowledge disadvantaged groups, therefore, would bring risks for those groups (and for the polity as a whole) that are far out of proportion to any of Brennan's hypothesized benefits. In the group-based competition for political power that constitutes modern political life, therefore, a nonnegotiable principle of universal suffrage serves as an indispensable safeguard of a reasonably level playing field.

8.4 The eyes of the people: Popular power without direct accountability

Thus far, my argument for electoral democracy has been largely a negative one. It supplies an explanation for the observed historical regularity that democratic systems have consistently outperformed all non-democratic alternatives—i.e., their greater resistance to manipulation and entrenchment—and thus offers decisive reasons not to experiment with any system that does away with competitive elections or universal suffrage. In that sense, it makes a critical advance over Churchill's formulation, as well as those of contemporary realists like Achen and Bartels, which rely entirely on the historical regularity itself. Yet this case has hinged on the dangers of alternatives, and it is worth exploring how electoral democracies work in positive terms. Before we investigate the additional tools that can help us keep public power *more* closely tethered to the public interest, that is, we should look more carefully at how a very loose, minimal tether can be achieved—under realistic conditions—by the practices of electoral democracy as such.

The first step is to relinquish what Jeffrey Green (2009) has called the "vocal" model of popular power, which emphasizes citizens' exercise of voice through voting and deliberation. In everyday democratic practice, Green shows, the "ocular" power of the people is far more important (see also Keane 2018; Manin 1997; Rosanvallon 2008; Thaa 2016). It is largely as spectators rather than active participants, for one, that citizens *experience* democracy. But Green's insight is not just phenomenological: it is also ocular pressure that most directly shapes the behavior of public officials. Given the dynamics explored in Chapter 2, the relationship between any particular action and a politician's prospects for re-election are so convoluted as to prevent any serious calculation of their marginal effects: as Achen and Bartels (2016: 147) put it, electoral competition resembles nothing so much as a game of "musical chairs." Instead, officials aim to manage their "image" in a more holistic way, responding directly not to precise shifts in predicted vote share but to the likely consequences for their reputation, more generally.

Of course, the leaders of authoritarian regimes are also constrained by ocular power and beholden to various interest groups in similar ways (Boix and Svolik 2013; Chen, Pan, and Xu 2016). The same could even be said of CEOs, religious leaders, and other public figures—all of whom are concerned for their public image, and are therefore subject to the discipline of ocular power. While a recognition of this continuity rightly blurs the line between democratic and nondemocratic modes of organization, however, it does not eliminate the distinction entirely. Elections rarely provide *direct* accountability, but leaders who are subject to electoral pressures do generally care *more* about their reputations, relative to other kinds of leaders. Even if rarely realized in practice, the threat of electoral removal still hovers over their heads—all the more frightening, perhaps, for its unpredictability—and this makes them relatively more susceptible to ocular discipline, causing them to respond to public pressure of all kinds.

On this model, politicians negotiate with diverse interest groups not because they can reliably estimate the electoral benefits of doing so, but precisely because they *cannot*. As long as the results are not *entirely* random, after all, competitors in a game of musical chairs do not stop playing to win. Similarly, politicians still regularly consider their electoral prospects in guiding their day-to-day actions, even though very few will ultimately prove decisive to their vote share. Because it is difficult to predict which *will* be decisive, they must play to win on all fronts—reliably adhering to "vague limits of permissiveness" set by public opinion (Achen and Bartels 2016: 318–319), for instance, and aiming to satisfy a range of interest groups without upsetting others too profoundly (Oppenheimer and Edwards 2012: 206–218).

To be sure, these efforts will often be superficial, and those with concentrated power will still have outsized influence. But democratic politicians must pay lip service to other groups as well, and that is not nothing. At the very least, it is a guaranteed foothold in the political system—something groups in nondemocracies do not have—which can become a focal point for other forms of popular organizing. What this means is that, rather than expressing the voice of the people through direct accountability, elections serve as an imprecise but reliable anchor for the people's *ocular* power, which can in turn be deployed for more targeted ends.

Of course, even ocular power is not wielded directly by "the people" in their millions. It is journalists and opposition politicians who expose the lies and misbehavior of officials; scholars and scientists who settle questions of fact; lawyers and judges who ensure that law effectively constrains officeholders. It is movement leaders who organize protests or boycotts; religious leaders and labor unions and media personalities who send signals about what to believe and value. It is mostly in an indirect sense, then, that politicians care about the scrutiny of "the people": more immediately, they care about the scrutiny of these mediating, mid-level elites.

This inevitably creates space for manipulation. As with representatives, the allegiance of citizens to particular mediating elites is driven by group identity more than rational argument, leaving those elites with significant latitude in shaping the beliefs and values of those who trust them. Nevertheless, their flexibility is not infinite. Everyone has multiple identities, which they interpret and weigh differently in different contexts, meaning that elites can never be secure in their ability to mobilize those identities for their ends. Despite the significant power they wield, then, intermediary elites in an open society depend on citizens too, and this standing reserve of popular power exerts some degree of discipline—however loose—on elites at all levels.

The error of commonsense "vocal" models of democracy, then, is not to value elections, but to overstate their significance. Democracy and nondemocracy are not two diametrically opposed forms of sovereignty: one enabling genuine collective self-rule by ordinary citizens, and the other granting citizens no influence whatsoever. This categorical distinction is not only false; it also makes demands on democracy that it can only fail to achieve. And when it does, the ordinary citizens who were promised genuine popular sovereignty will predictably lose faith, and may be tempted by authoritarian methods of realizing this dream (Müller 2016). My account, by contrast, directs us away from paradoxical and potentially dangerous questions of ultimate sovereignty, and towards more tractable questions of relative power. It views voting not as *the* democratic institution par excellence—capable of generating legitimate authority on its own—but simply as one form of power ordinary people should have at their disposal. In other words, it justifies an attitude of *measured appreciation* towards electoral democracy.

8.5 Measured appreciation: Reframing the significance of electoral democracy

Rather than reflecting the will of a collective subject, I have argued that political outcomes in both democracies and nondemocracies reflect the balance of power between state officials, a shifting class of intermediate elites, and the multitude of ordinary citizens, with no group holding ultimate sovereignty. Competitive elections are valuable, then, not because they enact a unique form of popular authorization, but rather because they prevent those at the top from ensuring they *remain* at the top. Given uncertainty about electoral outcomes and a strong opposition, democratic incumbents are more likely to exhibit restraint than their peers in noncompetitive systems. So long as they must fear electoral defeat, more substantively, they will have at least some incentive to respect the interests of all sizable voting blocs. Though hardly a sufficient safeguard of everyone's interests, much less an egalitarian one, universal suffrage thus ensures that all groups have *some* access to the tools of electoral and ocular discipline—and this, in turn, limits how far officials are likely to stray from broad public interests.

By allowing us to appreciate the genuine virtues of electoral democracy, while also keeping its shortcomings squarely in view, this account reframes its significance in crucial ways. While providing robust support for democratic procedures as the best available pragmatic response to the predicament of modern politics, for one, it rightly undermines the assumption—common to much political science, political philosophy, legal theory, and beyond—that the results of those procedures possess a special kind of authority or legitimacy. Regardless of whether some ideal version of democratic politics could generate truly collective decisions, no large-scale modern democracies come close to this ideal, and none are ever likely to do so. As such, we should not treat the actions of any actual democracies as if they are collectively authorized.

This conclusion, in turn, raises tough questions for legal and philosophical theories that rely on such collective authorization to ground claims in other domains. Consider the "transmission belt" theories of administrative legitimacy examined in Chapter 2. According to such theories, recall, state actions are legitimate or authoritative only because, and to the extent that, they have been made by certain democratically authorized representatives of the collective will (see Jackson 2022; Zacka 2022). Because such theories do not reflect an accurate picture of how democratic decisions actually get made, however, they fail to offer a persuasive defense of bureaucracy against increasingly aggressive right-wing critics (Walters 2022), and suggest an underwhelming agenda for democratic action and reform (Rosanvallon 2008, 2018).

Many theories in political philosophy also rely on standards of democratic authorization to ground important normative claims. Fairly typically, for instance, Annie Stilz argues that the right of a state to rule a population and territory hinges on whether it represents its subjects' "shared political will" (2019: 10). Similarly, Chiara Cordelli (2020) argues against privatizing many state functions on the grounds that doing so precludes properly collective authorization. Other accounts use criteria of collective authorization to determine whether citizens have duties to obey the law (Kolodny 2014b)—and what forms of resistance are justified, if not—as well as how active courts should be in overturning laws that seem to violate basic rights (Waldron 1999). And though it is beyond my scope here to give a thorough assessment of any particular theory, it is worth highlighting a dilemma facing any such account, to the extent that it makes key normative distinctions on the basis of the presence or absence of collective authorization.

If a demanding standard is used, on the one hand—requiring equal opportunity for political influence, perhaps—all systems will fail to meet it. Cordelli appears to take this horn of the dilemma, meaning that her account clearly explains why privatization is wrong, but in doing so also casts doubt on the legitimacy of existing nonprivatized bureaucratic agencies. If a minimal standard is used, on the other hand, it may confer a sheen of legitimacy on political systems that do not deserve it. Stilz appears to take this horn—and indeed, a minimal standard probably makes sense if our aim is merely to decide whether a state has certain basic territorial rights. Yet inferring the presence of a "shared will" from the existence of an open public sphere and other basic pre-conditions strains the ordinary meaning of the term, and threatens to inflate the normative significance of what is in reality a very minimal achievement. To be sure, each of these theories undoubtedly has resources for responding to these concerns. Still, it seems to me that any theory relying on collective authorization to ground other normative claims risks repeating the error of transmission-belt theories of administrative legitimacy: i.e., appropriating the prestige of democracy while obscuring the multiplicity and complexity of its demands.

Rather than tying normative judgments to a particular definition of collective authorization, I argue, we will get more reliable results if we ask, in a more open-ended way, which of the available options will best advance democratic ends on the whole. Given the deep complexity of this question, it will rarely be easy to answer. Yet the predictive inquiry it invites *can* yield decisive results in some cases—as with the categorical prohibition on coups defended in Chapter 7, or the robust support for competitive elections and universal suffrage defended here. Meanwhile, it is best not to suppress the genuine uncertainty that may remain.

Rather than making general pronouncements about the legitimacy or authority of states, the ideal of resisting state capture suggests a disaggregated, contextual, and pragmatic approach to the questions typically associated with democratic legitimacy and authority—one addressed to specific dilemmas faced by specific actors in their relations with specific states (for more, see Bagg 2016, 2022b, n.d.; Bagg and Knight 2014). Perhaps more importantly, it also suggests a more promising agenda for democratization. Just as the practices of electoral democracy are valuable because they obstruct the most pervasive and egregious forms of state capture, in short, deepening democracy beyond this baseline entails a diverse array of tactics aimed at further reducing the extent and severity of capture. Once we stop valorizing elections as the singular site of democratic sovereignty, in sum, we open ourselves to a far broader vision of what democracy means, why it matters, and how to make it better.

9
Fighting Power with Power

An Agenda for Democratic Policy

The demands of democracy give rise to a troubling dilemma. On the one hand, advancing democratic ends requires deploying the concentrated power of the state in ambitious ways, to undermine asymmetries of private power and balance the organizational capacity of different groups. On the other hand, empowering the state can be dangerous, since every time we give it new powers, we create new tools that could be co-opted by powerful groups to preserve and enhance their power. State power is one of the central means by which we can limit the outsized power of dominant groups, in other words, as well as one of the key mechanisms they use to perpetuate their dominance. A key question facing advocates of democracy, then, is how to deploy state power for democratic ends, while creating minimal opportunities for capture.

I call this the *dilemma of public and private power*, and the aim of this chapter is to grapple with it, by way of addressing three key questions. First, which *general approach* to state involvement in different areas of social and economic life will most likely minimize capture? Second, how can *substantive policy* tools be designed to achieve key democratic goals—like dispersing private power and balancing organizational capacity—while minimizing their susceptibility to capture? And third, what kinds of *procedural mechanisms* can most effectively insulate such ambitious forms of state action from capture? Before I address these questions directly, however, it is worth briefly clarifying why they are the right ones to ask. After all, this framing is already a significant departure from dominant approaches to democratic reform.

9.1 What sorts of policy reform does deeper democratization require?

Let us take stock of where we are. The previous chapter addressed the first key task of democratic theory outlined in Chapter 1: evaluating existing practices of electoral democracy. This chapter is addressed to the second: developing an agenda for the reform of law and policy. And as it turns out, we already have most of the answer. In any given context, for one, some of the policies we ought to pursue will be concerned with directly realizing the various first-order aims we might have, in response to concrete problems. In addition, previous chapters have argued that the overarching goal of democratic reform must be to disperse private power and organizational capacity, through policies of anti-monopoly, countervailing power, and systemic redistribution. This makes my approach relatively unique among accounts of democratic reform, whose scope is typically limited to the procedures by which political decisions are made. Though some do include certain substantive policies within their reform agenda, these are usually framed as establishing minimal preconditions for equal participation in those procedures, and thus have a somewhat limited scope. On my account, by contrast, the ambit of democratic reform includes any substantive policy that disperses private power and mitigates imbalances of organizational capacity. This ambition, however, only intensifies the challenge posed by the dilemma of public and private power: in short, any power structure we create in order to pursue democratic aims can be captured and used to undermine those aims. On my account, then, the most important challenge facing reformers is to successfully navigate this dilemma, pursuing maximal dispersion of power at minimal risk of capture.

On the one hand, I have argued, we cannot address the problems of concentrated private power by centralizing all of the major social functions otherwise performed by private actors, and subjecting them to collective control—as implied by the horizon of full socialization. Though it preserves significant scope for public ownership, my account is also acutely sensitive to the dangers of concentrating too much power in the hands of state actors—and, equivalently, of eliminating independent sources of power outside the state. A libertarian approach, on the other hand—minimizing state capture by minimizing what states are tasked with doing in the first place—simply denies another central observation of this book. Without a powerful state keeping them in check, certain private interests will accumulate more and more power, which in turn will enable them to capture whatever power the state does have. In addition to defensive limits, then, we must also take offensive action against the accumulation of private power.

Of course, I am hardly alone in rejecting such uncompromising calls for full centralization or decentralization of power. Most mainstream approaches accept the need for decentralized social and economic activity to be governed by a centralized state, while aiming to ensure that its intrusions into the private sphere are limited by individual rights and guided by a collective will. For some, democratic legitimacy requires only popular authorization of officials through free and fair elections. Meanwhile, those with higher standards usually locate the shortcomings of existing electoral institutions in their failure to realize a genuinely collective will. On such accounts, the task of deeper democratization is to bring state action into better alignment with the collective will—either through electoral reforms to make representatives more responsive, or through extra-electoral institutions enabling ordinary people to participate more directly.

Unfortunately, I have argued, neither strategy is sufficient to address the profound problems facing contemporary democracies, because both emphasize processes of collective decision-making that will always be susceptible to capture by those with outsized private power and organizational capacity. And while nothing we do can eliminate this danger entirely, my claim is that democratic actors can articulate a more promising agenda by focusing more squarely upon it: i.e., by orienting our democratic efforts towards an ideal of resisting state capture.

This perspective shift has two key implications for policy reform. First, it means explicitly designing political institutions to maximize resilience to capture, rather than responsiveness, participation, or any other intuitive measure of the "democraticity" (Landemore 2020) of their decision-making procedures. In other words, it means that more participation is *not* inherently more democratic. Even more importantly, it also means expanding the scope of "democratic" reform beyond the realm of narrowly political decisions, to include direct methods for dispersing private power. And it is this reframing of the problem, rather than any entirely novel policy recommendations, that most distinguishes my approach to deeper democratization. We cannot escape the dilemma of public and private power, I have argued, by making all private power public or making all public power private. Yet neither can democratic reformers confine their scope to the procedures that regulate public power, remaining neutral among substantive policies that organize and distribute private power in different ways. As libertarians and socialists both recognize in their own ways, rather, the character of the relationship between public and private power is crucial to the overall danger of capture in a regime, and negotiating its terms must be the first task of democratic reformers.

What this means is that rather than attempting to distinguish between a realm of human life that is properly subject to collective governance and a realm properly left to individual choice, I defend a pragmatic approach to the proper scope of government (Knight 2001; Knight and Johnson 2011). On my account, more specifically, democratic reformers begin by asking which general approach to state involvement in each policy area—ranging from full public ownership to basic policing of decentralized private interaction—will minimize capture overall, achieving maximum dispersion of private power at minimal risk of co-optation. They then use the same standard to guide the design of substantive reforms, asking how particular policies can be structured to minimize their susceptibility to capture. Only then do democratic reformers turn to the sort of questions with which they are traditionally occupied, regarding the procedures of political decision-making. And when they do, their aim of maximizing resilience to capture, rather than responsiveness or participation, suggests a different set of mechanisms.

Although tensions do arise between first-order and second-order aims, finally, I have argued (§1.5) that they are rarer than we might expect. In many cases, the choice of one policy over another will have few stakes for the structure and distribution of power. When comparing alternative sewer designs, for instance, we are unlikely to find clear and weighty second-order reasons to favor one over another. Thus, we can often resolve such technical questions entirely in terms of our first-order aims. When a policy proposal *would* clearly raise susceptibility to capture, on the other hand, this should almost always count decisively against it. This is not because second-order democratic reasons are inherently weightier than first-order reasons, but rather because they reveal *apparently* contradictory first-order reasons as illusory. Whatever its stated first-order goals, after all, a policy is unlikely to achieve them if the power structures it creates are highly susceptible to capture. As argued in Chapter 8, for instance, it would be a serious mistake to subvert democratic procedures to fight climate change—even if the need for climate action outweighs other first-order priorities. Because they require structures that are highly susceptible to capture, nondemocratic strategies are actually likely to *harm* climate action in the long run, and this voids any first-order reasons that might appear to speak in their favor.

None of this is to deny that there are hard cases. Especially when the second-order demands of democracy are weak or uncertain, they *will* stand in real tension with our first-order aims, and we should not pretend these conflicts are easy to resolve. In such cases, rather, the most a democratic theory can hope to do is clarify the stakes of our choices—and that, above all, is my aim in what follows.

9.2 Which general approach to state involvement is safest in each policy area?

We may begin by considering four stylized ways that states can be involved in those realms of social and economic life that are sometimes seen as constituting the "private sphere"—including both the market and civil society. In the first model of *full public provision*, private providers are rare or nonexistent, as with police and fire services. In the second model of *public participation*, the state owns or controls one competitor in an otherwise private system, as with education and postal services in most countries (see Sitaraman and Alstott 2019). In the third model of *substantive regulation*, states actively shape the outcomes of decentralized competition to ensure they serve public ends. This is the predominant way most modern states manage housing and finance, for instance—though some participate directly in these sectors as well, providing social housing, public financing for certain projects, postal banking services, and so on. Indeed, the borders between these stylized models are not meant to be stark.

This is especially true of the boundary between substantive regulation and the fourth model of *formal regulation*, which describes less active state involvement in a decentralized sphere. Some might be tempted to call this a "laissez-faire" or "free market" model, but these labels are seriously misleading in this context. No matter how "unregulated" it seems, every sphere of modern life is pervasively structured by states' background enforcement of private and criminal law. Terms like "laissez-faire," "free market," and "unregulated" occlude this reality, giving the false impression of a stark binary between spheres where a government "intervenes," and spheres where private actors choose "freely." By contrast, the distinction between formal and substantive regulation enables us to discuss real variation in the type of state involvement across different spheres—i.e., how detailed its policies are, how frequently they change, and how intentionally they pursue specific outcomes—without falsely implying that more proactive forms of involvement are necessarily more *consequential* for the distribution of power than the enforcement of "basic" legal structures that everyone simply takes for granted.

Even when they are written in general terms, stable over time, and not clearly intended to achieve particular outcomes, for instance, rules governing contracts, torts, intellectual property, and so on, still have enormous distributive implications (Kennedy 2002; Pistor 2019). Indeed, the very existence of a system of private law has immense distributive implications, and cannot simply be assumed as a neutral background (M. R. Cohen 1927; Hale 1923). The question we must ask, then, is not *whether* or *how much* a state ought to intervene within a preexisting private sphere, but rather *how* it ought to structure private interactions. More specifically, the choice between full public provision, public participation, substantive regulation, and formal regulation is not like choosing a point on a quantitative scale of state involvement, such that more *involvement* always brings greater risks of *capture*. Instead, the safest option in any case depends on particular features of the policy area or set of social functions under consideration.

Take the question of healthcare provision. Given its great complexity and central social importance, no reasonably advanced modern state engages only in basic formal regulation of actors in the healthcare industry. Most employ fully public provision, while others employ a mix of public participation and substantive regulation. If minimizing state involvement always reduces the overall risk of capture, substantive regulation should be the safest model. Yet a comparison between European-style public provision and the substantive regulation employed by the United States gives us reason to doubt this supposition, for the latter gives powerful private actors far more substantial opportunities to ensure that state policy serves their interests.

The very idea of structuring the healthcare system around private insurers was devised and implemented at the behest of the American Medical Association, over widespread protests that it would serve the interests of doctors above everyone else (Chapin 2015). The most significant revision of that system, meanwhile—the 2010 Affordable Care Act—was developed in close consultation with insurers and other industry giants, whose profits have soared in the years since it was passed (Herman 2018). This model of substantive regulation within an otherwise decentralized market is a major reason healthcare costs are so much higher in the US than in comparable countries (Galvani et al. 2020). Of course, systems of socialized medicine are also subject to various pathologies, and it is beyond my scope here to defend any particular way of organizing a healthcare system. The point is simply that a state whose involvement is more active and obvious is not automatically more prone to capture than a state that apparently stands back from the fray, serving only to police the competition of private actors.

On the contrary, in fact: the unmistakably *proactive* nature of the state's involvement in a system of public provision makes its activities salient in ways that may insure it against capture (see Persson and Rothstein 2015). Consider that if everyone uses services such as public transit, education, or healthcare on a regular basis, the quality of service provision will be salient for everyone, and the state actors responsible for it will have relatively little room to extract rents. If the role of the state in structuring a private market is hidden behind an impenetrable thicket of regulations and licensing rules, by contrast, its responsibility for undesirable outcomes will be far more opaque. As we saw in Chapter 2, this lack of clear accountability enables capture (see also Decanio 2015). In fact, Jon D. Michaels (2017) claims, this is precisely what has been accomplished by recent waves of privatization in many countries, which have given certain private interests exclusive access to the support of the state, while weakening transparency and democratic oversight of the broadly public functions they continue to serve.

Perhaps even more concerning, privatization of public service provision also creates actors outside of the state with a vested interest in shaping state policy in a particular direction, which will often not be aligned with that of the broader public. This is the dynamic that animates the "military-industrial complex," for instance—whereby private arms manufacturers have strong incentive to lobby state actors to pursue militaristic policy—as well as the "prison-industrial complex"—whereby prison operators have similarly strong incentives to lobby for aggressive policing and harsh sentencing. Similarly disturbing phenomena can be observed in many other sectors, such as energy—where private fossil fuel companies have strong incentives to sabotage everything from renewable energy projects to public transit infrastructure. My account thus provides robust democratic reasons to ensure that a wide range of goods and services are provided by public agents of the state, rather than private market actors, and thus to oppose most forms of neoliberal privatization. Unlike Cordelli (2020) and other critics of privatization, however, it does so without presuming that state actors possess a special kind of authority as representatives of a genuine popular (or "omnilateral") will.

As I pointed out in Chapter 5, finally, a policy of universal access or provision can limit the ability of state agents to dole out public services as a particularistic reward, thereby extracting rents or entrenching themselves in power. And this is yet another reason to expect that a system of public provision or participation may limit capture overall, in healthcare and many other areas, as compared to either formal or substantive regulation of decentralized markets.

Of course, direct public involvement will not minimize capture in *every* policy area. And in addition to sector-specific concerns, our judgments must also be sensitive to elements of the broader political context—such as the overall balance of power between state and nonstate actors, and the relative effectiveness of existing popular feedback mechanisms. We can only say so much without examining the details of particular contexts. My own view is that in most contemporary democracies, substantially expanding public participation in housing, finance, energy, and transport—without embracing *full* public provision—would reduce overall dangers of capture. If so, such reforms would be justifiable on purely democratic grounds, independent of their direct impact on the public interest—though in most cases, this would also be positive. Justifying these claims would take us much too far afield, however, so I proceed instead to the next step in a comprehensive agenda for democratic reform: the design of substantive policy tools. Taking the state's general approach to a given sector as fixed, in other words, how can we design policy instruments in a way that enables it to pursue ambitious democratic goals while minimizing the risks of capture along the way?

9.3 How can substantive policy be designed to limit susceptibility to capture?

The dilemma of public and private power arises from the fact that there are risks of capture involved any time we empower the state to take action—especially the ambitious kinds of action that are necessary to pursue the democratic demands of anti-monopoly, countervailing power, and systemic redistribution. In particular, I argue, we can identify three key risk factors for capture of substantive policy: the amount of discretion allotted to state actors, the number of levers for influencing policy open to private actors, and the independent capacity of private actors to perpetrate capture. In turn, focusing on these risk factors generates three principles for designing capture-resistant policy: simplicity, transparency, and adversarialism.

All three of these principles converge in the idea of "structuralist" regulation developed by K. Sabeel Rahman (2016). Rahman builds on the work of early twentieth-century US Progressives like Louis Brandeis and John Dewey, who faced a version of the dilemma of public and private power when they sought to enable the nascent administrative state to curb the power of big business, without succumbing to the forms of capture identified by right-wing critics. And in response, he shows, they developed a range of tools for democratizing the administrative state from within. During the New Deal era, however, these promising approaches were ultimately superseded by expert-driven or "managerialist" models of regulation, which set the tone for the subsequent development of the US administrative state (5–11, 31–53, see also Emerson 2019).

Managerialists did not ignore capture entirely, Rahman acknowledges, but their primary concern was to insulate bureaucrats from political conflict, on the supposition that expert administrators would better realize long-term common interests if not forced to cater to the short-term interests of politicians. And while that may be true, he points out, insulation from *all* political influence also opens these expert bodies to other forms of capture (8–9). On Rahman's telling, the result of New Dealers' managerialist confidence was a regulatory state that did manifest a number of pathologies, and when world events tested public confidence in experts during the 1970s, the neglected

Progressive alternative was overlooked in the course of a sharp turn back to the laissez-faire pole with the onset of neoliberalism (39–44).

Rejecting this binary between capture-prone managerialism and an uncompromising laissez-faire alternative, Rahman posits the early Progressives' ideas as a third way (11–16, 54–77; see also Stears 2010). Instead of abandoning the project of regulation altogether, more specifically, he argues that we should follow Brandeis and others in elaborating "structuralist" approaches to regulation that are more resistant to capture (116–165). And though his book primarily addresses financial regulation, the lessons of his broader narrative can be applied to many areas where substantive regulation is the appropriate model of state involvement.

On Rahman's account, the goal of managerialist regulation is to fine-tune market dynamics, and it thus trusts experts to get the details exactly right. And because this approach requires extremely detailed knowledge that can often be provided only by regulated firms themselves, it is especially ripe for the kinds of "information capture" (Wagner 2010) and "cultural capture" (Kwak 2013) discussed in Chapter 4. Like laissez-faire critics of the managerial state, then, Rahman counsels humility about the capacities of regulators to do such fine-tuning work. Yet unlike them, he is skeptical about the tendency of free markets to produce optimal results. Rather than abandoning regulation altogether, his preferred structuralist approach focuses less on fine-tuning market outcomes and more on formulating "bright-line" rules and changing the underlying structure of financial markets (128–136, see also Awrey 2012; Krugman 2009; Weber 2012). It accepts the broader social value of finance—i.e., allocating resources more efficiently than feasible alternatives—but given the systemic dangers inherent to innovation in this sphere, it puts the burden of proof on financial firms to prove that novel products are worth the risk, rather than on regulators to prove they are not. In other words, a *simple* and *transparent* mandate serves to minimize the amount of discretion allowed to state actors, as well as the number of opportunities available to industry actors for influencing the proceedings.

Crucially, it also enables regulators to take an *adversarial* stance towards those they seek to regulate. Where managerialist regulation aiming to exercise fine-grained control requires close collaboration between state and industry actors, a structural approach guards the public nature of state power more jealously. Indeed, hypervigilance towards industry actors is embedded within the substantive mandate for structural regulation, which seeks not only to make defensive regulatory policy that is relatively capture resistant, but also to go on the offensive by reducing the independent *capacity* for capture possessed by industry actors.

In other words, at least part of the job of regulators is to undermine the structures that might facilitate capture of *future* regulators. Capture is more likely where industries have united interests, for instance, or when particular companies wield immense power on their own, and less likely when there are diverse interests vying for a regulator's attention (Krippner 2011). Taking an adversarial stance, then, structuralist regulation aims to prevent these concentrations of power from arising—by separating commercial and investment banking (Pennacchi 2012), for instance, or limiting bank size (Macey and Holdcroft 2010). More broadly, it replaces a backward-looking, criminal model of regulation, where rule violations trigger discipline, with a forward-looking, prophylactic model. The idea is that by the time serious harm has been done, it is often too late, because the wrongdoers will have already captured or co-opted those who could have punished them. More urgent than punishing specific cases of wrongdoing, on this model, is preventing the conditions that would enable *future* wrongdoing to go unpunished. In line with the principles of anti-monopoly and countervailing power outlined in Chapter 6, in other words, we should recognize that bigness *itself* is a threat—enabling anti-competitive behavior and state capture—and that protecting competition thus requires active involvement by the state to weaken advantaged incumbents and support challengers.

This brings us back to the tension at the heart of this chapter: regardless of their intended aim, there is always the danger that policies empowering state actors to weaken certain parties and support others will be captured or co-opted by those with the most concentrated power, and used to perpetuate their advantages. In order to reliably advance the right sort of adversarial, prophylactic agenda, then, we must rely as far as possible on simple and transparent bright-line rules that will minimize this danger. Although the recent turn to a more aggressive "neo-Brandeisian" understanding of antitrust is *motivated* by the recognition that bigness itself is a threat, for instance, no one proposes that we simply give antitrust enforcers the discretion to decide when a company has become "too big." This would give them an almost impossibly open-ended "managerialist" task, rendering them highly susceptible to manipulation. Instead, neo-Brandeisians have proposed a variety of simpler and more transparent bright-line rules that policymakers might employ, such as setting a threshold of market concentration that firms are not allowed to cross, or decreeing that a single firm cannot serve as both platform and seller (Bagg 2023; Chopra and Khan 2020; Khan 2019; Naidu, Posner, and Weyl 2018; Rahman 2016; Wu 2017;).

This concern for simplicity and transparency also motivates my embrace of unconditional wealth transfers (UWTs) as the centerpiece of my utopian horizon. As noted in Chapter 7, theorists of property-owning democracy eschew such "redistributive" tax-and-transfer schemes in favor of various "pre-distributive" adjustments to market structure. Many pre-distributive policies can be pursued in broadly "structuralist" rather than "managerialist" ways, and I acknowledge that they may be the most promising tools for dispersing private power in many particular contexts. Yet none match the extraordinary simplicity and transparency of UWTs, since all confer some degree of discretion upon state officials. While they may or may not be the most effective transitional policy within any given context, UWTs have a unique ability to enact nearly unlimited redistribution at minimal risk of capture, making them a maximally efficient policy solution to the dilemma of public and private power.

That said, there is a reason I cast this solution as utopian. In practice, we will rarely if ever have the luxury of structuring policies in this maximally capture-resistant way. Most of the time, rather, democratic reformers cannot eliminate all official discretion or levers for outside influence—at least not without seriously constraining their ability to disperse private power and organizational capacity. While they should still try to structure the substantive policy tools they design as simply and transparently as possible, then, democratic reformers aiming to offset the risks of capture entailed by ambitious state action must also make use of the final tool in their arsenal: namely, *procedural* mechanisms of contestation and oversight.

9.4 How can state action be procedurally insulated from capture?

The most important "procedural" strategy for insulating states from capture is the practice of subjecting leaders to competitive elections. Yet as we have seen, capture remains rampant in electoral democracies, and no amount of electoral reform will be sufficient to address it. Nor can we rely upon more direct popular participation in policymaking—either at the mass scale of referendums, or the small scale of participatory governance. As Pierre Rosanvallon (2008, 2018) has argued, rather, democratization in modern mass democracies is best seen as a heterogeneous process, centering the publicity and legibility of decision-making, as well as open contestation among different interests, rather than mass authorization or participatory governance. This section examines three examples of what this alternative vision entails: institutionalized oppositional expertise, citizen oversight juries, and leverage points for popular mobilization. Though they hardly exhaust the procedural tools we can use within the state to minimize capture of public officials, they are especially promising and representative examples of my approach. While focused on particular decision nodes, all employ adversarial means rather than the collaborative orientation favored by practices of participatory inclusion, and are thus less apt to conceal and entrench deeper conflicts of interest and power asymmetries, or have their agenda entirely co-opted through back-channel influence.

9.4.1 Institutionalized oppositional expertise

As I have emphasized, adversarial competition can often serve to weaken the grip of concentrated private power, but whether it does so depends entirely on the way this competition is structured. In regulatory contexts, for instance, practices of lobbying predictably favor those with the strongest incentives to influence policy, the greatest capacity to coordinate, and the largest resource base. Unsurprisingly, the results are often contrary to the public interest. Yet the solution is not to eliminate lobbying, as some are tempted to suggest: lobbying serves too many important purposes in a complex and pluralistic society to be abandoned entirely. Nor is the solution to eliminate *regulation* itself, as public choice theorists propose. Instead, I argue that administrative procedures can best be protected from capture if we transparently embrace their adversarial nature, while leveling the playing field among groups with a clear interest in the outcome. As suggested in my discussion of countervailing power in Chapter 6, more specifically, the idea is to make rulemaking fairer not by stifling or concealing competition between interest groups, but by supporting those who are disadvantaged, and generally equalizing the terms on which that competition will inevitably take place.

Potential solutions include placing "contrarians" within regulatory agencies (McDonnell and Schwarcz 2011), reimbursing the costs of successful challenges from third parties (Schwarcz 2013), and giving oversight to courts (Magill 2013) or expert watchdogs (Livermore and Revesz 2013). In all these cases, however, the key point is that regulators must demonstrate to challengers that their decisions serve the public interest, rather than the private or factional interests of a corporation, industry, or lobby group. And thanks to this adversarial structure, such strategies have significant potential to disrupt cycles of capture within agencies. As always, my approach is to take the reality of partiality and unequal power for granted—rather than assuming that biases and asymmetries can be eliminated altogether—and to design institutions so that those power relations can at least be recognized and potentially contested (Walters 2022).

Even so, those with concentrated private power will predictably devise ways to manipulate such procedures to their advantage. In my view, therefore, institutionalizing opposition will be most successful when supplemented by the participation of ordinary people. As I have shown in Chapter 3, of course, popular participation does not always yield positive results. More broadly, managerialists are right to see *insulation* from political pressure as an important tool for resisting capture in certain contexts. Yet popular participation takes many forms, and it is perfectly consistent to insulate bureaucrats from the corrupting influences of legislative horse-trading and partisan mass politics while creating more *promising* levers for popular influence.

9.4.2 Randomly selected citizen oversight juries

One such mechanism involves random selection for office, also known as "sortition." Though this ancient idea is rapidly winning converts (Gastil and Wright 2019), recent discussion has been dominated by the idea of deliberative mini-publics (James Fishkin 1991). More generally, it assumes lotteries are mainly valuable as an alternative to representative elections, serving to more authentically interpret the popular will (Reybrouck 2016). In my view, this narrow focus obscures the full potential of sortition, directing reformist energy away from more fruitful goals. Though many advocates see sortition as an extension of deliberative democracy, whose role is to rejuvenate representation and popular sovereignty, the most astute analysts have seen its distinctive potential in its capacity to obstruct the capture of public power (Dowlen 2008; Guerrero 2014; Stone 2011). Rather than replacing existing legislatures, more specifically, I have argued elsewhere that the most promising use for sortition lies in "citizen oversight juries" within the administrative state (Bagg 2022c; Schulson and Bagg 2019).

This entails giving randomly selected citizens real power—unlike existing experiments with deliberative mini-publics, whose advice is often simply ignored (Sintomer 2018). Yet it would also avoid many of the serious objections to more radical "lottocratic" proposals that would give direct legislative power to randomly selected bodies. For one, the idea of replacing representative bodies faces extraordinary practical hurdles in most countries, and even if such obstacles could be overcome, the resulting system would likely face serious legitimacy issues (Abizadeh 2021). Perhaps most concerning, it would still depend heavily on agenda-setting procedures that are hidden from view, and thus would hardly be immune to the kinds of capture plaguing electoral democracy (Owen and Smith 2018). Understanding sortition as one among many methods for preventing capture and corruption, by contrast, suggests a role for ordinary democratic citizens that is realistic yet crucial. Without denying the importance of political elites in policy formation, it casts ordinary people as guardians of the public interest.

Why might this help to prevent capture? On the one hand, sortition introduces an element of *randomness* into political procedures that frustrates the attempts of powerful private actors to corrupt the public nature of those procedures. Popular election and meritocratic appointment have distinct advantages as methods of distributing political office, but they are also inevitably subject to various forms of manipulation and influence. As such, they are predictably biased towards the interests of those with concentrated power. By inserting a "blind break" (Dowlen 2008) that interrupts these influence channels, a truly random process levels the playing field.

On the other hand, those randomly selected for oversight roles would be *ordinary*. Given that wise political judgment often requires significant expertise and experience, of course, this requirement has obvious drawbacks. Indeed, that is one reason not to follow sortition's more radical proponents in demanding the complete replacement of elections with lotteries. At the same time, political naïveté has advantages as well. It is precisely because most participants would begin the process with *low* political knowledge and *few* ideological commitments that their deliberations could provide a distinctive check on career politicians and other official experts, whose judgments are intimately tied up with ideology and other identity commitments.

On the model I favor, moreover, ordinary citizens would be tasked not with general purpose legislation but with oversight on specific issues (Owen and Smith 2018). They would not be expected to generate an entire agenda, but simply to make yes or no judgments about particular cases. Oversight juries might be convened on an ad hoc basis in response to administrative decisions of a certain type or significance level—such as redistricting decisions, for instance, or merger approvals and defense contracts worth more than a billion dollars. Meanwhile, longer-standing councils could meet for several months to conduct a more general review of an administrative agency, or scrutinize interactions between legislators and lobbyists.

In each case, crucially, the process would include institutionalized opposition, so that the agency would be forced to defend its decisions as serving the public interest, while various adversaries would attempt to convince the jury otherwise. The jury would then decide to approve the policy, reject it, or send it for further review elsewhere—though in theory, juries would not need to reject policies very often, because the threat of exposure posed by this process would disincentivize capture from occurring in the first place. In many contexts, moreover, making these yes or no judgments would not require vast specialized knowledge. As with the citizens who make up trial juries, therefore, members of oversight juries could be educated largely by the agency and its opponents during the adversarial process. This would greatly reduce the ability of supposedly "neutral" facilitators and experts to set agendas or otherwise influence outcomes, thus insulating juries from capture.

As always, my aim here is not to defend any particular proposal as universally appropriate. Trial juries exhibit well-known pathologies, while oversight juries would face capture threats of their own, and certain questions may simply be too complex to accommodate this kind of popular input. My claim, rather, is that if designed and implemented carefully, *some* such policies could play a significant role in resisting capture—and, more generally, that the principle of random selection has a great deal of unrealized democratic potential.

Even in the best circumstances, however, citizen oversight juries would face various limitations, not least of which is their dependence on third parties and countervailing experts to raise challenges. More generally, the role of ordinary citizens in such procedures is to represent a generic public interest, arbitrating contests among various elites and experts. Yet ordinary people also have distinctive interests of their own. If institutionalized opposition and random selection are to reliably protect against capture, there must be organizations and experts that can be trusted to represent these interests. And while ordinary people themselves must drive the organizing that will enable them to press their distinctive interests, states can facilitate such efforts in various ways. In addition to the substantive policies discussed in §6.2 (see especiallyAndrias and Sachs 2020., more specifically, a key procedural tool to employ within the policy process is the creation of leverage points for popular mobilization.

9.4.3 Leverage points for popular mobilizing and organizing

The core idea here is simply to structure rulemaking so that disadvantaged groups have opportunities to exert meaningful leverage, outside of the electoral cycle, on issues that are relevant to their interests. These formal entry points into the policy process could then serve as focal points for mobilization and organizing in civil society, in turn enabling ordinary people to counter the extra-procedural pressure that well-resourced groups are routinely able to apply.

In Chapter 3, I highlighted the limitations of many existing participatory forums, which are generally designed to gather information and facilitate compromises among equally situated participants, not to accommodate coordinated opposition and popular pressure from below. In practice, such forums are often co-opted by groups with outsized organizational capacity, who can coordinate and exert pressure regardless of the formal characteristics of the decision-making process (Wagner, Barnes, and Peters 2011). In order to meaningfully level the playing field, then, leverage points must be carefully designed to minimize such co-optation. Again, an oppositional orientation is crucial for this (see e.g., Jaskoski 2020; Simonson 2017): forums designed to advance democratic goals should invite contestation, and provide active support for groups with fewer means to organize.

One way to accomplish this is to adapt existing proposals for institutionalizing oppositional expertise, such as the idea of reimbursing or rewarding groups for successful challenges. This has been analogized to the "tripartism" between employers, unions, and the state, where the union represents a source of countervailing power that is supported by the legal framework. Meanwhile, a more speculative possibility is raised by plebeian theorists of democracy, which entails excluding elites entirely from certain participatory forums—as with the institution of the tribunate in ancient Rome (J. Green 2016; McCormick 2001, 2011).

Both proposals are more promising than much of what passes for participatory democracy. Yet both are still quite limited in their ability to overcome deep-seated asymmetries of power. On the one hand, administrative tripartism enables people without many resources to contest bureaucratic policy on a more egalitarian footing, but is unlikely to generate broad participation among those whose interests are at stake. On the other hand, plebeian institutions may generate mass mobilization and identification with popular leaders, but they provide little incentive for healthy epistemic practices or long-term organizing. Ordinary people might participate, on this model, but only as an undifferentiated and easily co-opted mass.

In order to match the consistent pressure on agencies and other state actors that wealthy elites are routinely able to apply, ordinary people must somehow acquire a comparable capacity for coordinated and collective action, over sustained periods, in defense of specific goals. As I emphasized in Chapter 6, that requires organizing large numbers of people within a structure that accommodates long-term strategic planning. And though there is much that state policy can do to facilitate this process, what ultimately matters is simply that ordinary people decide to build and join such organizations. Without such independent organizations capable of asserting the collective power of ordinary people, moreover, there is little hope of achieving the necessary policies in the first place. As I have suggested throughout this book, then, the most pressing and fundamental question for those aiming at deeper democratization concerns how this sort of organized countervailing power can be built, sustained, and held accountable over time to the interests of ordinary people. That is the question I take up in the final chapter.

10
Organizing for Power

A Paradigm for Democratic Action

In all contemporary democracies, inequalities of private power and organizational capacity reliably enable certain advantaged groups to capture state power, ensuring that it serves their interests rather than a broader public interest. As such, a primary goal of democratic action and reform must be to mitigate these inequalities. And while this goal can be pursued through state policy, as outlined in the previous chapter, this strategy also faces an obvious challenge: if states are effectively captured by wealthy and powerful elites, they are unlikely to pursue policies that threaten the interests of those elites. Are we stuck, then, in a version of the infamous "paradox of politics" (Honig 2009), whereby the means for achieving democratic transformations are viable only if those transformations have already occurred?

Thankfully, this diagnosis is too pessimistic. Cracks always appear in any political order—in the form of conflicts among elite factions, for instance, or external shocks that disrupt ossified hierarchies—creating openings that can be exploited by various counter-hegemonic groups. Such opportunities will only be converted into lasting gains, however, if they are seized by durable organizations of countervailing power, outside of the state, which effectively defend the interests of ordinary people against those of elites. Building such organizations is thus the most important priority of deeper democratization, and this chapter asks how it can be done.

10.1 Countervailing power, democratic theory, and organizing for power

Democratic theorists have had strikingly little to say about countervailing power. Among theorists of collective self-rule who emphasize collaborative processes of will formation and decision-making, for one, the ongoing oppositional tasks of building countervailing power are typically relegated to subordinate status at best. Yet as I explored in Chapter 7, there are also several traditions of democratic thought that foreground the crucial role of contestation. Drawing on radical and poststructuralist thought, for instance, agonists have sought to unsettle liberal presumptions of neutrality, and thus emphasize the importance of conflictual rather than consensual discourse (Honig 1993; Mouffe 2000). Republicans highlight various forms of institutionalized contestation as bulwarks against domination—ranging from juridical forums (Pettit 1997, 2013) to citizens' assemblies (McCormick 2011; Vergara 2020) to competition between strong, responsible parties (Rosenbluth and Shapiro 2018; I. Shapiro 2016b). Those I labeled pluralists, finally, frame social movements and other oppositional forms of civil society as critical to democracy—understood as a never-ending process of overcoming concrete threats (Medearis 2015; see also Rosanvallon 2008; Sabl 2001; Stears 2010; Woodly 2015).

Even among those who adopt such allied perspectives, however, few democratic theorists have paid sufficient attention to what makes this contestation serve genuinely democratic ends, rather than simply providing additional vectors for capture by hegemonic groups. Embedding contestatory procedures within political decision-making structures provides formal tools that ordinary people can use to resist elite capture—and as I have argued, the oppositional framing preferred by republicans mitigates certain biases that are built into collaborative procedures. The same is true of the forms of adversarial discourse and oppositional civil society, external to formal decision-making institutions, which are promoted by agonists and pluralists. Unless counter-hegemonic groups are endowed with sufficient material and organizational resources to counter those wielded by hegemonic elites, however, those elites will likely find ways to turn all of these practices to their advantage as well. Ensuring that contestation actually serves to mitigate capture, in other words, requires countervailing organizations that can sustainably wield power over long periods of time, while remaining accountable to the interests of the ordinary people and counter-hegemonic groups whose interests they ostensibly serve. The key question, then, is how such countervailing organizations are actually constructed. And with a few notable exceptions (e.g., Rahman and Gilman 2019; Woodly 2021), unfortunately, this question has largely been neglected by agonists, republicans, and pluralists alike.

Perhaps the single most important intervention of this book is to demonstrate the urgency of this question. In one way or another, all of its arguments have led to the conclusion that the most pressing priority of deeper democratization is the development of durable, effective, and accountable organizations of countervailing power, which can reliably contest the influence of wealthy elites and other hegemonic groups, and thus limit the ability of those groups to capture state power for themselves. Democratic actors who aim to protect and enrich democracy must therefore be centrally concerned with how this can be done. And if they aim to articulate norms and recommendations that are relevant to those actors, so too must democratic theorists.

Unsurprisingly, the question of how to foster the development of durable, effective, and accountable organizations of countervailing power is enormously complex, and it is beyond my scope in this book to provide a comprehensive answer: given how little attention this question has received from democratic theorists, simply urging its necessity has been a tall enough order to occupy us for nine chapters. Still, it would also be deeply unsatisfying to reach the end of the book without reflecting on the question it presents as most important. Rather than either making an unsatisfactory attempt at a comprehensive answer, or punting this task entirely to future work, my aim in this final chapter is to examine one particularly promising approach in detail—both as an example of what democratic theorists might do, when drawing a more comprehensive picture, and also as an important element of that picture.

My focus is a distinctive set of practices that have been developed and refined over the last hundred years by overlapping communities of organizers working in labor unions, community organizations, and social movements—especially the Black freedom movement—largely but not only in the US. Following the labor organizer Jane McAlevey (2016), I use the phrase "organizing for power" to describe their approach, and in what follows, I highlight its unique ability to advance the goals of resisting state capture. Most directly, the practices of organizing for power facilitate sustained forms of collective action that threaten elite interests, and thereby enable ordinary people to extract concessions from better resourced opponents. Meanwhile, they also bring about forms of political socialization that help to resist capture indirectly. By encouraging healthier epistemic networks, stronger state–citizen linkages, and solidaristic transformations of identity among participants, more specifically, the practices of organizing for power can counteract various mechanisms of agenda control, identity manipulation, and ideological power that are frequently employed by elites to get their way behind the scenes. As I will demonstrate, in fact, these direct and indirect functions are closely connected.

Because they rely on face-to-face contact, the organizations that result from these practices are inevitably limited in scale, and organizing for power cannot be the only tool we rely upon in building countervailing power. At the very least, we also need organizations that can wield power at larger scales—most notably including political parties. Yet the smaller organizations discussed here can still play a key role, by leveraging local victories to foster solidarity and strategic alliances across municipal, regional, and national boundaries—a process that has been crucial, historically, for democratization (Rueschemeyer, Huber, and Stephens 1992; Usmani 2018). Indeed, ensuring that large-scale parties are connected to and dependent upon mid-level organizations built on face-to-face contact seems to be the most reliable way of keeping their leaders tethered to the interests of ordinary people (Bagg and Bhatia 2021). Though organizing for power in labor unions, community organizations, social movements, and other face-to-face contexts can only ever be a part of our broader agenda for democratic action, then, it seems to have unique potential to initiate virtuous cycles that shift the overall balance of power in society, and is thus likely to be an especially important component of that broader agenda.

This has practical implications for all sorts of democratic actors. If my argument is right, for instance, young idealists should consider developing their talents as organizers, rather than pursuing more familiar careers in public service or nonprofit work. Journalists and media-makers with the ability to shape public attitudes should frame organizing practices as central to democratic life. Philanthropic foundations seeking to have a high impact should direct more resources toward groups that employ an organizing-for-power model (Villanueva 2018). Most generally, activists, radicals, and reformers of all stripes should orient their action—like the organizers I discuss—towards building enduring and effective forms of countervailing power, while ordinary citizens should join, support, and become leaders in the resulting organizations.

Finally, my argument also entails that the members of my most immediate audience—i.e., democratic theorists—should devote much more attention to organizing, as practiced in the traditions I discuss and beyond. Although there is growing recognition that social movements and other forms of oppositional civil society are indispensable elements of democracy, it is rarely spelled out what this might mean in practice, or how exactly these calls differ from the generic paeans to civic virtue long made by nearly all democratic theorists. There are important exceptions, of course, and I have relied heavily on their work, along with that of historians and social scientists who study organizers and their tactics.[1] And in addition, I am clearly indebted to the democratic actors who developed and refined these insights in the

---

[1] Political theorists who have written about organizing include Andy Sabl (2001), Rom Coles (2005), Paul Apostolidis (2010), Harry Boyte (2010), Jeffrey Stout (2012), Luke Bretherton (2014), Laura Grattan (2016), Vijay Phulwani (2016), Mie Inouye (2019, 2022), and Deva Woodly (2021). Historians and social scientists whose work has been influential for my account include Charles Payne (1995), Barbara Ransby

first place.[2] Still, existing analysis has typically focused on the dynamics of particular organizations, rather than the broader role of organizing practices in a democracy, and its impact in democratic theory has been limited. This chapter seeks to rectify that, insisting that these organizing traditions, and the questions they raise, must be central to democratic theory. And in doing so, it gives a distinctive answer—albeit a partial one—to the third key task of democratic theory outlined in Chapter 1: i.e., setting priorities for civic action and participation outside the state.

10.2 The distinctive practices of organizing for power

As noted, the model of organizing for power combines insights from several overlapping traditions. It is perhaps most directly inspired by the confrontational practices of the early Congress of Industrial Organizations (CIO) and other radical labor unions (see especially McAlevey 2016, 2020). Yet many tactics employed by labor organizers are not directly applicable outside of the workplace, and given my aim of articulating a more general model for building countervailing power, I also draw from two other traditions. The first comes from Saul Alinsky and his successors at the Industrial Areas Foundation (IAF), who explicitly sought to translate the CIO's aggressive and oppositional tactics to community contexts (Bretherton 2014; Phulwani 2016; Sabl 2001; Stout 2012). The second builds on the work of Civil Rights organizers like Septima Clark, Ella Baker, and Bob Moses, and their successors in the tradition of "movement organizing" (Woodly 2021). These traditions differ in important ways, and are usually treated separately, but they were in conversation from the beginning—notably through Myles Horton's Highlander Folk School—and they converge on several crucial points.

One of their commonalities, for instance, is a conviction that organizing is importantly distinct from other modes of contentious political action, such as advocacy, mobilizing, activism, protest, and prefigurative politics. To be sure, each of these other tactics has a role to play in efforts to achieve political change, but as organizers across all of these traditions are at pains to insist, there is something special about engaging ordinary people on their

(2003), Francesca Polletta (2002), John Ahlquist and Margaret Levi (2013), Hahrie Han (2014), and Eitan Hersh (2020).

[2] Two organizers whose approach is especially influential on contemporary thinking about organizing are Saul Alinsky and Ella Baker (Sabl 2001). While Alinsky published two books (1946, 1971), Baker's model was most prominently articulated by her colleague Bob Moses (1989). Contemporary organizers with influential accounts include Jane McAlevey (2016, 2020), Jonathan Smucker (2017), and adrienne marie brown (2017).

own terms, in face-to-face conversations, over the long term. In Ella Baker's words, this is the difficult and unglamorous "spadework" that is nevertheless required to build genuine power (Battistoni 2019)—and in many circles, only such practices earn the honorific title of *organizing*. In seeking to understand the distinctive features of organizing, therefore, we can begin by comparing it to the other forms of political action with which it if sometimes confused.

Fairly typically, for example, McAlevey contrasts organizing with both *advocacy* and *mobilizing*.[3] Advocates, for their part, aim to persuade political leaders to adopt certain reforms through rational argument and moral suasion, and can often achieve limited objectives like "forcing car companies to install seatbelts or banishing toys ... that infants might choke on" (2016: 9). Yet in her view, "advocacy fails to use the only concrete advantage ordinary people have over elites: large numbers"—and this "severely limits serious challenges to elite power." When facing opponents with massive incentives to defend the status quo, and vast resources to expend in doing so, appealing to moral or technocratic sensibilities will only get you so far.

Massive demonstrations and protests, by contrast—characteristic of the technique known as *mobilizing*—do take advantage of the power of numbers. As McAlevey points out, however, there are stark limits here as well, given that the vast majority of participants in such events are already disposed to agree with the aims of the mobilizers, and already see themselves as the kind of people who do things like go to protests (2016: 10). Too often, moreover, they are mobilized only for particular events, which do not in themselves threaten elite power. After all, demonstrations are only likely to be effective if they demonstrate something specific: i.e., the collective power of an organized group that is able to impose real costs on powerful actors.

As the organizer Jonathan Smucker (2017) points out, more broadly, the sharp distinction between "activists" and "normal" people is a fairly recent invention that serves to undermine movement-building—generating insular communities who have trouble engaging broader audiences. These small but committed groups may be able to motivate participation from "the usual suspects" in endless marches, protests, boycotts, and even costlier forms of direct action. At the same time, however, their insularity limits the reach of their message, and—consequently—their ability to wield collective power.

---

[3] Nearly everyone writing about organizing contrasts it with mobilizing, often tracing the distinction to the account of Ella Baker's approach developed by Moses et al. (1989). Many also discuss a third category similar to McAlevey's advocacy, while Sabl combines mobilizing and advocacy in his archetype of *moral advocacy*—modeled on Martin Luther King, Jr. and contrasted to the model of organizing adopted by Ella Baker.

As long as opponents can successfully paint them as an idiosyncratic fringe group with extreme views, activists may be safely ignored.

A common tactic that may appear to transcend these limits, finally, is the kind of canvassing undertaken by electoral campaigns and advocacy organizations, in an effort to drive turnout, collect signatures, or raise money. After all, its express purpose is to reach out beyond core activists. Yet engagement remains superficial and short-lived—taking people neither on their own terms nor as agents in their own struggles (Hersh 2020).[4] Where canvassers airdrop into a community every few years with instructions on who to vote for or where to donate money, organizers build trust and listen to community members over an extended period, ultimately developing a political analysis and a collective strategy that responds to their concerns.

Crucially, then, the role of organizers is not to indoctrinate community members or even to "lead" them in any traditional sense, but to help them find their *own* leaders and build their *own* power. Organizers may provide guidance, but community members themselves participate actively in building the organization, setting its goals, and making strategic decisions (see also Freire 1970). More broadly, organizers are wary of strong and charismatic leadership styles, which may be effective at drawing elite attention and even mobilizing large numbers of people in the short term, but can undermine the long-term success of efforts to build power by preventing ordinary people from feeling ownership and agency over their own struggles.

For instance, scholars of the Civil Rights movement contrast the public role of Martin Luther King Jr. and Stokely Carmichael—not to mention Lyndon Johnson—with that of organizers like Septima Clark and Ella Baker (Moses et al. 1989; Payne 1995; Ransby 2003; Sabl 2001). Though the latter were much less visible, historians argue that their "spadework" laid the foundation for achievements more commonly associated with their male counterparts, and should be conceived as equally essential—if not more so. Especially in recent years, indeed, suspicion of charismatic leaders has converged with a "margin-to-center" ethic (hooks 1984) that seeks to transcend the dominance of white and male leaders—and their traditionally domineering leadership styles—by centering women of color (brown 2017; Carruthers 2018).

At the same time, organizers understand the need for leadership of some kind, and as such, their approach is often situated *between* the extremes of leaderless "horizontalism" and fully centralized "vanguardism"

---

[4] On the basis of field experiments (e.g., Kalla and Broockman 2020), Hersh is more optimistic about a practice called 'deep canvassing'. Though it does not fit the model of organizing for power—and is unlikely to alter deep asymmetries of private power—this practice may have potential to shift popular views about certain issues.

(Bretherton 2014: 185; Stout 2012: 19). One of the main tasks of organizers who come from outside a given community or workplace, for instance, is to find and develop "organic" leaders: i.e., community members who have earned the trust of neighbors or coworkers, and can therefore lead both more effectively *and* more accountably than any outside organizer (Stout 2012: 93–113). Often, the role of organizers themselves is conceived not in terms of leadership at all, but rather in terms of creating *new* leaders and organizers, or perhaps simply "making democratic agents" (Inouye 2019; Phulwani 2016).

It is difficult to say precisely what this looks like—and as we shall see, that remains one of the main points of contention *between* the traditions of organizing discussed in this chapter. Nevertheless, all of these traditions share a number of convictions about what true organizing requires. On the one hand, organizers must seek to engage large numbers of ordinary people—reaching beyond the elite audience characteristic of advocacy efforts, as well as the "usual suspects" involved in insular forms of activism. On the other hand, this engagement cannot be either episodic or unidirectional, as with mobilizing and canvassing: instead, organizers must adopt a long time horizon, while ensuring that rank-and-file members participate actively in formulating both the ends and the means pursued by their organization.

This emphasis on widespread participation by ordinary people is shared, of course, by the forms of participatory inclusion whose inadequacies I discussed at length in Chapter 3. What separates the practices discussed in this chapter, however, is their relentless focus on questions of power and the power structure, as well as their partisan, oppositional framing. The point of organizing is not to find consensus or compromise, in other words, among members of a political community who are presumed to relate on equal terms. Instead, it starts with the far more realistic assumption that groups relate to one another on vastly unequal terms, and aims to contest this status quo through partisan action on behalf of those at the bottom.

As a result, organizers also place far less emphasis on formal political procedures and other moments of collective decision-making. They aim instead to undermine pervasive asymmetries in the distribution of power, by building robust organizations capable of continuously exerting collective countervailing power. More specifically, the model of "organizing for power" enables a community to act collectively in ways that impose costs on powerful elites, and this, in turn, allows them to extract impressive concessions. As I shall argue, therefore, widespread participation is desirable in this particular context not because it has generic *intrinsic* value—reflecting yet another opportunity to exercise collective self-rule—but rather because it plays a crucial *instrumental* role in threatening elite interests and thus building countervailing power.

Any attempt to fit diverse traditions within a common theoretical mold, of course, will end up glossing over certain differences and particularities. For one, many labor unions, community organizations, and movement groups do not embrace the long-term, oppositional, participatory methods of organizing for power. Even those which do, meanwhile, may still reject my exclusive focus on the aim of *countervailing* power, embracing other logics of power-building—such as mutual aid or autonomy—in addition to the oppositional goals of organizing for power.

To be clear, then: I do not claim that building countervailing power is the only valid aim for organizers to adopt; nor that organizing for power is the only way of doing so. My claims are rather as follows: (a) building countervailing power is a *particularly important* democratic goal; (b) the model of organizing for power outlines a *particularly potent* set of interlocking strategies for doing so; and (c) this model figures significantly within each of the traditions I have discussed. On the one hand, then, my account of the crucial democratic role of organizing for power—i.e., helping to resist state capture by ensuring greater balance in the organizational capacity available to different social groups—may be useful to organizers in understanding and contextualizing their practices. On the other hand, it implies that these organizing practices should play a much larger role in our broader agenda for democratization.

10.3 Collective action against elite interests: The origins of countervailing power

The basic idea of organizing for power is that by making use of their numerical superiority, those with few resources can threaten the material interests of those who individually possess much greater power, thereby forcing them to make concessions. In order to make use of their greater numbers in this way, however, a counter-hegemonic group must be able to coordinate on forms of mass collective action that actually pose a threat to elite interests—often easier said than done. As such, generating this capacity is the primary goal of organizing for power.

Different types of collective action will be available to different types of communities. The paradigm case of countervailing power under modern conditions is that wielded by organized workers, who can extract huge concessions from capital owners by threatening to collectively withhold their labor until certain demands are met. That said, the industrial and political context always mediates the effectiveness of this threat—which diminishes if striking workers may face violent repression or legal sanction, for instance, or if employers can easily replace them or relocate capital investments. Since the 1970s, indeed, a concerted effort to undermine the social, legal, and economic foundations of union power—amid accelerating globalization and automation—has successfully weakened the ability of workers to wield this threat across the North Atlantic world, and especially in the United States (McAlevey 2020).

Labor unions can and must be rejuvenated, especially in less mobile sectors like education and healthcare: on my account, indeed, this is a crucial priority for democratization. As radicals have long appreciated, denying profits to the owners of capital through the strike remains one of the most powerful weapons ordinary people have at their disposal, and this explains why labor unions have often provided a blueprint for organizers in other contexts. As I demonstrate below, moreover, unions also have much broader benefits for the distribution of power, which only grow more significant when they adopt the sort of confrontational tactics and participatory methods suggested by the model of organizing for power. On my account, therefore, democracy demands not only that unions grow their membership, but also that they adopt a more oppositional stance, and focus on the long-term tasks of building countervailing power.

Nevertheless, labor organizing also has certain inherent limitations. Strikes can be quite risky, for instance, and workplaces generate distinctive obstacles for the solidarity required to motivate such risks. In large companies, workers are often drawn from many social groups and divided into many job categories, creating cleavages that employers can exploit: indeed, they have often been constructed for precisely that purpose.[5] Meanwhile, labor unions will always be vulnerable to global economic trends and hostile political regimes. As such, they must also be joined by other forms of countervailing power, built along alternative lines of solidarity.

Thankfully, the workplace strike is hardly the *only* threatening form of collective power available to ordinary people. For one, something resembling

---

[5] In the United States, for instance, job categories often break down along racial lines, which facilitates the sort of 'divide-and-conquer' strategy discussed in Chapter 2. Perhaps most notoriously, Southern Democrats ensured that the Wagner Act and other key parts of the New Deal excluded domestic workers and farmworkers—jobs held disproportionately by nonwhites—from protection (Katznelson 2005). Nor have these tactics disappeared in the modern era: see McAlevey's discussion of how the bosses at Smithfield Foods in North Carolina, for instance, have recently used racial divisions to undermine potential worker coalitions (2016: 143–178).

the strike model can be applied to contexts outside the workplace. If tenants and debtors collectively withhold rent and loan payments, for instance, they can conceivably impose steep costs on landlords and creditors (Bangs 2018; Hampton 2015). Indeed, the debt strike is perhaps the oldest form of (nonviolent) mass collective action, and it was certainly the most common before the modern era (Appel 2015). Rent and debt strikes enjoy little legal protection at present, and thus entail greater risks. Yet the same was once true of workplace strikes: legal protection was a hard-fought victory for organized labor, and it is plausible that skyrocketing housing costs and ballooning debt burdens could generate similar momentum for tenants' and debtors' unions.

Threatening profits from the other end of the production process, meanwhile, ordinary people can also coordinate consumer boycotts to extract concessions from producers—as with the 1981 boycott that forced Coca-Cola to work with more Black-owned businesses and hire more Black executives. Alternatively, an organization may seek to damage the value of a brand by precipitating a public relations disaster. The more diffuse the threat, of course, the weaker it will be, but capital markets can be skittish about scandals, and corporations have been known to respond to pressures of this kind—indeed, it is increasingly deployed by unions themselves, either as a replacement for or supplement to strikes and walkouts (McAlevey 2016: 208–10).

Finally, similar dynamics can also be observed in politics. Where profits respond directly to scandals and other challenges, of course, politicians must depend on indirect indicators of their popularity—such as press coverage and polls—to estimate their likelihood of victory in the next elections. This attenuates the ability of ordinary people to clearly and credibly threaten their interests. Nevertheless, it is not impossible for organized groups to make demands and extract concessions from politicians by employing various forms of mass collective action. Indeed, public sector unions have often been quite successful, despite the fact that their employers are typically elected politicians, and thus face the same set of incentives.

The most obvious bargaining chip an organization can deploy with political leaders is the ability to deliver a reliable voting bloc. Given the vast array of influences on voting behavior, only the largest and most disciplined of organizations—such as political parties—will be able to make such claims with high credibility on a large scale. While parties represent important vectors of organization on the national scale, however, local organizations can often maximize their leverage by remaining distant from established party structures. Local races are small enough that a voting bloc need not be larger than a few hundred to potentially tip the scales, thereby generating significant leverage for the bloc and its leaders (Hersh 2020: 64–73).

Meanwhile, influence over a particular voting bloc is only the most direct form of leverage that well-organized communities can wield with politicians. As I argued in Chapter 8, vague threats of bad press or voter pressure can carry significant weight with elected officials. Indeed, uncertainty about the electoral impact of any particular incident can make fears of public relations disasters *more* salient. Especially at local and regional levels, meanwhile, government policies often require extensive material support and cooperation from community members, and withdrawing that support can often inflict serious costs on government actors.

As an example of how community organizations might wield this leverage to maximum effect, consider Stout's (2012: 45–52) description of the "accountability sessions" run by IAF affiliates. Ideally conducted by organic leaders, on the community's turf, and before a large audience of engaged members, these sessions invite local politicians to listen to community concerns before being asked whether they support a series of concrete proposals. Threatened with a silenced microphone and other sanctions if they are evasive, candidates are effectively forced to embody the democratic virtue of "candor" (J. Green 2009), giving simple answers to direct questions and making public yes or no commitments to very specific demands. Such events can be quite uncomfortable for candidates, but if the community is sufficiently well-organized, savvy politicians know that they cannot afford to decline the invitation.

As a very different example of community power, we might also consider the celebrated bus boycott of 1955–56 in Montgomery, Alabama—as well as the years of patient organizing that made it possible. As every US schoolchild knows, Rosa Parks was arrested for refusing to give up her seat on a segregated bus, sparking a boycott of public transit among Montgomery's Black community that ended with the integration of buses. This conclusion was reached only after the intervention of the US Supreme Court, and is thus not a simple case of a community extracting concessions *directly* from powerful opponents. Still, it does illustrate several of the tools of community leverage we have just discussed, merging the immediate economic and political pressures of a boycott with legal challenges and a national public relations campaign.

Even more relevant to our discussion of organizing, however, are the features of the boycott that are often *obscured* by its canonical portrayal as a spontaneous reaction to Parks' arrest, spearheaded by the charismatic leadership of Martin Luther King, Jr. In reality, a boycott of this magnitude would have been impossible without a great deal of preparation. Parks herself was fresh off a training at Myles Horton's Highlander Folk School, and even more crucially, organizations like the Women's Political Council of Montgomery had spent years laying the groundwork for some sort of boycott in the Black community.

Indeed, the truly extraordinary feature of the Montgomery bus boycott is not that a single woman was willing to be arrested, but rather that thousands of ordinary people were willing to skip the bus, day after day, and walk to work or school instead—which often took hours, under threat of violence from white mobs—for 381 straight days. King's inspirational rhetoric surely played a role in motivating this remarkable commitment as well. Yet the singular focus King receives in American historical memory here—as in other well-known episodes of the Civil Rights movement—reflects a common temptation to overlook the slower and less glamorous organizing efforts that nearly always lie behind such achievements.

10.4 Identity, collective action, and the entangled aims of organizing for power

This brings us to the crux of my argument in this chapter. Throughout the previous section, we have seen that the most potent forms of countervailing power are made possible only by sustained and widespread commitment to costly forms of collective action. My claim, then, is that practices of organizing for power are uniquely capable of motivating this commitment. That explains why diverse traditions of labor, community, and movement organizing have converged upon them—and it is also what makes them so essential for democratization.

The crucial factor, more specifically, is the attention organizers devote to shaping identity. Where advocacy involves little mass participation, and mobilizing often engages only the "usual suspects," organizing is unique in its emphasis on bringing in new people (Smucker 2017). Opponents of unionization must become union members willing to go on strike (McAlevey 2016, 2020). People who are disillusioned with politics—often with good reason—must become the kinds of people who take substantial risks and devote significant time to political action (Payne 1995; Ransby 2003). Atomized individuals with fairly parochial interests must learn to forge solidarity and make sacrifices for one another (Battistoni 2019; Blanc 2019). At a very basic level, in other words, organizing for power is about shifting the *subjectivity* of the organized (Inouye 2022; Woodly 2021).

A core theme of this book has been that achieving such shifts is extraordinarily difficult. Drawing on extensive research in political psychology, I have argued that political behavior is driven largely by social identity, which is highly resistant to change. That is why practices of participatory inclusion help participants overcome information deficits and reach compromises when there is little of salience at stake, for instance, yet make less progress on polarized issues characterized by greater asymmetries of power, or more basic political values (Bagg 2018a), which are more intimately connected with identity (Goodman and Bagg 2022). The practices of organizing for power, by contrast, are distinguished by their capacity to bring about such subjective transformations. Unlike reformers touting superficial participatory forums as the solution to deep power asymmetries, organizers appreciate just how demanding political transformation really is. Rather than hoping to change minds through mass persuasive speech or isolated bouts of reasonable deliberation among strangers, organizers understand that the only route to meaningful political change is through transforming citizens' identities, and the practices of organizing for power are appropriate to the magnitude of this task.

To begin with, organizations may engage in explicit forms of political education, as well as more implicit forms of political socialization—exposing members to certain news sources, for instance. Despite their biases, epistemic networks founded in sophisticated journalistic and scholarly practices tend to weed out blatantly fake news and crass forms of conspiracism. By providing access to information that is driven neither by the political projects of wealthy moguls nor by consumer demand for sensationalized clickbait, face-to-face organizations can thus keep their members tethered to basic political realities.[6] At the same time, they can also represent feedback mechanisms, highlighting elite blind spots and biases by transmitting the perspectives of ordinary people back up the chain. Neither elite-driven dissemination nor undisciplined speculation from below can generate trustworthy knowledge on its own, but both can contribute to a healthier epistemic ecology, which is more resistant to elite efforts to control the agenda and shape public opinion through ideological propaganda (Rosenfeld 2018).

Similarly, organizations built on long-term, face-to-face contact are often the most trusted points of connection between ordinary people and the faceless bureaucracies that govern their lives. As such, they can serve as focal

---

[6] Hacker and Pierson (2011: 139–158), for instance, argue that a major reason for the increasing inequality in the US since 1970 is the withdrawal of the informational function of unions. For a more comprehensive account of these and other functions of unions, see O'Neill and White (2018).

points for accessing and disseminating important legal or medical information that might otherwise be inaccessible—especially in communities facing barriers of language or migration status (Hersh 2020). Aside from helping people *access* the information they need to defend their interests within the state and other distant, impersonal institutions, moreover, these organizations also prepare people to take *action*, by habituating them to making and winning demands of powerful actors in those institutions (Ahlquist and Levi 2013). Ordinary people who are actively engaged with such organizations are not only better informed about the structures of power they face, in other words, they are also more likely to see themselves as potentially efficacious political agents within those structures.

By far the most important and distinctive feature of organizing for power, however—which sets it apart from other voluntary organizations and civil society groups—is precisely its emphasis on mass collective action in opposition to elites with concentrated private power. If political beliefs largely follow from social identity, after all, efforts to cultivate political education, socialization, and state–citizen linkage are unlikely to bear fruit unless accompanied by more powerful emotional experiences as well: i.e., the sort of experiences that might shape the identities of adults who are otherwise quite accustomed to their place in the world.

This is a tall order indeed. As organizers recognize, however, the ordeal of fighting powerful opponents and winning improbable victories through mass collective action can often yield just the profound sort of experiences necessary to meet it. In other words, it is the *process* of organizing, acting collectively, and extracting concessions from elites that has the greatest potential to shift participants' social identity and political orientation. In all of the traditions I have discussed, therefore, the experience of forging solidarity through oppositional collective action is understood as the most promising fount of transformational change.

What this means is that the aims of building countervailing power and shifting participants' identities are fully interdependent. On the one hand, organizations must bring about substantial shifts in the identities of rank-and-file members in order to generate sustained commitment to collective action and thereby create countervailing power. In order to pull off costly collective actions, that is, people must become the kinds of people who do things like participate in costly collective actions. And on the other hand, organizations must successfully extract concessions from elite interests through mass collective action in order to generate lasting shifts in the identities of participants. Or, to put it even more succinctly: successful organizing depends on shifting the identity of the organized, and shifting the identity of the organized depends on successful organizing. The genius of organizing for power, I argue, is that it creates profound experiences of collective struggle and success that can and do change political identities.

10.5 Building countervailing power: A roadmap for transformation

To begin with, one of the most noticeable features that sets organizing for power apart from other forms of political activism is its long time horizon. Successful mobilizing may generate momentary bursts of collective action, but unless high levels of mobilization are sustained, elites can simply weather the storm—using their greater resources to sustain temporary losses in the service of long-term goals. As organizers recognize, anyone hoping to credibly threaten elite interests must be able to continue the fight as long as it takes.

At the same time, organizers also recognize the importance of breaking down seemingly impossible long-term challenges into more manageable short- and medium-term goals. A small core of activists may be willing to spend their entire lives fighting for a revolutionary dream that may never arrive, but most people need a reasonable prospect of concrete victories to stay motivated. Meanwhile, the most powerful forms of collective solidarity are forged when participants share the fruits of victory with one another. Though often motivated by radically transformative visions themselves, therefore, effective organizers steer communities towards concrete intermediate aims that are at least potentially achievable. This, in turn, requires an accurate "power analysis" identifying the forms of leverage that a community and its potential allies might be able to wield, as well as the kinds of concessions this leverage might enable them to extract from their opponents (McAlevey 2016: 2–9, 58–70; Stout 2012: 21–33).

Rather than moving directly to a costly action such as a strike, meanwhile, organizers typically stage a series of "structure tests" requiring increasing commitment. On the one hand, this allows them to assess organizational strength, and thereby avoid demoralizing participants and undermining future organizing efforts by attempting high-profile actions that are doomed from the start. On the other hand, it gives potential participants a less intimidating path towards more costly forms of participation. As noted, the key to successful organizing for power is engaging many people who are new to collective political action, and do not yet understand themselves as efficacious political agents. The escalating series of structure tests enables them to gradually become such agents, rather than demanding an instantaneous transformation.

Adopting concrete and limited goals is also crucial for engaging the widest possible range of participants. Effective organizing must always reject the sort of purity tests that generate internal cleavages and relegate activist groups to a radical fringe. And in certain contexts, at least, the only way those with radical goals will have a chance of winning concrete victories is by working in a broad-based coalition that includes moderates and even avowed conservatives.

As the journalist Eric Blanc (2019) observes, for instance, substantial participation from conservative educators was critical to the success of the 2018 "Red for Ed" movement, which saw education workers in West Virginia, Oklahoma, and Arizona use supermajority strikes to win enormous concessions from Republican-led state governments. And as Blanc's interviews make clear, this united front was possible only because people of color in the movement were willing to temporarily set aside the casual racism and reactionary views of white colleagues in order to fight for the interests they shared in common. Disagreements could be had—as a space of solidarity, in fact, the picket line is a fertile ground for conversations about difficult topics—but they could not endanger participants' ability to work together. People of color thus needed to see Trump-voting whites as possible allies, rather than eternal political enemies—which, in turn, meant keeping certain controversial demands off the agenda. As Blanc found, however, these were sacrifices that many Black and Latino/a education workers in West Virginia, Oklahoma, and Arizona were willing to make, in order to defeat more immediate foes.

To state the obvious, members of disadvantaged groups have every reason to be wary of processes that require them to stand in solidarity with those who subject them to racism, sexism, and other harms. All too often, minorities who have participated in collective struggle alongside hegemonic groups have been excluded from the spoils of victory, and in light of this history, distrust and withdrawal are perfectly rational responses. Despite this, many members of disadvantaged groups are willing to take the leap of faith required to work with members of hegemonic groups—and in some cases, that gamble pays enormous dividends. In the Red for Ed strikes, for instance, Black and Latino/a education workers won the same benefits for themselves and their students as their white colleagues. Even more significantly, Blanc reports, the ordeal of standing in solidarity with coworkers, in opposition to powerful interests, and winning real concessions from a common enemy, had a transformative effect on a substantial number of the conservative white education workers who participated in the strikes.

In particular, Blanc's interviews suggest that a surprising number of conservative Trump voters grew skeptical of Republican state officials, who deployed a barrage of duplicitous methods in their efforts to divide workers and break the strikes. Others were especially moved by experiences of solidarity with Black and Latino/a coworkers, voicing newfound dedication to anti-racist struggles in their workplaces and beyond. This is the sort of transformation that social identity theory tells us is extremely rare, but as I have suggested, winning concessions from powerful opponents through mass collective action seems to be among the few experiences that can bring them about. Needless to say, such transformations would have been impossible if participants were required to agree on more than a few concrete aims at the outset.

The idea here is not to actively *cater* to bigotry in framing demands, but simply to *set aside* the most contentious questions, tactically and temporarily, in making demands that will motivate maximum participation by generating benefits for everyone. And when implemented correctly, this universalizing imperative actually *serves* racial justice. Some participants in the "Red for Ed" strikes, for instance, would have preferred to limit the strike to teachers, who are disproportionately white. In every case examined by Blanc, however, strike leaders insisted on including more racially diverse support staff as well—on the grounds that doing so made the strikes more *effective*. Because cooks, janitors, and bus drivers were also on strike, schools had to be shut down entirely, rather than simply making do without the teachers, and this drastically increased the pressure on state leaders to meet the strikers' demands.

Counterintuitive as it may seem, more broadly, appeals to self-interest can also help to facilitate solidarity over the long term. Disinterested concern for justice may motivate certain people to participate in costly collective action, but especially at the outset, the most reliable way of motivating many rank-and-file members is to demonstrate the concrete benefits of participation for themselves, their families, and their communities. As we shall see, organizers disagree about whether these discrete and broadly self-interested goals must be situated within a broader orienting vision or ideology. Yet organizers across all the traditions I discuss recognize that concrete victories serve to motivate participation and foster solidarity. As such, they tend to pursue short- and medium-term aims that are not just realistically achievable and broadly appealing, but also at least partly grounded in some form of self-interest.

Perhaps the most crucial tactic for shifting the identities of rank-and-file members of an organization, however—and thereby generating maximum participation in costly forms of collective action—is to engage them actively in building the organization, setting its goals, and making strategic decisions. When an organization is highly centralized, rank-and-file members will feel little investment in the organization or its activities, and its leaders will have difficulty motivating the participation needed to generate meaningful threats. In an organization characterized by significant input and investment from ordinary rank-and-file members, by contrast, they are much more likely feel a strong and durable connection to their fellow members, the organization, and the forms of collective action they themselves have decided to pursue. Under these conditions, commitment will be far more forthcoming.

More broadly, this is another reason to insist on face-to-face conversations, existing social networks, and organic leaders who have earned the community's trust. As Stout (2012: 149) writes, "when organizers take shortcuts and rely too much on more distant forms of interaction, the organizations become less powerful ... because the people who claim to lead them have done less to earn the entitlement to represent those on whose behalf they speak." Similarly, Sabl (2001: 264) observes that "*nonrational* assessments of another's character are the best way to get people to trust one another when they have limited time and resources, limited formal education and ability to assess complicated propositions, and little political experience." As Deva Woodly (2021) surmises, therefore, the formation of "political friendships" must take place "in a register that is explicitly both emotional and political."

Thus far, of course, my claims about the virtues of organizing for power have been supported entirely by qualitative and anecdotal evidence, provided by scholars and journalists studying the tactics of specific organizers and movements, as well as the accounts of organizers themselves. Many of these accounts focus on the cases they consider to be most successful—or in other words, they "select on the dependent variable"—and their authors are often invested, to some degree, in vindicating the practices they describe. In the absence of more systematic quantitative data, then, we might worry that the success stories I have discussed are simply exceptional cases, with little external or general validity. Does organizing for power really generate the sort of collective power and solidaristic identity transformations claimed by its advocates, or have they just cherry-picked the most promising examples?

Given the limitations of existing evidence, and the difficulty of causal inference about such matters more generally, this worry cannot be entirely assuaged. Nevertheless, there are several reasons to remain confident that organizing for power does indeed possess the advantages I have claimed for it. For one, historians, journalists, and organizers do typically confine their attention to success cases, but several of the qualitative, small-n studies I have relied upon most heavily (e.g., Han 2014, McAlevey 2016) are designed expressly to avoid this problem of selecting on the dependent variable. Although the evidence from large-n quantitative studies is necessarily less fine-grained, meanwhile, it generally points in the same direction as well.

The main problem with using large-n quantitative studies to gather fine-grained evidence about the effectiveness of organizing for power lies in organizational heterogeneity. Simply put, not all labor unions, community organizations, and movement groups employ practices of organizing for power, and it will often require extensive qualitative study—like that undertaken by Han and McAlevey—to discover whether, and to what extent, they do so. Thus, while many studies have demonstrated that high social capital and a strong civil society are associated with a variety of positive democratic outcomes (e.g., Putnam 1993, 2001), few differentiate among organizations on the basis of their social function or strategic orientation, and so the evidence they provide is not directly relevant to the specific question at hand: i.e., whether a model of organizing for power is especially effective at generating collective action and solidaristic identity transformations. (It goes without saying, meanwhile, that we cannot randomly assign this strategic orientation to different organizations, to observe the causal effect experimentally.)

Nevertheless, other kinds of quantitative evidence do lend indirect support to the claims of organizers—perhaps most notably including studies of the effects of union density on broad social outcomes, as well as the effects of union membership on individual political behavior.[7] To the extent that they do not differentiate between unions that adopt the methods of organizing for power and those that do not, large-n studies that measure the impact of labor unions as such cannot directly test the effectiveness of those methods. Yet given that many unions do employ such methods—and that unions have done so more extensively than any other organizations in modern

---

[7] For good summaries of this evidence, see O'Neill and White (2018) and Ahlquist (2017). For a related example, outside the context of labor unions, see Kenneth Andrews' (2004) finding that Mississippi counties with more movement infrastructure during the Civil Rights era demonstrated higher levels of Black political participation and office-holding two decades later.

history—union density and union membership are decent proxy measures for social and individual exposure to those methods. And the evidence we get by employing these proxies suggests quite strongly that organizing for power has precisely the sort of transformative, democracy-enhancing effects observed in journalistic, historical, and qualitative accounts.

On the level of broader social outcomes, for one, union density and other measures of the overall strength of labor are strongly correlated with a more egalitarian distribution of private power and organizational capacity in almost every relevant respect (Ahlquist 2017; Becher and Stegmueller 2021; Bradley et al. 2003; Freeman and Medoff 1984). Focusing narrowly on formal access to political power, a strong labor movement is associated with earlier and more durable democratization (Kadivar, Usmani, and Bradlow 2020; Rueschemeyer, Huber, and Stephens 1992; Usmani 2018). Union strength is also associated with a less skewed distribution of private power—as reflected in greater after-tax redistribution as well as more compressed pretax wage distributions (Farber et al. 2021; Kerrissey 2015; Pontusson 2013). The evidence for these correlations—from cross-national studies as well as detailed studies of change over time within individual countries (e.g., Hacker and Pierson 2011)—is overwhelming. And while it is always difficult to tease out the relative causal contributions of the various factors that might explain such broad correlations, it is also hard to believe that the strength of the labor movement has no causal role whatsoever in generating the relatively egalitarian political and economic circumstances with which it is so strongly associated (Streeck and Hassel 2003).

Meanwhile, quantitative evidence also confirms that unions shape the political subjectivity of individual union members in ways that tend to strengthen democracy on the whole. To start with, union membership induces people to participate more frequently, and experience greater political efficacy (D'Art and Turner 2007; Flavin and Radcliff 2011; Kerrissey and Schofer 2013, 2018; Radcliff and Davis 2000; Terriquez 2011). More substantively, union members are more likely to identify as working class (Franko and Witko 2023) and prefer redistributive policy (Macdonald 2019; Rueda and Pontusson 2000). Although some unions have historically served to reinforce racial cleavages, finally, union membership under contemporary conditions tends to reduce racial animus among whites (Frymer and Grumbach 2021). And despite the difficulty of making these fine-grained distinctions using quantitative data, what evidence we do have suggests that all of these transformative effects on individual political behavior and identity are stronger in unions that employ confrontational, participatory methods (Ahlquist, Clayton, and Levi 2014; Kim and Margalit 2017; Mosimann and

Pontusson 2017)—i.e., just the sort of methods favored by the model of organizing for power.

What should we conclude from this? Although we cannot claim absolute certainty about any particular element of the picture I have drawn in this chapter, convergent evidence from journalistic narratives, qualitative scholarship, and quantitative studies suggests that there is something genuinely special about the model of organizing for power. This evidence gives us very good reason, in other words, to believe what organizers in labor unions, community organizations, and the Black freedom movement have long insisted: i.e., that practices of face-to-face organizing with an explicit oppositional orientation, a long time horizon, a participatory methodology, and an emphasis on winning concrete victories within a given power structure, are uniquely capable of advancing the entangled democratic aims of building enduring capacity for collective action and inciting solidaristic transformations of identity.

10.6 The dilemmas of democratic transformation

Before we wholeheartedly endorse the model of organizing for power, however, we must address a final set of worries, arising from the fact that no organization is immune to capture. After all, more than a few labor unions have been involved in political corruption and even organized crime. More broadly, unions have often been accused of protecting the interests of their members at the expense of the general public. Why should we not expect the practices of organizing for power to simply be co-opted in just the same way as the conventional methods of democratic action and reform I have rejected in earlier chapters?

One version of this worry can be dismissed fairly quickly, based on what has already been said about the dilemmas inherent to the task of fighting power with power. Given that capture can never be entirely eliminated, for one, I have argued that the best way for democratic actors to minimize its overall prevalence and severity is to focus their limited resources on countering those hegemonic groups whose interests are most reliably served by contemporary democratic states, thanks to their outsized private power and organizational capacity—especially wealthy elites and those advantaged by categorical inequalities. What looks like capture at a local scale may thus be democratically justified, on the whole, if it has the effect of reducing capture at larger scales. If a political party is faced with an opponent that seeks to undermine democratic institutions, for instance, I have argued that the best way for it to protect democracy might be to engage in certain self-limiting and reciprocal forms of "hardball" that would otherwise be considered anti-democratic (Bagg and Tranvik 2019; Faris 2018; Schedler 2021).

In a similar spirit, we might imagine a coalition of labor unions that effectively captures a city council, and makes policies that serve the interests of unionized workers above those of other groups. In a world that is otherwise characterized by a perfectly egalitarian balance of power, this would clearly increase the overall level of capture, relative to a baseline of zero, and would rightly be considered anti-democratic. In the actual world, however, it is easy to imagine how a labor coalition might use its outsized control over a city council as a base from which to build countervailing power and contest the advantages of the wealthy elites who remain hegemonic in the broader society—thus making organizational capacity more balanced on the whole, and reducing the overall prevalence and severity of capture. In doing so, there are certain methods they must avoid categorically, such as suppressing opposition, because they are overwhelmingly likely to have counterproductive effects in the long run. If they simply use the power they have won through fair electoral procedures to pursue the sectional interests of labor on a local scale, however, the unions who have "captured" this city council may actually be protecting public interests on a broader national or global scale—and if so, what appears as capture locally may serve democratic ends from a broader perspective.

Of course, this democracy-enhancing outcome is hardly guaranteed. Fighting power with power is always a risky business, and the history of the labor movement in particular is full of unions exercising power in ways that even the most charitable observer could not interpret as serving democratic ends on any scale. Such unions should clearly be opposed by democratic actors. Meanwhile, there may be certain types of unions whose interests are structurally tied to those of hegemonic groups—such as police unions—which are likely to exert a pernicious influence on democracy on the whole, and which democratic actors thus have strong reasons to oppose. And if such cases were the rule rather than the exception, my counsel would be to limit union power, rather than fostering it. As it happens, however, the evidence surveyed above favors the opposite conclusion quite strongly. Overall and in the long run, it seems, union power reliably leads to a more egalitarian balance of organizational capacity. Overall and in the long run, then, labor unions deserve robust support on democratic grounds.

Similar considerations apply to the other civic groups I have discussed: rather than offering a generic endorsement of all civil society organizations, the ideal of democracy as resisting state capture endorses only those that reliably serve the interests of counter-hegemonic groups. Even as it stresses the critical importance of community organizations and social movements in general, then, it also gives democratic actors unambiguous reasons to oppose any groups that serve hegemonic interests, such as racially exclusive community organizations and regressive social movements. This is yet another of its advantages. If democracy is presented as a perfectly neutral ideal, we will struggle to explain what is anti-democratic about these organizations. On my account, by contrast, the asymmetry is clear: because they exacerbate inequalities of private power and organizational capacity, they do not deserve support on democratic grounds.[8]

Beyond specifying the substantive goals that civic organizations should pursue and the kinds of organizations most likely to pursue them, finally, this chapter has primarily been concerned with *how* these goals can best be pursued. Unlike approaches such as advocacy or mobilizing, for instance, the model of organizing for power emphasizes the need for small-scale, face-to-face interaction and consistent participation by rank-and-file members. Yet this participation is not valued categorically, or for its own sake—as with ideals of participatory inclusion—but only when and because it facilitates more powerful forms of collective action. Unlike the conventional approaches to democratic reform examined in earlier chapters, more specifically (see especially §3.3), the model of organizing for power requires an oppositional rather than a neutral or collaborative orientation—focused explicitly on addressing particular problems with identifiable opponents. As such, it is more likely to expose power inequalities and conflicts of interest, and less likely to present any agreements as final and authoritative. Because it adopts a long time horizon, and emphasizes the need for continuous power-building rather than decision-making at specific points in time, meanwhile, it is better able to expose and contest the background agenda-setting use by elites to co-opt conventional decision-making institutions and participatory reforms. While not entirely immune to capture, this structure reduces the likelihood that leaders will be able to co-opt the organization to serve the interests of a hegemonic elite. If the arguments of this chapter have been at all persuasive, then, we can dismiss the concern that organizing for power will be captured by hegemonic elites *just as easily* as other modes of democratic action and reform.

Even if we set aside the possibility of co-optation by hegemonic elites, however, subtler concerns remain about the relationship between organizers and

---

[8] Again, this does not mean they should be suppressed: there are strong reasons to protect their rights to organize, demonstrate, and so on. The point is simply that we need not treat them as equally democratic in every context of judgment: in at least some cases, rather, a stance of corrective partiality will be warranted.

rank-and-file participants—especially when it comes to the proper role of organizers' broader ideological visions. Even if solidaristic transformations have democratic effects, in short, we might worry that there is something undemocratic about organizers actively trying to shape participants' identities in a particular direction. In Mie Inouye's (2019) words, therefore, the key dilemma of democratic transformation is as follows: "how can participants in processes of organization or education that aim at liberating the oppressed reconcile the necessity of some form of external intervention with the imperative of treating the organized or educated as agents?" Indeed, this is a central concern of organizers themselves, and a key point of contention between traditions.

At one end of the spectrum is the approach of Saul Alinsky, who had radical ambitions to redistribute power yet was thoroughly anti-communist and allergic to anything that smacked of "ideology" (Bretherton 2014; Phulwani 2016; Sabl 2001; Stout 2012). As a result, IAF organizers are supposed to rely entirely on goals expressed by community members in building collective power, and to refrain from guiding community members towards any broader vision. Understandable as it is, however, this "hands-off" approach brings dangers of its own. Perhaps most notoriously, the first community organization Alinsky founded—the Back of the Yards Neighborhood Council (BYNC), in a poor, white neighborhood in Chicago—ended up using its substantial collective power to exclude Blacks from the neighborhood. Indeed, Alinsky himself maintained that he did not regret building the organization; insisting instead that the best response was proliferating *further* countervailing organizations among Black communities (Phulwani 2016: 874). Yet many organizers have understood the BYNC as a cautionary tale.

For some—including Alinsky's friend and fellow organizing innovator Myles Horton—the BYNC was proof that organizing must be grounded in broader ideals like "democracy and brotherhood" rather than focusing *solely* on narrowly self-interested goals (Horton 1998). More generally, the tradition of movement organizing—which has long centered Black and female leadership—usually insists on the importance of broader liberatory visions. Where IAF organizers assume that people's interests "are material and will always be self-evident," Woodly (2021) writes, the contemporary movement organizers involved in groups like the Movement for Black Lives "know that the value of the lives of Black people are not self-evident or universally legible in the hegemonic culture of anti-Blackness." As a result, she argues, "it is necessary but insufficient to target discrete policies and practices," and this concrete focus must be supplemented by a kind of "pragmatic imagination." For their part, finally, McAlevey and other radical unionists generally have no problem centering concrete, self-interested demands, but they often understand ideological lenses as crucial to an accurate power analysis, and therefore necessary in achieving those demands.

Alinsky might argue that this commitment to broader political ideals and ideologies makes the practices of movement organizers and radical unionists less democratic—or, in the terms of this book, more prone to capture. In my view, however, this accusation is largely unfounded. As I have argued, organizers have strong *tactical* reasons to emphasize concrete, self-interested goals, and to refrain from broadcasting controversial ideological positions that might alienate potential members and allies. Yet movement organizers and radical unionists appreciate these reasons just as well as community organizers trained by Alinsky's IAF. Meanwhile, no *principled* distinction can be drawn between the sort of influence each exerts. Where an IAF organizer might elicit certain concerns and interpret them as reflecting material interests, suggesting a localized power analysis, a movement organizer or radical unionist might elicit different concerns, and read them through lenses of white supremacy or capitalism. Each approach has strengths and weaknesses, but neither can claim to be *neutral*.

As I have argued in Chapter 2, after all, multidimensional group preferences generate no unique collective will—especially when those preferences are shallow and unstable in the first place. As such, it is idle to seek direction from a pure popular will in setting organizational priorities. More broadly, our preferences are always shaped by a churning maelstrom of factors, such that no one who engages in the social world can avoid exerting some influence on others (Bagg 2021). As recent theorists of representation have insisted, more specifically, ordinary people who do not devote their lives to politics will always need their interests filtered and interpreted politically by various representative claim-makers (Disch 2021; Saward 2010).

Thus, what is troubling is not the fact of social influence as such, nor even the existence of leaders who exert more influence than others. As Stout (2012: 94) observes, indeed, ordinary people can wield effective countervailing power "only if some of them acquire the moral authority to lead, represent, and advise their associates and only if those associates are prepared to acknowledge whatever moral and intellectual authority their leaders, representatives, and advisors have earned." What is troubling, rather, is the *capture* of such influence channels, by leaders, for their own private purposes. As Stout concludes, therefore, "democracy has more to do with structures of earned and accountable authority than it does with leveling" (94). And despite the real differences between them, organizers in the traditions I have examined are unanimous and unwavering in their commitment to such structures.

The reason for this follows from my earlier analysis. Collective action poses the greatest threat to elite interests when it involves sustained and widespread commitment to costly forms of participation. If an organization is to wield significant countervailing power, therefore, its members must feel strongly invested in the cause, their fellow members, and the organization itself. And as I have argued, a crucial way of fostering this kind of solidarity is to ensure that rank-and-file members are actively engaged in organization-building and decision-making. Effective organizers thus demand participatory practices even when it limits their own influence. We should not deny the tradeoffs here: not only are participatory practices time-consuming and often contentious, they also allow rank-and-file members to derail strategic plans developed by more experienced organizers—timidly avoiding reasonable risks, for instance, or naïvely demanding too much. In the long run, however, good organizers understand that excluding rank-and-file members from these key decisions will only *inhibit* their ability to wield collective countervailing power. And that is the whole point of organizing for power.

Conclusion

Once-urgent claims about the crisis of democracy are by now—in 2023, as I write these concluding remarks—almost banal. Over the course of the long gestation of this book, a cottage industry has arisen that is devoted to "fixing" or "saving" democracy, generating countless articles, books, podcasts, think tanks, institutes, and beyond.

There is good reason to be concerned. The past decade has witnessed serious challenges to basic democratic norms in some of the world's largest and most powerful democracies, such as the US, Brazil, and India. In places like Hungary, Turkey, and the Philippines, authoritarian encroachment has advanced much further. And around the world, a great many other societies have experienced rising polarization, disinformation, party system volatility, and far-right mobilization—alongside declining social trust and commitment to democracy—which may signal more turbulence in the years ahead. These challenges vary from country to country, but they are driven by worldwide trends towards globalization, class dealignment, climate stress, migration, and the rise of social media; as well as global shocks like the wars in Afghanistan, Iraq, and Ukraine, the 2008 financial crisis, and COVID-19.

It is worth clarifying why these acute problems have received so little direct discussion in a book that purports to address the central challenges facing contemporary democracies. It is not because I think they are illusory or insignificant. To be sure, some radicals see the liberal, electoral form of democracy as a hollow sham, and thus dismiss the apparent crises it faces as little more than pearl-clutching by liberal elites. Meanwhile, certain empirical measures suggest that widespread perceptions of a "democratic recession" are overstated (Little and Meng 2023). Despite electoral democracy's many deficits, however, this book has argued that no alternative regime can protect public power more reliably. And even if many pundits have exaggerated how sharply our current moment differs from prior eras, it seems obvious to me that the global situation of democracy in the twenty-first century is indeed distinctive—and distinctively troubling.

So why have I devoted so little space to what may seem the most obvious challenges facing contemporary democracies? One reason is simply that they *are* so obvious—and that as a result, addressing issues like polarization and disinformation already tops the agenda for democratic reformers. Another is that, like most political theorists and philosophers, I aim to speak beyond the narrow temporal and geographic context in which I write. Though inevitably rooted in that context, I hope that the theory of democracy I have presented may be useful in any society that faces the predicament of modern politics. And while polarization and disinformation may be with us for some time, they are not constitutive features of modern democracy.

The chief reason I have not focused on these acute challenges, though, is that doing so risks addressing the symptoms without curing the underlying disease—much less identifying those responsible for spreading it. Problems like polarization and disinformation are very serious, but if the scope of democratic reform ends with strategies that target them directly, it will inevitably fail to achieve its long-term goals. These problems are often symptoms of a deeper dysfunction—one that is sometimes invisible in the political discourse. The work of my book has been to bring that dysfunction to the surface, name it, and examine it from all sort of angles. In short, I have suggested, many of the problems that most immediately afflict democracies today are rooted in vast inequalities of private power and organizational capacity among groups—and the myriad forms of capture perpetrated by those at the top. And if that is right, the democratic agenda I have outlined in response will be essential, in the long run, for meeting whatever challenges appear most acute in *any* particular democracy.

To be sure: defending any particular democracy does require many short-term strategies that can directly address its most immediate problems. As discussed in Chapter 7, however, there are very few hard-and-fast rules we can follow in responding to acute threats such as anti-democratic parties or hyperpolarization—nor even a general direction that can be safely pursued. In some cases, bending democratic norms or deepening polarization will be necessary to fend off even more severe problems, while in other cases, these same tactics will only make things worse. Addressing such acute challenges thus requires careful attention to context—and even then, our conclusions will admit of very little certainty.

By contrast, I have argued, we can have far more confidence in the democratic virtues of the broader agenda outlined in this book, oriented towards a more egalitarian balance of social forces. In addition to those short-term strategies that address acute challenges, in other words, any plausible agenda for defending democracy must also aim to disperse private power and organizational capacity among groups, rather than allowing it to accumulate in the hands of a narrow elite. In terms of policy reform, this entails enacting the various forms of corrective partiality outlined in Chapter 6—including policies of antimonopoly, countervailing power, and systemic redistribution. In terms of civic action, meanwhile, it means building enduring organizations of oppositional collective power, such as strong labor unions.

Take, for instance, the interlocking threats of disinformation and authoritarian populism. Elites often blame these problems on "too much democracy," embracing greater technocratic control as the solution (e.g., Jones 2020). And if we presume a crude definition that equates democracy with any form of mass participation, their diagnosis has some validity. Once we are armed with the more nuanced perspective on democracy proposed in this book, however—which sees it as a diverse set of tools, working together to protect public power from capture—this self-serving elite narrative falls apart.

Viewing authoritarian populism through the lens of state capture, for instance, allows us to see that much of its contemporary appeal derives from economic hardship, instability, and precarity caused by technocratic policies that served the interests of wealthy elites (Azmanova 2020; Rodrik 2018). Meanwhile, the scale of disinformation has exploded in the past decade at least partly because its spread served the interests of social media companies, who deployed substantial private power to evade regulation and oversight (Bernstein 2021). Looking at such trends through the lens of resisting state capture, it is still possible to see their proximate causes, from troll farms to lax content moderation standards. But it also highlights how capture by wealthy elites—and the broader inequalities it feeds on—have facilitated their emergence. As a result, it suggests an approach to reform that goes beyond fact-checking, content moderation, and civic education, addressing the deeper dysfunctions that give rise to these acute symptoms in the first place. More broadly, it explains why the solution to the problems of democracy really is *more democracy*—so long as we have the right account of what democracy means.

Citizen juries and other adversarial oversight mechanisms, for instance, can reduce the sort of bitter resentment that fuels authoritarian impulses, while channeling legitimate skepticism and anger towards practices that actually keep officials accountable to broad public interests. Meanwhile, organizations that successfully foster collective power via sustained face-to-face contact—including certain kinds of unions, community groups, social movements, and political parties—succeed in part because they encourage healthy epistemic networks that counteract disinformation, as well as broad-based solidarities that transcend traditional social divisions. And indeed, many observers point to the declining power of civic associations in general, and the labor movement in particular, as a key enabling factor behind most of the acute challenges facing twenty-first-century democracies (Hacker and Pierson 2011; McAlevey 2020; Skocpol 2003). While we cannot (and should not) revive the mid-twentieth-century labor movement just as it was, a central priority of democratic action must therefore be to generate new forms of solidarity and collective power among ordinary people—building on the interests they share not only as precarious workers, but also as tenants, debtors, neighbors, young people, and beyond.

Even more than any of its specific implications for action or reform, finally, the most central intervention of this book ultimately concerns the way we *think* about democracy. Drawing on convergent insights from realist and radical traditions, I began by showing why prevailing ideals of responsive representation and participatory inclusion fail to explain the value of existing institutions or provide a promising agenda for democratization. And in both cases, I argued, their deficits reflect a common underlying commitment to seeing democracy as a way of making decisions together. This vision is—and always will be—a mirage. Even under the best conditions, the results of mass elections, small-scale participatory procedures, and any other process of will formation and decision-making will reliably favor groups with outsized private power. Many such processes are indeed critical for democracy, but not because any of them reflects a fully equal, genuinely collective process of self-rule.

As modern humans subject to the authority of vast and powerful states, it is not surprising that many of us hold out hope for this sort of collective self-rule. We desperately want to be able to render that authority legitimate; to own the rules that govern our lives, or understand them as consistent with our autonomy. And so we search for some way to reconcile our conflicting wills fairly and without remainder, despite our plurality—some way for free and equal beings to live together on genuinely free and equal terms. Beyond the realm of democratic theory, indeed, much the same dream motivates many philosophical accounts of justice, legitimacy, authority, and public reason. It pervades legal doctrine, as well as broader public conceptions of constitutional authority, popular sovereignty, and the social compact.

The problem with this dream is not just that it is impossible to achieve in full: that much is acknowledged by nearly anyone who has given it serious thought. The problem is that when we allow it to structure our aspirations, this impossible dream tends to distort our understanding of the present and our priorities for the future. Again, this is not *always* or *necessarily* the case: it is possible to define collective self-rule in such a way that its practical implications converge with those defended here, and certain recent trends in political theory may even point in that direction. As I have catalogued throughout, however, seeing democracy principally as a way of making decisions often leads us astray—inviting us either to overstate the legitimacy of existing decision procedures or to focus on improving those procedures at the expense of the underlying power relations that determine the results of whatever procedures we use.

One way to read this book is as a call to change how we pursue this dream. Its core lesson, on this reading, is that we must divorce the ideal of collective self-rule from any particular processes of will formation and decision-making, and interpret it instead in terms of an egalitarian balance of social forces. It should be pursued, more specifically, via practices that make it more difficult for any group to capture public power for itself, and thus more likely that public power will be used to advance public interests. This entails liberal practices of constitutionalism, competition, and universalism—which structure public power to make it less hospitable to capture—as well as radical practices of antimonopoly, countervailing power, and systemic redistribution, which structure private power to obstruct the ability of any group to perpetrate capture. And indeed, if this book convinces democratic actors to consistently understand the ideal of self-rule in these terms, it will have achieved its primary aim.

Yet the book also invites a more radical reading, which dares us to let go of this dream altogether: i.e., to accept that the world was not made for us; that it contains contradictions that cannot be reconciled; that the rules governing our lives will always remain foreign to us. On this view, it is neither possible nor desirable to eliminate all asymmetries of private power, or the forms of capture to which they give rise. And under these circumstances, my suspicion is that anyone holding on to the dream of full legitimation and complete reconciliation will always be tempted to ignore certain inconvenient remainders. My wager, then, is that we are better off embracing a view of democracy as a never-ending struggle. If we accept that we live in a fallen and tragic world, in other words—a world under no obligation to live up to our expectations for it—we can more easily get down to the business of making it better.

Bibliography

Abizadeh, Arash. 2021. "Representation, Bicameralism, Political Equality, and Sortition: Reconstituting the Second Chamber as a Randomly Selected Assembly." *Perspectives on Politics* 19(3): 791–806.

Abramovitz, Mimi. 1988. *Regulating the Lives of Women: Social Welfare Policy from Colonial Times to the Present*. Boston: South End Press.

Acemoglu, Daron, and James Robinson. 2012. *Why Nations Fail: The Origins of Power, Prosperity, and Poverty*. New York: Crown Business.

Achen, Christopher H., and Larry M. Bartels. 2016. *Democracy for Realists: Why Elections Do Not Produce Responsive Government*. Princeton: Princeton University Press.

Addams, Jane. 1902. *Democracy and Social Ethics*. London: Macmillan.

Adkins, Lisa, Melinda Cooper, and Martijn Konings. 2020. *The Asset Economy*. Medford: Polity.

Afsahi, Afsoun. 2021. "Gender Difference in Willingness and Capacity for Deliberation." *Social Politics: International Studies in Gender, State & Society* 28(4): 1046–1072.

Agmon, Shai. 2021. "Undercutting Justice—Why Legal Representation Should Not Be Allocated by the Market." *Politics, Philosophy & Economics* 20(1): 99–123.

Agrawal, Arun. 2005. "Environmentality: Community, Intimate Government, and the Making of Environmental Subjects in Kumaon, India." *Current Anthropology* 46(2): 161–90.

Ahlquist, John S. 2017. "Labor Unions, Political Representation, and Economic Inequality." *Annual Reviews in Political Science* 20: 409–32.

Ahlquist, John S., Amanda B. Clayton, and Margaret Levi. 2014. "Provoking Preferences: Unionization, Trade Policy, and the ILWU Puzzle." *International Organization* 68(1): 33–75.

Ahlquist, John S., Nahomi Ichino, Jason Wittenberg, and Daniel Ziblatt. 2018. "How Do Voters Perceive Changes to the Rules of the Game? Evidence from the 2014 Hungarian Elections." *Journal of Comparative Economics* 46(4): 906–19.

Ahlquist, John S., and Margaret Levi. 2013. *In the Interest of Others: Organizations and Social Activism*. Princeton: Princeton University Press.

Albertus, Michael. 2015. *Autocracy and Redistribution: The Politics of Land Reform*. Cambridge University Press.

Alence, Rod, and Anne Pitcher. 2019. "Resisting State Capture in South Africa." *Journal of Democracy* 30(4): 5–19.

Alexander, Michelle. 2010. *The New Jim Crow*. New York: The New Press.

Alinsky, Saul. 1946. *Reveille for Radicals*. Chicago: University of Chicago Press.

———. 1971. *Rules for Radicals: A Pragmatic Primer for Realistic Radicals*. New York: Random House.

Allen, Theodore. 1994. *The Invention of the White Race (Vol. 1)*. London: Verso.

———. 1997. *The Invention of the White Race (Vol. 2)*. London: Verso.

Althusser, Louis. 1971. "Ideology and Ideological State Apparatuses." In *Lenin and Philosophy and Other Essays*. New York: Monthly Review Press, 127–86.

Anderson, Elizabeth. 2010. *The Imperative of Integration*. Princeton: Princeton University Press.

———. 2014. "Dewey's Moral Philosophy." In *The Stanford Encyclopedia of Philosophy*, ed. Edward N. Zalta. http://plato.stanford.edu/archives/spr2014/entries/dewey-moral/ (April 23, 2014).
Andrews, Kenneth. 2004. *Freedom Is a Constant Struggle*. Chicago: University of Chicago Press.
Andrias, Kate. 2015. "Separations of Wealth: Inequality and the Erosion of Checks and Balances." *University of Pennsylvania Journal of Constitutional Law* 18(2): 419.
Andrias, Kate, and Benjamin I. Sachs. 2020. "Constructing Countervailing Power: Law and Organizing in an Era of Political Inequality." *Yale Law Journal* 130(3): 546–635.
Annunziata, Rocío. 2015. "Ciudadanía Disminuida: La Idea de La 'construcción de Ciudadanía' En Los Dispositivos Participativos Contemporáneos." *Temas y Debates*.
Anria, Santiago. 2016. "Delegative Democracy Revisited: More Inclusion, Less Liberalism in Bolivia." *Journal of Democracy* 27(3): 99–108.
Anria, Santiago, and Kenneth M. Roberts. 2019. "Bolivia After Morales: What Lies in Store for the Country." *Foreign Affairs* 21.
Ansell, Ben W., and David Samuels. 2014. *Inequality and Democratization: An Elite-Competition Approach*. New York: Cambridge University Press.
Apostolidis, Paul. 2010. *Breaks in the Chain: What Immigrant Workers Can Teach America about Democracy*. Minneapolis: University of Minnesota Press.
Appel, Hannah. 2015. "You Are Not a Loan: Strike Debt and the Emerging Debtors Movement." *Tikkun* 30(1): 28–30.
Arlen, Gordon. 2021. "Citizen Tax Juries: Democratizing Tax Enforcement after the Panama Papers." *Political Theory*.
Arneson, Richard. 2004. "Democracy Is Not Intrinsically Just." In *Justice and Democracy: Essays for Brian Barry*, eds. Keith Dowding, Robert Goodin, and Carole Pateman. Cambridge: Cambridge University Press, 40–58.
Arnstein, Sherry R. 1969. "A Ladder of Citizen Participation." *Journal of the American Institute of Planners* 35(4): 216–24.
Aronoff, Kate, Alyssa Battistoni, Daniel Aldana Cohen, and Thea Riofrancos. 2019. *A Planet to Win: Why We Need a Green New Deal*. London: Verso Books.
Arrow, Kenneth. 1951. *Social Choice and Individual Values*. New York: John Wiley & Sons.
Ash, Elliott, Daniel L. Chen, and Suresh Naidu. 2022. "Ideas Have Consequences: The Impact of Law and Economics on American Justice." https://www.nber.org/papers/w29788 (January 24, 2023).
Aspinall, Edward, and Ward Berenschot. 2019. Democracy for Sale *Democracy for Sale: Elections, Clientelism, and the State in Indonesia*. Ithaca: Cornell University Press.
Atkinson, Anthony B., Thomas Piketty, and Emmanuel Saez. 2011. "Top Incomes in the Long Run of History." *Journal of Economic Literature* 49(1): 3–71.
Auyero, Javier. 2001. *Poor People's Politics: Peronist Survival Networks and the Legacy of Evita*. Durham: Duke University Press.
Avi-Yonah, Reuven S. 2002. "Why Tax the Rich? Efficiency, Equity, and Progressive Taxation," ed. Joel B. Slemrod. *The Yale Law Journal* 111(6): 1391–416.
Awrey, Dan. 2012. "Complexity, Innovation, and the Regulation of Modern Financial Markets." *Harvard Business Law Review* 2: 235–94.
Azmanova, Albena. 2020. *Capitalism on Edge: How Fighting Precarity Can Achieve Radical Change Without Crisis or Utopia*. New York: Columbia University Press.
Bagg, Samuel. 2016. "Between Critical and Normative Theory: Predictive Political Theory as a Deweyan Realism." *Political Research Quarterly* 69(2): 233–44.
———. 2018a. "Can Deliberation Neutralise Power?" *European Journal of Political Theory* 17(3): 257–79.

———. 2018b. "The Power of the Multitude: Answering Epistemic Challenges to Democracy." *American Political Science Review* 112(4): 891–904.

———. 2021. "Beyond the Search for the Subject: An Anti-Essentialist Ontology for Liberal Democracy." *European Journal of Political Theory* 20(2): 208–231.

———. 2022a. "Do We Need an Anti-Oligarchic Constitution?" *European Journal of Political Theory* 21(2): 399–411.

———. 2022b. "Realism Against Legitimacy: Towards an Action-Centered Political Realism." *Social Theory and Practice* 48(1): 29–60.

———. 2022c. "Sortition as Anti-Corruption: Popular Oversight against Elite Capture." *American Journal of Political Science* (online ahead of print)

———. 2023. "Whose Coordination? Which Democracy?" *Politics & Society* (online ahead of print)

———. 2023. "Beyond Democratic Authorization." Paper presented at APSA Annual Conference in Los Angeles.

Bagg, Samuel, and Udit Bhatia. 2022. "Intra-Party Democracy: A Functionalist Account." *Journal of Political Philosophy* 30(3): 347–369.

———. 2021. "Acting Democratically against Clientelism." Paper presented at APSA Annual Conference (online)

Bagg, Samuel, and Ying Chan. 2022. "The Irrelevance of Benevolence: On the Role of Benign Despots in Political Theory." Paper presented at PPE Society Annual Conference in New Orleans.

Bagg, Samuel, and Jack Knight. 2014. "Legitimacy." *Encyclopedia of Political Thought*.

Bagg, Samuel, and Isak Tranvik. 2019. "An Adversarial Ethics for Campaigns and Elections." *Perspectives on Politics* 17(4): 973–87.

Baiocchi, Gianpaolo. 2001. "Participation, Activism, and Politics: The Porto Alegre Experiment and Deliberative Democratic Theory." *Politics & Society* 29(1): 43–72.

———. 2005. *Militants and Citizens: The Politics of Participatory Democracy in Porto Alegre*. Stanford: Stanford University Press.

Baiocchi, Gianpaolo, and Ernesto Ganuza. 2014. "Participatory Budgeting as If Emancipation Mattered." *Politics & Society* 42(1): 29–50.

———. 2016. *Popular Democracy: The Paradox of Participation*. Stanford: Stanford University Press.

Balfour, Lawrie. 2003. "Unreconstructed Democracy: W. E. B. Du Bois and the Case for Reparations." *American Political Science Review* 97(1): 33–44.

Bangs, Christopher. 2018. "A Union for All: Collective Associations Outside the Workplace Notes." *Georgetown Journal on Poverty Law and Policy* 26(1): 47–164.

Baradaran, Mehrsa. 2017. *The Color of Money: Black Banks and the Racial Wealth Gap*. Cambridge: Harvard University Press.

Barber, Benjamin R. 1984. *Strong Democracy: Participatory Politics for a New Age*. Berkeley: University of California Press.

Barnhill, Anne, and Brian Hutler. 2021. "SNAP Exclusions and the Role of Citizen Participation in Policy-Making." *Social Philosophy and Policy*.

Barrow, Clyde W. 1993. *Critical Theories of the State: Marxist, Neomarxist, Postmarxist*. Madison: University of Wisconsin Press.

Bartels, Larry M. 2002. "Beyond the Running Tally: Partisan Bias in Political Perceptions." *Political Behavior* 24(2): 117–50.

———. 2009. *Unequal Democracy: The Political Economy of the New Gilded Age*. Princeton: Princeton University Press.

Battistoni, Alyssa. 2017. "Bringing in the Work of Nature: From Natural Capital to Hybrid Labor." *Political Theory* 45(1): 5–31.

———. 2019. "Spadework: On Political Organizing." *n+1* (34). https://nplusonemag.com/issue-34/politics/spadework/ (March 24, 2020).
Baum, Bruce. 2007. "JS Mill and Liberal Socialism." In *JS Mill's Political Thought: A Bicentennial Reassessment*, eds. Nadia Urbinati and Alex Zakaras. Cambridge: Cambridge University Press, 98–123.
Beauvais, Edana. 2019. "Discursive Inequity and the Internal Exclusion of Women Speakers." *Political Research Quarterly*: 1065912919870605.
Bebchuk, Lucian Arye, and Jesse M. Fried. 2003. "Executive Compensation as an Agency Problem." *Journal of Economic Perspectives* 17(3): 71–92.
Becher, Michael, and Daniel Stegmueller. 2021. "Reducing Unequal Representation: The Impact of Labor Unions on Legislative Responsiveness in the U.S. Congress." *Perspectives on Politics* 19(1): 92–109.
Beitz, Charles R. 1989. *Political Equality: An Essay in Democratic Theory*. Princeton: Princeton University Press.
Bell, Daniel A. 2006. *Beyond Liberal Democracy: Political Thinking for an East Asian Context*. Princeton: Princeton University Press.
———. 2015. *The China Model: Political Meritocracy and the Limits of Democracy*. Princeton: Princeton University Press.
Bell, Derrick. 1992. "Racial Realism." *Connecticut Law Review* 24(2): 363–80.
Benhabib, Seyla, ed. 1996. *Democracy and Difference: Contesting the Boundaries of the Political*. New York: Cambridge University Press.
Benvenisti, Eyal. 2016. "Democracy Captured: The Mega-Regional Agreements and the Future of Global Public Law." *Constellations* 23(1): 58–70.
Berman, Elizabeth Popp. 2023. *Thinking like an Economist: How Efficiency Replaced Equality in U.S. Public Policy*. Princeton: Princeton University Press.
Bernstein, Joseph. 2021. "Bad News: Selling the Story of Disinformation." *Harper's Magazine* September 2021. https://harpers.org/archive/2021/09/bad-news-selling-the-story-of-disinformation/ (March 23, 2023).
Beyer, Daniela, and Miriam Hänni. 2018. "Two Sides of the Same Coin? Congruence and Responsiveness as Representative Democracy's Currencies." *Policy Studies Journal* 46(S1): S13–47.
Bhatia, Udit. 2020. "Rethinking the Epistemic Case against Epistocracy." *Critical Review of International Social and Political Philosophy* 23(6): 706–31.
Bingham, Lisa Blomgren, Tina Nabatchi, and Rosemary O"Leary. 2005. "The New Governance: Practices and Processes for Stakeholder and Citizen Participation in the Work of Government." *Public Administration Review* 65(5): 547–58.
Blanc, Eric. 2019. *Red State Revolt: The Teachers" Strike Wave and Working-Class Politics*. London: Verso.
Blau, Adrian. 2018. "Cognitive Corruption and Deliberative Democracy." *Social Philosophy and Policy* 35(2): 198–220.
Boehm, Christopher. 1999. *Hierarchy in the Forest: The Evolution of Egalitarian Behavior*. Cambridge: Harvard University Press.
Bohman, James. 1998. "Survey Article: The Coming of Age of Deliberative Democracy." *Journal of Political Philosophy* 6(4): 400–25.
Boix, Carles, and Milan W. Svolik. 2013. "The Foundations of Limited Authoritarian Government: Institutions, Commitment, and Power-Sharing in Dictatorships." *The Journal of Politics* 75(2): 300–16.
Bonilla-Silva, Eduardo. 1997. "Rethinking Racism: Toward a Structural Interpretation." *American Sociological Review* 62(3): 465–80.

———. 2003. *Racism without Racists: Color-Blind Racism and the Persistence of Racial Inequality in the United States*. Rowman & Littlefield.
Bork, Robert. 1978. *The Antitrust Paradox*. New York: Free Press.
Bowles, Samuel, and Herbert Gintis. 1976. *Schooling in Capital America*. New York: Basic Books.
Boyte, Harry C. 2010. *Everyday Politics: Reconnecting Citizens and Public Life*. Philadelphia: University of Pennsylvania Press.
Bradley, David et al. 2003. "Distribution and Redistribution in Postindustrial Democracies." *World Politics* 55(2): 193–228.
Brandeis, Louis. 1913. "The Curse of Bigness." *Harper's Weekly*.
Brennan, Jason. 2016. *Against Democracy*. Princeton: Princeton University Press.
Bretherton, Luke. 2014. *Resurrecting Democracy: Faith, Citizenship, and the Politics of a Common Life*. New York: Cambridge University Press.
Brettschneider, Corey. 2010. *Democratic Rights: The Substance of Self-Government*. Princeton: Princeton University Press.
Brill, Steven. 2015. *America's Bitter Pill: Money, Politics, Backroom Deals, and the Fight to Fix Our Broken Healthcare System*. New York: Random House.
Britton-Purdy, Jedediah, David Singh Grewal, Amy Kapczynski, and K. Sabeel Rahman. 2020. "Building a Law-and-Political-Economy Framework: Beyond the Twentieth-Century Synthesis." *Yale Law Journal* 129(6): 1784–835.
Brooks, Clem, and Jeff Manza. 2006. "Social Policy Responsiveness in Developed Democracies." *American Sociological Review* 71(3): 474–94.
brown, adrienne maree. 2017. *Emergent Strategy: Shaping Change, Changing Worlds*. Chico, CA: AK Press.
Brown, Dorothy A. 2022. *The Whiteness of Wealth: How the Tax System Impoverishes Black Americans—and How We Can Fix It*. New York: Crown.
Brown, Wendy. 2015. *Undoing the Demos: Neoliberalism's Stealth Revolution*. New York: Zone Books.
Brulle, Robert J. 2018. "The Climate Lobby: A Sectoral Analysis of Lobbying Spending on Climate Change in the USA, 2000 to 2016." *Climatic Change* 149(3): 289–303.
Buchanan, James M., Robert D. Tollison, and Gordon Tullock. 1980. *Toward a Theory of the Rent-Seeking Society*. College Station, TX: Texas A & M University Press.
Bullard, Robert. 1990. *Dumping in Dixie: Race, Class, and Environmental Quality*. Boulder: Westview Press.
Burstein, Paul. 2003. "The Impact of Public Opinion on Public Policy: A Review and an Agenda." *Political Research Quarterly* 56(1): 29–40.
Byrne, Monica. 2021. *The Actual Star*. New York: Harper Voyager.
Cagé, Julia. 2020. *The Price of Democracy: How Money Shapes Politics and What to Do about It*. Cambridge: Harvard University Press.
Cain, Bruce E. 2011. "More or Less." In *Race, Reform, and Regulation of the Electoral Process: Recurring Puzzles in American Democracy*, Cambridge Studies in Election Law and Democracy, eds. Guy-Uriel E. Charles, Heather K. Gerken, and Michael S. Kang. Cambridge: Cambridge University Press, 263–86.
Calabresi, Steven G., Mark E. Berghausen, and Skylar Albertson. 2012. "The Rise and Fall of the Separation Powers Symposium." *Northwestern University Law Review* 106(2): 527–50.
Campbell, Angus, Philip E. Converse, Warren E. Miller, and Donald E. Stokes. 1960. *The American Voter*. Chicago: University of Chicago Press.
Caplan, Bryan. 2007. *The Myth of the Rational Voter: Why Democracies Choose Bad Policies*. Princeton: Princeton University Press.

Carnes, Nicholas. 2013. *White-Collar Government: The Hidden Role of Class in Economic Policy Making*. Chicago: University of Chicago Press.

Carpenter, Daniel. 2013. "Corrosive Capture." In *Preventing Regulatory Capture*, eds. Daniel Carpenter and David A. Moss. New York: Cambridge University Press, 152–72.

Carruthers, Charlene. 2018. *Unapologetic: A Black, Queer and Feminist Mandate for Radical Movements*. Boston: Beacon Press.

Casassas, David. 2016. "Economic Sovereignty as the Democratization of Work: The Role of Basic Income." *Basic Income Studies* 11(1): 1–15.

Caughey, Devin, and Christopher Warshaw. 2018. "Policy Preferences and Policy Change: Dynamic Responsiveness in the American States, 1936–2014." *American Political Science Review* 112(2): 249–66.

Chambers, Clare. 2008. *Sex, Culture, and Justice: The Limits of Choice*. University Park, PA: Penn State University Press.

Chambers, Simone. 1996. *Reasonable Democracy: Jürgen Habermas and the Politics of Discourse*. Ithaca: Cornell University Press.

Chapin, Christy Ford. 2015. *Ensuring America's Health*. New York: Cambridge University Press.

Chen, Jidong, Jennifer Pan, and Yiqing Xu. 2016. "Sources of Authoritarian Responsiveness: A Field Experiment in China." *American Journal of Political Science* 60(2): 383–400.

Chopra, Rohit, and Lina M. Khan. 2020. "The Case for 'Unfair Methods of Competition' Rulemaking." *The University of Chicago Law Review* 87(2): 357–80.

Christiano, Thomas. 1996. *The Rule of the Many: Fundamental Issues in Democratic Theory*. Boulder: Westview Press.

———. 2008. *The Constitution of Equality: Democratic Authority and Its Limits*. Oxford: Oxford University Press.

Christophers, Brett. 2020. *Rentier Capitalism: Who Owns the Economy, and Who Pays for It?* London: Verso.

Coates, Ta-Nehisi. 2014. "The Case for Reparations." *The Atlantic* 313(5): 54–71.

Coglianese, Cary. 1997. "Assessing Consensus: The Promise and Performance of Negotiated Rulemkaing." *Duke Law Journal* 46(6): 1255–350.

Cohen, G. A. 2008. *Rescuing Justice and Equality*. Cambridge: Harvard University Press.

———. 2009. *Why Not Socialism?* Princeton: Princeton University Press.

Cohen, Morris R. 1927. "Property and Sovereignty." *Cornell Law Quarterly* 13(1): 8–30.

Coles, Romand. 2005. *Beyond Gated Politics: Reflections for the Possibility of Democracy*. Minneapolis: University of Minnesota Press.

Conley, Dalton. 1999. *Being Black, Living in the Red: Race, Wealth, and Social Policy in America*. Berkeley: University of California Press.

Connaughton, Jeff. 2012. *The Payoff: Why Wall Street Always Wins*. Westport, CT: Prospecta Press.

Connolly, William E. 1991. *Identity, Difference: Democratic Negotiations of Political Paradox*. Minneapolis: University of Minnesota Press.

———. 1999. *Why I Am Not a Secularist*. Minneapolis: University of Minnesota Press.

———. 2002. *Neuropolitics: Thinking, Culture, Speed*. Minneapolis: University of Minnesota Press.

Cook, Philip J., and Robert H. Frank. 2010. *The Winner-Take-All Society: Why the Few at the Top Get So Much More Than the Rest of Us*. London: Virgin Books.

Cordelli, Chiara. 2020. *The Privatized State*. Princeton: Princeton University Press.

Coulthard, Glen Sean. 2014. *Red Skin, White Masks: Rejecting the Colonial Politics of Recognition*. Minneapolis: University of Minnesota Press.

Courant, Dmitri. 2021. "The promises and disappointments of the French Citizens' Convention for Climate." *Deliberative Democracy Digest*. https://www.publicdeliberation.net/the-promises-and-disappointments-of-the-french-citizens-convention-for-climate/. (June 9, 2021).

Cowen, Tyler. 2013. *Average Is Over: Powering America Beyond the Age of the Great Stagnation*. New York: Dutton.

Crabtree, John, and Francisco Durand. 2017. *Peru: Elite Power and Political Capture*. London: Zed Books.

Crotty, James. 2019. *Keynes Against Capitalism: His Economic Case for Liberal Socialism*. Routledge.

Cuellar, Mariano-Florentino. 2005. "Rethinking Regulatory Democracy." *Administrative Law Review* 57: 411–500.

Culpepper, Pepper D. 2010. *Quiet Politics and Business Power: Corporate Control in Europe and Japan*. New York: Cambridge University Press.

———. 2015. "Structural Power and Political Science in the Post-Crisis Era." *Business & Politics* 17(3): 391–409.

Culpepper, Pepper D., and Kathleen Thelen. 2020. "Are We All Amazon Primed? Consumers and the Politics of Platform Power." *Comparative Political Studies* 53(2): 288–318.

Dahl, Robert A. 1957. "The Concept of Power." *Behavioral Science* 2(3): 201–15.

———. 1961. *Who Governs?* New Haven: Yale University Press.

Darity, William et al. 2017. "Stratification Economics: A General Theory of Intergroup Inequality." In *The Hidden Rules of Race: Barriers to an Inclusive Economy*, eds. Andrea Flynn, Dorian T. Warren, Felicia J. Wong, and Susan R. Holmberg. Cambridge: Cambridge University Press.

D'Art, Daryl, and Thomas Turner. 2007. "Trade Unions and Political Participation in the European Union: Still Providing a Democratic Dividend?" *British Journal of Industrial Relations* 45(1): 103–26.

De Loecker, Jan, Jan Eeckhout, and Gabriel Unger. 2020. "The Rise of Market Power and the Macroeconomic Implications∗." *The Quarterly Journal of Economics* 135(2): 561–644.

Decanio, Samuel. 2015. *Democracy and the Origins of the American Regulatory State*. New Haven: Yale University Press.

DellaVigna, Stefano, and Ethan Kaplan. 2007. "The Fox News Effect: Media Bias and Voting." *The Quarterly Journal of Economics* 122(3): 1187–234.

Dewey, John. 1927. *The Public and Its Problems*. Athens, OH: Swallow Press.

Dhillon, Jaskiran K. 2017. *Prairie Rising: Indigenous Youth, Decolonization, and the Politics of Intervention*. Toronto: University of Toronto Press.

Dietsch, Peter. 2015. *Catching Capital: The Ethics of Tax Competition*. New York: Oxford University Press.

Dietsch, Peter, François Claveau, and Clément Fontan. 2018. *Do Central Banks Serve the People?* Medford, MA: Polity Press.

Dietsch, Peter, and Thomas Rixen, eds. 2016. *Global Tax Governance: What's Wrong, and How to Fix It*. Colchester: Rowman & Littlefield International.

Director, Aaron, and Edward H. Levi. 1956. "Law and the Future: Trade Regulation." *Northwestern University Law Review* 51(2): 281–96.

Disch, Lisa. 2011. "Toward a Mobilization Conception of Democratic Representation." *American Political Science Review* 105(1): 100–14.

———. 2021. *Making Constituencies: Representation as Mobilization in Mass Democracy*. Chicago: University of Chicago Press.

Domhoff, G. William. 1967. *Who Rules America?* Englewood Cliffs, NJ: Prentice Hall.

Dowlen, Oliver. 2008. *The Political Potential of Sortition: A Study of the Random Selection of Citizens for Public Office*. Exeter, UK: Imprint Academic.

Downs, Anthony. 1957. *An Economic Theory of Democracy*. New York: Harper.

Drutman, Lee. 2020. *Breaking the Two-Party Doom Loop: The Case for Multiparty Democracy in America*. New York: Oxford University Press.

Du Bois, W. E. B. 1935. *Black Reconstruction in America*. New York: Harcourt Brace.

Dunn, John. 2014. *Breaking Democracy's Spell*. New Haven: Yale University Press.

Dworkin, Ronald. 1996. *Freedom's Law: The Moral Reading of the American Constitution*. Cambridge: Harvard University Press.

Eckerd, Adam. 2017. "Citizen Language and Administrative Response: Participation in Environmental Impact Assessment." *Administration & Society* 49(3): 348–73.

Ehs, Tamara and Monika Mokre. 2021. "Deliberation against Participation? Yellow Vests and Grand Débat: A Perspective from Deliberative Theory." *Political Studies Review* 19(2): 186–192

El Amine, Loubna. 2016. "Beyond East and West: Reorienting Political Theory through the Prism of Modernity." *Perspectives on Politics* 14(1): 102–20.

Elhauge, Einer. 2016. "Horizontal Shareholding." *Harvard Law Review* 129: 1267.

Elkjær, Mads Andreas, and Michael Baggesen Klitgaard. 2021. "Economic Inequality and Political Responsiveness: A Systematic Review." *Perspectives on Politics* (online ahead of print).

Elster, Jon. 1999. "Arguing and Bargaining in Two Constituent Assemblies." *University of Pennsylvania Journal of Constitutional Law* 2: 345.

Emerson, Blake. 2019. *The Public's Law: Origins and Architecture of Progressive Democracy*. New York: Oxford University Press.

Erikson, Robert S. 2015. "Income Inequality and Policy Responsiveness." *Annual Review of Political Science* 18(1): 11–29.

Estlund, David. 2008. *Democratic Authority: A Philosophical Framework*. Princeton: Princeton University Press.

Faguet, Jean-Paul. 2018. "Latin America's Shifting Politics: The Lessons of Bolivia." *Journal of Democracy* 29(4): 89–101.

Farber, Henry S, Daniel Herbst, Ilyana Kuziemko, and Suresh Naidu. 2021. "Unions and Inequality over the Twentieth Century: New Evidence from Survey Data∗." *The Quarterly Journal of Economics* 136(3): 1325–85.

Faris, David. 2018. *It's Time to Fight Dirty: How Democrats Can Build a Lasting Majority in American Politics*. Brooklyn: Melville House.

Fearon, James. 1999. "Electoral Accountability and the Control of Politicians: Selecting Good Types versus Sanctioning Poor Performance." In *Democracy, Accountability, and Representation*, eds. Bernard Manin, Adam Przeworski, and Susan C. Stokes. Cambridge: Cambridge University Press. 55–97.

Ferguson, James. 2015. *Give a Man a Fish: Reflections on the New Politics of Distribution*. Durham: Duke University Press.

Fishkin, James. 1991. *Democracy and Deliberation: New Directions for Democratic Reform*. New Haven: Yale University Press.

Fishkin, Joseph, and William E. Forbath. 2014. "The Anti-Oligarchy Constitution." *Boston University Law Review* 94(3): 669–96.

Flavin, Patrick, and Benjamin Radcliff. 2011. "Labor Union Membership and Voting across Nations." *Electoral Studies* 30(4): 633–41.

Flynn, Andrea, Dorian T. Warren, Felicia J. Wong, and Susan R. Holmberg. 2017. *The Hidden Rules of Race: Barriers to an Inclusive Economy*. New York: Cambridge University Press.

Foa, Roberto Stefan, and Yascha Mounk. 2016. "The Democratic Disconnect." *Journal of Democracy* 27(3): 5–17.

Ford, Martin. 2016. *Rise of the Robots: Technology and the Threat of a Jobless Future.* Basic Books.

Fox, Eleanor M. 2019. "Platforms, Power, and the Antitrust Challenge: A Modest Proposal to Narrow the US-Europe Divide Symposium." *Nebraska Law Review* 98(2): 297–318.

Frank, Robert H. 2016. *Success and Luck: Good Fortune and the Myth of Meritocracy.* Princeton: Princeton University Press.

Franko, William W., and Christopher Witko. 2023. "Unions, Class Identification, and Policy Attitudes." *The Journal of Politics* 85(2): 553–567.

Fraser, Nancy. 1990. "Rethinking the Public Sphere: A Contribution to the Critique of Actually Existing Democracy." *Social Text* (25/26): 56–80.

———. 2013. *The Fortunes of Feminism: From Women's Liberation to Identity Politics to Anti-Capitalism.* Brooklyn: Verso Books.

Frazer, Elizabeth, and Kimberly Hutchings. 2019. *Can Political Violence Ever Be Justified?* Cambridge: Polity.

Freeman, Richard, and James L. Medoff. 1984. *What Do Unions Do?* New York: Basic Books.

Freire, Paulo. 1970. *Pedagogy of the Oppressed.* New York: Continuum.

Fricker, Miranda. 2009. *Epistemic Injustice: Power and the Ethics of Knowing.* Oxford: Oxford University Press.

Frost, Samantha. 2016. *Biocultural Creatures: Toward a New Theory of the Human.* Durham: Duke University Press.

Frymer, Paul, and Jacob M. Grumbach. 2021. "Labor Unions and White Racial Politics." *American Journal of Political Science* 65(1): 225–40.

Fuller, Lon L. 1978. "The Forms and Limits of Adjudication." *Harvard Law Review* 92(2): 353–409.

Fung, Archon. 2003. "Survey Article: Recipes for Public Spheres: Eight Institutional Design Choices and Their Consequences." *Journal of Political Philosophy* 11(3): 338–67.

———. 2005. "Deliberation before the Revolution: Toward an Ethics of Deliberative Democracy in an Unjust World." *Political Theory* 33(3): 397–419.

Fung, Archon, and Erik Olin Wright, eds. 2003. *Deepening Democracy: Institutional Innovations in Empowered Participatory Governance.* London; New York: Verso.

Galbraith, John Kenneth. 1952. *American Capitalism: The Theory of Countervailing Power.* Boston: Houghton Mifflin.

———. 1954. "Countervailing Power." *The American Economic Review* 44(2): 1–6.

Galeotti, Anna Elisabetta. 2018. *Political Self-Deception.* Cambridge: Cambridge University Press.

Galston, William. 2018. *Anti-Pluralism: The Populist Threat to Liberal Democracy.* New Haven: Yale University Press.

Galvani, Alison P. et al. 2020. "Improving the Prognosis of Health Care in the USA." *The Lancet* 395(10223): 524–33.

Gastil, John, and Erik Olin Wright, eds. 2019. *Legislature by Lot: Transformative Designs for Deliberative Governance.* London: Verso Books.

Gaventa, John. 1980. *Power and Powerlessness: Quiescence and Rebellion in an Appalachian Valley.* Oxford: Clarendon Press.

Gerber, David J. 2019. "Comparative Competition Law." In *The Oxford Handbook of Comparative Law*, eds. Mathias Reimann and Reinhard Zimmerman. Oxford: Oxford University Press, 1169–92.

Giger, Nathalie, Jan Rosset, and Julian Bernauer. 2012. "The Poor Political Representation of the Poor in a Comparative Perspective." *Representation* 48(1): 47–61.

Gilens, Martin, and Benjamin I. Page. 2014. "Testing Theories of American Politics: Elites, Interest Groups, and Average Citizens." *Perspectives on Politics* 12(03): 564–81.

Giridharadas, Anand. 2018. *Winners Take All: The Elite Charade of Changing the World*. New York: Knopf.

Goetz, Edward G. 2013. *New Deal Ruins: Race, Economic Justice, and Public Housing Policy*. Ithaca: Cornell University Press.

Golway, Terry. 2014. *Machine Made: Tammany Hall and the Creation of Modern American Politics*. New York: Liveright.

Goodman, Rob, and Samuel Bagg. 2022. "Preaching to the Choir? Rhetoric and Identity in a Polarized Age." *Journal of Politics* 84(1): 511–524.

Gordon, Scott. 1999. *Controlling the State: Constitutionalism from Ancient Athens to Today*. Cambridge: Harvard University Press.

Gourevitch, Alex. 2015. *From Slavery to the Cooperative Commonwealth*. New York: Cambridge University Press.

———. 2016. "The Limits of a Basic Income: Means and Ends of Workplace Democracy." *Basic Income Studies* 11(1): 17–28.

Gowder, Paul. 2016. *The Rule of Law in the Real World*. New York: Cambridge University Press.

Gramsci, Antonio. 1971. *Selections from the Prison Notebooks*, eds. Quintin Hoare and Geoffrey Nowell Smith. New York: International Publishers.

Grattan, Laura. 2016. *Populism's Power: Radical Grassroots Democracy in America*. New York: Oxford University Press.

Green, Donald, Bradley Palmquist, and Eric Schickler. 2002. *Partisan Hearts and Minds: Political Parties and the Social Identity of Voters*. New Haven: Yale University Press.

Green, Jeffrey. 2009. *The Eyes of the People: Democracy in an Age of Spectatorship*. Oxford: Oxford University Press.

———. 2016. *The Shadow of Unfairness: A Plebeian Theory of Liberal Democracy*. Oxford: Oxford University Press.

Grewal, David Singh, and Jedediah Purdy. 2014. "Introduction: Law and Neoliberalism." *Law and Contemporary Problems* 77: 1.

Grumbach, Jacob. 2022. *Laboratories against Democracy: How National Parties Transformed State Politics*. Princeton: Princeton University Press.

Guerrero, Alexander A. 2014. "Against Elections: The Lottocratic Alternative." *Philosophy & Public Affairs* 42(2): 135–78.

Gutmann, Amy, and Dennis Thompson. 1996. *Democracy and Disagreement*. Cambridge: Harvard University Press.

———. 2004. *Why Deliberative Democracy?* Princeton: Princeton University Press.

Habermas, Jürgen. 1975. *Legitimation Crisis*. Boston: Beacon Press.

———. 1984. *The Theory of Communicative Action, Vol. 1: Reason and the Rationalization of Society*. Boston: Beacon Press.

———. 1987. *The Theory of Communicative Action, Vol. 2: Lifeworld and System*. Boston: Beacon Press.

———. 1990. *Moral Consciousness and Communicative Action*. Cambridge: MIT Press.

———. 1996. *Between Facts and Norms*. Cambridge: MIT Press.

Hacker, Jacob S., and Paul Pierson. 2002. "Business Power and Social Policy: Employers and the Formation of the American Welfare State." *Politics & Society* 30(2): 277–325.

———. 2011. *Winner-Take-All Politics: How Washington Made the Rich Richer—and Turned Its Back on the Middle Class*. New York: Simon & Schuster.

Hagglund, Martin. 2019. *This Life: Secular Faith and Spiritual Freedom*. New York: Penguin Random House.

Hale, Robert L. 1923. "Coercion and Distribution in a Supposedly Non-Coercive State." *Political Science Quarterly* 38(3): 470–94.

———. 1952. *Freedom Through Law: Public Control of Private Governing Power*. New York: Columbia University Press.

Hall, Richard L., and Alan V. Deardorff. 2006. "Lobbying as Legislative Subsidy." *American Political Science Review* 100(1): 69–84.

Hamburger, Philip. 2014. *Is Administrative Law Unlawful?* Chicago: University of Chicago Press.

Hamilton, Lawrence. 2014. *Freedom Is Power: Liberty through Political Representation*. Cambridge: Cambridge University Press.

Hampton, Paul A. 2015. "Power without the King: The Debt Strike as Credible Threat." *Tikkun* 30(1): 31–4.

Han, Hahrie. 2014. *How Organizations Develop Activists: Civic Associations and Leadership in the 21st Century*. Oxford: Oxford University Press.

Hanlon, Joseph, Armando Barrientos, and David Hulme. 2010. *Just Give Money to the Poor: The Development Revolution from the Global South*. Sterling, VA: Kumarian Press.

Hansen, Marianne Nordli, and Maren Toft. 2021. "Wealth Accumulation and Opportunity Hoarding: Class-Origin Wealth Gaps over a Quarter of a Century in a Scandinavian Country." *American Sociological Review* 86(4): 603–638.

Hartung, William D. 2012. *Prophets of War: Lockheed Martin and the Making of the Military-Industrial Complex*. New York: Bold Type Books.

Hasen, Richard L. 2016. *Plutocrats United: Campaign Money, the Supreme Court, and the Distortion of American Elections*. New Haven: Yale University Press.

Havel, Vaclav. 1985. *The Power of the Powerless*. London: Hutchison.

Hawkins, Kirk A. 2016. "Chavismo, Liberal Democracy, and Radical Democracy." *Annual Review of Political Science* 19(1): 311–29.

Hayward, Clarissa Rile. 2000. *De-Facing Power*. Cambridge: Cambridge University Press.

———. 2013. *How Americans Make Race: Stories, Institutions, Spaces*. New York: Cambridge University Press.

———. 2021. "Why Does Publicity Matter? Power, Not Deliberation." *Journal of Political Power* 14(1): 176–95.

Hazan, Reuven Y., and Gideon Rahat. 2010. *Democracy within Parties: Candidate Selection Methods and Their Political Consequences*. Oxford: Oxford University Press.

Herman, Bob. 2018. "The ACA Has Helped, Not Hurt, the Health Care Industry." *Axios*. https://www.axios.com/aca-health-care-industry-insurance-hospitals-profit-856273fc-4248-4021-adf3-dfda8bc13040.html (February 24, 2020).

Hersh, Eitan. 2020. *Politics Is for Power: How to Move Beyond Political Hobbyism, Take Action, and Make Real Change*. New York: Scribner.

Hertel-Fernandez, Alex. 2019. *State Capture: How Conservative Activists, Big Businesses, and Wealthy Donors Reshaped the American States—and the Nation*. New York: Oxford University Press.

Hicken, Allen. 2011. "Clientelism." *Annual Review of Political Science* 14(1): 289–310.

Hindmoor, Andrew, and Josh McGeechan. 2013. "Luck, Systematic Luck and Business Power: Lucky All the Way down or Trying Hard to Get What It Wants without Trying?" *Political Studies* 61(4): 834–49.

Hobsbawm, Eric. 1962. *The Age of Revolution: Europe, 1789–1848*. London: Weidenfeld & Nicolson.

Holdo, Markus, and Lizzie Öhrn Sagrelius. 2020. "Why Inequalities Persist in Public Deliberation: Five Mechanisms of Marginalization." *Political Studies* 68(3): 634–652

Honig, Bonnie. 1993. *Political Theory and the Displacement of Politics*. Ithaca: Cornell University Press.
———. 2009. *Emergency Politics: Paradox, Law, Democracy*. Princeton: Princeton University Press.
hooks, bell. 1982. *Ain't I a Woman: Black Women and Feminism*. London: Pluto Press.
———. 1984. *Feminist Theory: From Margin to Center*. London: Pluto Press.
Hopkin, Jonathan, and Julia Lynch. 2016. "Winner-Take-All Politics in Europe? European Inequality in Comparative Perspective." *Politics & Society* 44(3): 335–43.
Horton, Myles. 1998. *The Long Haul: An Autobiography*, eds. Judith Kohl and Herbert Kohl. New York: Teachers College Press.
Hualing, Fu. 2015. "Wielding the Sword: President Xi's New Anti-Corruption Campaign." In *Greed, Corruption and the Modern State: Essays in Political Economy*, eds. Susan Rose-Ackerman and Paul Lagunes. Northampton, MA: Edward Elgar Publishing, 134–59.
Humphrey, Mathew. 2007. *Ecological Politics and Democratic Theory: The Challenge to the Deliberative Ideal*. New York: Routledge.
Ingham, Sean. 2019. *Rule by Multiple Majorities*. Cambridge: Cambridge University Press.
Inouye, Mie. 2019. "Myles Horton on the Paradox of Democratic Transformation." Paper presented at APSA Annual Meeting in Washington, DC.
———. 2022. "Starting with People Where They Are: Ella Baker's Theory of Political Organizing." *American Political Science Review* 116(2): 533–546.
Islam, Nazrul, and John Winkel. 2017. *Climate Change and Social Inequality*. United Nations Department of Economic and Social Affairs Working Paper No. 152. https://www.un.org/esa/desa/papers/2017/wp152_2017.pdf.
Issacharoff, Samuel. 2010. "On Political Corruption." *Harvard Law Review* 124: 118.
Issacharoff, Samuel, and Pamela S. Karlan. 1999. "Hydraulics of Campaign Finance Reform." *Texas Law Review* 77: 1705.
Issacharoff, Samuel, and Richard H. Pildes. 1998. "Politics as Markets: Partisan Lockups of the Democratic Process." *Stanford Law Review* 50(3): 643–717.
Jackson, Kate. 2022. "All the Sovereign's Agents: The Constitutional Credentials of Administration." *William & Mary Bill of Rights Journal* 30(3): 777.
Jacobs, Lawrence R., and Desmond King. 2017. *Fed Power: How Finance Wins*. New York: Oxford University Press.
Jacobs, Lawrence R., and Robert Y. Shapiro. 2000. *Politicians Don't Pander: Political Manipulation and the Loss of Democratic Responsiveness*. Chicago: University of Chicago Press.
Jaffrelot, Christophe, Atul Kohli, and Kanta Murali, eds. 2019. *Business and Politics in India*. Oxford: Oxford University Press.
Jaskoski, Maiah. 2020. "Participatory Institutions as a Focal Point for Mobilizing: Prior Consultation and Indigenous Conflict in Colombia's Extractive Industries." *Comparative Politics* 52(4): 537–56.
Johnson, McKenzie F. 2019. "Strong (Green) Institutions in Weak States: Environmental Governance and Human (in)Security in the Global South." *World Development* 122: 433–45.
Johnston, Michael. 2005. *Syndromes of Corruption: Wealth, Power, and Democracy*. Cambridge: Cambridge University Press.
———. 2013. *Corruption, Contention, and Reform: The Power of Deep Democratization*. Cambridge: Cambridge University Press.
Jones, Garett. 2020. *10% Less Democracy: Why You Should Trust Elites a Little More and the Masses a Little Less*. Stanford: Stanford University Press.
Kadivar, Mohammad Ali, Adaner Usmani, and Benjamin H. Bradlow. 2020. "The Long March: Deep Democracy in Cross-National Perspective." *Social Forces* 98(3): 1311–38.

Kahan, Dan M. et al. 2007. "Culture and Identity-Protective Cognition: Explaining the White-Male Effect in Risk Perception." *Journal of Empirical Legal Studies* 4(3): 465–505.

———. 2012. "Why We Are Poles Apart on Climate Change." *Nature* 488(7411): 255–255.

Kalla, Joshua L., and David E. Broockman. 2020. "Reducing Exclusionary Attitudes through Interpersonal Conversation: Evidence from Three Field Experiments." *American Political Science Review* 114(2): 410–425.

Kampourakis, Ioannis. 2021. "Bound by the Economic Constitution: Notes for 'Law and Political Economy' in Europe." *Journal of Law and Political Economy* 1(2): 301–32.

Kapczynski, Amy. 2011. "The Cost of Price: Why and How to Get beyond Intellectual Property Internalism." *UCLA Law Review* 59(4): 970–1027.

———. 2020. "The Law of Informational Capitalism." *Yale Law Journal* 129(5): 1460–515.

Katz, Richard S., and Peter Mair. 2018. *Democracy and the Cartelization of Political Parties*. Oxford: Oxford University Press.

Katznelson, Ira. 2005. *When Affirmative Action Was White: An Untold History of Racial Inequality in Twentieth-Century America*. New York: W. W. Norton & Company.

———. 2013. *Fear Itself: The New Deal and the Origins of Our Time*. New York: Liveright.

Keane, John. 2018. *Power and Humility: The Future of Monitory Democracy*. Cambridge: Cambridge University Press.

Keck, Thomas M. 2022. "Court-Packing and Democratic Erosion." In *Democratic Resilience: Can the United States Withstand Rising Polarization?*, eds. Robert C. Lieberman, Suzanne Mettler, and Kenneth M. Roberts. Cambridge: Cambridge University Press.

Kelly, Nathan J. 2020. *America's Inequality Trap*. Chicago: University of Chicago Press.

Kennedy, Duncan. 2002. "The Political Stakes in Merely Technical Issues of Contract Law." *European Review of Private Law* 1: 7–28.

Kerr, Gavin. 2019. *The Property-Owning Democracy: Freedom and Capitalism in the Twenty-First Century*. London: Routledge.

Kerrissey, Jasmine. 2015. "Collective Labor Rights and Income Inequality." *American Sociological Review* 80(3): 626–53.

Kerrissey, Jasmine, and Evan Schofer. 2013. "Union Membership and Political Participation in the United States." *Social Forces* 91(3): 895–928.

———. 2018. "Labor Unions and Political Participation in Comparative Perspective." *Social Forces* 97(1): 427–64.

Khan, Lina M. 2016. "Amazon's Antitrust Paradox." *Yale Law Journal* 126(3): 710–805.

———. 2018. "The New Brandeis Movement: America's Antimonopoly Debate." *Journal of European Competition Law & Practice* 9(3): 131–2.

———. 2019. "The Separation of Platforms and Commerce." *Columbia Law Review* 119(4): 973–1098.

Kim, Sung Eun, and Yotam Margalit. 2017. "Informed Preferences? The Impact of Unions on Workers' Policy Views." *American Journal of Political Science* 61(3): 728–43.

King, Jr., Martin Luther. 1967. *Where Do We Go from Here: Chaos or Community?* Boston: Beacon Press.

Kirshner, Alexander S. 2014. *A Theory of Militant Democracy: The Ethics of Combatting Political Extremism*. New Haven: Yale University Press.

———. 2016. "Legitimate Opposition, Ostracism, and the Law of Democracy in Ancient Athens." *The Journal of Politics* 78(4): 1094–106.

Klobuchar, Amy. 2021. *Antitrust: Taking on Monopoly Power from the Gilded Age to the Digital Age*. New York: Random House.

Knight, Jack. 2001. "A Pragmatist Approach to the Proper Scope of Government." *Journal of Institutional and Theoretical Economics (JITE)/Zeitschrift für die gesamte Staatswissenschaft* 157(1): 28–48.

Knight, Jack, and James Johnson. 1994. "Aggregation and Deliberation: On the Possibility of Democratic Legitimacy." *Political theory* 22(2): 277–96.

———. 2011. *The Priority of Democracy: Political Consequences of Pragmatism*. Princeton: Princeton University Press.

Kolodny, Niko. 2014a. "Rule Over None I: What Justifies Democracy?" *Philosophy & Public Affairs* 42(3): 195–229.

———. 2014b. "Rule Over None II: Social Equality and the Justification of Democracy." *Philosophy & Public Affairs* 42(4): 287–336.

Kozol, Jonathan. 1992. *Savage Inequalities: Children in America's Schools by Jonathan Kozol*. New York: Harper.

Kramm, Matthias, and Ingrid Robeyns. 2020. "Limits to Wealth in the History of Western Philosophy." *European Journal of Philosophy* 28(4): 954–69.

Krippner, Greta R. 2011. *Capitalizing on Crisis: The Political Origins of the Rise of Finance*. Cambridge: Harvard University Press.

Krugman, Paul. 2009. "How Did Economists Get It so Wrong?" *New York Times* 2(9): 2009.

Kunda, Ziva. 1990. "The Case for Motivated Reasoning." *Psychological Bulletin* 108(3): 480–98.

Kwak, James. 2013. "Cultural Capture and the Financial Crisis." In *Preventing Regulatory Capture*, eds. Daniel Carpenter and David A. Moss. New York: Cambridge University Press. 71–98.

Lafont, Cristina. 2019. *Democracy without Shortcuts: A Participatory Conception of Deliberative Democracy*. Oxford; New York: Oxford University Press.

Landa, Dimitri and Ryan Pevnick. 2021. "Is Random Selection a Cure for the Ills of Electoral Representation?" Journal of Political Philosophy 29(1): 46–72.

Landemore, Hélène. 2012. *Democratic Reason: Politics, Collective Intelligence, and the Rule of the Many*. Princeton: Princeton University Press.

———. 2020. *Open Democracy: Reinventing Popular Rule for the 21st Century*. Princeton: Princeton University Press.

Le Guin, Ursula K. 1974. *The Dispossessed*. New York: Harper and Row.

Lee, Caroline W. 2014. *Do-It-Yourself Democracy: The Rise of the Public Engagement Industry*. Oxford: Oxford University Press.

Lee, Caroline W., Michael McQuarrie, and Edward T. Walker, eds. 2015. Democratizing Inequalities: Dilemmas of the New Public Participation. New York: NYU Press

Leipold, Bruno, Karma Nabulsi, and Stuart White, eds. 2020. *Radical Republicanism: Recovering the Tradition's Popular Heritage*. New York: Oxford University Press.

Lenowitz, Jeffrey A. 2021. "The People Cannot Choose a Constitution: Constituent Power's Inability to Justify Ratification Referendums." *The Journal of Politics* 83(2): 617–32.

Leonard, Christopher. 2019. *Kochland*. New York: Simon & Schuster.

Lepoutre, Maxime. 2018. "Rage inside the Machine: Defending the Place of Anger in Democratic Speech." *Politics, Philosophy & Economics* 17(4): 398–426.

———. 2020. "Democratic Group Cognition." *Philosophy & Public Affairs* 48(1): 40–78.

Leslie, Christopher R. 2013. "Antitrust Made (Too) Simple Symposium: Robert Bork and Antitrust Policy." *Antitrust Law Journal* 79(3): 917–40.

Lessig, Lawrence. 2011. *Republic, Lost: How Money Corrupts Congress—and a Plan to Stop It*. New York: Twelve.

Levinson, Daryl J., and Richard H. Pildes. 2006. "Separation of Parties, Not Powers." *Harvard Law Review* 119(8): 2311–86.

Levitsky, Steven, and James Loxton. 2013. "Populism and Competitive Authoritarianism in the Andes." *Democratization* 20(1): 107–36.

Levitsky, Steven, and Lucan Way. 2010. *Competitive Authoritarianism: Hybrid Regimes after the Cold War*. New York: Cambridge University Press.

———. 2022. *Revolution and Dictatorship: The Violent Origins of Durable Authoritarianism*. Princeton: Princeton University Press.

Levitsky, Steven, and Daniel Ziblatt. 2018. *How Democracies Die*. New York: Crown.

Levy, Jacob T. 2007. "Federalism, Liberalism, and the Separation of Loyalties." *American Political Science Review* 101(3): 459–77.

———. 2015. *Rationalism, Pluralism, and Freedom*. Oxford: Oxford University Press.

Lindblom, Charles E. 1982. "The Market as Prison." *The Journal of Politics* 44(2): 324–36.

Lindsey, Brink, and Steven Teles. 2017. *The Captured Economy: How the Powerful Enrich Themselves, Slow Down Growth, and Increase Inequality*. New York: Oxford University Press.

Lippmann, Walter. 1922. *Public Opinion*. New York: Harcourt Brace.

Liscow, Zachary. 2018. "Is Efficiency Biased?" *University of Chicago Law Review* 85(7): 1649–718.

Little, Andrew, and Anne Meng. 2023. "Subjective and Objective Measurement of Democratic Backsliding." https://papers.ssrn.com/abstract=4327307 (March 21, 2023).

Livermore, Michael, and Richard Revesz. 2013. "Can Executive Review Help Prevent Capture?" In *Preventing Regulatory Capture*, eds. Daniel Carpenter and David A. Moss. New York: Cambridge University Press, 420–50.

Lodge, Milton, and Charles S. Taber. 2013. *The Rationalizing Voter*. Cambridge; New York: Cambridge University Press.

Loewenstein, Karl. 1937a. "Militant Democracy and Fundamental Rights, I." *American Political Science Review* 31(3): 417–32.

———. 1937b. "Militant Democracy and Fundamental Rights, II." *American Political Science Review* 31(4): 638–58.

Longino, Helen E. 2013. *Studying Human Behavior: How Scientists Investigate Aggression and Sexuality*. Chicago: University of Chicago Press.

López-Guerra, Claudio. 2014. *Democracy and Disenfranchisement: The Morality of Electoral Exclusions*. Oxford: Oxford University Press.

Lovett, Frank. 2010. *A General Theory of Domination and Justice*. Oxford: Oxford University Press.

———. 2016. *A Republic of Law*. Cambridge: Cambridge University Press.

———. 2022. *The Well-Ordered Republic*. Oxford: Oxford University Press.

Luban, David. 1988. *Lawyers and Justice: An Ethical Study*. Princeton: Princeton University Press.

Lui, Meizhu et al. 2006. *The Color of Wealth: The Story Behind the U.S. Racial Wealth Divide*. New York: The New Press.

Lukes, Steven. 1974. *Power: A Radical View*. London: Macmillan.

Lupu, Noam, and Zach Warner. 2022. "Affluence and Congruence: Unequal Representation Around the World." *Journal of Politics* 84(1): 276–290.

Lynn, Barry C. 2011. *Cornered: The New Monopoly Capitalism and the Economics of Destruction*. Hoboken: John Wiley & Sons.

Macdonald, David. 2019. "Labor Unions and Support for Redistribution in an Era of Inequality∗." *Social Science Quarterly* 100(4): 1197–214.

Macedo, Stephen, ed. 1999. *Deliberative Politics: Essays on Democracy and Disagreement*. Oxford: Oxford University Press.

Macey, Jonathan R., and James P. Jr. Holdcroft. 2010. "Failure Is an Option: An Ersatz-Antitrust Approach to Financial Regulation." *Yale Law Journal* 120: 1368–419.

MacGilvray, Eric. 2021. "Liberal Freedom, the Separation of Powers, and the Administrative State." *Social Philosophy and Policy* 38(1): 130–51.
Mackie, Gerry. 2003. *Democracy Defended*. Cambridge: Cambridge University Press.
MacKinnon, Catherine. 1989. *Toward a Feminist Theory of the State*. Cambridge: Harvard University Press.
MacLean, Nancy. 2017. *Democracy in Chains: The Deep History of the Radical Right's Stealth Plan for America*.London: Scribe.
Magill, M. Elizabeth. 2013. "Courts and Regulatory Capture." In *Preventing Regulatory Capture*, eds. Daniel Carpenter and David A. Moss. New York: Cambridge University Press, 397–419.
Mahmood, Saba. 2015. *Religious Difference in a Secular Age: A Minority Report*. Princeton: Princeton University Press.
Mainwaring, Scott, and Aníbal Pérez-Liñán. 2015. "Cross-Currents in Latin America." *Journal of Democracy* 26(1): 114–27.
Mair, Peter. 2013. *Ruling the Void: The Hollowing of Western Democracy*. London: Verso
Malm, Andreas. 2015. *Fossil Capital: The Rise of Steam-Power and the Roots of Global Warming*. London: Verso.
Maloy, J. S. 2019. *Smarter Ballots: Electoral Realism and Reform*. New York: Palgrave Macmillan.
Manin, Bernard. 1997. *The Principles of Representative Government*. Cambridge: Cambridge University Press.
Mansbridge, Jane. 1980. *Beyond Adversary Democracy*. Chicago: University of Chicago Press.
———. 2010. "The Place of Self-Interest and the Role of Power in Deliberative Democracy." *Journal of Political Philosophy* 18(1): 64–100.
Mansbridge, Jane, et al. 2012. "A Systemic Approach to Deliberative Democracy." In *Deliberative Systems: Deliberative Democracy at the Large Scale*, eds. John Parkinson and Jane Mansbridge. New York: Cambridge University Press 1–26.
Marks, Jonathan. 2009. *Why I Am Not a Scientist: Anthropology and Modern Knowledge*. Berkeley: University of California Press.
Martin, Gregory J., and Ali Yurukoglu. 2017. "Bias in Cable News: Persuasion and Polarization." *American Economic Review* 107(9): 2565–99.
Mason, J. W. 2018. "The Market Police." *Boston Review*. http://bostonreview.net/class-inequality/j-w-mason-market-police.
Mason, Lilliana. 2018. *Uncivil Agreement: How Politics Became Our Identity*. Chicago: University of Chicago Press.
Mattiuzzi, Elizabeth, and Margaret Weir. 2020. "Governing the New Geography of Poverty in Metropolitan America:" *Urban Affairs Review* 56(4): 1086–1131
Mattli, Walter, and Tim Buthe. 2013. *The New Global Rulers: The Privatization of Regulation in the World Economy*. Princeton: Princeton University Press.
Mayer, Jane. 2016. *Dark Money: The Hidden History of the Billionaires Behind the Rise of the Radical Right*. New York: Doubleday.
Mayer, Rob. n.d. "Assassinating Hitler: An Ethical Analysis." Unpublished Manuscript
Mayka, Lindsay. 2019. *Building Participatory Institutions in Latin America: Reform Coalitions and Institutional Change*. Cambridge; New York: Cambridge University Press.
McAlevey, Jane. 2016. *No Shortcuts: Organizing for Power in the New Gilded Age*. New York: Oxford University Press.
———. 2020. *A Collective Bargain: Unions, Organizing, and the Fight for Democracy*. New York: Harper Collins.

McCabe, David. 2020. "Lawmakers From Both Sides Take Aim at Big Tech Executives." *The New York Times*. https://www.nytimes.com/live/2020/07/29/technology/tech-ceos-hearing-testimony (June 3, 2021).

McCarty, Nolan, Keith T. Poole, and Howard Rosenthal. 2013. *Political Bubbles: Financial Crises and the Failure of American Democracy*. Princeton: Princeton University Press.

McCormick, John P. 2001. "Machiavellian Democracy: Controlling Elites with Ferocious Populism." *American Political Science Review* 95(2): 297–314.

———. 2011. *Machiavellian Democracy*. Cambridge: Cambridge University Press.

———. n.d. "Democracy, Plutocracy and the Populist Cry of Pain." Unpublished Manuscript.

McDonnell, Brett, and Daniel Schwarcz. 2011. "Regulatory Contrarians." *North Carolina Law Review* 89(5): 1629.

McGoey, Linsey. 2015. *No Such Thing as a Free Gift: The Gates Foundation and the Price of Philanthropy*. London: Verso Books.

McKay, Amy Melissa. 2018. "Fundraising for Favors? Linking Lobbyist-Hosted Fundraisers to Legislative Benefits." *Political Research Quarterly* 71(4): 869–80.

McKee, Martin, and David Stuckler. 2010. "How Cognitive Biases Affect Our Interpretation of Political Messages." *BMJ* 340: c2276.

McNamee, Stephen J., and Robert K. Miller. 2013. *The Meritocracy Myth*. Lanham: Rowman & Littlefield.

McNay, Lois. 2014. *The Misguided Search for the Political: Social Weightlessness in Radical Democratic Theory*. Cambridge: Polity.

Meade, James. 1993. *Liberty, Equality, and Efficiency*. London: Macmillan.

Medearis, John. 2005. "Social Movements and Deliberative Democratic Theory." *British Journal of Political Science* 35(1): 53–75.

———. 2015. *Why Democracy Is Oppositional*. Cambridge: Harvard University Press.

Medina, José. 2012. *The Epistemology of Resistance: Gender and Racial Oppression, Epistemic Injustice, and Resistant Imaginations*. Oxford: Oxford University Press.

Meehan, Johanna. 2017. "Feminism and Rethinking Our Models of the Self." *Philosophy & Social Criticism* 43(1): 3–33.

Mendelberg, Tali, and John Oleske. 2000. "Race and Public Deliberation." *Political Communication* 17(2): 169–91.

Michaels, Jon D. 2017. *Constitutional Coup: Privatization's Threat to the American Republic*. Cambridge: Harvard University Press.

Michels, Robert. 1915. *Political Parties: A Sociological Study of the Oligarchical Tendencies of Modern Democracy*. New York: Hearst's International Library Co.

Mickey, Robert. 2015. *Paths Out of Dixie: The Democratization of Authoritarian Enclaves in America's Deep South, 1944–1972*. Princeton: Princeton University Press.

Mildenberger, Matto. 2020. *Carbon Captured: How Business and Labor Control Climate Politics*. Cambridge: MIT Press.

Miliband, Ralph. 1969. *The State in Capitalist Society*. London: Weidenfeld & Nicolson.

Mills, C. Wright. 1956. *The Power Elite*. Oxford: Oxford University Press.

Mittiga, Ross. 2022. "Political Legitimacy, Authoritarianism, and Climate Change." *American Political Science Review* 116(3): 998–1011.

Moore, Barrington. 1966. *Social Origins of Dictatorship and Democracy*. Boston: Beacon Press.

Morgenson, Gretchen and Joshua Rosner. 2011. *Reckless Endangerment*. New York: Times Press.

Moses, Robert, Mieko Kamii, Susan McAllister Swap, and Jeffrey Howard. 1989. "The Algebra Project: Organizing in the Spirit of Ella." *Harvard Educational Review* 59(4): 423–43.

Mosimann, Nadja, and Jonas Pontusson. 2017. "Solidaristic Unionism and Support for Redistribution in Contemporary Europe." *World Politics* 69(3): 448–92.
Mouffe, Chantal. 2000. *The Democratic Paradox*. London: Verso.
———. 2005. *The Return of the Political*. London: Verso.
Mounk, Yascha. 2018. *The People vs. Democracy: Why Our Freedom Is in Danger and How to Save It*. Cambridge: Harvard University Press.
Moyn, Samuel. 2018. *Not Enough: Human Rights in an Unequal World*. Cambridge: Harvard University Press.
Muldoon, James, ed. 2018. *Council Democracy: Towards a Democratic Socialist Politics*. New York: Routledge.
———. 2022. "A Socialist Republican Theory of Freedom and Government." *European Journal of Political Theory* 21(1): 47–67
———. 2020. *Building Power to Change the World: The Political Thought of the German Council Movements*. Oxford: Oxford University Press.
Müller, Jan-Werner. 2016. *What Is Populism?* Philadelphia: University of Pennsylvania Press.
Murray, Charles A. 2006. *In Our Hands: A Plan to Replace the Welfare State*. Washington, D.C.: AEI Press.
Naidu, Suresh. 2020. "Modern Market Power." Presented at the Anti-Monopoly and Regulated Industries Summer Academy, Law and Political Economy Project. Online conference (June 9, 2020).
Naidu, Suresh, Eric A. Posner, and Glen Weyl. 2018. "Antitrust Remedies for Labor Market Power." *Harvard Law Review* 132(2): 536–601.
Nall, Clayton. 2018. *The Road to Inequality: How the Federal Highway Program Polarized America and Undermined Cities*. Cambridge: Cambridge University Press.
Nathan, Andrew. 2016. "Contribution to Symposium on Bell's China Model." *Perspectives on Politics* 14(1): 154–5.
Neblo, Michael. 2015. *Deliberative Democracy between Theory and Practice*. New York: Cambridge University Press.
Nichols, Tom. 2017. *The Death of Expertise: The Campaign Against Established Knowledge and Why It Matters*. New York: Oxford University Press.
North, Douglass C., John Joseph Wallis, and Barry R. Weingast. 2009. *Violence and Social Orders: A Conceptual Framework for Interpreting Recorded Human History*. Cambridge: Cambridge University Press.
Novak, William. 2013. "A Revisionist History of Regulatory Capture." In *Preventing Regulatory Capture*, eds. Daniel Carpenter and David A. Moss. New York: Cambridge University Press, 25–48.
———. 2019. "Institutional Economics and the Progressive Movement for the Social Control of American Business." *Business History Review* 93(4): 665–96.
Nyhan, Brendan, and Jason Reifler. 2010. "When Corrections Fail: The Persistence of Political Misperceptions." *Political Behavior* 32(2): 303–30.
O'Connor, Cailin. 2019. *The Origins of Unfairness: Social Categories and Cultural Evolution*. Oxford: Oxford University Press.
Olson, Joel. 2004. *Abolition of White Democracy*. Minneapolis: University of Minnesota Press.
Olson, Mancur. 1965. *The Logic of Collective Action*. Cambridge: Harvard University Press.
O'Neill, Martin. 2020. "Social Justice and Economic Systems: On Rawls, Democratic Socialism, and Alternatives to Capitalism." *Philosophical Topics* 48(2): 159–201.
O'Neill, Martin, and Stuart White. 2018. "Trade Unions and Political Equality." In *Philosophical Foundations of Labour Law*, eds. Hugh Collins, Gillian Lester, and Virginia Mantouvalou. Oxford: Oxford University Press.

O'Neill, Martin, and Thad Williamson, eds. 2012. *Property-Owning Democracy: Rawls and Beyond*. Malden, MA: Wiley-Blackwell.

Ong, Lynette. 2016. "Contribution to Symposium on Bell's China Model." *Perspectives on Politics* 14(1): 156–7.

Oppenheimer, Danny, and Mike Edwards. 2012. *Democracy Despite Itself: Why a System That Shouldn't Work at All Works So Well*. Cambridge: MIT Press.

O'Shea, Tom. 2020. "Socialist Republicanism." *Political Theory* 48(5): 548–72.

Owen, David, and Graham Smith. 2018. "Sortition, Rotation, and Mandate: Conditions for Political Equality and Deliberative Reasoning." *Politics & Society* 46(3): 419–34.

Pachirat, Timothy. 2013. *Every Twelve Seconds: Industrialized Slaughter and the Politics of Sight*. New Haven: Yale University Press.

Page, Benjamin I., Jason Seawright, and Matthew J. Lacombe. 2018. *Billionaires and Stealth Politics*. Chicago: University of Chicago Press.

Parvin, Phil. 2021. "The Participatory Paradox: An Egalitarian Critique of Participatory Democracy." *Representation* 57(2): 263–85.

Pateman, Carole. 1970. *Participation and Democratic Theory*. Cambridge: Cambridge University Press.

———. 2006. "Democratizing Citizenship: Some Advantages of a Basic Income." In *Redesigning Distribution: Basic Income and Stakeholder Grants as Cornerstones for an Egalitarian Capitalism*, ed. Erik Olin Wright. London: Verso, 101–19.

Paul, Sanjukta. 2020. "Antitrust as Allocator of Coordination Rights." *UCLA Law Review* 67(2).

Payne, Charles M. 1995. *I've Got the Light of Freedom: The Organizing Tradition and the Mississippi Freedom Struggle*. Berkeley: University of California Press.

Peck, Reece. 2019. *Fox Populism: Branding Conservatism as Working Class*. New York: Cambridge University Press.

Pennacchi, George. 2012. "Narrow Banking." *Annual Review of Financial Economics* 4(1): 141–59.

Persson, Anna, and Bo Rothstein. 2015. "It's My Money: Why Big Government May Be Good Government." *Comparative Politics* 47(2): 231–49.

Peters, Yvette, and Sander J. Ensink. 2015. "Differential Responsiveness in Europe: The Effects of Preference Difference and Electoral Participation." *West European Politics* 38(3): 577–600.

Peterson, Ruth D., and Lauren J. Krivo. 2010. *Divergent Social Worlds: Neighborhood Crime and the Racial-Spatial Divide*. New York: Russell Sage Foundation.

Pettit, Philip. 1997. *Republicanism: A Theory of Freedom and Government*. Oxford: Oxford University Press.

———. 2013. *On the People's Terms: A Republican Theory and Model of Democracy*. Cambridge: Cambridge University Press.

Philippon, Thomas. 2019. *The Great Reversal: How America Gave Up on Free Markets*. Cambridge: Belknap Press.

Phillips, Anne. 2021. *Unconditional Equals*. Princeton: Princeton University Press.

Phulwani, Vijay. 2016. "The Poor Man's Machiavelli: Saul Alinsky and the Morality of Power." *American Political Science Review* 110(4): 863–75.

Piano, Natasha. 2019. "Revisiting Democratic Elitism: The Italian School of Elitism, American Political Science, and the Problem of Plutocracy." *The Journal of Politics* 81(2): 524–38.

Pierson, Paul. 1993. "When Effect Becomes Cause: Policy Feedback and Political Change." *World Politics* 45(4): 595–628.

Piketty, Thomas. 2014. *Capital in the Twenty-First Century: The Dynamics of Inequality, Wealth, and Growth*. Cambridge: Belknap Press.

Pildes, Richard H. 1999. "The Theory of Political Competition Symposium: The Law and Economics of Elections." *Virginia Law Review* 85(8): 1605–26.
Piliavsky, Anastasia, ed. 2014. *Patronage as Politics in South Asia.* Cambridge: Cambridge University Press.
Pistor, Katharina. 2019. *The Code of Capital: How the Law Creates Wealth and Inequality.* Princeton: Princeton University Press.
Pitofsky, Robert. 1978. "Political Content of Antitrust." *University of Pennsylvania Law Review* 127(4): 1051–75.
Piven, Frances Fox. 1971. *Regulating the Poor: The Functions of Public Welfare.* New York: Random House.
Pogrebinschi, Thamy. 2023. *Innovating Democracy?: The Means and Ends of Citizen Participation in Latin America.* Cambridge: Cambridge University Press.
Polanyi, Karl. 1944. *The Great Transformation.* New York: Farrar and Reinhart.
Polletta, Francesca. 2002. *Freedom Is an Endless Meeting: Democracy in American Social Movements.* Chicago: University of Chicago Press.
Pontusson, Jonas. 2013. "Unionization, Inequality and Redistribution." *British Journal of Industrial Relations* 51(4): 797–825.
Posner, Eric A., and Adrian Vermeule. 2011. *The Executive Unbound: After the Madisonian Republic.* New York: Oxford University Press.
Posner, Gerald. 2020. *Pharma: Greed, Lies, and the Poisoning of America.* New York: Simon & Schuster.
Poulantzas, Nicos. 1969. "The Problem of the Capitalist State." *New Left Review* 0(58): 67–78.
Przeworski, Adam. 1991. *Democracy and the Market: Political and Economic Reforms in Eastern Europe and Latin America.* Cambridge: Cambridge University Press.
———. 1999. "Minimalist Conception of Democracy: A Defense." In *Democracy's Value*, eds. Ian Shapiro and Casiano Hacker-Cordon. Cambridge: Cambridge University Press.
———. 2005. "Democracy as an Equilibrium." *Public Choice* 123(3-4): 253–73.
———. 2018. *Why Bother with Elections?* Cambridge: Polity.
Przeworski, Adam, and Michael Wallerstein. 1982. "The Structure of Class Conflict in Democratic Capitalist Societies." *The American Political Science Review* 76(2): 215–38.
Purdy, Jedediah. 2018. "Beyond the Bosses' Constitution: The First Amendment and Class Entrenchment Essays." *Columbia Law Review* 118(7): 2161–86.
———. 2019. *This Land Is Our Land.* Princeton: Princeton University Press.
Purdy, Jedediah, and David Grewal. 2017. "Inequality Rediscovered." *Theoretical Inquiries in Law* 18: 61–82.
Putnam, Robert. 1993. *Making Democracy Work: Civic Traditions in Modern Italy.* Princeton: Princeton University Press.
———. 2001. *Bowling Alone: The Collapse and Revival of American Community.* New York: Simon & Schuster.
Quadagno, Jill. 1994. *The Color of Welfare: How Racism Undermined the War on Poverty.* New York: Oxford University Press.
Radcliff, Benjamin, and Patricia Davis. 2000. "Labor Organization and Electoral Participation in Industrial Democracies." *American Journal of Political Science* 44(1): 132–41.
Radford, Gail. 1997. *Modern Housing for America: Policy Struggles in the New Deal Era.* Chicago: University of Chicago Press.
Rahman, K. Sabeel. 2016. *Democracy against Domination.* Oxford: Oxford University Press.
———. 2018a. "Infrastructural Regulation and the New Utilities." *Yale Journal of Regulation* 35: 911–39.
———. 2018b. "The New Utilities: Private Power, Social Infrastructure, and the Revival of the Public Utility Concept." *Cardozo Law Review* 39(5): 1621–92.

Rahman, K. Sabeel, and Hollie Russon Gilman. 2019. *Civic Power: Rebuilding American Democracy in an Era of Crisis*. Cambridge: Cambridge University Press.
Rana, Aziz. 2014. *The Two Faces of American Freedom*. Cambridge: Harvard University Press.
Ransby, Barbara. 2003. *Ella Baker and the Black Freedom Movement*. Chapel Hill: University of North Carolina Press.
Rawls, John. 1971. *A Theory of Justice*. Cambridge: Belknap Press.
———. 1993. *Political Liberalism*. New York: Columbia University Press.
Reardon, Sean F., and Ann Owens. 2014. "60 Years After Brown: Trends and Consequences of School Segregation." *Annual Review of Sociology* 40(1): 199–218.
Reeves, Richard. 2017. *Dream Hoarders: How the American Upper Middle Class Is Leaving Everyone Else in the Dust, Why That Is a Problem, and What to Do about It*. Washington, D.C: Brookings Institution.
Reybrouck, David Van. 2016. *Against Elections: The Case for Democracy*. London: Random House.
Riker, William H. 1982. *Liberalism Against Populism: A Confrontation Between the Theory of Democracy and the Theory of Social Science*. San Francisco: Freeman Press.
Roberts, William Clare. 2016. *Marx's Inferno: The Political Theory of Capital*. Princeton: Princeton University Press.
Robertson, David Brian. 2012. *Federalism and the Making of America*. New York: Routledge.
Robeyns, Ingrid. 2017. "Having Too Much." In *NOMOS LVIII: Wealth*, eds. Jack Knight and Melissa Schwartzberg. New York: NYU Press, 1–44.
———. 2022. "Why Limitarianism?*." *Journal of Political Philosophy* 30(2): 249–70.
Robinson, James A., Ragnar Torvik, and Thierry Verdier. 2006. "Political Foundations of the Resource Curse." *Journal of Development Economics* 79(2): 447–68.
Rodrik, Dani. 2018. "Is Populism Necessarily Bad Economics?" *AEA Papers and Proceedings* 108: 196–9.
Roediger, David R., and Elizabeth D. Esch. 2012. *The Production of Difference: Race and the Management of Labor in U.S. History*. New York: Oxford University Press.
Roemer, John E. 1996. *Equal Shares: Making Market Socialism Work*. London: Verso.
Roithmayr, Daria. 2010. "Racial Cartels." *Michigan Journal of Race and Law* 16(1): 45–79.
———. 2021. *Reproducing Racism: How Everyday Choices Lock in White Advantage*. New York: NYU Press.
Rosanvallon, Pierre. 2008. *Counter-Democracy: Politics in an Age of Distrust*. Cambridge: Cambridge University Press.
———. 2018. *Good Government: Democracy beyond Elections*. Cambridge: Harvard University Press.
Rosenbluth, Frances McCall, and Ian Shapiro. 2018. *Responsible Parties: Saving Democracy from Itself*. New Haven: Yale University Press.
Rosenfeld, Sophia. 2018. *Democracy and Truth: A Short History*. Philadelphia: University of Pennsylvania Press.
Rothstein, Richard. 2017. *The Color of Law: A Forgotten History of How Our Government Segregated America*. New York: Liveright.
Rubin, Lillian B. 1969. "Maximum Feasible Participation: The Origins, Implications, and Present Status." *The ANNALS of the American Academy of Political and Social Science* 385(1): 14–29.
Rueda, David, and Jonas Pontusson. 2000. "Wage Inequality and Varieties of Capitalism." *World Politics* 52(3): 350–83.
Rueschemeyer, Dietrich, Evelyne Huber, and John D. Stephens. 1992. *Capitalist Development & Democracy*. Chicago: University of Chicago Press.

Sabl, Andrew. 2001. *Ruling Passions: Political Offices and Democratic Ethics*. Princeton: Princeton University Press.
———. 2017. "Realist Liberalism: An Agenda." *Critical Review of International Social and Political Philosophy* 20(3): 366–84.
Saez, Emmanuel, and Gabriel Zucman. 2019. *The Triumph of Injustice: How the Rich Dodge Taxes and How to Make Them Pay*. New York: Norton.
Sagar, Paul. 2018a. *The Opinion of Mankind*. Princeton: Princeton University Press.
———. 2018b. "We Should Look Closely at What Adam Smith Actually Believed." *Aeon*. https://aeon.co/essays/we-should-look-closely-at-what-adam-smith-actually-believed (April 15, 2020).
Samuels, David. 2001. "Money, Elections, and Democracy in Brazil." *Latin American Politics and Society* 43(2): 27–48.
Sanders, Lynn M. 1997. "Against Deliberation." *Political Theory* 25(3): 347–76.
Sartori, Giovanni. 1962. "Constitutionalism: A Preliminary Discussion." *The American Political Science Review* 56(4): 853–64.
Saward, Michael. 2010. *The Representative Claim*. Oxford: Oxford University Press.
Schakel, Wouter. 2021. "Unequal Policy Responsiveness in the Netherlands." *Socio-Economic Review* 19(1): 37–57.
Schattschneider, Elmer Eric. 1960. *The Semisovereign People: A Realist's View of Democracy in America*. New York: Holt, Reinhart, and Wilson.
Schedler, Andreas. 2021. "Democratic Reciprocity." *Journal of Political Philosophy* 29(2): 252–278.
Schimmelfennig, Frank. 2001. "The Community Trap." *International Organization* 55(1): 47–80.
Schlozman, Kay Lehman, Henry E. Brady, and Sidney Verba. 2018. *Unequal and Unrepresented: Political Inequality and the People's Voice in the New Gilded Age*. Princeton: Princeton University Press.
Schulson, Michael, and Samuel Bagg. 2019. "Give Political Power to Ordinary People." *Dissent Magazine*. https://www.dissentmagazine.org/online_articles/give-political-power-to-ordinary-people-sortition.
Schumpeter, Joseph. 1942. *Capitalism, Socialism, and Democracy*. New York: Harper.
Schwab, Klaus. 2017. *The Fourth Industrial Revolution*. New York: Crown Business.
Schwarcz, Daniel. 2013. "Preventing Capture through Consumer Empowerment Programs: Some Evidence from Insurance Regulation." In *Preventing Regulatory Capture*, eds. Daniel Carpenter and David A. Moss. New York: Cambridge University Press, 365–98.
Schwartz, Louis. 1979. "Justice and Other Non-Economic Goals of Antitrust." *University of Pennsylvania Law Review* 127(4): 1076.
Shapiro, Ian. 1999. "Enough of Deliberation: Politics Is about Interests and Power." In *Deliberative Politics: Essays on Democracy and Disagreement*, ed. Stephen Macedo. New York: Oxford University Press.
———. 2003. *The State of Democratic Theory*. Princeton: Princeton University Press.
———. 2016a. "Against Impartiality." *The Journal of Politics* 78(2): 467–80.
———. 2016b. *Politics against Domination*. Cambridge: Belknap.
———. 2017. "Collusion in Restraint of Democracy: Against Political Deliberation." *Daedalus* 146(3): 77–84.
Shapiro, Thomas M., and Melvin L. Oliver. 1995. *Black Wealth/ White Wealth: A New Perspective on Racial Inequality*. New York: Routledge.
Shelby, Tommie. 2014. "Integration, Inequality, and Imperatives of Justice: A Review Essay." *Philosophy & Public Affairs* 42(3): 253–85.

Shklar, Judith N. 1989. "The Liberalism of Fear." In *Political Liberalism: Variations on a Theme*, ed. Nancy Rosenblum. Cambridge: Harvard University Press, 21–38.

Sidman, Professor Andrew H. 2019. *Pork Barrel Politics: How Government Spending Determines Elections in a Polarized Era*. New York: Columbia University Press.

Simonson, Jocelyn. 2017. "Democratizing Criminal Justice Through Contestation and Resistance." *Northwestern University Law Review* 111(6): 1609–24.

Singer, Abraham. 2018. *The Form of the Firm: A Normative Political Theory of the Corporation*. New York: Oxford University Press.

Sintomer, Yves. 2018. "From Deliberative to Radical Democracy? Sortition and Politics in the Twenty-First Century." *Politics & Society* 46(3): 337–57.

———. 2020. "The Contrasted Models of Democracy in Sortition-Based Innovations." Paper presented at Association for Political Thought (APT UK) in Oxford.

Sitaraman, Ganesh, and Anne Alstott. 2019. *The Public Option: How to Expand Freedom, Increase Opportunity, and Promote Equality*. Cambridge: Belknap Press.

Skocpol, Theda. 1985. "Bringing the State Back In: Strategies of Analysis in Current Research." In *Bringing the State Back In*, eds. Peter B. Evans, Dietrich Rueschemeyer, and Theda Skocpol. Cambridge: Cambridge University Press, 3–38.

———. 2003. *Diminished Democracy: From Membership to Management in American Civic Life*. University of Oklahoma Press.

Skocpol, Theda, and Alexander Hertel-Fernandez. 2016. "The Koch Network and Republican Party Extremism." *Perspectives on Politics* 14(3): 681–99.

Slobodian, Quinn. 2018. *Globalists: The End of Empire and the Birth of Neoliberalism*. Cambridge: Harvard University Press.

Smith, Adam. 1904. *An Inquiry into the Nature and Causes of The Wealth of Nations*. London: Meuthen.

Smith, Graham. 2009. *Democratic Innovations*. Cambridge: Cambridge University Press.

Smith, Mark. 2000. *American Business and Political Power: Public Opinion, Elections, and Democracy*. Chicago: University of Chicago Press.

Smith, Rogers M. 1993. "Beyond Tocqueville, Myrdal, and Hartz: The Multiple Traditions in America." *American Political Science Review* 87(3): 549–66.

Smucker, Jonathan. 2017. *Hegemony How-To: A Roadmap for Radicals*. Chico: AK Press.

Somin, Ilya. 2016. *Democracy and Political Ignorance: Why Smaller Government Is Smarter*. 2d ed. Stanford: Stanford University Press.

———. 2020. *Free to Move: Foot Voting, Migration, and Political Freedom*. New York: Oxford University Press.

Spies, Dennis C., and André Kaiser. 2014. "Does the Mode of Candidate Selection Affect the Representativeness of Parties?" *Party Politics* 20(4): 576–90.

Srnicek, Nick. 2016. *Platform Capitalism*. Cambridge: Polity.

Srnicek, Nick, and Alex Williams. 2015. *Inventing the Future: Postcapitalism and a World Without Work*. London: Verso.

Standing, Guy. 2011. *The Precariat: The New Dangerous Class*. New York: Bloomsbury.

———. 2017. *Basic Income*. New York: Penguin.

Stark, Johanna. 2019. *Law for Sale: A Philosophical Critique of Regulatory Competition*. Oxford: Oxford University Press.

Stears, Marc. 2010. *Demanding Democracy: American Radicals in Search of a New Politics*. Princeton: Princeton University Press.

Steinmetz-Jenkins, Daniel, and Daniel Zamora. 2019. "Socialism Beyond Equality." *Dissent Magazine* (Summer). https://www.dissentmagazine.org/article/socialism-beyond-equality (April 2, 2020).

Stigler, George J. 1971. "The Theory of Economic Regulation." *The Bell Journal of Economics and Management Science* 2(1): 3–21.
Stilz, Anna. 2019. *Territorial Sovereignty: A Philosophical Exploration*. Oxford: Oxford University Press.
Stinchcombe, Arthur L. 1985. "The Functional Theory of Social Insurance." *Politics & Society* 14(4): 411–30.
Stokes, Susan C. 2005. "Perverse Accountability: A Formal Model of Machine Politics with Evidence from Argentina." *American Political Science Review* 99(3): 315–25.
Stoller, Matt. 2019. *Goliath: The 100-Year War Between Monopoly Power and Democracy*. New York: Simon & Schuster.
Stone, Peter. 2011. *The Luck of the Draw: The Role of Lotteries in Decision Making*. Oxford: Oxford University Press.
Stout, Jeffrey. 2012. *Blessed Are the Organized: Grassroots Democracy in America*. Princeton: Princeton University Press.
Stovall, Tyler. 2021. *White Freedom: The Racial History of an Idea*. Princeton: Princeton University Press.
Streeck, Wolfgang. 2014. *Buying Time: The Delayed Crisis of Democratic Capitalism*. London: Verso.
Streeck, Wolfgang, and Anke Hassel. 2003. "Trade Unions as Political Actors." In *International Handbook of Trade Unions*, eds. John T. Addison and Claus Schnabel. Edward Elgar, 335–65.
Sunstein, Cass R. 1987. "Lochner's Legacy." *Columbia Law Review* 87(5): 873–919.
Susskind, Lawrence, and Gerard McMahon. 1985. "The Theory and Practice of Negotiated Rulemaking." *Yale Journal on Regulation* 3(1): 133–66.
Svolik, Milan W. 2019. "Polarization versus Democracy." *Journal of Democracy* 30(3): 14.
Szwarcberg, Mariela. 2015. *Mobilizing Poor Voters: Machine Politics, Clientelism, and Social Networks in Argentina*. Cambridge University Press.
Tait, Allison Anna. 2019. "The Law of High-Wealth Exceptionalism." *Alabama Law Review* 71(4): 981–1038.
Táíwò, Olúfẹ́mi O. 2022a. *Elite Capture: How the Powerful Took Over Identity Politics*. Chicago: Haymarket Books.
———. 2022b. *Reconsidering Reparations*. New York: Oxford University Press.
Talisse, Robert B. 2019. *Overdoing Democracy: Why We Must Put Politics in Its Place*. New York: Oxford University Press.
Taylor, Astra. 2020. *Democracy May Not Exist, but We'll Miss It When It's Gone*. New York: Metropolitan Books.
Taylor, Charles. 1992. *Multiculturalism and "the Politics of Recognition"*, ed. Amy Gutmann. Princeton: Princeton University Press.
Taylor, Keeanga-Yamahtta. 2019. *Race for Profit*. Chapel Hill: The University of North Carolina Press.
Taylor, Robert S. 2017. *Exit Left: Markets and Mobility in Republican Thought*. Oxford: Oxford University Press.
Teachout, Zephyr. 2016. *Corruption in America: From Benjamin Franklin's Snuff Box to Citizens United*. Cambridge: Harvard University Press.
———. 2020. *Break 'Em Up: Recovering Our Freedom from Big Ag, Big Tech, and Big Money*. New York: Macmillan.
Teles, Steven M. 2012. *The Rise of the Conservative Legal Movement: The Battle for Control of the Law*. Princeton: Princeton University Press.

Terriquez, Veronica. 2011. "Schools for Democracy: Labor Union Participation and Latino Immigrant Parents' School-Based Civic Engagement." *American Sociological Review* 76(4): 581–601.

Thaa, Winfried. 2016. "Issues and Images: New Sources of Inequality in Current Representative Democracy." *Critical Review of International Social and Political Philosophy* 19(3): 357–75.

Thiele, Leslie Paul. 2006. *The Heart of Judgment: Practical Wisdom, Neuroscience, and Narrative*. Cambridge: Cambridge University Press.

Thomas, Alan. 2016. *Republic of Equals: Predistribution and Property-Owning Democracy*. New York: Oxford University Press.

Tilly, Charles. 1999. *Durable Inequality*. Berkeley: University of California Press.

Tronto, Joan C. 2013. *Caring Democracy: Markets, Equality, and Justice*. New York: NYU Press.

Trounstine, Jessica. 2018. *Segregation by Design: Local Politics and Inequality in American Cities*. Cambridge: Cambridge University Press.

Tsebelis, George. 2002. *Veto Players: How Political Institutions Work*. Princeton: Princeton University Press.

Usher, Nikki. 2021. *News for the Rich, White, and Blue: How Place and Power Distort American Journalism*. New York: Columbia University Press.

Usmani, Adaner. 2018. "Democracy and the Class Struggle." *American Journal of Sociology* 124(3): 664–704.

Vaheesan, Sandeep. 2020. "Privileging Consolidation and Proscribing Cooperation: The Perversity of Contemporary Antitrust Law." *Journal of Law and Political Economy* 1(1) 28–45.

Van der Veen, Robert, and Philippe Van Parijs. 1986. "A Capitalist Road to Communism." *Theory and Society* 15(5): 635–55.

Van Parijs, Philippe. 2006. "Basic Income: A Simple and Powerful Idea for the Twenty-First Century." In *Redesigning Distribution: Basic Income and Stakeholder Grants as Cornerstones for an Egalitarian Capitalism*, ed. Erik Olin Wright. London: Verso, 3–42.

Van Parijs, Philippe, Joshua Cohen, and Joel Rogers. 2001. *What's Wrong with a Free Lunch?* Boston: Beacon Press.

Vergara, Camila. 2020. *Systemic Corruption: Constitutional Ideas for an Anti-Oligarchic Republic*. Princeton: Princeton University Press.

Viehoff, Daniel. 2014. "Democratic Equality and Political Authority." *Philosophy & Public Affairs* 42(4): 337–75.

Villanueva, Edgar. 2018. *Decolonizing Wealth: Indigenous Wisdom to Heal Divides and Restore Balance*. Oakland, CA: Berrett-Koehler.

Vogel, David. 1983. "The Power of Business in America: A Re-Appraisal." *British Journal of Political Science* 13(1): 19–43.

———. 1987. "Political Science and the Study of Corporate Power: A Dissent from the New Conventional Wisdom." *British Journal of Political Science* 17(4): 385–408.

Wagner, Wendy. 2010. "Administrative Law, Filter Failure, and Information Capture." *Duke Law Journal* 59(7): 1321–432.

———. 2013. "The Participation-Centered Model Meets Administrative Process *Wisconsin Law Review* 2013(2): 671–94.

Wagner, Wendy, Katherine Barnes, and Lisa Peters. 2011. "Rulemaking in the Shade: An Empirical Study of EPA's Airr Toxic Emission Standards." *Administrative Law Review* 63(1): 99–158.

Waldron, Jeremy. 1987. "Theoretical Foundations of Liberalism." *The Philosophical Quarterly* 37(147): 127–50.

———. 1999. *Law and Disagreement*. Oxford: Clarendon Press.

Walker, Edward T., 2015. "Legitimizing the Corporation through Public Participation." In *Democratizing Inequalities: Dilemmas of the New Public Participation*, eds. Lee, Caroline W., Michael McQuarrie, and Edward T. Walker. New York: NYU Press. 66–82.

Walker, Renee E., Christopher R. Keane, and Jessica G. Burke. 2010. "Disparities and Access to Healthy Food in the United States: A Review of Food Deserts Literature." *Health & Place* 16(5): 876–84.

Wall, Steven. 2007. "Democracy and Equality." *The Philosophical Quarterly* 57(228): 416–38.

Walters, Daniel E. 2022. "The Administrative Agon: A Democratic Theory for a Conflictual Regulatory State." *Yale Law Journal* 132: 1.

Walzer, Michael. 1983. *Spheres of Justice*. New York: Basic Books.

———. 1984. "Liberalism and the Art of Separation." *Political Theory* 12(3): 315–30.

Warren, Mark. 2004. "What Does Corruption Mean in a Democracy?" *American Journal of Political Science* 48(2): 328–43.

———. 2011. "Voting with Your Feet: Exit-Based Empowerment in Democratic Theory." *The American Political Science Review* 105(4): 683–701.

Weale, Albert. 2018. *The Will of the People: A Modern Myth*. Cambridge: Polity.

Weber, Robert F. 2012. "Structural Regulation as Antidote to Complexity Capture." *American Business Law Journal* 49(3): 643–738.

Weeks, Kathi. 2011. *The Problem with Work: Feminism, Marxism, Antiwork Politics, and Postwork Imaginaries*. Durham: Duke University Press.

Wenar, Leif. 2016. *Blood Oil: Tyrants, Violence, and the Rules That Run the World*. Oxford: Oxford University Press.

Wenman, Mark. 2013. *Agonistic Democracy: Constituent Power in the Era of Globalisation*. Cambridge: Cambridge University Press.

Wertheimer, Alan. 1988. "The Equalization of Legal Resources." *Philosophy & Public Affairs* 17(4): 303–22.

Weschle, Simon. 2022. *Money in Politics: Self-Enrichment, Campaign Spending, and Golden Parachutes*. New York: Cambridge University Press.

Williams, Eric. 1944. *Capitalism and Slavery*. Chapel Hill: University of North Carolina Press.

Wilson, James. 2019. *Democratic Equality*. Princeton: Princeton University Press.

Wilson, James Q. 1980. *The Politics of Regulation*. New York: Basic Books.

Winters, Jeffrey A. 2011. *Oligarchy*. Cambridge; New York: Cambridge University Press.

———. 2017. "Wealth Defense and the Complicity of Liberal Democracy." In *NOMOS LVIII: Wealth*, eds. Jack Knight and Melissa Schwartzberg. New York: NYU Press, 158–225.

Wollmann, Thomas G. 2019. "Stealth Consolidation: Evidence from an Amendment to the Hart-Scott-Rodino Act." *American Economic Review: Insights* 1(1): 77–94.

Woo, Su Yun. 2023. *Deliberation with Chinese Characteristics: A Tale of Two Chinese Cities' Participatory Budgeting Experiences*. New York: Routledge.

Woodly, Deva R. 2015. *The Politics of Common Sense: How Social Movements Use Public Discourse to Change Politics and Win Acceptance*. New York: Oxford University Press.

———. 2021. *Reckoning: #BlackLivesMatter and the Democratic Necessity of Social Movements*. Oxford: Oxford University Press.

Wootton, David. 2006. "Liberty, Metaphor, and Mechanism: 'Checks and Balances' and the Origins of Modern Constitutionalism." In *Liberty and American Experience in the Eighteenth Century*, ed. David Womersley. Indianapolis: Liberty Fund.

Wright, Erik Olin. 2006a. "Basic Income, Stakeholder Grants, and Class Analysis." In *Redesigning Distribution: Basic Income and Stakeholder Grants as Cornerstones for an Egalitarian Capitalism*, ed. Erik Olin Wright. London: Verso, 91–100.

———, ed. 2006b. *Redesigning Distribution: Basic Income and Stakeholder Grants as Cornerstones for an Egalitarian Capitalism*. London: Verso.

———. 2010. *Envisioning Real Utopias*. London: Verso.
Wu, Tim. 2017. "Antitrust via Rulemaking: Competition Catalysts." *Colorado Technology Law Journal* 16(1): 33–64.
———. 2018. *The Curse of Bigness: Antitrust in the New Gilded Age*. New York: Columbia Global Reports.
Yackee, Susan Webb. 2013. "Reconsidery Agency Capture During Regulatory Policymaking." In *Preventing Regulatory Capture*, eds. Daniel Carpenter and David A. Moss. New York: Cambridge University Press, 292–325.
Yang, Tsemin. 2019. "The Emergence of the Environmental Impact Assessment Duty as a Global Legal Norm and General Principle of Law." *Hastings Law Journal* 70(2): 525–572
Young, Iris Marion. 1990. *Justice and the Politics of Difference*. Princeton: Princeton University Press.
———. 2001. "Activist Challenges to Deliberative Democracy." *Political Theory* 29(5): 670–90.
Young, Kevin A., Tarun Banerjee, and Michael Schwartz. 2018. "Capital Strikes as a Corporate Political Strategy: The Structural Power of Business in the Obama Era." *Politics & Society* 46(1): 3–28.
———. 2020. *Levers of Power: How the 1% Rules and What the 99% Can Do about It*. London: Verso.
Yuen, Samson. 2014. "Disciplining the Party: Xi Jinping's Anti-Corruption Campaign and Its Limits." *China Perspectives* 2014(3): 41–47.
Zacka, Bernardo. 2022. "Political Theory Rediscovers Public Administration." *Annual Review of Political Science* 25(1): 21–42.
Zaller, John. 1992. *The Nature and Origins of Mass Opinion*. New York: Cambridge University Press.
Zelleke, Almaz. 2008. "Institutionalizing the Universal Caretaker Through a Basic Income?" *Basic Income Studies* 3(3).
Zucman, Gabriel. 2019. "Global Wealth Inequality." *Annual Review of Economics* 11(1): 109–38.

Index

For the benefit of digital users, indexed terms that span two pages (e.g., 52–53) may, on occasion, appear on only one of those pages.

accountability
  elections as accountability mechanism, 6, 37–48, 158–159, 200–201
  electoral reforms to enhance accountability, 52–53
  nonelectoral methods of accountability, 122, 205–211, 223, 241–242
  obstacles to accountability, *see* state capture, methods of
  ocular power as indirect accountability, 190–192
  perverse accountability under clientelism, 88
  within organizations, 31, 173–174, 213–214, 233–238
activism, *see* civic virtue; civil society; organizing, distinctive features of
Administrative Procedures Act (APA), 59–60, 66–67
administrative state, *see* bureaucracy
adversarialism (as key principle of democracy), 6–7, 9, 27–28, 64–66, 73, 111, 113, 115–116, 140, 143*t*, 148–150, 155–160, 183, 203–211, 213, 219, 221, 226, 235, 240–241, *see also* competition
affirmative action, 95, 137, 139–140, 143*t*, *see also* corrective partiality
agency, *see* freedom; political ontology
agonism
  as category of allied approaches to democratic theory, 156, 212–213
  as general democratic principle, *see* adversarialism
Alinsky, Saul, 160, 215–216 n.2, 216–217, 236–237

anti-monopoly, 5, 8, 19, 30, 109, 126–131, 143*t*, 146, 150, 152, 160, 195–196, 202–205, 240–241, 243, *see also* Brandeis, Louis; corrective partiality; Progressivism; taxation
Aristotle, 85–86
arms races, 114–115, 171, 173–174, 187, 233–234
artificial intelligence, 140–141 n.8
Athens, ancient, 56, 61, 91–92, 129
authoritarianism, *see* autocracy
authority, *see* legitimacy
authorization, *see* collective will; legitimacy
autocracy, 8, 18–19, 22, 33, 51, 75, 80, 85–91, 97, 109–112, 116–117, 161–163, 168–174, 180–185, 190–192, 239, 241–242
autonomy, *see* freedom; political ontology

Baker, Ella, 160, 215–216 n.2, 216–217 n.3, 218
balance of power, 3–5, 25–31, 34*t*, 37, 48, 135, 141–142, 143*t*, 149–150, 159, 165–166, 171, 173–174, 192, 195–196, 201–202, 220, 234, 240–241, 243; *see also* organizational capacity
basic income, *see* unconditional wealth transfers (UWTs)
Bell, Daniel A., 119–120, 177–186
Bell, Derrick, 95
benevolent despotism, 33, 163, 179, 184–185, 198, *see also* epistemic arguments for and against democracy; intrinsic *vs.* instrumental accounts of democracy's value; political violence
billionaires, 80, 98–99, 102–104; *see also* oligarchy

Index

Black Freedom Movement, 51–52, 92–95, 114, 214, 216, 218, 222–224, 231–232 n.7; *see also* Baker, Ella; King Jr., Martin Luther
Bolsonaro, Jair, 22
Brandeis, Louis, 126–128, 202, 203; *see also* anti-monopoly; Progressivism
Brazil, 22, 61, 93–94, 100–101, 103, 153–154 n.2, 239
Brennan, Jason, 119–120, 177–180, 185–189
bureaucracy
  agency discretion, 50
  capture of, *see* regulation, capture of
  democratization of, 59–73, 111, 115, 202–211, 225–226
  as democratizing force, 18–19, 126–131, 164–168, 195–202
  independence of, as a democratic value, 202–203, *see also* meritocracy; neutrality
  theories of administrative legitimacy, 49–50, 193–194, 197, 201

campaign finance, 21–22, 29–30, 36–37, 39–40, 52–53, 103, 131
capital mobility, *see* power, structural forms of
capitalism
  markets, *see* competition, market competition
  Marxist critiques of, *see* Marx and Marxism; socialism
  relation to dispersion of power ideal, 152–155
  as tool of analysis, 132, 237
caste and caste systems, *see* inequality, categorical inequality; race and racism
Chavez, Hugo, 169, 172–174
checks and balances, *see* constitutionalism
Chinese Communist Party (CCP), 70–71, 180–185
Christiano, Thomas, 23–24, 74, 119–120, 179
citizens, *see* ordinary people
citizens' assemblies, 18, 29, 61, 67–68, 212–213, *see also* deliberation; participatory inclusion; sortition
Citizens' Convention on Climate (CCC), 1–3

citizenship, *see* civic virtue; civil society; organizing; ordinary people, proper democratic role of
civic virtue, *see also* civil society; participatory inclusion
  as component of republican theory, 157–158
  as component of ideal of participatory inclusion, 56–58, 62
  in comparison to more specific demand for organized countervailing power, 29–31, 34*t*, 72–73, 132, 160, 182–183, 212–220, 225, 233–235, 241
civil liberties, *see* rights
Civil Rights Movement, *see* Black Freedom Movement; Jim Crow; race and racism
civil society, 115–116, 132, 143*t*, 157–158, 160, 191–192, 198–199, 209–213, 215–216, 226, 231, 234–235, *see also* pluralism; social movements
class, 6, 26–27, 46–47, 56–57, 92, 93–96, 99–101, 111–112, 139–142, 143*t*, 156–157, 188–189, 220–221, 227–233, 239, 242
clientelism, 8, 52, 72, 80, 86–88, 120
climate change, 1–2, 33, 106–107, 138–139 n.4, 183–185, 198, 239, *see also* fossil fuel interests
cognitive science, *see* motivated reasoning, Social Identity Theory (SIT)
collaboration, *see* cooperation
collective action, 9, 22–23, 26–28, 30–31, 39–40, 115–116, 131–136, 149–150, 157, 210–211, 214, 220–227, 230, 233, 235, 238
  obstacles to, 133–134, 228–229
collective authorship, *see* collective will; cooperation
collective self-rule, ideal of, *see also* collective will; cooperation; popular sovereignty
  comparison with resisting state capture, 3–5, 15, 23–31, 34*t*, 147, 149–150, 155–156
  definition of, 5–9, 20–25
  expansive versions of, 23–25, 73–76
  participatory inclusion as version of, 8, 55–56, 61–62, *see also* participatory inclusion

responsive representation as version of, 8, 36–37, *see also* representation
summary of problems with, 6–7, 22–23, 63–64
utopian horizons of, 21, 34*t*, 147–150
varieties of, 2–3, 20–22
collective will
as source of democratic authority, 2, 21–22, 36–37, 49–50, 52, 59, 62, 108, 149, 157, 190, 193–194, 196–197, 207
processes of formation, 20–22, 25, 29, 34*t*, 44, 57, 58, 61–62, 149, 212–213
summary of problems with, 8, 37–42, 48–49, 63–64, 70, 79, 193–194, 197, 237
colonialism, 69–70, 91–95, *see also* race and racism
competition
as core principle of democracy, 8, 113–118, 143t
dangers of, 114–115, 143t
electoral competition, 8–9, 56–57, 87, 112–114, 124, 157–159, 161, 165–166, 170–171, 180–185, 192–194
ideal of egalitarian competition, 4–5, 25–31, 34*t*, 109, 117–118, 123, 124–125, 141–145, 150–152, 155–160
market competition, 89–91, 116–117, 126–129, 134, 143*t*, 148–149, 152–155, 160, 198–202
principle of adversarial contestation, *see* adversarialism
complexity
as challenge for political theorizing, *see* empirical claims; imprecision
as tool of capture, 37–38, 70, 85, 101–103, 115–121, 129, 158–159, 188 n.5, 199–205, *see also* publicity; simplicity
congruence, *see* representation
consequentialism, *see* intrinsic *vs.* instrumental accounts of democracy's value; pragmatism; utilitarianism
constitutionalism
as core principle of democracy, 8, 90–91, 109–112, 143*t*, 132, 146, 172–173, 178, 180–181, 243
countervailing power and, 127, 132
materialist constitutionalism, 111–112, 127, *see also* plebeianism
separation of powers, 86, 111, 143*t*, 157–158, 169

constitutional hardball, *see* arms races
contestation and contestatory institutions, *see* adversarialism; agonism; competition; republicanism
cooperation
central place in ideals of collective self-rule, 4, 22, 34*t*, 55, 58–66, 69–70, 152, *see also* deliberation; participatory inclusion
human psychology and, 153
limitations of, 6, 9, 26–30, 34*t*, 55–56, 63–64, 66–73, 155–156, 212–213, 235, *see also* adversarialism
value and importance within dispersion of power framework, *see* solidarity
Cordelli, Chiara, 193–194, 201
corrective partiality, 30, 34*t*, 96, 123, 124–125, 128, 130–131, 143*t*, 146, 149–150, 234–235, 240–241, *see also* affirmative action; anti-monopoly; countervailing power; neutrality, limitations of
corruption, *see also* clientelism; regulation, capture of; state capture
in civil society organizations, 233
definition of, 85–86
diverse varieties of, 85–87, 102–103, 120
as form of state capture, 8, 52, 80, 85, 87, 90–91, 97–98, 180–184
mechanisms for combatting, 115, 126, 129, 205–211
counter-hegemonic groups, 8–9, 30–31, 34*t*, 137–138, 142, 143*t*, 149–151, 160, 188–189, 206–207, 212, 234–235, *see also* countervailing power; hegemonic groups; ordinary people; organizational capacity
definition of, 131, 133, 136–137
types of, 133–134, 220–224
counter-majoritarian institutions, 32, 51–52, *see also* bureaucracy; judicial review; US Supreme Court
countervailing power, *see also* civil society; counter-hegemonic groups; labor unions; organizing; political parties; social movements; strikes
as core principle of democracy, 5, 8–9, 31, 46, 109, 124–125, 131–136, 143*t*, 146, 150, 152, 168, 195–196, 202, 204, 212–216, 240–241, 243

274 Index

countervailing power (*Continued*)
  contrast with more cooperative modes of pursuing deeper democratization, 34*t*, 68, 132, 148–149, *see also* adversarialism; cooperation, limitations of
  dangers of co-optation, 233–238
  definition of, 131–133
  examples of, 132–136, 143*t*, 158–160, 173, 206–207, 209–211
  obstacles to, 133–136
  organizing for power as method for generating, 216–233, 238
  policies to facilitate, 134–135, 209–211
creative destruction, 89, 116–117
critical realist approach, *see also* empirical claims; ideal and nonideal theory; imprecision; normative foundations; metaethics; pragmatism
  core principles of, 5–9, 13–20, 22, 25–26
  implications of, 55, 147
  limitations of, 31–33
critical theory, 6, 58–59, *see also* critical realist approach; Habermas, Jürgen; neutrality, as tool for capture
cultural capture, 40, 85, 203, *see also* power, cultural and ideological forms of

Dahl, Robert, 21, 159
decentralization, 72, 93–96, 113–114, 137, 143*t*, 158, 183, 196–202; *see also* competition
decision-making
  as core focus on ideals of collective self-rule, 2–6, 20–25, 34*t*, 43–44, 53–55, 57–58, 61–62, 147–149
  limitations of, as core focus of democratic theory, 2–4, 6–8, 25–31, 34*t*, 36–42, 48–50, 55–56, 63–64, 66, 72–73, 79, 101–102, 150; *see also* collective will; Social Choice Theory (SCT)
deliberation, 2–3, 34*t*, 43–44, 53–54, 57, 58–59, 61–63, 121–122, 225, *see also* participatory Inclusion
  mini-publics, 22, 61, 67–68, 121, 207–208, *see also* sortition
  deliberative systems theory, 23–24, 73–76
  utopian horizon of, 21, 147, 149–151

Democracy for Realists (Christopher Achen and Larry Bartels), 6, 36 n.1, 44 n.6, 113–114, 178–179, 187–191
democratic authority, *see* legitimacy
democratic backsliding, 51, 168–174, 239–241, *see also* autocracy; hybrid regimes; political stability
democratic innovations, *see* democratic reform, strategies for
democratic instrumentalism, *see* intrinsic *vs.* instrumental accounts of democracy's value
democratic minimalism, *see* elections, real value of; elite theories of democracy; realism; Przeworski, Adam
democratic reform, strategies for
  according to collective self-rule ideals, 8–9, 22, 51–54, 59, 63–65
  according to dispersion of power ideal, 5, 30–31, 65–66, 124–125, 135, 150–151, 160, 194, 198–211, 213–214, 220, 240–242
  summary and comparison of approaches, 9, 34*t*, 48, 73, 195–198
Democratic Party (US), 60, 140–141 n.7, 170, 186, 221 n.5
democratization
  as process of deepening democracy beyond electoral minimalism, *see* democratic reform, strategies for
  as process of institutionalizing basic electoral democracy, 87, 89–90, 97, 116–117, 179, 184, 214–215, 232
depoliticization, 6, 68–70, 92–96, 108, 199–200, *see also* individualization; neutrality
Dhillon, Jaskiran, 6, 69–70
direct democracy, 1, 18–19, 21–22, 38 n.2, 50, 53, 57, 61–62, 64, 205–206
Disch, Lisa, 36 n.1, 46–48, 134, 159–160, 237
disadvantaged groups, *see* counter-hegemonic groups; inequality; ordinary people
domination, 33, 109–110, 120, 154, 156–160, 213, *see also* power; republicanism
Du Bois, William Edward Burghardt, 46, 134, 164–167

economic growth, 16–17, 88–91, 116–117, 126, 127–129, 138–139 n.4, 141, 177–179, 198–202
education, 45, 53, 58, 125, 140–141, 143t, 165–166, 180–183, 186, 187–188, 198–201, 221, 225, 235–236, *see also* civic virtue; political socialization
efficiency, 89, 119, 121–122, 141, 179, 203
elections, *see also* representation
   design and reform of, 3, 8, 21–22, 29–30, 34t, 36, 52–53, 57
   limitations of, 28–29, 34t, 37–48, 101–102
   real value of, 6, 28, 29, 34t, 36–37, 56–57, 87, 113–114, 119–120, 157–160, 168, 170, 180–194
elite capture, *see* inequality; power; state capture
elite theories of democracy, 47–48, 56–58, 190–194, *see also* Schumpeter, Joseph
elites, definition of, 39–40, *see also* hegemonic groups; ordinary people; organizational capacity
empirical claims, role of in normative political theory, 32, 79–80, 82–83, 106–107, 125, 174, *see also* critical realist approach; imprecision; pragmatism; realism
empowerment
   ineffective strategies for, *see* participatory inclusion
   optimal strategies for, *see* ordinary people, proper democratic role of; organizing
environment
   climate issues, *see* climate change
   environmental regulation, 16–17, 60, 67–69, 93, 94, *see also* regulation
epistemic arguments for and against democracy, 51, 119–120, 177–189, *see also* intrinsic vs. instrumental accounts of democracy's value; procedure vs. substance
equality
   dispersion of power ideal and, 19, *see also* normative foundations
   ideal of equal control over collective decisions, *see* collective self-rule
   political equality as justification of democracy, 20–21, 23–25, 34t, 73–76, 119–120, 163–168, 179, 193, *see also* intrinsic vs. instrumental accounts

of democracy's value; Christiano, Thomas; Kolodny, Niko; Waldron, Jeremy
Erdoğan, Recep Tayyip, 22, 169
ethnicity, *see* inequality, categorical inequality; race and racism
exit, 104–105, 114, 141–142, *see also* competition; decentralization; power, structural power
experimentalism, 58, 61; *see also* decentralization
expertise
   in healthy relationship with ordinary people, 2, 207–211
   necessity of, 44, 58, 62, 85, 108, 191, 202–203, *see also* bureaucracy, as democratizing force
   oppositional forms of, 205–207, 210–211
   as vehicle for capture, 85, 158–159, 202–203

federalism, *see* decentralization
feminism, *see* gender; patriarchy
Ferguson, James, 153–155
financial industry, 84–85, 101, 105–106, 130, 198–199, 201–204
first-past-the-post electoral systems, *see* elections, design and reform of
fossil fuel interests, 1–3, 33, 101, 184–185, 201
Frankfurt School, *see* Habermas, Jürgen
freedom
   as normative ideal of collective autonomy, *see* collective self-rule; collective will
   as normative ideal of individual autonomy, 19, 23–25, 43–44, 48–49, 74, 118–119, 242
   as political practice of protecting individual rights and liberties (e.g., freedom of speech, freedom of the press), 88, 91–92, 108, 109–110, 143t, 146–147, 163, *see also* rights

Galbraith, John Kenneth, 132–133
gender
   as basis for oppression, *see* patriarchy
   as an identity, 46–47, 80, 92, 113–114, 121–122, 134, 139–140 n.6, 143t

gerrymandering, 36–37, 52–53, 170, 182, 186, 208, *see also* elections, design and reform of; political parties
global justice, 32–33, 95, 104–106
grassroots movements, *see* organizing; social movements
Green, Jeffrey, 6, 36 n.1, 52–53, 129–130, 190, 210, 223
group theory of democracy, 4–5, 26–27, 34t, 44–48, 88–91, 132–138, 159–160, 165–168, 187–192, 209–211, 224–227

Habermas, Jürgen, 53, 58–59, 61
healthcare policy, 13, 120, 140–141, 200–201, 221
hegemonic groups, 5, 30–31, 34t, 65–66, 73, 96–97, 135–136, 142, 143t, 150, 213, *see also* counter-hegemonic groups; elites; inequality
  definition of, 131, 133, 136–137, 149, 233–234, *see also* elites, definition of; organizational capacity
  examples of, 91–107, 132–133
  methods of achieving and maintaining hegemonic status, *see* power; state capture
  organizing by, 234–235
heuristics, 7, 13–16, 24–26, 34t, 81, 160–161; *see also* ideal and nonideal theory; judgment; pragmatism; tasks of democratic judgment
Hobbes, Thomas, 26
Horton, Myles, 216, 223–224, 236–237
housing policy, 93, 134, 198–199, 201–202, 221–222
human interests, *see also* political ontology
  as foundational normative commitment, 4, 16–18, 27, 28, 31–32
human nature, *see* human interests; political ontology
human rights, *see* global justice; rights
humility as a theoretical virtue, *see* imprecision; judgment; political ontology
hybrid regimes, 87, 172–174
hydraulic model of capture, 91–92, 103

ideal and nonideal theory, 15–16, 73–76, *see also* critical realist approach; empirical claims; imprecision; pragmatism; realism
ideology
  as form of power, *see* power, cultural and ideological forms of
  as orienting political vision, 22, 44–45, 208, 229–230, 235–238, *see also* Social Identity Theory (SIT)
identity construction, *see* Social Identity Theory (SIT)
impartiality, *see* neutrality
imprecision, as a theoretical virtue, 7, 15–16, 19, 23–24, 31–32, 75, 79, 81–83, 124 n.1, 125, 138–139 n.4, 147, 152, 153, 161–163, 172, 174, 194, 198, 233, 240–241
inclusion
  importance of, as democratic value, *see* universalism
  ineffective strategies for, *see* participatory inclusion
  optimal strategies for, *see* ordinary people, proper democratic role of; organizing
indeterminacy
  in collective will-formation, *see* collective will; Social Choice Theory (SCT)
  in individual will-formation, *see* voter ignorance; Social Identity Theory (SIT)
  as a theoretical virtue, *see* imprecision
India, 22, 93–94, 103, 239
Indigenous groups, 14, 69, 70, 93–94
individualization
  political dangers of, 63–73, 93–96, 153–155, 187–188, 220, 224–227, 229–230, *see also* neoliberalism
  theoretical dangers of, 9, 22–23, 30, 61–65, 152, *see also* group theory of democracy
Industrial Areas Foundation (IAF), 216, 223, 236–237
interests, *see* human interests; public interest; organizing, self-interest and
inequality, *see also* hegemonic groups; organizational capacity
  categorical inequality, 91–97, 143t, *see also* race and racism; patriarchy
  economic inequality, 97–107, 130–131, 136–145, 143t, *see also* class; oligarchy

political inequality, 39–40, 45, 47, 51–52, 101–106, 142, *see also* clientelism; hybrid regimes
information capture, 85, 203, *see also* expertise
Ingham, Sean, 41, 103, 157
intellectual property, 43, 84–85, 100–102, 143*t*, 199–200
intra-party democracy, 18–19, 31, 52, 60, 158, 180–181; *see also* workplace democracy
intrinsic *vs.* instrumental accounts of democracy's value, 31, 34*t*, 51, 119–120, 161–163, 166–168, 177–181, 219–220, *see also* pragmatism; realism
issue salience, 38, 43, 45–47, 101–103, 113–114

Jackson, Kate, 49–50, 193
Jim Crow, 51–52, *see also* Black Freedom Movement; race and racism; Reconstruction (US historical era)
Johnston, Michael, 86–87, 97–98
judgment, 4, 7, 13–16, 32–33, 81–83, 110, 122, 133, 147, 152–153, 160–163, 172, 174, 194, 201–202, 208, *see also* imprecision; heuristics; pragmatism; tasks of democratic judgment
judicial review, 32, 34*t*, 146–147, 158, 193, *see also* US Supreme Court
judicial independence, *see* neutrality
jurisprudence, 49–50, 121–123, 170
justice, *see also* equality; global justice; normative foundations; property-owning democracy
  democracy and, 18–19, 24–25, 138, 151–153, 164–168, 242

King Jr., Martin Luther, 140–141 n.8, 217 n.3, 218, 223–224
Kirshner, Alexander, 129, 162–168
Kolodny, Niko, 21, 23–24, 74, 119–120, 179, 193

labor unions, 8–9, 30–31, 45, 46, 57, 70–73, 80–81, 101–102, 125, 131–136, 143*t*, 148–149, 173, 191, 210, 214–238, 240–242, *see also* class; counter-hegemonic groups; countervailing power; organizational capacity; organizing; strikes
Latin America, 61, 86, 93–94, 100–101, 103, 110, 153–154 n.2, 172–174, 239
leadership, 18–19, 22, 31, 44, 47, 56–57, 162–163, 170–171, 180–185, 189, 190–192, 214–215, 218–220, 223–224, 230, 235–238; *see also* organizational capacity; organizing; political parties; representation
Lefort, Claude, 160
legal realism, 94, 100–101, 117, 199–200, *see also* neutrality, as tool of capture; Progressivism
legitimacy, *see also* collective will; intrinsic *vs.* instrumental accounts of democracy's value
  perceived legitimacy as tool of capture, 7–8, 21, 34*t*, 40–41, 63, 66–73, 95–96, 98–99, 164, 177
  theories of, 49–50, 74–76, 180–181, 192–194, 196–197, 242–243
Levy, Jacob, 114–116, 160
liberalism, *see also* constitutionalism; competition; pluralism; universalism
  deficits of, 91, 96, 122–125, 131, 132, 137, 139–140, 143*t*, 197–198
  importance of, 88–91, 108–123, 143*t*, 177–180, 239, *see also* elections, real value of
  historical origins of, 16–17
  tensions with democracy, 17–20, 108–109
  tensions with radical principles, 122–123, 146–147, 157–158, 160, 164–174
libertarianism, 49, 84–85, 105–106, 110–111, 140–141 n.8, 177–178, 196, 199, 202–203, *see also* neoliberalism
liberty, *see* freedom
limitarianism, *see* anti-monopoly
lobbying, 36, 40, 102–104, 206, *see also* money in politics; regulation, capture of
Locke, John, 55, 111
lotteries, *see* sortition

Machiavelli, Niccolo, 129, 156–157
MacKinnon, Catherine, 95–96
Macron, Emmanuel, 1–4, 9, 55, 70–71
Madison, James, 86, 111–112, 156–157, 169
majority rule, *see* collective will

Index

Mansbridge, Jane, 23–24, 53, 58, 65, 74
marketplace of ideas, 115–116, 143t, *see also* deliberation; media; power, cultural and ideological forms of
markets, *see* competition, market competition
Marx and Marxism, 55, 58–59, 99–101, 104–107, 153–154, 156–157, *see also* socialism
mass politics, 37–38, 46–47, 52, 53–54, 56–59, 61–62, 64, 133–134, 179, 205–206, 210, 220, 226–227, 241, *see also* elite theories of democracy; political parties; representation
McAlevey, Jane, 214, 216–217, 220–221 n.5, 222, 224, 227, 231, 236–237, 241–242
McCormick, John, 112, 129, 156–157, 210, 212–213
Medearis, John, 65 n.2, 115, 160, 212–213
media
  capture of, 39, 45–46, 66, 103–104, 136–137
  democratic role of, 87, 115–116, 121, 142, 173, 182–183, 190–192, 225
  social media, 239
meritocracy
  political meritocracy, 180–185
  problems with, 121–122, 134, 183–184, 208, *see also* neutrality, objections to
  real value of, 18–19, 118, 121–122, 143t, 160, 181, *see also* bureaucracy, as democratizing force
metaethics, 14, *see also* ideal and nonideal theory; normative foundations
militant democracy, 161–168, *see also* autocracy; hybrid regimes; political violence; populism
minority rights, *see* rights
mobilization
  as conception of representation, *see* Disch, Lisa
  as distinctive political tactic, *see* organizing, distinctive features of
modern states, 4, 16–17, 81, 95, 97
Modi, Narendra, 22
money in politics, 40, 47–48, 102–104, *see also* billionaires; elites; hegemonic groups; inequality; oligarchy; state capture, methods of

Montesquieu, Charles Louis de Secondat, Baron de, 55, 86, 111–112, 156–157, 160
Morales, Evo, 169, 172–174
motivated reasoning, 6, 8, 26–27, 44–45, 64, 121, 162–163, *see also* Social Identity Theory (SIT)
Müller, Jan-Werner, 18–19, 22, 51, 192

National Environmental policy Act (NEPA), 59–60, 67, 68, 70
neoliberalism, 105–106, 127–128, 133–134, 152, 201–203, 220–221, *see also* depoliticization; individualization; libertarianism; privatization
neutrality
  attractions of, 62–63
  limitations of, 7, 122–124, 132, 136, 146, 156–159, 197, 199–200, 234–235, 237, *see also* corrective partiality
  real value of, 30, 34t, 65–66, 90–91, 119, 120–122, 125, 131, 143t, 168, 239–240, *see also* bureaucracy, as democratizing force; meritocracy, real value of; publicity
  as tool of capture, 38–39, 66–71, 92–98, 118, 121–125, 131, 143t, *see also* depoliticization; hydraulic model of capture
New Deal (US policy era), 59–60, 104–105, 140–141 n.7, 202–203, 221 n.5, *see also* welfare state
normative foundations, 7, 13–16, 19–20, 24–25, 32–33, 73–76, 80–83, 108–109, 118–119, 242–243, *see also* metaethics; ideal and nonideal theory; pragmatism
norms
  as normative principles and heuristics to guide action, 213–214, *see also* heuristics
  as procedural norms sustaining democratic institutions, 110, 169–171, 173, 182–183, 239, 240
  as public, mutually-shared norms of deliberation and evaluation, 22, 121–122, 143t, *see also* deliberation; meritocracy; neutrality
  as values and cultural scripts taken up by individuals, 13, 95–96, 134, 136–137,

143t, 149, 172 *see also* power, cultural and ideological forms

oligarchy, 8, 57, 80, 85–86, 91, 97–100, 128, 130, 172, *see also* billionaires; capitalism; elites; hegemonic groups; inequality; money in politics
opposition
  democratic importance of, *see* adversarialism; competition; Medearis, John
  institutionalization of, 27–28, 33, 65–66, 86–87, 111–113, 115–116, 124–125, 131–133, 143t, 168, 170–171, 173–174, 182–183, 191, 205–211, 212–214, *see also* countervailing power; labor unions; political parties
oppression, 33, 93–96, 137, *see also* power
Orbán, Viktor, 18–19, 22, 169
ordinary people, *see also* counter-hegemonic groups; elites; plebeianism
  competence of, *see* epistemic arguments for and against democracy; voter ignorance
  definition of, 39–40
  proper democratic role of, 5, 9, 30–31, 33, 34t, 49, 51, 68, 113, 130, 135, 157, 189–192, 207–238, 241–242, *see also* countervailing power; organizing; solidarity; sortition
  uncritical valorization of, *see* participatory inclusion
  vulnerability to elite manipulation, 44–48, 102, 103–104
organizational capacity
  definition and components of, 7, 39–40
  egalitarian balance of, as democratic ideal, 25, 27–31, 34t, 42, 124–125, 133, 136–137, 150–151, 165–166, 173–174, 195–196, 220, 232, 240–241, *see also* balance of power; corrective partiality
  imbalances of, as driver of capture, 29–30, 42–43, 48, 63, 65–68, 73, 83–84, 89, 101–102, 113–114, 122–124, 131, 136, 138, 150, 210, 212
organizing
  challenges of, 133–136, 225, 226, 228–229, 233–238

  democratic importance of, 5, 8–9, 30–31, 34t, 40, 64–67, 70, 72–73, 143t, 159–160, 165–166, 212–216, 241–242, *see also* countervailing power, as core principle of democracy
  distinctive features of, 213–220, 225–227, *see also* Alinsky, Saul; Baker, Ella; McAlevey, Jane
  policies to facilitate, 134–135, 209–211
  self-interest and, 229–230
  varieties of, 132–134, 220–224, *see also* Black Freedom Movement; Industrial Areas Foundations (IAF); labor unions; social movements; strikes
oversight, 8–9, 30, 34t, 65–66, 73, 105–106, 143t, 200–201, 205–209, 241–242

participatory inclusion
  definition of, 23, 55–56, 65
  examples of, 29, 59–73, *see also* Citizens' Convention on Climate (CCC); intra-party democracy; workplace democracy
  historical and theoretical roots of, 52–54, 56–63
  limitations of, 3, 6, 23, 55–56, 63–73, 148–149, 210, 219, 225, *see also* adversarialism
  participatory budgeting, 29–30, 61, 67, 71–72
  participatory governance, 60, 69–70, 205–206
  as version of collective self-rule, 22–23, 34t
partisanship, 26–29, 38, 45–46, 111, 159 n.4, 170, 182, 186–189, 207, 214–215, 228–229, 239–240, *see also* arms races; clientelism; Democratic Party (US); polarization; Republican Party (US); Social Identity Theory (SIT); solidarity
patriarchy, 6, 91, 95–96, 118, 134, 137, 140–141 n.7, 141–142, 153–154, 188, 218, 228–229
Pettit, Philip, 111, 156–158, 212–213
philanthropy, 40, 103–104, 215
Piketty, Thomas, 99–101, 106–107, 128–129
plebeianism, 156–157, 210
pluralism
  as category of allied approaches, 147, 156, 159–160, 212–213

pluralism (*Continued*)
  as paradigm in political science, 113–114, 159
  as non–sovereigntist theory of state power, 25–26, 157, 192
  value of social pluralism, 115–116, 121–122, 143t, 148–150, 191, 206, *see also* civil society; competition
plutocracy, *see* billionaires; oligarchy
polarization, 46–47, 146–147, 182–183, 225, 239–240, *see also* adversarialism; arms races; competition, dangers of; partisanship
policy feedback, 45, 134–135, 200–202, 209–211, 231–233, *see also* individualization; privatization; welfare state
political equality, *see* equality; inequality, political inequality
political obligation, *see* legitimacy
political ontology, 16, 31–32, 118–119, 147, 152–155, 197–198, 237–238, 242–243
political parties, *see also* Democratic Party (US); intra-party democracy; Republican Party (US)
  as participants in institutionalized competition for power, 18–19, 43, 52–53, 60, 87, 111, 113–114, 125, 143t, 158–160, 170, 182, 212–213, 239, 240
  as representatives of groups, identities, and interests, 26–29, 31, 33, 38–39, 46–47, 52, 56–57, 60, 72, 132–133, 159, 173, 187–189, 214–215, 222–223, *see also* countervailing power; leadership; representation
  as vectors of state capture, 46, 52–53, 70–71, 86, 87, 103, 115–116, 146–147, 161, 170, 173–174, 182, 186–187, 233–234, 240, *see also* clientelism; gerrymandering
political socialization, 33, 148, 153, 182–183, 214, 225–227, 231–232
political stability and instability, 39, 67–68, 89–90, 97–100, 110, 113, 120, 167–168, 170–171, 179, 182–183, 199–200, *see also* political violence
political violence
  avoidance of, as key achievement of electoral democracy, 4–5, 28, 89–90, 114–115

  in service of revolutionary goals, 56–57, 75, 148, 171–172, 184–185, *see also* benevolent despotism
  justification of, 161–163, 166–167, 169–172, *see also* militant democracy
  as threat to human interests, 16–17, 28
  as tool of state capture, 86, 89, 90, 98–99, 101, 114–115, 201, 220–221, 224
popular sovereignty, 18–19, 26, 49–51, 157, 159, 192–194, 207, 242–243, *see also* collective self-rule; collective will
popular will, *see* collective will
populism, 1, 22, 51, 57, 108, 168–174, 178, 188 n.4, 192, 241; *see also* plebeianism; polarization; popular sovereignty
power, *see also* domination; hegemonic groups; oppression; patriarchy; race and racism; state capture
  cultural and ideological forms of, 20–21, 45–48, 53–54, 58–59, 98–100, 103–106, 134, 136–137, 142, 143t, 153–155, 177–178, 214, 225, *see also* cultural capture; media
  instrumental forms of, 39–40, 46, 48, 83–88, 100, 101–106, 126–128, 136–137, *see also* organizational capacity
  structural forms of, 38–39, 42, 99–100, 104–106, 114, 128–129, 140–141 n.8, 220–221, *see also* exit; information capture; state capture, inherent vulnerability of collective choice procedures to
pragmatism, 14 n.2, 53, 58, 119–120, 163, 171–172, 194, 197–198, 202, 236–237, *see also* critical realist approach; empirical claims; ideal and nonideal theory; imprecision; intrinsic *vs.* instrumental accounts of democracy's value; legal realism; Progressivism; realism
preference aggregation, 2–3, 36–44, 47, 48–49, 64, 101–102, 158–159 n.4, 237, *see also* collective will; representation; Social Choice Theory (SCT)
private domination, 33, 157 n.3, *see also* republicanism
private law, 94, 100–102, 199–200, *see also* competition, market competition; intellectual property; legal realism; private property

Index 281

private property, 56–57, 97–99, 133–134, 151–153, 155, *see also* competition, market competition; intellectual property; property-owning democracy; socialism
privatization, 84–85, 193–194, 200–201, *see also* individualization; neoliberalism
proceduralism, *see* intrinsic *vs.* instrumental accounts of democracy's value; equality, political equality as justification of democracy; procedure *vs.* substance, dilemmas of; Waldron, Jeremy
procedure *vs.* substance, dilemmas of, *see also* intrinsic *vs.* instrumental accounts of democracy's value
  case studies of, 164–174, 233–238
  theoretical approach to, 17–20, 33, 108–109, 120–125, 146–147, 157, 160–163, 179, 195–198, *see also* corrective partiality; neutrality
Progressivism (US political movement), 52–53, 57–60, 85, 126–128, 202–203, *see also* anti-monopoly; Brandeis, Louis; legal realism; pragmatism
property-owning democracy, 151–152, 155, 204–205, *see also* Rawls, John
proportional representation, *see* elections, design and reform of
protest, 1–2, 36, 170, 191, 216–218 *see also* organizing, distinctive features of; Yellow Vests (*gilets jaunes*)
Przeworski, Adam, 100, 113, 179 n.1, 182
psychology, *see* motivated reasoning, Social Identity Theory (SIT)
public choice theory, 40, 83–85, 206
public interest
  definition of, 19–20, 27, 79–83, 85
  protection of, as indirect goal of democracy, 4, 7, 16–18, 25, 29, 34*t*, 50, 65–66, 79, 106, 108–111, 113, 123, 127, 129–131, 138–139, 146, 150, 177, 184–185, 190, 192, 206–209, 212, 234, 241–243
public power
  importance of, 16–17, 79, 195–198, *see also* bureaucracy, as democratizing force; public interest
  origins of, *see* modern states
  threats to, *see* state capture

public reason, 121–122, 156, 242, *see also* deliberation; Habermas, Jürgen; neutrality; publicity; Rawls, John
publicity, democratic role of, 82–83, 121, 128–130, 143*t*, 200–206, 223

race and racism, *see also* Black Freedom Movement; colonialism; inequality, categorical inequality; Jim Crow; Reconstruction (US historical period); slavery
  as basis of solidarity, 46–47, 133–134, 143*t*, 222–224, 228–229, 236–237
  as "divide-and-conquer" strategy, 46–47, 57, 134, 221
  as system of categorical inequality and disadvantage, 6, 51–52, 91–97, 118, 121–122, 139–140
Rahman, K. Sabeel, 57, 85, 115, 126, 128, 202–204, 213
Rawls, John, 59, 138–139 n.4, 151–152
realism, *see also* critical realist approach; legal realism; pragmatism
  democratic realism, 6–7, 22, 25, 56–58, 158–159, 178–179, 190, 242, *see also Democracy for Realists* (Christopher Achen and Larry Bartels); elections, real value of; elite theories of democracy; Green, Jeffrey; Przeworski, Adam; Shapiro, Ian
  importance of setting realistic expectations, 5, 8–9, 50–51, 147, 165–167, 177–180, 192–194, 207–208, 219
Reconstruction (US historical period), 46, 164–168
redistribution, *see also* corrective partiality; reparations
  as demand of democracy, 8, 18, 42, 109, 123–125, 136–145, 143*t*, 164–167, 202, 205, 232, 240–241
  dilemmas of redistributive populism, 168–174
  in contrast to pre-distribution, *see* property-owning democracy
  in contrast to pre-distribution, *see* property-owning democracy
  as effect of creative destruction, 90, 116–117
  as part of utopian horizon, 150
  as social insurance, *see* welfare state

redistribution (*Continued*)
   upward redistribution, 84–85, 125, 129
   wealth as proper medium for, 138–141, *see also* unconditional wealth transfers (UWTs)
referendums, *see* direct democracy
regulation, *see also* anti-monopoly; bureaucracy
   capture of, 66–69, 83–85, 99, 101–105, 182
   democratization of, 205–211
   types of, 198–202
relational equality, *see* equality
religion, 26–27, 46–47, 80, 89, 92, 95, 109–111, 115–116, 143*t*, 191, *see also* civil society; pluralism, value of social pluralism; secularism
rent-seeking, 83–84, 89–91, 116, *see also* public choice theory
reparations, 139–141, 143t
representation
   constructivist theories of, 46–47, 237, *see also* Disch, Lisa
   descriptive representation, 61, 67–68, *see also* sortition
   direct representation, *see* populism
   ideal of responsive representation, 8, 23, 34*t*, 36–54, 196–197
   interest representation, 73, 136, 159, 189, 191–192, 209, 230, *see also* leadership; organizational capacity
   legal representation, 115, 131
   principal-agent model of, 36, 42, 44, 47, 193, 201*see also* collective will
   representative democracy, 1–3, 57, 72–73, 207–208, *see also*, elections, real value of
Republican Party (US), 164–167, 170, 186, 228–229
republicanism
   as a category of allied approaches, 147, 156–158, 212–213
   civic republicanism, 56, *see also* civic virtue
   labor republicanism, 57
   liberal *vs.* radical republicanism, 111–112, 156–157
   socialist republicanism, 148
resisting state capture, ideal of
   comparison with allied approaches, 155–160
   comparison with collective self-rule, 3–5, 15, 23–31, 34*t*, 147, 149–150, 155–156
   definition of, 25–31, 80–83
   utopian horizons of, 147–155
responsiveness, *see* representation
rights, 17–18, 20–21, 32, 34*t*, 74, 87, 108–110, 118–121, 130–131, 143*t*, 146–147, 161–163, 177–178, 193, 196–197, 234–235 n.8, *see also* constitutionalism; freedom; universal suffrage; universalism
Rome, ancient, 56, 98, 111–112, 210
Rosanvallon, Pierre, 52, 160, 190, 193, 205–206, 212–213
Rousseau, Jean-Jacques, 26, 55, 74
rule of law, 17–19, 87, 98, 109–111, 130, 143*t*, 170, *see also* constitutionalism

Schumpeter, Joseph, 56–57, 91–92 n.1, 158, *see also* creative destruction; elite theories of democracy
scientific progress, 16–17, 58, 116, 191, *see also* expertise; meritocracy
   comparison with politics, 183–184
secularism, 118
separation of powers, *see* constitutionalism
settler states, 69–70, 91–94, *see also* colonialism; Indigenous groups; race and racism
sexism, *see* patriarchy
Shapiro, Ian, 108, 113, 158–159, 182, 186, 212–213
Shklar, Judith, 115–116, 160
simplicity, as tool of resisting capture, 120, 202–205, 223, *see also* publicity
slavery, 46, 91–93, 110, 139–140, 164, *see also* colonialism; race and racism
Slobodian, Quinn, 105–106
Smith, Adam, 84
Social Choice Theory (SCT), 6, 8, 37–42, 47, 48–49, 63–64, 101–102, 177, *see also* collective will; decision-making; Ingham, Sean
social democracy, *see* welfare state
Social Identity Theory (SIT), 6, 26–29, 42–49, 64, 101–102, 104, 177, 187–189, 191–192, 208, 225–227, 229; *see also* empirical claims; epistemic arguments

for and against democracy; group theory of democracy; motivated reasoning; partisanship; policy feedback; political socialization; race and racism; representation; solidarity; subjectivity
social movements, 31, 45, 53, 58, 73, 132–133, 137, 212–216, 234–235, 241–242, *see also* Black Freedom Movement; civil society; countervailing power; organizing
social norms, *see* norms
social science and political theory, *see* empirical claims
socialism, *see also* capitalism; Chinese Communist Party (CCP); Marx and Marxism; Morales, Evo
  dispersion of power and, 123, 148–149, 153–155
  historical socialists, 56–57, 173, 177–178, 188–189, 197, 216
  utopian horizon of full socialization, 21, 34*t*, 147–148, 196
solidarity, 22–23, 31, 46–47, 133–136, 143*t*, 157, 160, 214–215, 221, 224–238, 241–242; *see also* counter–hegemonic groups; countervailing power; labor unions; political socialization; social movements
sortition, 1, 22, 61, 67–68, 121, 130, 180 n.2, 207–209, *see also* deliberation
South Africa, 80, 91–94, 100–101, 153–154 n.2
spontaneity as a democratic virtue, 31, 223–224
state capture
  authoritarianism and, 87, *see also* autocracy
  categorical inequality as a form of, 91–97, *see also* class; inequality; race and racism
  clientelism as a form of, 87–88, *see also* clientelism
  corruption as a form of, 85–87, *see also* corruption
  definition of, 8, 80–83; *see also* public interest
  inherent vulnerability of collective choice procedures to, 37–42, 63–64, 101–102
  limitations of, as a concept, 31–33, *see also* global justice; private domination
  methods of, 37–48, 63–73, 83–88, 91–107
  oligarchy as a form of, 97–100, *see also* oligarchy
  regulatory capture as a form of, 83–85, *see also* cultural capture; regulation, capture of
  political violence and, 89–90, *see also* political violence
  wealth inequality as a form of, 99–107; *see also* class
Stilz, Anna, 193–194
Stout, Jeffrey, 160, 215–216 n.1, 216, 218–219, 223, 227, 230, 236–238
strikes
  2018 "Red for Ed" teacher strikes (US), 228–229
  capital strikes, *see* power, structural forms of
  labor strikes, 70–71, 135, 170, 221–222, 224, 227–230
  rent and debt strikes, 221–222
  the right to strike, 19, 133–135, 220–221
subjectivity, 69, 118–119, 224–225, 232–233

tasks of democratic judgment, 15–16, 24, 34*t*, 48–54, 75–76, 81, 83, 142–147, 155–156, 160–161, 174, 177, 192–196, 215, 239–242, *see also* heuristics; judgment
taxation
  citizen tax juries, 130, *see also* sortition
  drawbacks of tax-and-transfer schemes, *see* property-owning democracy
  tax evasion, 99–100, 102, 104–105, 130
  tax competition, 104–106, 114, *see also* arms races; power, structural forms of
  wealth taxes as democratic demand, 1–2, 30, 99, 128–129, 138–139 n.4, 140–141, 143*t*, *see also* unconditional wealth transfers (UWTs)
technocracy, *see* bureaucracy; meritocracy
Tocqueville, Alexis de, 56, 91–92, 160
trade unions, *see* labor unions
transparency, *see* publicity
Turkey, 22, 162, 169, 239
tyranny, *see* autocracy

uncertainty
  as challenge for political theorizing, *see* empirical claims; imprecision

uncertainty (*Continued*)
  as democratic value, 87, 89, 113, 182–183, 192, 223, *see also* creative destruction; hybrid regimes; Przeworski, Adam
unconditional wealth transfers (UWTs)
  as compared to welfare state policies and basic income, 138–141, 143*t*, *see also* property-owning democracy; welfare state
  as core component of dispersion of power ideal, 19, 30, 141–145, 143*t*, 153–155, 204–205
unions, *see* labor unions
universal basic income (UBI), *see* unconditional wealth transfers (UWTs)
universal suffrage, 28, 56, 91–92 n.1, 115, 119–120, 122–123, 143*t*, 161–163, 165, 177, 185–189, 192, *see also* elections; rights; universalism
universalism
  as core principle of democracy, 118–123
  deliberation, publicity, and transparency, as reflection of, *see* deliberation; publicity
  impartiality and neutrality as reflections of, *see* neutrality
  limitations of, *see* neutrality, limitations of; participatory inclusion, limitations of
  universal rights, *see* constitutionalism; rights; universal suffrage
  universal social programs, *see* policy feedback; unconditional wealth transfers (UWTs); welfare state
US Supreme Court, 85–86, 95, 158–159, 169, 223
utilitarianism, 19
utopianism
  dispersion of power as utopian horizon, 34*t*, 140–145, 143*t*, 148–155
  horizon of full socialization, 21, 34*t*, 148, *see also* collective self-rule; socialism
  horizon of ideal deliberation, 21, 34*t*, 149, *see also* collective self-rule; deliberation
  limitations of, *see* ideal and nonideal theory; realism
  necessity and usefulness of, 147

Vergara, Camila, 86, 111–112, 156–157, 212–213
violence, *see* political violence
Violence and Social Orders (Douglass North, John Wallis, and Barry Weingast [NWW]), 88–92, 96, 97–99, 106–107, 116
voter ignorance, 44, 177–178, *see also* epistemic arguments for and against democracy; Social Identity Theory (SIT)
voting rules, *see* elections

Waldron, Jeremy, 5–6, 20–21, 32, 108, 118, 193
Walzer, Michael, 122–123
war, *see* political violence
Weale, Albert, 6, 18–19, 21, 38–39, 43 n.5, 64
welfare state, *see also* New Deal; policy feedback; property-owning democracy; unconditional wealth transfers (UWTs)
  as achievement of social democratic parties, 46–47, 188–189, 232–233
  as component of collective self-rule, 29, 34*t*, 138–139
  as focal point for organizing, 133–134, 143*t*
  capture of, 84, 87–88, 140–141 n.7, 171, 198–202, 221 n.5, *see also* regulation, capture of
  limitations of, 99–100, 139, 140–141, 151, 152–155, 188–189
  weakness of, in the US, 46, 169
Westminster system, 111, 158–159
Why Nations Fail (Daron Acemoglu and James Robinson [A&R]), 88–92, 96, 97–99, 106–107, 116
Winters, Jeffrey, 97–101, 129
white supremacy, *see* colonialism; race and racism; settler states
Woodly, Deva, 160, 212–213, 216, 224, 230, 236–237
workplace democracy, 18–19, 31, 34*t*, 53, 58, 112, 143*t*, 148–149, *see also* intra-party democracy; labor unions

Yellow Vests (*gilets jaunes*), 1–4, 9, 55

Zacka, Bernardo, 49–50, 193